# ALASKA–YUKON
## ADVENTURES

FRASER BRIDGES

An On-Route Communications Book

PRIMA PUBLISHING

PRIMA PUBLISHING, ROAD TRIP ADVENTURES, and colophons are registered trademarks of Prima Communications, Inc.

Library of Congress Cataloging-in-Publication Data

Bridges, Fraser
   Alaska–Yukon Adventures: / Fraser Bridges.
      p.   cm.
   Includes index.
   ISBN 0-7615-0226-2
     1. Alaska—Guidebooks. 2. Yukon Territory—Guidebooks. 3. Automobile travel—Alaska—Guidebooks. 4. Automobile travel—Yukon Territory—Guidebooks. I. Title. II. Series.
F902.3.B744  1996
917.9804'5—dc20
                                      96-8048
                                        CIP

96 97 98 99 00 01 HH 10 9 8 7 6 5 4 3 2 1

Printed in the United States of America

**How to Order:**
Single copies may be ordered from Prima Publishing, P.O. Box 1260BK, Rocklin, CA 95677; telephone (916) 632-4400. Quantity discounts are also available. On your letterhead, include information concerning the intended use of the books and the number of books you wish to purchase.

# ALASKA–YUKON
## ADVENTURES

## ALSO BY FRASER BRIDGES

*Pacific Coast Adventures*
*Southwest Adventures*
*Rocky Mountain Adventures*
*Natural Places of the Northwest*
*Natural Places of the Southwest*

### Coming Soon

*Natural Places of the Gulf Coast from Florida to Texas*
*Gulf Coast and Texas Adventures*

# Contents

## YUKON

## ACCESS ROUTES

# Using This Travelguide

The *Road Trip Adventures* series of guidebooks is designed to make it easy to plan your trip, and to travel with peace of mind. Each chapter is divided into three main sections.

## Drives

Use the highway log pages while you're traveling. They are meant to be read at the start of the day and especially while on the road. You'll discover the next picnic park, gas stations ahead, parks and campgrounds, and upcoming scenic views. If you like getting out of the car and enjoying the natural environment, the logs will tell you where to stop to walk, hike, swim, fish, and view wildlife. In addition to covering the Alaska Highway and the other major routes, the log pages include suggestions for scenic sidetrips. Three spectacular routes lead to untouched northern wilderness. The Dempster Highway, starting at Dawson City, and the Dalton Highway, starting near Fairbanks, both lead north of the Arctic Circle. The Liard/Mackenzie Route provides a circular path from B.C. into the Northwest Territories, and returns through Alberta.

## Destinations

Destinations pages contain the information you need to plan your northern adventure trips, and will help you enjoy your visit. You can read about the cities and towns along the way, things to do and see, and historical information on the fascinating regions of Alaska, the Yukon, and Canada's western Arctic. We've included recommendations on a range of places to eat.

### Places to Stay

When visiting the north country, planning overnight stays is essential. We've recommended a wide variety of accommodations, including hotels, motels, inns, and lodges, ranging from inexpensive to super-deluxe. Private campgrounds and RV parks in or close to the major tourist destinations are included in these sections.

# Recommendations and Costs

### Places to Stay

You'll find a broad selection of motels, hotels, inns, bed and breakfasts, resorts, lodges, campgrounds, and RV parks in the Places to Stay section. Whether you're traveling deluxe or on a tight budget, you will find a range of recommended hotels, motels, inns, lodges, and camping places for each of the cities and towns.

All hotels, motels, lodges, and bed-and-breakfast homes are shown with price ranges with the following designations:

- **Inexpensive ($):**
  under 65 dollars

- **Moderate ($$):**
  66–100 dollars

- **Deluxe ($$$):**
  101–150 dollars

- **Super Deluxe ($$$+):**
  over 151 dollars

Deluxe and super-deluxe accommodations are found in the large city hotels and in unique and specialized resort hotels, inns, and lodges.

There is a good supply of campgrounds and RV parks throughout the regions. Public campgrounds (national, provincial, state, and municipal parks) have minimal facilities, sometimes with pit toilets and without hot water.

Private campgrounds and RV parks are better equipped, almost always with hookups, hot water, showers, flush toilets, water piped to sites, and electrical supply. Prices for government campgrounds range from $4 to $8. Private facilities run from $10 to $20.

## Where to Eat

Our recommended restaurants, delis, cafés, and pubs are listed in the Destinations pages for the larger towns and cities. We have not included fast-food chains, as these are easy to spot along the roadside, and the prices are consistent. Many of the restaurants are found in hotels or attached to motels along the highways. On the other hand, we have made an effort to include the smaller, more interesting local eating places that serve local food and specialties found only in that location. A selection of neighborhood bars or pubs that serve meals is included. We have found that pubs often serve simple, nourishing meals which are usually less expensive than in standard restaurants. We encourage you to picnic along the way. Many scenic picnic parks are noted in the logs opposite the strip maps and in the city pages in the Destinations pages.

# Introduction

## Explorations

It's hard to think of adequate superlatives when describing the magic and the inspiration of the northwest corner of North America. The geography of Alaska and the Yukon is truly magnificent and awe-inspiring, from the highest mountains on the continent, to the icefields and glaciers that are unique to this region of the world, and then to the far north and the tundra with its ancient stunted trees and changing muted colors throughout the spring, summer, and fall seasons.

But the Alaska-Yukon adventure is more than scenery, as spectacular as it may be. The North is its native people, and its history of settlement and development. A traveler can't help being caught and entranced by the lore of the north, from the early explorations of the Russians in Alaska, the Hudson's Bay Company and Northwest Company in the Yukon and British Columbia, and the pioneers of the fabled Klondike Gold Rush adventure at the turn of the century, to the more recent oil discoveries which have opened up Alaska as never before.

All this is for the modern traveler to explore, from the fabulous fishing rivers of the north coast of British Columbia and the Alaskan Panhandle to the bustling cultural life of the Yukon and Alaskan cities. A journey north gives the traveler a chance to sample it all: 1898-style dancing girls in Dawson City; hunting and fishing in the Alaskan wilderness; music festivals almost everywhere; quiet exploration of the mountains, glacial rivers, and national parks; and sampling the everyday life of the fishing villages in Alaska and along Canada's Arctic coast.

It was 1959 when I first came into contact with the immensity of the north and the northern experience. As a young broadcaster, I went northwest to take a job in Whitehorse, and spent the next two years working and traveling in the Yukon and Alaska.

At the beginning of the 1960s, Alaska was a fledgling 49th state. The Alaska Highway was unpaved and it was a daunting experience to drive from Dawson Creek to Fairbanks. Dawson Creek was then no more than a village at the lowest part of its up-and-down cycle. Tourists of the day were exceptionally hardy types and we called them "adventurers" or "explorers". They came to take part in rugged river trips and mountain climbing expeditions or to take away game trophies.

What a change the next 40 years would bring!

Those years brought prosperity to Alaska with huge oil revenues. In addition, the Yukon and Alaska have become major tourist destinations for people of all kinds, not just the rugged explorers of the past. The recreational vehicle helped to bring about this revolution in northern travel, and vacationing in the north became possible for seniors, who are now the most prominent group of travelers to this far-flung region.

The early 1960s began a renaissance in Dawson City, and climbing gold prices in later years revived mining in the fabled Klondike gold fields. Dawson was renewed, becoming a wonderful echo of the 1898 gold stampede, now visited by travelers from around the world.

Farther south, cruise ships now sail the remarkable Inside Passage. These floating resorts bring thousands of people in comfort each year to the unique communities of the Alaska Panhandle. Tourism has brought new life and meaning to such communities as Skagway and Sitka.

Denali National Park has now become so popular (and so busy) that dedicated outdoor adventurers often travel farther, to more isolated places including Brooks Camp in Katmai National Park and the islands of the Bering Sea.

The main function of this book is to provide highway maps and practical information on what to see and do, as well as where to stay and eat. However, I hope that the book will help to heighten an appreciation of the wilderness in this frontier region of our continent, and to pay tribute to the Native Americans, Canadians, and rugged pioneers who came to the north looking for gold and other resources, or those who settled the north in order to live singular lifestyles in this serene environment.

The towns and cities of this vast wilderness area are featured in later pages of the book. In this introduction, we pass over the enticements of the urban areas to look at some of the outdoor adventure opportunities available to all those who travel slightly off the beaten track—taking the time to savor the outdoors experiences that wait throughout Alaska and the Yukon Territory.

This book is directed at the motoring traveler: all but one of the following adventures and explorations are readily accessible from the roads of the north. They all, however, require leaving your vehicle to enjoy the special experience of the wilderness through outdoor adventuring.

### Hiking in Southeastern Alaska

The national forests of the Alaska Panhandle offer superb wilderness hiking on hundreds of miles of trails. Several communities, including Sitka, Juneau, and Haines, provide easy hiking experiences for those who wish to take accessible day hikes.

Three-quarters of a mile from the former Russian capital of Sitka sits Sitka National Historic Park. Here you will find a fort built by the Tlingit people. A trail winds through the park forest, reaching a beach and picnic area. There are totem poles in the park, and the Native Arts Workshop teaches and displays Tlingit arts and crafts.

An outstanding climb can be taken up Harbor Mountain (Gavan Hill) beginning from downtown. This 6-mile round trip takes you up to 2,700 feet (823 meters) to superb views of the surrounding areas. Campsites along the trail serve as picnic spots.

The more strenuous climb to the top of Mount Verstova is also accessible from downtown Sitka. It offers outstanding views. This trail takes some caution because of steep drop-offs. The Indian River trail is less exacting: a ten-mile hike with the trailhead 2.5 miles from town. The trail traverses forest and winds beside the river, crossing some muskeg along the way. The Forest Service (2045 Siginaka Way) and the city offices (Lake Street) have brochures on Sitka hikes.

More than 20 hiking trails are easily accessible from Juneau, the state capital. A brochure is available from the USDA Forest Service at the Centennial Hall Information Center (101 Egan Drive). A stairway at the end of Sixth Street is the start of the Mount Roberts Trail, a climb of almost 4,000 feet. Three other Forest Service trails lead from Gold Street to Basin Road and across Gold Creek. These are the Mount Juneau, Perseverance, and Granite Creek trails. Perseverance is, paradoxically, the shortest of the three.

Several trails lead from the visitor center at Mendenhall Glacier, ranging from a 1.5-mile loop to longer hikes. This is the best way to observe the icefields. The Salmon Creek trail crosses muskeg and the Kowee Creek trail travels through beautiful forest and meadow land. This trail includes a boardwalk over the muskeg.

Haines has one of the most scenic townsites on the Panhandle. The visitor center (at Second and Wuillard) has a brochure on several day hikes you can take from downtown. The Mount Ripinski Trail takes you above the tree line to an elevation of 3,500 feet, where the viewpoint offers stunning views of the snow-clad peaks beside the Lynn Canal. For full information on hiking from Haines, phone the town information center at (907) 766-2202.

### Chilkoot Trail

The town of Skagway, at the head of the Lynn Canal, is a scenic historic site evocative of the Klondike Stampede of 1897 and

1898. The former townsite of Dyea, a few miles to the south, marks the start of the celebrated Chilkoot Trail, used during those Stampede years.

Supervised by the National Park Service, the lower part of the trail begins as a riverside walk, climbing to the top of the Chilkoot Pass into Canada and to the shores of Lake Bennett, where the stampeders built boats and rafts for their long journey down the Yukon River to Dawson City.

The park service advises hikers to take at least four days to hike the 33 miles from Dyea to Bennett The trail climbs 4,700 feet through rugged countryside that is sometimes boggy. Necessary equipment includes a camp stove and fuel, warm clothing and good hiking boots, plenty of food and water, and a first-aid kit.

Artifacts of the 1898 gold rush can be found along the trail, including parts of wagons, stoves, and other supplies left behind in the rush to get to Lake Bennett. The parks service requests that hikers not disturb these "museum pieces" of the stampede.

There are many things to see along the Chilkoot Trail, including several biotic zones ranging from rain forest at the start, past the tree line to alpine areas. Once at the top of the pass and into Canada, you will notice the climate change. This dry region is in the shadow of the Coast range, and the landscape features stands of pine and fir with small lakes and streams beside and crossing the path.

Hikers can return to Skagway by the scenic White Pass and Yukon Railway (in summer months) or by local transportation, which should be arranged in Skagway before starting the trip. A printed guide to the Chilkoot Trail is available from the National Park Service Information Center in downtown Skagway.

## Yukon River Adventure

The Yukon River journey from Whitehorse or Carmacks to Dawson City offers one of the ultimate canoe trips, filled with the history of the early explorers and gold rush pioneers of the Yukon Territory.

A combination of floating sedately and hurtling wildly through the challenging Five Finger Rapids, a Yukon river trip explores the route of the Klondike gold prospectors. Along the way abandoned villages, tumble-down cabins, and wrecked sternwheelers can be spotted. Starting from Whitehorse, the canoe trip begins with a paddle down Lake Laberge, a widening of the river. Those who drive downriver to start at Carmacks save a day or two. A map that gives details of several Yukon wild river voyages is available from the Yukon Conservation Society, P.O. Box 4136, Whitehorse, Y.T. Y1A 3T3.

Several Yukon companies offer guided river trips. These include Karpes and Pugh Company, P.O. Box 4531, Whitehorse, Y.T. Y1A 4S3, and Yukon Tours, 200-3067 Jarvis Street, Whitehorse, Y.T. Y1A 2H3.

Canoes are available from Listers Rentals in Whitehorse. A full list of outfitters is included in a Yukon government publication, available from Tourism Yukon, P.O. Box 2703, Whitehorse, Y.T. Y1A 2C6, or call (403) 667-5340.

## Outdoors in Dempster Country

The Dempster Highway starts at the Klondike River, near Dawson City, and traverses three mountain ranges. It crosses the Arctic Circle, reaching the flatlands of the Mackenzie River Delta in Canada's Northwest Territories. The southern portion of the Dempster route offers wonderful hiking experiences in country crossed by large herds of caribou during spring and fall migration seasons. The mountain ranges feature unusual geological formations and several climatic regions. The landscape varies from boreal forest to alpine tundra.

An easy hike 6.5 kilometers from the southern end of the highway provides an historical focus. The North Fork power plant opened in 1911 to provide electricity to the Klondike gold dredges. Eventually providing most of the power for the Dawso City area, the plant operated until 1955, when gold dredging came unprofitable. Hikers will enjoy the walk to the North penstock and gatehouse. Walk west from the highway at KM 6.5 for 6 kilometers (4 miles). The trail parallels a ditch. The gatehouse is well preserved and machinery is scattered around the property.

The Grizzly Valley offers a hike of four to eight kilometers, starting at KM 59.3 (mile 36.8). Park at the gravel pit and enter the valley by walking northwest. The trail lies between Grizzly and Cairnes creeks and rises after one kilometer. After two, the peak of Mount Monolith is visible at an elevation of 270 meters (900 feet). You may wish to continue for another two kilometers to a viewpoint at 1,500 meters elevation to see the whole Grizzly Valley.

A number of hikes available in the Tombstone Range are reached through the Grizzly, Wolfe, and North Klondike valleys. The Wolfe Creek valley is the southernmost. The Upper Klondike valley is accessed at KM 76 (mile 47). An excellent eight-hour hike begins from the territorial campground, ending at Divide Lake. This walk is for sturdy and experienced hikers.

Farther north, close to the Arctic Circle, hikes are available along the Continental Divide. At KM 420 (mile 261), hills within an hour's walk provide views of the "midnight" sun at summer solstice. These and other hikes in this region are described in Walter Lanz's excellent book *Along the Dempster,* available at book stores in the Yukon.

### Volcanoes and Bears: Katmai National Park

The forces of the earth are always in evidence in Katmai. In 1912 this park of over four million acres was the scene of one of the greatest volcanic eruptions of all time. A vent named Novarupta blew its top and Mount Katmai collapsed into itself, losing 2,000 feet of height in the process. The intense heat and a layer of ash up to 12 feet deep devastated a wide area. Fumaroles in the "Valley of the Ten Thousand Smokes" gave out sulfur steam for years.

The mountains are mostly quiet now, and Katmai has be- one of the special wilderness destinations in Alaska, accessible only by plane. Most visitors fly via King Salmon to Brooks Camp, where there is a lodge, campground, and park interpretive center. Here, in rushing streams, bears fish for salmon and trails lead to a very special wilderness where more than 40 varieties of songbirds gather each summer.

Katmai is wild country and an unforgettable rugged wilderness experience. To properly plan for a visit, write the National Park Service, P.O. Box 7, King Salmon, AK 99613, or phone (907) 246-3305.

All of the above adventures in the Alaska-Yukon outdoors are there for you to seek and enjoy. For some, simply making the trip and relaxing in campgrounds and scenic parks along the way is taxing enough and quite satisfying. For others, adventure means high mountain climbing or running swift rivers in canoe or kayak. For me, a combination of the two fills the bill. I best enjoy a trip when I can savor some of the local history, putting my sightseeing within an historical context, even if it means only visiting a local museum, having a beer in an antique pub, or staying in a hotel room first occupied by a gold rush stampeder. This rich history is what makes a regular trip to this part of the world so rewarding. Add to that the continuing pioneer activity and spirit, and you know why some visitors return regularly—some every year.

# *Alaska*

The "Great Land" is exactly that, offering a staggering number of northern adventures in its varied regions.

Southeast Alaska is "the Panhandle", a 600-mile long strip of fjords, glaciers, forests and fishing towns hugging the Coast Mountains. The Inside Passage provides ferry and cruise routes to Alaska, and jumping-off points to the Alaskan interior and to the Yukon.

South-central Alaska is a wildlife wonderland including the recovering Prince William Sound, the Kenai Peninsula, and the city of Anchorage.

The Alaska Interior is the home of the state's Arctic Inuit and Native American villages located along the Yukon River and its tributaries. Fairbanks is the staging point for visits to Denali National Park and the Arctic. Nome, situated on the Bering Sea, was the site of the famous 1899 gold rush. Kotzebue is one of Alaska's oldest and largest Inuit communities. Barrow, on the Arctic Ocean, is the northernmost settlement in North America and is the center for oil exploration and development on the Alaskan North Slope.

Southwest Alaska is the remote section of the state that includes the Alaskan Peninsula, Kodiak Island, and the Aleutian island chain.

## Climate and Geography

The maritime climate of the Panhandle and Prince William Sound provides moderate temperatures year-round, much like the north coast of B.C. The interior and far north regions have much more varied weather with sunny, warm (even hot) summer temperatures and dry, biting winter cold. Alaskans face snow from October through April and into early May, except in the mainly snow-free southeast region.

Two mountain ranges separate Alaska into distinct regions: the Alaskan Range in the south-central area includes Mount McKinley in Denali, the highest mountain in the U.S.; and the Brooks Range runs east to west in the northern region and separates the Alaskan interior from the north coast and Prudhoe Bay. The interior's main geographic feature is the Yukon River, which passes Eagle at the Yukon border and snakes through the state to its mouth at the Bering Sea.

The Coast Mountains anchor the Alaskan Panhandle, providing a thrilling backdrop for the communities of the southeast region, including several historic villages and the state capital, Juneau. Many of Alaska's 3,000 glaciers are here.

The Inside Passage is the route of cruise ships that travel to sightseeing points in Alaska from Vancouver, B.C. The Alaska Marine Highway ferry service links the lower 48 with southeastern Alaska via Inside Passage cruises from its terminal in Bellingham, Washington.

## Traveling to Alaska

Visitors have the choice of air travel, the Alaska Marine Highway and B.C. ferry systems, and two highways that run through British Columbia. The Alaska ferry system operates two unconnected services. On the southeastern route, ferries connect Bellingham, Washington, Ketchikan, Wrangell, Petersburg, Sitka, Juneau, Haines, and Skagway. On the southwestern route, ferries stop at Kodiak, Port Lions, Homer, Seldovia, Seward, Valdez, Cordova, and Whittier.

Highway travelers can take their cars and RVs from the ferries and continue by several routes.

- From terminals at Skagway and Haines in the southeast region and then by highway through the Yukon to join the Alaska Highway.

- From the ferry terminal at Valdez and along the Richardson Highway to Fairbanks. You should be aware that the southeastern ferries do not connect with this system.

- From ferry terminals on the Kenai Peninsula to Anchorage and the interior.

- Via the Alaska Highway, starting in Dawson Creek, B.C., at "Mile 0". After 1,969 kilometers (1,190 miles) the highway enters Alaska south of Tok, after traversing the Yukon Territory.

## Population Centers

The largest city in Alaska is Anchorage, the commercial center of the state, with a population of 250,000, hotels of all kinds, good shopping and plenty of things to see and do. Fairbanks, in the interior, is the end of the Alaska and Richardson highways. With a population of 75,000, it is home to the University of Alaska and is the launching point for trips to Denali National Park.

The truly adventurous should think about traveling by air to the northern settlements, including Nome and Barrow. Over $3 million in gold was taken from the sands of Nome during the gold rush of 1899. Barrow is located 300 miles north of the Arctic Circle. Visitors here experience the midnight sun, which doesn't set for 82 days each year. Two hundred miles east, Prudhoe Bay supplies crude oil to the Alaska Pipeline.

Southeast Alaska includes the state capital, Juneau. The fishing towns of Ketchikan, Wrangell, Petersburg, and Sitka reflect the Russian settlement of the area, before Russia sold Alaska to the United States. Skagway, at the top of the Lynn Canal, relives the gold rush days of 1897 and 1898, with an outstanding summer train trip up the White Pass, as well as the thrilling hike along the Chilkoot Trail. Haines enjoys a spectacular location on the Lynn Canal.

# The Yukon

The Yukon Territory is a fascinating mixture of history and modern adventure. Before the gold rush days at the turn of the century, the Yukon was a vast wilderness populated by Athabaskan people and by a very few Europeans, Canadians, and Americans who came to the area in the 1800s to establish fur-trading forts and to search for minerals.

The fabulous Klondike Gold Rush of 1898 changed the Yukon forever, as Dawson City for a short time became the largest western North American city north of San Francisco. The intrepid gold seekers also established Whitehorse as a riverside way station on the way to the Klondike. Today the Yukon is a favorite destination for anglers and hunters. Most of all, it is Canada's finest accessible wilderness adventure area, with unique cities and towns offering a wonderful historical experience, many related to the Klondike Gold Rush.

The summer months of the Yukon offer varied attractions and entertainment mirroring the Gold Rush days, including cabaret and theater performances in Whitehorse and Dawson City, as well as a tent "canteen show" in Watson Lake that re-creates the days during the Second World War when the Alaska Highway was constructed in less than a year. Dawson City itself is a national historic site with several significant buildings maintained by the federal government and open to tourists during the busy summer season.

## Climate and Geography

The climate of the Yukon is easy to describe: dry and mostly sunny. Yukon summers are warm through the June-to-September months. Temperatures rise into the high 20°C (80°F). Daylight hours are long throughout the territory, with midnight sun in the more northern regions during June and July. Whitehorse, in the southern Yukon, has about 20 hours of sunlight in June and 18 hours in July.

Winter days are short, with cold, dry weather. This dry and frigid weather can be quite comfortable if you are properly dressed.

The Yukon includes Mount Logan, the highest mountain in Canada (6,050 meters or 19,850 feet), located on the western edge of the territory within Kluane National Park. The remaining expanse is a combination of mountains, river valleys, and plains, with a new view around every turn.

The primary geological feature is the Yukon River with its source near the Pacific Coast just across the mountain ridge from Skagway, Alaska. The river winds across the southern Yukon, through Whitehorse to Dawson City, and then turns northwest to cross the Alaska border at Eagle.

The other great northern river is the Porcupine, with the Native American village of Old Crow sitting beside the Porcupine and accessible only by air.

## Traveling Through the Yukon

Four routes bring highway travelers to the Yukon from the south:

- On the Alaska Highway (Highway 97) beginning at Dawson Creek, B.C., and entering the Yukon south of Watson Lake, where it becomes Highway 1.

- On the Stewart/Cassiar Highway (Highway 37), beginning at the Yellowhead Highway near Terrace, B.C., and entering the Yukon at Upper Liard, north of Watson Lake.

- On the Klondike Highway (Highway 2) which begins at Skagway, Alaska.

- On the Haines Road (Highway 3) which starts at Haines, Alaska, on the Lynn Canal, joining the Alaska Highway at Haines Junction, north of Whitehorse.

Four other highways offer interesting scenic alternatives:

- Atlin Road (Highway 7) joins the Alaska Highway south of Whitehorse and winds for 95 KM (40 miles) south to the village of Atlin, B.C., and beautiful Atlin Lake.

- The Silver Trail (Highway 11) branches off the Klondike Highway at Stewart Crossing and goes on to Mayo and the closed silver mines at Elsa.

- The Top of the World Highway (Highway 9) joins the Alaska Highway at Tok, Alaska, and ends at Dawson City. This road is closed during winter months but is an unforgettable trip from late June to October.

- The Dempster Highway (Highway 5) runs north from Dawson to the Arctic town of Inuvik (see the Dempster Highway section).

## Population Centers

Whitehorse is the modern capital and the largest community in the Yukon, a transportation hub with a population of 19,500, good shopping, hotels, and other tourist facilities. You can take advantage of a fascinating museum of early Yukon life, boat trips on the Yukon River, and entertainment. Watson Lake, farther south with a population of 1,600, is also located on the Alaska Highway. Carcross, Tagish, and Teslin are small, scenic communities near the Yukon's southern border. Carmacks is a Yukon

River community on the way to Dawson City, while the mining towns of Faro and Elsa are located in the central interior.

Dawson City, 530 KM (329 miles) north of Whitehorse, is still a gold-mining center with a permanent population of 1,600. During the summer months, visitors relive the Klondike Gold Rush days of 1898 in this town that still has its false fronts, boardwalks, and the only licensed casino in Canada, where "dancing girls" in 1898 costume entertain the customers.

# Dempster Country

Inuvik is the population center for the western Arctic and the end of the fascinating Dempster Highway. Since 1978, adventurers have traveled this route to experience an unforgettable trip to Canada's northern frontier. This road starts near Dawson City, winding across three mountain ranges and some of the most awesome scenery in North America. Most people take two days to travel the Dempster, starting near Dawson and crossing the Ogilvie Mountains—the same migration route as thousands of northern caribou in the spring and fall. Unusual rock formations are a strong feature of the route, with government campgrounds providing stopping points for noon-time picnics and overnight stays. Hiking is a popular pastime along the route.

After crossing the Richardson Mountains just north of the Arctic Circle, travelers can take a ferry that lands near Fort McPherson, a Kutchin (Loucheux) settlement. Farther north lies the majestic Mackenzie River, where a second ferry lands at Arctic Red River and crosses the Mackenzie, letting travelers rejoin the Dempster Highway as it continues across the muskeg to Inuvik.

## Climate and Geography

The climate of Dempster Country is varied, with dry and sunny weather during summer periods in the Yukon section, and misty mountains beside the river delta to the north. Summer temperatures are pleasant, with snow arriving in late September or early

October. With its crisp mornings and warm days, September is a good month to travel the Dempster. The Ogilvie Mountains lie across the southern part of the route, with several ranges following each other. The Tombstone range is particularly scenic with its castellated ridge tops. The northernmost mountains, north of Eagle Plains and the Arctic Circle, are the unusual and beautiful Richardsons. These most northerly of the Rocky Mountains are unusual for their softly sculptured shapes, caused by a lack of glaciation and many centuries of erosion by wind and water. Sunrises and sunsets on the Richardsons are not to be missed. North of the mountain pass at the Arctic Circle is the Mackenzie River Delta with its many river channels, flat muskeg, and abundant wildlife.

## Where to Stay

An easy day's drive north of Dawson City is Eagle Plains, a unique, privately owned settlement that includes a motel, restaurant, lounge, and service station. It's 30 kilometers (19 miles) south of the Arctic Circle, beside the Richardson Mountain Range. At the end of the road lies Inuvik, a community of 4,000 people including Inuit, Dene and Caucasians, with hotels, stores, restaurants, and other tourist services.

# Liard/Mackenzie Country

The Liard and Mackenzie highways provide an exhilarating summer circle route, which can be taken in a clockwise direction starting at Fort Nelson, B.C., or counter-clockwise from Dawson Creek, B.C., or points north of Edmonton, Alberta.

This drive is described fully in the Liard/Mackenzie highway logs and in the Yukon/Northwest Territories destinations pages. The trip can take eight days or a month or two, with rewards along the way each day. The Liard Highway stretches north from its junction with the Alaska Highway to join the Mackenzie Highway near Fort Simpson in the Northwest Territories. Travelers have the opportunity to visit Nahanni National Park, which has its headquarters in Fort Simpson. If you're touring in a clockwise direction, the Mackenzie Highway then takes you east, turning north past the riverside village of Fort Providence and on to Yellowknife, the government center for the Northwest Territories. You'll be surprised at the high level of tourist services in this modern Arctic community.

Our route then reverses itself, retracing the drive south to the Mackenzie Highway, and then leading southeast to the town of Hay River, a water transportation center and great fishing spot. The route runs south into the province of Alberta, giving you the choice of returning to B.C. and Dawson Creek or continuing south to Edmonton and Calgary.

This route does not take you as far north as the Dempster Highway does, but the climate is similar during summer months, and there is a variety of scenery along the two highways, although the mountain ranges are seen at some distance compared to the underfoot Dempster experience. You can see the Liard range to the west, along almost the entire length of the Liard Highway. Nahanni National Park is situated in this range, not reachable by car but accessible by air from Fort Liard and Fort Simpson. Short sightseeing tours of the park are available.

The Mackenzie Highway travels over the relatively flat river plain, with muskeg along much of the way to and from Yellowknife. This is fishing country, with pike, pickerel, grayling, and whitefish to be found along the route.

Hotels, motels, and campgrounds are available along the entire route, although at some distance from each other. Overnight motel stops are best planned for Fort Liard, Fort Simpson, Fort Providence, Yellowknife, and Hay River. All are within an easy day's drive as you proceed along the circle drive.

## British Columbia

British Columbia is a vast, mountainous land, with its population largely located in the southwest corner of the province, in the Vancouver and Victoria regions.

The southern interior region is dominated by the Coast and Cascade mountain ranges, which separate the province into quite different regions, including wide plains where some of the largest cattle ranches in the world are located, the lake region of the Okanagan Valley, and the southeastern region, which includes the Kootenay mountain and lakes area and the B.C. Rockies.

The northern half of the province, located north of the Yellowhead Highway dividing line, is almost pure wilderness with only scattered settlement.

The area south of the Yellowhead is fully described in our companion book *Rocky Mountain Adventures*.

Access routes through southern B.C. are described in this book to guide travelers to adventures farther north. We have chosen two access routes that lead from the southwestern corner of the province. Starting in Vancouver, you travel on the Trans-Canada Highway (Highway 1) to Hope and Cache Creek through the scenic Fraser River Canyon, then north on the Cariboo Highway (Highway 97) through 100 Mile House and Williams Lake to Prince George. The final leg of the interior access route is the Hart Highway (Highway 97), starting in Prince George and running north to Dawson Creek and "Mile 0" of the Alaska Highway.

The second adventure route to northern British Columbia leads from the Vancouver area or from Washington state, by ferry to Vancouver Island. Victoria is the major city at the southern end of the island. The Island Highway (Highway 1, changing to Highway 19) leads north through Nanaimo, Parksville, and Campbell River to the island's northern tip at Port Hardy. Travelers to Prince Rupert and points north take the B.C. car ferry *Queen of the North*.

## Climate and Geography

Northern B.C. has three main climate zones. On the north coast, the weather is gentle, warmed by the Japan current, which sweeps up the coastline toward Alaska. It is a land of mists, rain forests, and magnificent fjords.

As you travel through several mountain ranges in the inland region, the weather will be drier and much colder during the fall and winter months. The summers in the Cariboo district are warm—even hot—and dry. The northeast corner of the province is an extension of the Canadian prairie, with dry weather and pleasant summer temperatures. During the winter, this region is sunny and dry with very cold temperatures.

## Traveling through Northern British Columbia

The Yellowhead Highway (Highway 16) is the main east-west route, leading from Jasper in the Rocky Mountains to the coastal city of Prince Rupert.

Once arriving at the Yellowhead Highway, you can choose from three ways of traveling to the more northern adventure destinations.

- By the Alaska Marine Highway (ferry system) from Prince Rupert to several southeast Alaska communities including Juneau, the state capital.
- On the Stewart/Cassiar Highway (Highway 37) which meets the Yellowhead between Terrace and Hazelton. It leads to the Alaska Highway just west of Watson Lake, Yukon. This wilderness trip is the shortest route to the Yukon Territory and Alaska for motorists starting their driving trip from Prince Rupert.
- By the Hart Highway (Highway 97), which joins the Yellowhead at Prince George and leads you to the Alaska Highway at "Mile 0" in Dawson Creek, B.C. It is possible to take a shortcut, bypassing Dawson Creek and traveling from Chetwynd to just northwest of Fort St. John.
- Bus transportation to the Yukon and Alaska is available from Prince George. This bus service originates in Vancouver.

## Population Centers

Northern B.C. towns are few and far between. The major city on the west coast is Prince Rupert, a fishing port and lumber center.

It is the launching point for trips by ferry to Alaska and to Canada's Queen Charlotte Islands. These islands, some 100 kilometers off the coast, form a unique archipelago with rain forests, historic settlements of the Haida people, and a fascinating ecosystem. The major communities here are Skidegate and Masset on Graham Island, and Sandspit on Moresby Island.

Along the Yellowhead Highway east of Prince Rupert, the larger towns are Terrace, Hazelton, Vanderhoof, and Prince George. Of these, Prince George is the largest: a bustling resource-based city with all of the big town amenities. The city is the junction of the main north-south highway route (the Cariboo, Highway 97) and the Yellowhead. Terrace and Hazelton are worth a pause for their Native American cultures and historic sites. K'san Village, near Hazelton, is a tribute to B.C. native culture. The village includes authentic longhouses and a museum and cultural center with carving demonstrations. Hazelton has Canada's largest collection of historic totem poles. Stewart, B.C., and Hyder Alaska are reached via the Stewart/Cassiar Highway.

# Planning Your Trip

Driving an automobile or recreational vehicle is the best way to experience the north country, and this guidebook is designed to help you get the most out of your driving trip.

An auto club membership is useful for planning your vacation and especially for coping with problems you may have on the highways. Should you not have an auto club membership before you leave home, a convenient office of the British Columbia Automobile Association (BCAA) is located at 999 West Broadway in Vancouver, B.C. Other BCAA offices are located in B.C. cities including Victoria, Prince George, and Prince Rupert.

### Money

At the time this book was going to print, the Canadian dollar was worth about 80 cents in U.S. currency. Americans get good value for their dollars in Canada. To exchange U.S. dollars to Canadian currency, we suggest that you use a bank for the best exchange rates. However, U.S. dollars are accepted in most Canadian stores, hotels, and restaurants.

Avoid carrying large amounts of cash while on the road. Travelers' checks are widely available in Canada, as in the U.S. The two most widely used travelers' checks are American Express (available at most banks and credit unions and at BCAA offices in B.C.) and Visa. Canadian banks and credit unions are affiliated with major credit card companies and give cash advances on credit cards. Automated teller machines (ATMs) are widely available in Canadian cities for such networks as Cirrus, Interact, Plus, and Exchange.

## What to Wear

Summer visitors to northern regions generally enjoy warm sunny days. Residents tend to wear informal clothing, and visitors may dress in a relaxed fashion almost anywhere. Evenings and early mornings may be crisp. Light jackets, sweaters, and light gloves are advised. You'll want shorts during the day as well as sunglasses and a hat. Shoes suitable for hiking and off-road walking are a necessity. And don't forget rainwear for those off moments when heavy mists and rains descend.

The spring and fall months provide great opportunities for northern travel. Warmer clothing is needed during these periods, including garb suitable for temperatures down to the freezing point. A light ski jacket is ideal for early mornings and evenings.

## Budget Hostels

Directories are available from the Canadian Hostelling Association, 1515 Discovery Street, Vancouver, B.C. V6R 4K5, or phone (604) 224-7111. The guide to Canadian hostels is free. The U.S. hostel handbook costs $6.00.

## Border Crossings

For U.S. and Canadian tourists, visas are not necessary for the border crossings into Canada and Alaska. If you are 18 or older, you may import goods into Canada duty free: 200 cigarettes or 50 cigars or 3 pounds of tobacco, 40 ounces of liquor or 24 bottles of beer, a small amount of perfume and other goods up to the value of $40. Seeds, plants, meat, and fruit are not allowed to cross the borders.

If you're passing through B.C. and going into Alaska and are 21 or older, you may import free of duty the following: 200 cigarettes or 50 cigars or 3 pounds of tobacco, and 1 U.S. quart of alcohol. All travelers are entitled to take into the U.S. gifts to a value of $100. Plants, fruit, seeds, and meat are not allowed past U.S. borders.

Possession of "controlled substances" can result in fines, jail terms, and seizure of your vehicle—or all three. Tourists are strongly advised not to carry illegal drugs. It's a bad way to abruptly end a vacation!

### Flying Rocks, Dust, Mud, and Other Joys

Throughout British Columbia, the Yukon, and Alaska, the major roads are paved and are generally in good condition. However, there is always reconstruction, and drivers are urged to be patient when encountering road stoppages. Highways in this region are engineering marvels and at times rock scaling or other improvements have to take place to protect the safety of travelers. You may encounter muddy roads as well, and should not be concerned when your car becomes caked with fine mud. Car washes are located along the routes.

Flying gravel is a hazard on some northern highways. Portions of the Alaska Highway north of Fort Nelson are not paved and will not be paved in the near future. Motorists should be wary of stones flying from the tires of large trucks. Many thousands of windshields, including mine on several occasions, have been cracked by rocks from fast moving trucks. It helps to slow almost to a stop when encountering these speeding behemoths.

We recommend that you drive with your lights on when on any of the northern highways. Driving with lights on is mandatory in the Yukon Territory, and should be in other jurisdictions as well. Lights are particularly helpful when meeting other vehicles on dusty roads, and there are dusty roads throughout the northland. Canadian cars purchased in the past few years are equipped with daytime driving lights.

## Area Codes

Telephone area codes for the regions covered in this book are:

Alaska: 907

Yukon Territory: 403

British Columbia: 604

Alberta: 403

Northwest Territories: 403 and 819

## Map Key

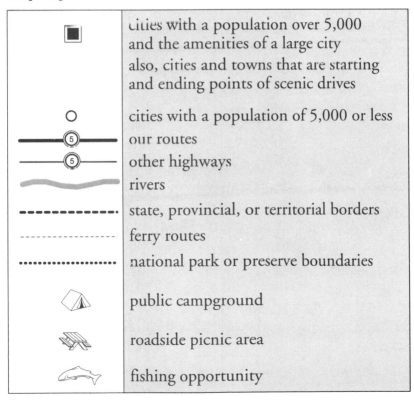

| | |
|---|---|
| ■ | cities with a population over 5,000 and the amenities of a large city also, cities and towns that are starting and ending points of scenic drives |
| ○ | cities with a population of 5,000 or less |
| ──⑤── | our routes |
| ──⑤── | other highways |
| ~~~~~ | rivers |
| – – – – – – | state, provincial, or territorial borders |
| - - - - - - | ferry routes |
| •••••••••• | national park or preserve boundaries |
| ⛺ | public campground |
| 🪑 | roadside picnic area |
| 🐟 | fishing opportunity |

# The Ten Best Places

The following recommendations (sorted into 3 lists of 10) provide a highly personal, and purely subjective, listing of our most enjoyable experiences while traveling through northern British Columbia, the Yukon, Alaska and Canada's western Arctic.

Everyone has a different view of what he or she wants in a vacation experience, and there are many, varied experiences to be had in this wonderful north country: the drive itself, enjoying the natural surroundings of the wilderness, hunting and fishing, hiking along the scenic mountain trails, enjoying the amenities found along the routes in hotels, restaurants, pubs, and special attractions such as historical restorations, hot spring pools, wild animal parks, vaudeville shows, boat rides, and train trips.

We hope that these "Top Ten" lists will help you to plan your northern adventure trip by focusing on some of the outstanding circle routes and one-day sidetrips, as well as telling you about some of the unique and historic hotels and about the special eating and socializing to be done.

Much of the attraction of the North is its people. Northerners live here because they like to do so. They are, for the most part, individualists who chose to live in the North because of the seasons, the lure of the great outdoors, some isolation from "outside" society, and the influence of the area's wonderful history.

This part of the world was founded by adventurers who came to take part in some of the most rugged and challenging adventures known to humanity: from the early explorations by Russian, Spanish, British, and American sea captains and traders, to the intrepid adventurers of the gold rush era, to the farmers who pulled up stakes in southern areas and moved to the North to challenge the bushland and the forbidding climate. We hope that you will make opportunities to meet the people of the north, and to get to know them.

## Circle Routes and Sidetrips

This list is not presented in any particular order of preference. It is simply a listing of our most remembered adventures, and we hope that it will be helpful to you in planning your northern adventure vacation.

### 1. The Dempster Highway

Although Dempster enthusiasts (some of whom return year after year) spend a major part of their vacation along the Dempster, we made the trip in five days, spending one whole day in Inuvik. You can go on by air to Tuktoyaktuk to enjoy the unique setting of the Arctic coast. The wonderful scenery of the Dempster, with its mountain ranges, rivers, alpine tundra, sunsets, and wildlife, is unforgettable, and this trip past the Arctic Circle was the most memorable.

### 2. Dawson City

For history buffs, Dawson is the mecca. This town is filled with ghosts from the 1898 Klondike Gold Rush. The Midnight Dome presents a panoramic view of the historic gold fields and the Yukon Valley. The boardwalks, the false fronts, the tumble-down structures and the new buildings constructed in turn-of-the-century style, the abandoned and present-day gold diggings on the creeks and the Yukon River—they all add up to an unforgettable experience.

### 3. Skagway and the Klondike Highway

The second historic town is Skagway, another "must" for Gold Rush fans. Skagway is a much neater town than Dawson, lovingly restored and preserved by the people of Skagway and the

National Parks Service. The downtown area is a living memorial to the rough-and-ready days of "Soapy" Smith, Frank Reid, and the earlier days of Captain John Moore. But the most memorable part of our Skagway visit was seeing the former site of Dyea, the start of the long climb up the Chilkoot Trail, and the slide cemetery. Here, you realize the truly incredible human challenges of the Klondike adventure.

### 4. Kenai Peninsula

As mentioned earlier, if you can visit only one part of Alaska, the Kenai Peninsula and its towns present a microcosm of the state, within a route with a diversity of scenery and historic significance, all covered within a few days out of Anchorage. Take the Sterling Highway to Soldotna, Kenai, Homer, and the Kenai National Wildlife Refuge. Take the Seward Highway through the Chugach and Kenai mountains and the Chugach National Forest to beautiful Resurrection Bay, the town of Seward, and Kenai Fjords National Park.

### 5. Kodiak Island

Kodiak is the most accessible part of southwestern Alaska. It is a 45-minute flight from Anchorage. You can get there by the Alaska Marine Highway system from Homer and Seward on the Kenai Peninsula. Kodiak echoes the early history of Alaska with its reminders of the Russian explorations and fur traders. Now a thriving commercial fishing center, Kodiak is equipped with resort lodges, motels, and campgrounds. Its crab festival each May is an enjoyable special event. Several beautiful and unpopulated beaches provide excellent places for beachcombing and picnics-in-the-wild.

### 6. Denali National Park

Although other national parks and forest preserves offer more true wilderness experiences without great numbers of people around every corner, Mount McKinley makes Denali National Park a memorable experience. The mountain overshadows the whole park, sometimes glistening white on sunny days, sometimes poking out of the clouds and mists, sometimes completely hidden. The subalpine meadows are magnificent, with carpets of tiny flowers.

### 7. Glacier Watching

There are glaciers in every corner of Alaska, and the glaciers that calve icebergs into the sea are a prime destination for many visitors. Outstanding amongst the many glaciers are: the Columbia Glacier in Prince William Sound, viewed from the Alaska ferry which cruises between Valdez and Cordova or from a local Valdez cruise boat; Glacier Bay National Park, 100 miles by boat or air from Juneau, with a collection of glaciers that once filled the entire bay, and is a favorite place for cruise ships and for shorter charter boat trips from Juneau; glaciers on the Kenai Peninsula include those in the vast Harding Icefield in Kenai Fjords National Park.

### 8. Stewart, B.C., and Hyder, Alaska

These towns rub up against each other at the Canada/U.S. border. The short trip on the road to Stewart offers a scenic drive beside the Bear Glacier to the Tongass National Forest. The two towns provide an interesting overnight stop and several area tours.

### 9. The Alaska Highway Rockies

Stone Mountain and Muncho Lake provincial parks contain incredible views of the Rocky Mountains, excellent camping facilities, and fishing opportunities.

### 10. Liard Hot Springs

Last but certainly not least is the set of two wilderness hot springs pools in Liard Provincial Park, in northern British Columbia. Olympic-sized indoor hot pools are fine, but after you've experienced these natural pools in the northern forest, all other hot springs pale by comparison.

### Inns and Lodges

### 1. Golden North Hotel—Skagway ($ to $$)

This original hotel, dating from 1898 and the gold rush days, is a wonderful place to start an exploration of the Klondike Gold

Rush trail. The rooms of the hotel are each decorated and furnished with care in period furnishings and wallpaper. The café and bar reflect the turn-of-the-century era. The hotel is located in the midst of the historic restored downtown area of Skagway, close to the National Historic park headquarters and a short walk from anywhere in Skagway. The second floor corner room in the tower, dedicated to Mrs. Pullen, one of the original 1897 Skagway pioneers, is especially interesting.

**2. Kenai Princess Lodge—Kenai Peninsula ($$$)**

Located near Cooper Landing on 1,900 feet of riverfront, this deluxe lodge in some ways resembles the cruise ships operated by its parent company. You don't have to leave the lodge to get everything you want in the way of pampering, including fine dining, and the outdoor recreation provided includes fishing, hiking, flightseeing, and river rafting. The resort has indoor and outdoor whirlpools. It's open from mid-May to mid-September. There is also an RV park associated with the lodge with full hookups and laundry. Camp and—if you're tired of cooking your own meals—go next door to the lodge (907) 258-5993 or 800-541-5174.

**3. Quiet Place Lodge—Halibut Cove, Alaska ($$)**

This is only one of a dozen bed-and-breakfast places in Homer, Alaska, and neighboring Halibut Cove (you have to get to Halibut Cove by boat). This charming little community has boardwalks connecting artists galleries and some fine restaurants. Call the lodge at (907) 235-7847. This is one of the most scenically blessed areas in Alaska, at the southern end of the Kenai Peninsula. Other B & B homes in the Homer area include the Wild Rose Bed and Breakfast, with a lovely homestead and cabins, overlooking Kachemak Bay, two miles from downtown Homer (907) 235-8780; and the Beach House, situated on the beach at Homer, with spectacular views of the bay and the mountains beyond. There is a deluxe suite here with whirlpool and balcony. This B & B is open year-round (907) 235-5945.

## 4. Liard River Lodge—Liard ($ to $$)

This rustic Alaska Highway lodge is staffed by friendly owners, Anne and Gene Beitz. Good food is served in its log-sided dining room and (best of all) it's just across the road from Liard Provincial Park and its hot spring pools. An overnight stay here will take the aches out of your bones, expose you to a very fascinating ecosystem in the park, and allow you to experience the hospitality of one of the best of the traditional highway lodges. For information and reservations, call (604) 776-7341. If this lodge is full, Trapper Ray's Liard Hot Springs Lodge, a newer log inn, is close by.

## 5. Westminster Hotel—Dawson City ($)

This hotel is not for travelers who want all of the creature comforts available in top-class hotels. This is a true original, virtually untouched from its early days in 1898, with bare rooms, floors sloping from the permafrost, and a very noisy bar downstairs. Yet the rooms are clean, a lot less expensive than the deluxe hotels down the street, and full of character. It's not everyone's cup of tea but it is an experience! (403) 993-5463.

## 6. Downtown Hotel—Dawson City ($$)

Here is the other face of Dawson City: a modern hotel which looks like it was built during the gold rush, with false front and the obligatory saloon. This is a comfortable place. The Jack London Grill serves seafood and steaks and there's a hot tub in the annex. It's a good place to stay if you want comfort and convenience (403) 993-5076.

## 7. Eagle Plains Hotel—Northern Yukon ($$)

Halfway up the Dempster Highway, this oasis owes its special character to its location. It's a completely self-contained community in the middle of nowhere: actually on top of a ridge in the Eagle Plains, just a few miles south of the Arctic Circle. The Eagle Plains Hotel is a convenient overnight stopping place on your way to Inuvik. The walls are covered with historical black and white photos of early Royal Canadian Mounted Police (RCMP) exploits and the great reindeer drive (403) 979-4187.

### 8. Denali Wilderness Lodge—Denali National Park ($$$)

Visiting Denali National Park south of Fairbanks can be accomplished with a train tour via the Alaska Railroad, with an overnight stay at the Denali National Park Hotel or the McKinley Resort and Lodge, or by taking a plane ride into the park interior and experiencing the park from the inside. The Denali Wilderness Lodge is one of these rustic lodges which are a 15-minute plane ride from the park airstrip. The accommodations are cozy, there's evening entertainment with an open bar, copious quantities of food, riding opportunities, and more hiking trails than you could walk in a month (at least 450 miles of trails in the immediate area). The lodge has more than 25 log buildings in an unparalleled scenic setting. Who could ask for more? Write the lodge at P.O. Box 50, Denali Park, Alaska 99755 or phone 800-541-9779.

### 9. Anchorage Hotel ($$ to $$$)

This restored historic hotel is one of the most pleasant places to stay in Anchorage, and it's close to everything downtown. The rooms are large and well appointed. The service is excellent. There are restaurants of all kinds nearby. For an urban stay, this is it! (907) 277-4483.

### 10. Glacier Bay Lodge—Glacier Bay National Park ($$$)

A superb wilderness lodge with accommodations from deluxe to dormitory, a dining room, and lounge. You can find scenery like this nowhere else in the world. For reservations call 800-451-5952.

## Restaurants and Pubs

### 1. An Alaska Salmon Bake

We couldn't settle on just one to list here. There are salmon bakes throughout the state. Haines puts up a good one, on the Parade Grounds at the old Fort Seward. There are two in Fairbanks, including one in Alaskaland, the pioneer theme park. Salmon bakes are available in all of the southeastern Alaska seaside communities. Wherever you are, just look for a salmon bake. You'll probably find one that serves tasty barbecued salmon.

## 2. The Back Room Restaurant—Inuvik

Hidden behind a pizza take-out place, the Back Room is a very good licensed restaurant that serves dishes using western Arctic ingredients, including Arctic char, caribou (the burgers are great), and reindeer meat. The Back Room also has standard southern-type meals. But if you travel all that distance, why not try the local cuisine?

## 3. Diamond Tooth Gertie's—Dawson City

This is neither a restaurant nor a bar, although you can eat and drink here. Operated by the Klondike Visitor's Association, the group that promotes tourism in the Klondike area, it's Canada's only licensed casino featuring eating, drinking, and dancing girls—almost as it was done during the Klondike Gold Rush days. Gertie's casino is open evenings during the summer months. Gertie herself introduces the acts.

## 4. Red Onion Saloon—Skagway

The Red Onion conveys the mood of Skagway's "Soapy Smith" period, when it was a rough-and-ready town filled with characters, and character. It's a good place to have a light meal and some Chinook beer—Alaska's own. The saloon is at Broadway and Second, across the street from the National Park headquarters, close to the ferry terminal.

## 5. Sawlty Dawg Saloon—Homer

Part of the attraction of Homer is the four-mile spit of sand that dominates this community. Along the Homer Spit are boardwalks and a collection of stores, restaurants, the Land's End Hotel, a small boat basin, and other places catering to tourists. The renowned Sawlty Dawg Saloon is here on the spit and well worth the visit to wet your whistle and take in the local color.

## 6. Malamute Saloon and North Country Inn—Fairbanks

There are musical revues and period entertainment shows throughout the Yukon and Alaska. They're all worth a visit to catch the northern mood, depending on where your trip takes you. There are two of these places near Fairbanks, where the beer flows and the audience often becomes part of the act. Try the Malamute Saloon, in the pretend gold mining camp at Ester. There is sawdust on the floor, the tables are made out of beer barrels and there's a nightly revue with Robert Service recitations. The North Country Inn, off the Steese Highway in Fox, also has a vaudeville show and the audience gets to can-can. It's all good fun and more appropriate than going to a Hollywood movie.

### 7. Hotel Hälsingland—Haines

Not being able to get the Hälsingland into the top ten places to stay (it's close), we should say here that the seafood restaurant in the former officers' quarters in historic Fort Seward is excellent. This hotel is part of the old Fort Seward complex overlooking Lynn Fjord. The white Victorian buildings, neatly arranged, make staying here a pleasure. There's a lounge in the hotel, and a salmon bake too. Call (907) 766-2000 or 800-542-6363.

### 8. The Pump House—Fairbanks

Part of this excellent restaurant used to be a pump house that supplied water to gold diggings outside of Fairbanks. It's located at mile 1.3, Chena Pump Road. It sits beside the Chena River, and features an outdoor eating and drinking area as well as a series of good-sized rooms inside. The menu is eclectic, ranging from steaks to fresh seafood (including an oyster bar) and continental dishes. Draft beer is served as well as wines and a generous selection of imported beers. All in all, an excellent place to eat. Reservations: (907) 479-8452.

### 9. Braeburn Lodge (café)—Mile 55.6, Klondike Highway

This Klondike Highway café is famous solely for its cinnamon buns. But oh what buns they are! This roadhouse is north of Whitehorse, on the way to Dawson City. Bush pilots fly across the wilderness to land at the lodge's airstrip to pick up some of these large, gooey cinnamon buns. Need we say more? Okay, see the next entry.

## 10. Chicken Creek Mercantile and Saloon—Chicken, Alaska

Chicken, Alaska, being what it is, there is no doubt in my mind that eating at the Chicken Creek Saloon will be talked about long after you've left this windswept spot along the Taylor Highway between Dawson City and Tok. I slowly chased a trotting moose with my car along the Taylor for about a mile, and it just wouldn't get off the road. I've never been able to forget it. This restaurant will affect you the same way; it's one of a kind in a community that is ditto. Actually, the café, saloon, and store are the remnants of old gold country, among the last remaining such buildings in Alaska. It's still a trading post and eating place for local miners, with burgers, fries, very good pies, and fine cinnamon buns taking up much of the menu.

# The Alaska Highway

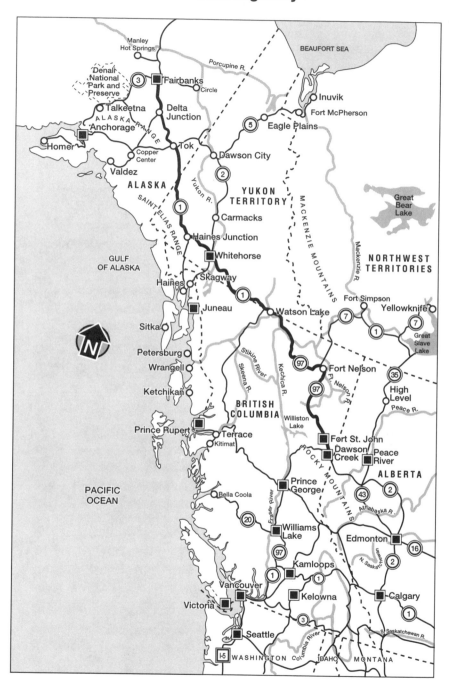

# The Alaska Highway
## *Drives*

In June of 1942, more than 10,000 U.S. troops had moved into northern Canada to begin what quickly became one of the world's most impressive and unusual engineering feats: the construction of the Alaska-Canada Military Highway (Alcan). The task of building an all-weather overland route between the 48 states and Alaska had begun on February 11th, when U.S. president Franklin D. Roosevelt authorized construction. At the time, Alaska was felt to be vulnerable to Japanese attack.

The road was designed to link a chain of existing airfields that dotted the landscape between Edmonton, Alberta, and Fairbanks, Alaska. More than 8,000 warplanes were ferried up this route from Great Falls, Montana, to Fairbanks, and then flown on to Russia as part of a joint military program.

Canada agreed to have the road constructed and provided construction materials along the route. Road-building equipment, trucks of all sizes, tents for accommodation, portable kitchens, and massive amounts of food were taken north. Once construction had started, the work never stopped. Soldiers and civilians alike worked eight or more hours a day, seven days a week. Forests were cleared and a rough wagon track began to take shape. The bulldozers and trucks worked their way across marshes and bogs, over the Rocky Mountains north of Fort Nelson, B.C., then through river canyons and—for the final 500 miles—across muskeg in the Yukon Territory and Alaska. In the northern reaches, the muskeg topsoil was removed and filled with rock, which disappeared into the thawed mud after spring arrived. Hundreds of vehicles were lost, sinking in bogs, swamps, and quicksand.

A ribbon-cutting ceremony was held on November 20th beside Kluane Lake, north of Whitehorse. The Alcan Highway was an extremely rough road—no more than a rugged, rutted track, suitable for only the most hardy military vehicles—but it worked! And amazingly it was built in only six months.

After the war, the Canadian section of the highway was turned over to Canada for use as a public highway, opening to the public in 1948. Since then, the re-named Alaska Highway has been continually improved and is paved for much of the distance between Dawson Creek and Fairbanks.

# Alaska Highway Drives

### Dawson Creek to Fort Nelson

The first part of the Alaska Highway drive from Dawson Creek to Fort Nelson, B.C., is uneventful, crossing northern British Columbia prairie, with the foothills of the Rockies many miles to the west. The Alaska Highway bears none of the old rutted trappings of the original military route for this first 465-kilometer (238-mile) section to Fort Nelson. Because this is an inhabited area, you will find plenty of stopping places for food and gas. Several roadside provincial parks offer picnic areas and overnight campsites.

**Dawson Creek**, the start of the drive, is a trading center for northeastern British Columbia, located 591 kilometers (367 miles) northwest of Edmonton, Alberta, and 402 KM (250 miles) north of Prince George, B.C. It, like Dawson City, was named for George Mercer Dawson, a Canadian government surveyor who mapped almost all of the region. This agricultural country is famous for its honey and other farm products, including eggs and beef. Canola grows here, along with cereal grains. It is a railway terminus and a major highway hub. It also supplies the oil and gas industry, and the large coal-mining operation located southwest of the town. Dawson Creek boasts a dozen hotels and motels, with several RV parks located along the highway. You can purchase your "I Drove the Alaska Highway" T-shirt at Treasure House Imports.

## Along the Way

**Taylor** This town on the Peace River services the petro-chemical industry. A pipeline transports gas to Vancouver, B.C., and the U.S.

**Fort St. John** At KM 75.5 (mile 47), this town was established as a Hudson's Bay post, and has grown into a busy, modern town on the northern prairie. Charlie Lake, just north of Fort St. John, is the junction point for the alternate route to the Hart Highway, offering a sidetrip to the picturesque town of Hudson's Hope, a hydro project, and a museum.

**Pink Mountain** A haven in the open countryside, this roadside oasis at KM 226 (mile 140.4) offers gas stations, 2 motels, and a bar. Additional roadside gas stations and cafés, about every 80 KM (50 miles), are listed in the following Highway Log.

## Mile (kilometer) Posts

Travelers along the Alaska Highway should make note of the milepost system established when the road was constructed. Several of the highway communities have their original milepost location in their name, including Wonowon. Improvements to the road have made the original numbers obsolete. Many sections have been strengthened, reducing their length; Whitehorse is almost 35 miles closer to Dawson Creek than it was in 1944. However, many of the places still bear the original milepost numbers. To add to the confusion, Canada switched to the metric system and re-numbered the posts, using kilometers. Kilometer posts appear at three-mile intervals along the British Columbia section.

When entering the Yukon, you'll notice that the posts carry both kilometers and miles. While the B.C. posts correctly state today's actual kilometers, those in the Yukon hold to the original 1940s numbers. The following highway log begins your journey along the Alaska Highway, with a little foreshadowing of what is to come in the way of scenic wonders a few hundred miles to the north.

# HIGHWAY LOG
## Dawson Creek to Fort Nelson
### 465 KM (283 miles)—5 hours, 30 minutes

"Mile 0" A signpost in downtown Dawson Creek, a block from Hwy. 7. For the real Alaska Hwy., take Hwy. 97 northwest.

**Junction–Hart Highway** (KM 1.9, mile 1.2) Route from Prince George.

**Turnoff to Old Alaska Highway and Kiskatinaw Provincial Park** (KM 27.8, mile 17.3). A private campground and RV park. Just before Kiskatinaw Provincial Park is an original curved, wooden Alaska Hwy. bridge.

**Junction–Road to Taylor Landing Provincial Park** (KM 54.7, mile 34) Camping, picnic area, fishing. A causeway leads to Peace Island Regional Park which has camping, a trail, and fishing.

**Taylor** (KM 56.3, mile 35) An industrial town with motels, hotel, food, stores, gas, and post office.

**Fort St. John** (KM 75.6, mile 47) Southern access to the city is via 100th Street. The Infocentre is found at 9323 100th Street, behind the oil derrick. The city has a full range of visitor services including hotels, motels, gas, and shopping.

**Beatton Provincial Park** (KM 79.6, mile 49.5) The park is 8 KM (5 miles) east of the highway. Camping, swimming, fishing.

Charlie Lake (KM 81.4, mile 50.6) A small village with gas, store, pub, RV park.

Junction–Highway 29 (KM 86.4, mile 53.7) to Hudson's Hope and the John Hart Hwy. The large power dam in Hudson's Hope houses a museum displaying fossils unearthed when the dam was constructed.

Charlie Lake Provincial Park (KM 86.4, mile 53.7) East of the hwy. with camping, fishing for walleye and northern pike, picnic area.

Wonowon (KM 161.7, mile 101) A village with gas, restaurants, motels, camping, store, pub, and post office.

Pink Mountain (KM 225.9, mile 140.4) A way station in the wilderness with motels, café, lounge, camping, gas, and post office. There is a time-zone change 12 KM (7.5 miles) north of Pink Mountain. Set your watches back one hour to Pacific Time.

Sikanni Chief (KM 256.5, mile 159.4) Gas, café, lodging and camping.

Highway Services (KM 232.5, mile 144.5) Café and gas.

Buckinghorse Provincial Park (KM 278.7, mile 173.2) Camping, picnic tables.

Prophet River Provincial Park (KM 349.3, mile 217.2) Off the hwy. with campsites, picnic tables, trail.

Prophet River (KM 365.8, mile 227) Café, gas, camping, lodging.

Andy Bailey Provincial Park (KM 427, mile 265.5) Found 11 KM (6.8 miles) off the highway. Camping, picnic tables, fishing.

Fort Nelson (KM 455.4, mile 283) The last major community before Watson Lake, Y.T. The Infocentre is located next to the museum on the Alaska Hwy. at the west end of town. Fort Nelson has a good supply of hotels, motels, food, shopping, gas, etc.

## Fort Nelson to Watson Lake

Of all the sections of the Alaska Highway, the portion from Fort Nelson to Watson Lake most realizes the romantic expectations most people have for the trip. The road climbs, winds, and descends through the Rocky Mountains. Rushing rivers make a path for the roadway. High mountain lakes and rivers offer great fishing for Dolly Varden, lake and rainbow trout, and grayling.

Highway lodges, motels, and campgrounds permit visitors to spend several enjoyable days in this area and we highly recommend doing so. Wildlife abounds in the Rockies and you stand a good chance of seeing Stone sheep, caribou, and moose at the edge of the highway.

## Along the Way

**Crossing the Rockies**   Leaving Fort Nelson, the highway begins climbing through the Rockies. Steamboat Mountain is the first rise, providing good views from the summit. Sixteen KM (10 miles) beyond the Steamboat Café you'll find a view of Indian Head, a mountain ridge shaped somewhat like the profile of a person.

**Tetsa River Provincial Park**   This is the first of four B.C. parks located on or near this Rocky Mountain stretch of the highway. They all offer unbeatable scenery and recreational opportunities, including fishing. Tetsa River is a fine place for anglers to pitch their tents or trailers. The campground is on the river, with grayling and Dolly Varden available. The park is 1.9 KM (1.2 miles) south of the highway, via a gravel road. Tetsa River Outfitters, with a store, gas, cabins, and food, is located on the highway.

**Stone Mountain Provincial Park**   The route enters this large park about 142 KM (88 miles) from Fort Nelson, winding through the park for ten miles, passing over the mountain crest and past the small community of Summit Lake, which has Mount St. George in the Stone Mountain Range as a backdrop. Summit Lake Campground is situated on a beautiful, small lake offering rainbow and lake trout and whitefish.

**Toad River**   This village sits along the highway. Toad River Lodge is a year-round operation, with rooms and cabins, plus a café with a large collection of baseball caps fastened to the ceiling. Toad River presents another fine fishing spot. Moose are usually seen just north of the community, beyond the bridge.

**Wildlife Viewing**   Just beyond Toad River, the highway turns north. Watch for a large turnout with litter barrels to the north of the highway. This is an excellent place to see Stone sheep. They may even stand right on the road. They have little fear of vehicles, and you can often drive through the flock and take photos through the car window. This same turnout is also often occupied by caribou, with moose and black bears seen in the early mornings and late evenings.

**Muncho Lake Provincial Park**   The most beautiful mountain lake along the B.C. section of the Alaska Highway is this vivid blue-green lake, colored by a small amount of copper oxide suspended in the water. The colors—almost iridescent—change with the time of day. Huge fish live here, and all are naturally bred. Lake trout as large as 50 pounds have been taken from Muncho Lake. Campsites are located here, and boats can be rented from several lodges along the highway.

**Liard Hot Springs**   Our favorite highlight of the trip (always) is Liard Hot Springs Provincial Park. This unique park, located 30 miles north of Muncho Lake and just south of the B.C./Yukon border, features two natural thermal pools, and a unique ecosystem warmed by the steaming spring water. Boardwalks take you to the hot pools, over a warm swamp fed by the outflow. Two lodges are located nearby, offering overnight accommodations and meals. See page 63 for more on this delightful area.

# HIGHWAY LOG
## *Fort Nelson to Watson Lake*
### 523 KM (325 miles)—6 hours, 30 minutes

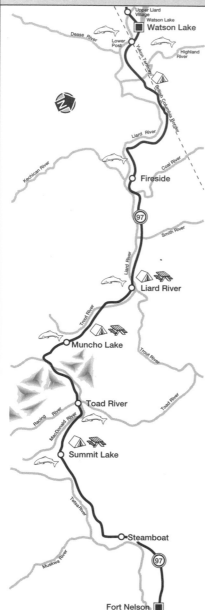

This is by far the most mountainous section of the Alaska Hwy. Driving north from Fort Nelson offers a spectacular range of scenery and wildlife, particularly in Stone Mountain Provincial Park.

Hwy. services are scattered with long intervals between gas pumps and restaurants. A picnic lunch beside a river or small lake is often a good idea.

**Junction–Liard Highway (#77)** (KM 484, mile 301) North to Fort Liard and Fort Simpson.
**Bridge over Steamboat Creek** (KM 519.3, mile 322.7) Begin steep climb up Steamboat Mountain.
**Steamboat** (KM 535.8, mile 333) Gas, café. The hwy. continues to climb with good views of the Muskwa Valley and the Rockies.
**Tetsa River Provincial Park** (KM 557.6, mile 346.5) 2 KM south of highway. Camping, picnic tables.
**Highway Services** (KM 575.3, mile 371.5) Gas and camping.
**Stone Mountain Provincial Park** (KM 597.8, mile 371.5) Entrance to a large wilderness park.
**Summit Lake** (KM 599.7, mile 373.3) Gas, café, store, lodging. The nearby peak is Mt. St. George.
**East End of Summit Lake** (KM 600.7, mile 373.6)

Campground, picnic tables, boat launch, trails, fishing for lake and rainbow trout and whitefish. Caribou and Stone sheep are often seen here. Roadside kilometer posts are off by 21 KM at this point.

**Picnic Area** (KM 605, mile 376) on Rocky Crest Lake.

**Highway Services** (KM 609.2, mile 378.6) Gas, store, lodging, campground.

**Provincial Campground** (KM 618, mile 384.2) Picnic tables, fishing for Dolly Varden and grayling.

**Highway Services** (KM 628.4, mile 390.5) Gas, café, lodging, RV parking.

**Toad River** (KM 651, mile 404.5) Gas, café, lodging, private campground. Toad River Lodge.

**Highway Services** (KM 655.7, mile 407.5) Gas, café, private campground.

**Muncho Lake Provincial Park** (KM 658.5, mile 409.2) The road follows the Toad River westbound. Fishing for Dolly Varden. Watch for Stone sheep on hwy. for next 30 KM.

**Muncho Lake** (KM 702.4, mile 436.5) Gas, lodges, cafés, campground.

**Strawberry Flats Campground** (KM 704.4, mile 437.7) Picnic tables, fishing for Dolly Varden, whitefish, grayling, lake trout.

**Highway Services** (KM 711.6, mile 442.2) Gas, café, private campground.

**Highway Services** (KM 714, mile 443.7) Gas, café, lodging, campground.

**Liard River** (KM 768, mile 477) Gas, store, Liard River Lodge, RV parking, camping.

**Liard Hot Springs Provincial Park** (KM 768.7, mile 477.7) Camping, hot springs pools, picnic tables, trails. Café across the hwy.

**Highway Services** (KM 827, mile 514) Gas, café, lodging, campground.

**Fireside** (KM 844, mile 524.2) Gas, café. In burn area left by a large forest fire burning more than 400,000 acres in 1982.

**Picnic Area** (KM 914, mile 568) At the Contact Creek Bridge. On this spot, the Alaska Hwy. was completed with road builders from the north and south meeting for a ceremony on September 24, 1942.

**Highway Services** (KM 917.3, mile 570) Gas, café, lodging, campground.

**Highway Services** (KM 927, mile 576) Gas, café, lodging.

**Yukon Border** (KM 973.6, mile 605) The first of seven crossings.

**Watson Lake** (KM 986.5, mile 613) Gas, cafés, stores, motels, camping. The southern Yukon Infocentre is behind the sign forest.

## Watson Lake to Whitehorse

The highway between Watson Lake and Whitehorse is a well-maintained paved roadway. We have left the Rocky Mountain sections of the highway, and now the road runs through the long valley between the Simpson range of the Pelly Mountains to the north and the Coast Mountains, looming to the south.

The following highway log includes several notes about fishing, for good reason. The southern Yukon is an angler's paradise, with ample stocks of grayling, northern pike, Dolly Varden, and whitefish. If you're coming north just to fish, you don't have to proceed much farther than this southern Yukon town. The information center at Watson Lake has details on the best fishing periods.

## Along the Way

**Watson Lake**   This small town was a crucial staging point during the building of the Alaska Highway. To get an understanding of what a tremendous feat the highway project was, visit the Alaska Highway Interpretive Centre, located beside the town's Visitor Centre, behind the famed sign forest, and accessed via the Campbell Highway. A 40-minute film shows scenes from the construction days, and displays have artifacts from the period. The sign forest began in 1941 when a homesick soldier posted a sign from his hometown. The display has grown each year, with the town placing more poles as necessary to accommodate the additional thousands of signs.

**More Mountains**   The ranges in this area are really extensions of the Rockies, although they are given other names (Cassiar, Pelly, Omineca). The drive leads between the ranges, not over them, providing a flat drive past Whitehorse. A spring trip offers snow-capped ranges on both sides of the highway. Although snowfall is not abundant in the cold, super-dry winter climate, there is enough snowpack to provide a series of beautiful vistas through June.

**Rancheria River**   After leaving Watson Lake, the highway climbs slightly as it runs beside the Rancheria River. This extremely scenic river is thought by some to have been named by surveyor George Dawson after a stream in California, as he traveled and mapped the northern river routes before the turn of the century. There is a Rancheria Creek about a mile from my home in the Sierra Foothills gold country; possibly the two names are connected. The California creek was named during the 1849 gold rush.

**Teslin**   Teslin is a picturesque Native American community situated at the junction of the Nisutlin River and Teslin Lake, at KM 1250 (mile 779). This is the first of three large lakes between here and Whitehorse. The Nisutlin Bay Bridge is the longest overwater span on the Alaska Highway, crossing the arm of Teslin Lake. The town has a fascinating local museum, devoted to the Native American history of the region. It also has good places to stay, eat, and shop for travel supplies.

**Jake's Corner and the Atlin Road**   The road to Atlin is just about the most scenic short sidetrip from the Alaska Highway. Jake's Corner, not identified as such, is the home of Jake's Crystal Palace, a restaurant and gas station at the Atlin Road junction. The sideroad leads 95 kilometers (59 miles) into the region called Canada's Little Switzerland. The route offers stupendously beautiful scenery, with snowcapped peaks and hanging glaciers, two beautiful lakes (Big and Little Atlin), great fishing, and lots of wildlife. At the end is the village of Atlin, with overnight accommodations (see page 64) and several places to eat. This route offers a marvelous two-day sojourn.

**Klondike Highway**   Another scenic route, Highway 2 runs to tidewater at Skagway, Alaska, at the head of Lynn Canal. This route is covered in detail, starting on page 178. The route passes through the Yukon village of Carcross, and then alongside Lake Bennett, a prime location for stampeders during the Klondike Gold Rush. The junction is located 18 kilometers (11 miles) from the southern entrance road to Whitehorse.

# HIGHWAY LOG
## *Watson Lake to Whitehorse*
### 436 KM (271 miles)—5 hours

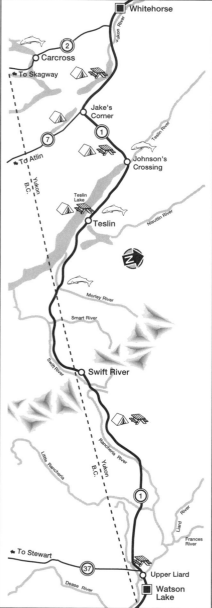

Turnoff to Watson Lake Recreation Park (KM 990.2, mile 615.3) 3 KM (1 mile) off highway. Camping, picnic tables, shelters, swimming.

Upper Liard Village (KM 957.7, mile 620) Private RV and camping park, café, motel.

Junction–Stewart/Cassiar Highway (#37) (KM 1007.7, mile 626.2) Gas, store, café, lodging, camping.

Big Creek Picnic Area (KM 1048, mile 651.2) Drinking water.

Turnout–Lower Rancheria River (KM 1068.7, mile 664.1) The hwy. follows the river for the next 57 KM (35 miles). Good fishing for Dolly Varden and grayling.

Scenic River Viewpoint (KM 1070.3, mile 665.1) Views of the Rancheria valley.

Highway Services (KM 1106, mile 687.2) Gas, café, motel, camping.

Highway Services (KM 1124, mile 698.4) Gas, café, lodging, campground.

Turnout–Great River Divide (KM 1125, mile 699.1) Division of the Mackenzie and Yukon watersheds.

**Swift River** (KM 1142.6, mile 710) Gas, café, lodging. The hwy. re-enters B.C. for 68 KM (42 miles).
**Turnout–Swan Lake** (KM 1158, mile 719.6) Good fishing for whitefish and lake trout.
**Morley River Picnic Area** (KM 1210, mile 752) Shelter, drinking water. We're now back in the Yukon after nine border crossings. Fishing in Morley Bay (Teslin Lake) and the river for grayling, northern pike, and lake trout.
**Highway Services** (KM 1211.6, mile 752.9) Gas, café, RV park, and camping.
**Campground** (KM 1238.5, mile 769.6) Hookups.
**Teslin** (KM 1249.2, mile 776.3) Turn to village at north end of the bridge. Gas, cafés, stores.
**Highway Services** (KM 1253.8, mile 779.1) Gas, café, campground, lodging.
**Highway Services** (KM 1262, mile 784.3) Café, lodging, RV park, hookups.
**Teslin Lake Campground** (KM 1263.6, mile 785.2) Picnic tables.
**Junction–Canol Road** (KM 1291, mile 802.2) To Ross River. This gravel road meets the Robert Campbell Hwy.

**Bridge–Teslin River** (KM 1301.7, mile 808.9) At Johnson's Crossing. Private campground, café, store at north end of bridge. Fishing for grayling.
**Squanga Lake Campground** (KM 1320.2, mile 820.4) Picnic tables, shelter. Northern pike, grayling, whitefish, and rainbow trout.
**Jake's Corner** (KM 1346.6, mile 836.8) At Junction with Hwy. 7 (to Atlin). Access to Carmacks and Klondike Hwy. (to Skagway).
**Pullout to Marsh Lake** (KM 1375, mile 854.4) Boat ramp to the west.
**Marsh Lake Campground** (KM 1383.8, mile 859.9) Picnic tables, shelter, drinking water.
**Picnic Park** (KM 1395.7, mile 867.3) From turnoff near historic marker.
**Wolfe Creek Campground** (KM 1411, mile 876.8) Via 1.3 KM road.
**South Access Road** to the Yukon capital city of Whitehorse (KM 1422.6, mile 884).

Whitehorse has tourist services in the downtown area and the Alaska Hwy. For the north (main) entrance to the city, stay on the Alaska Hwy. and turn onto 4th Avenue (Two-Mile Hill).

## Whitehorse to Alaska Border

The tiny town of Beaver Creek lies about 32 KM (20 miles) south of the Yukon/Alaska border. The 282-mile (470-KM) route between Whitehorse and Beaver Creek starts off as an easy, flat drive on a wide highway for two hours—to Haines Junction. The only community between the two towns is Champagne, a small Native American village, which provides no tourist facilities. It takes less than two hours to reach Haines Junction (98 miles, 163 KM) and the headquarters for Kluane National Park. Destruction Bay, with a motel, lodge, restaurant, and gas station, is located 67 miles (108 KM) beyond Haines Junction. With another 117 miles (188 KM) to Beaver Creek, the end of the delivery route for gasoline, it makes sense to plan ahead to buy gas in Haines Junction or Destruction Bay. Gas prices in Beaver Creek are usually the highest on the highway.

Beside the small towns along this route, several highway lodges offer food and overnight accommodations, including MacIntosh Lodge, Bayshore Motel, Burwash Landing (on Kluane Lake), Bear Flats Lodge, and White River Lodge. For details on these accommodations outside the towns, see page 255.

## Along the Way

**Aishihik Lake and Bridge**   This large lake offers anglers good opportunities to catch grayling and lake trout. The Yukon Government Campground is located at the south end of the lake (41.8 KM, 26 miles from the highway on Aishihik Road). There's a day-use park at 30 KM (18 miles) along this same road, with picnic tables, outhouses, and boat ramp. Along the main highway two bridges cross Aishihik River. The original bridge was built in 1920, long before the highway was constructed on a wagon route to Silver City on Kluane Lake. The new highway bridge was built in 1987.

**Haines Junction and Kluane National Park**   Before reaching Haines Junction, you'll have increasingly good views of the St. Elias Mountains, including the Kluane Icefields. To the north a turnout with markers provides information on the Kluane Ranges. Haines Junction is a small three-corners community at the junction of the Alaska and Haines highways. The town has full visitor services, including the visitor center for Kluane National Park. The park lies west of town. This impressive wilderness area has no roads into the interior, and hiking is necessary to see the abundant wildlife and mountain wonders. There is one campground, located 27 KM (16 miles) south of town, on the Haines Highway.

**Kluane Lake**   Kluane National Park is on the west side of the highway from Haines Junction to Burwash Landing. The lake is to the immediate east. Sheep Mountain, seen first from the bridge which crosses one of the lake's arms, is the home of a large herd of Dall sheep, the only pure white mountain sheep on the continent. May is the best month to see the sheep in large numbers, close to the highway. A Parks Canada information station is located at the base of the mountain.

### *Approaching Alaska*

A word of caution is necessary at this point. Between Burwash Landing and the Alaska boundary, the paved road is less than satisfactory. Paving this section, previously a fine piece of gravel road, may have been a mistake. Frost heaving has caused sloping pavement, dips, and bumps along much of the route. The no-man's-land between the Canadian Customs station, near Beaver Creek, and the U.S. Customs station at Port Alcan (only 20 miles away) has always been a notorious stretch of extremely bad highway. Let's hope recent roadwork by the Shakwak Reconstruction Project has helped to improve this boggy, bumpy stretch, and that your passage through this forbidding territory will be a lot more pleasant than mine. Beaver Creek in summer is an interesting, funky place to stay. For details, see page 251.

# HIGHWAY LOG
## *Whitehorse to Alaska Border*
### 486 KM (302 miles)—5 hours, 45 minutes

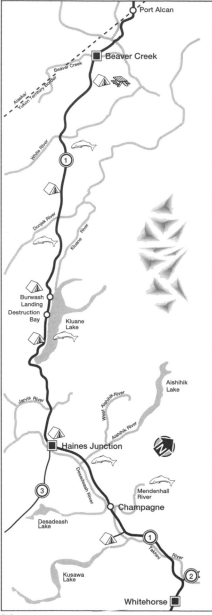

**North Entrance to Whitehorse** (KM 1420, mile 887.4) At top of Two Mile Hill.

**Turnoff–Fish Lake Road** (KM 1431.3, mile 889.4) Historic marker at 4 KM (2.5 miles) on copper mining.

**Turnoff–Porter Creek** (KM 1433.8, mile 891) Gas, store.

**Turnoff–Azure Road** (KM 1435.4, mile 892) RV park, hookups.

**Junction–Klondike Highway North** (Hwy. 2) (KM 1440, mile 894.8) Route for Takhini Hot Springs and Dawson City.

**Turnout–Marker** (KM 1490.2, mile 926) Fires in 1958 destroyed more than 1.5 million acres of forest.

**Turnoff–Kusawa Lake** (KM 1492.3, mile 927.3) Campground (24 KM, 15 miles).

**Champagne** (KM 1568.4, mile 974.6) Village of Champagne-Aishihik Indian Band. A roadhouse was built here in 1902, on the old Dalton Trail to Dawson City.

**Turnoff–Aishihik Road** (KM 1552.3, mile 964.6) Yukon campground on Aishihik Lake 40 KM (25 miles). Reached by this narrow, winding road. Good fishing for grayling, lake trout.

**Viewpoint–Canyon Creek Bridge** (KM 1554, mile 965.6) Built in 1920.

**Turnout–Markers** (KM 1572.4, mile 977.1) View of Kluane mountain ranges. The peaks of Mt. Kennedy and Mt. Hubbard are seen on clear days.
**Pine Lake Campground** (KM 1578.5, mile 980.9) Picnicking, boat launch, swimming, drinking water.
**Haines Junction** (KM 1584.8, mile 984.8) Turn onto Kluane St. for the Kluane National Park Visitor Centre.
**Junction–Haines Highway** (#4) (KM 1585, mile 985) Haines Junction lies on the eastern edge of Kluane National Park. There are motels, gas stations, restaurants, stores, and other visitor services.
**National Park Headquarters** (KM 1589.6, mile 987.8) There is an information desk and displays in this building.
**Highway Services** (KM 1595.7, mile 991.6) Gas, store, camping, lodging.
**Bear Creek Summit** (KM 1609.4, mile 1000.1) Highest point on the hwy. between Whitehorse and Fairbanks.
**Turnoff–Viewpoint** (KM 1635.8, mile 1016.5) Kluane Mountains.
**Turnoff** (KM 1642, mile 1020.3) To old Silver City townsite.
**Highway Services** (KM 1647.4, mile 1023.7) Gas, RV park, Kluane Lake Lodge, café.
**Park Information** (KM 1656, mile 1029) Trailer at Sheep Mountain

(open May-September). A sign marks the official opening of the Alaska Hwy. here, on Nov. 20, 1942.
**Highway Services** (KM 1660.6, mile 1031.9) Gas, café, camping, hookups. From here you will find hwy. services every 30 to 40 miles.
**Private Campground** (KM 1665.5, mile 1034. 9)
**Congdon Creek Campground** (KM 1673.5, mile 1039.9) Picnic tables, shelters, drinking water. On Kluane Lake.
**Destruction Bay** (KM 1692.2, mile 1051.5) Gas, café, camping, RV hookups, lodging.
**Turnoff–Burwash Landing** (KM 1708.2, mile 1061.5) Gas, restaurant, lounge, lodging. Museum on east side of hwy.
**Lake Creek Campground** (KM 1800.4, mile 1118.8) Picnic tables, shelter.
**Turnoff–Snag Junction Campground** (KM 1859, mile 1155.2) Picnic tables, swimming.
**Beaver Creek** (KM 1878.3, mile 1167.2) The last Yukon community before the Alaska border. Gas, motels, restaurants, stores. The infocenter is on the hwy.
**Canada Customs Station** (KM 1883.6, mile 1170.5)
**U.S. Customs Station** (KM 1914.7, mile 1189.8) At Port Alcan. Time zone change.

## Alaska Border to Fairbanks

The time zone changes at the Alaska Border, just north of Beaver Creek. Through the Canadian section of the highway, we have indicated mileage by kilometers first and miles second. Now that we're dealing with Alaska mileposts and signs that use miles, we shift to listing miles first and kilometers second.

While they are somewhat lacking in northern B.C. and the Yukon, mileposts in Alaska come at steady one-mile intervals. A suitable number of mileage signs keep travelers well informed.

Beside the U.S. border station is a large Alaska sign. Travelers stop here to shoot photos to celebrate their arrival. The border is marked with a 20-foot swath of clearing in the bush. You can see the seemingly endless clearing by walking down to the border.

The 125 miles (201 KM) of highway between the border and Tok offers a well-maintained roadway, but not much in the way of scenic variety.

### Along the Way

**Wildlife and Recreation**   The 950,000-acre Tetlin National Wildlife Refuge is a bird-watchers' paradise, particularly for summer waterfowl nesting. The small town of Northway lies inside the preserve. After passing Border City Lodge, you'll notice a pulloff with a large parking area to the southwest. This is an interpretive marker put here by the U.S. Fish and Wildlife Service, providing information on the geography of the area and on migrating birds. Another mile along the highway is the USFWS log cabin visitor center, with displays and a viewing deck. Nature talks are given twice daily during summer months. Eight miles farther north is the Hidden Lake Trail, a one-mile walk to a wildlife viewing area, and fishing for rainbow trout. The trail leads through black spruce bogs. Deadman Lake State Campground offers fishing for northern pike, a fish not well appreciated by resident Alaskans.

**Tok**   This roadside town (rhymes with *poke*), at the junction of the Alaska Highway and the Tok Cutoff to the Glenn Highway, takes advantage of its location to offer services to travelers year-round. You can experience your first Alaska salmon bake of the season here. This is the one sizable town between Whitehorse and Fairbanks. Newcomers to the state can pick up information and permits required for a vacation here. The town information center sits at the highway junction. The museum at the information center depicts the history of the area, and displays stuffed wildlife—a common feature of Alaska museums. State park passes, other permits, and free coffee are available at the Alaska Public Lands Information Center, at milepost 1314.1. Tok has a range of visitor services including hotels, motels, B & B homes, restaurants, gas stations, and stores.

**Delta Junction** Delta residents will tell you that this town is the real end of the Alaska Highway. Strictly speaking, this is true, for the rest of the road to Fairbanks is the northern part of the Richardson Highway, which joins Valdez on Prince William Sound, to Fairbanks. However, most visitors consider Fairbanks the end of the Alaska Highway, and so does Fairbanks. Sitting beside the Delta River, for which it was named, the town is 108 miles north of Tok, and a highway service center. The Trans-Alaska Pipeline crosses through the area, and the best place to see it is along the Alaska/Richardson Highway, nine miles (15 KM) north of town. Pump Station No. 9 offers a free 45-minute tour daily.

Before reaching the pump station and the Tanana River Bridge, visit Big Delta State Historical Park for a glimpse of early Alaskan society. This is the rebuilt Rika's Roadhouse, originally established in 1910 as an overnight stop on the trail between Valdez and Fairbanks, mainly on the route now taken by the Richardson Highway. Breakfast and lunch are served here.

# HIGHWAY LOG
## Alaska Border to Fairbanks
### 330.5 miles (540 KM)—6 hours, 30 minutes

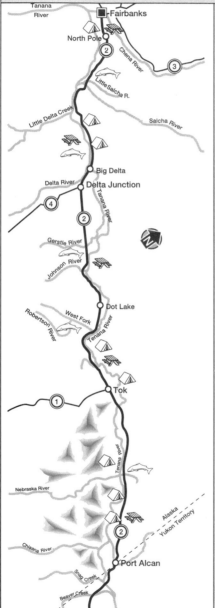

**Highway Services** (Mile 1225.6, KM 1972. 3) Gas, café, lodging. 3.5 miles (5.6 KM) north of the border station at Port Alcan.

**U.S. Forest and Wildlife Service** (Mile 1227.9, KM 1976.1) Information sign, picnic tables, view west to Wrangell Mountains.

**USFWS Information Center** (Mile 1229, KM 1980.9)

**Deadman Lake Campground** (Mile 1249.3, KM 2010.5) Found 1.5 miles (2.4 KM) off highway. Picnic tables, swimming, fishing for northern pike.

**Rest Area** (Mile 1250.2, KM 2012) Picnic tables.

**Lakeview Campground** (Mile 1256.7, KM 2022.5) On Yarger Lake, with good views of the Wrangell and St. Elias ranges.

**Highway Services** (Mile 1263, KM 2032.5) Gas, café, lodging, RV hookups.

**Northway Junction** (Mile 1264, KM 2034.2) Camping, café, store, gas. Road to Northway (7 miles, 11.3 KM).

**Midway Lake** (Mile 1289, KM 2074.4) The Tetlin Native American village is located 10 miles (16 KM) southwest (not accessible by road).

**Tetlin Junction** (Mile 1301.7, KM 2094.8) Village at junction of

Taylor Hwy., the route to Dawson City via Taylor and Top of the World hwys. (see drive, page 186). Café, store, camping, RV hookups at Tetlin Junction.

**Tanana River Bridge** (Mile 1303.3, KM 2097.4) From here, the Alaska Hwy. parallels the Tanana to Fairbanks.

**Highway Services** (Mile 1309.2, KM 2106) Gas, café, RV hookups, store.

**Tok** (Mile 1314.2, KM 2115) Junction of Alaska and Glenn hwys. (to Anchorage). State Information Center on the hwy. is open year-round.

**Tanacross Junction** (Mile 1325.8, KM 2133.7) Turnoff for village of Tanacross, just off highway.

**Moon Lake State Campground** (Mile 1331.9, KM 2143.5) Picnic tables, drinking water, swimming.

**Dot Lake** (Mile 1361.3, KM 2190.7) Small village with gas, café, car wash, camping, lodging.

**Picnic Park** (Mile 1393, KM 2241.8) Beside Gerstle River.

**Clearwater Campground** (Mile 1415, KM 2277) Camping 2.8 miles (4.5 KM) from hwy. with picnic area, boat launch. Fishing, in season, for grayling, whitefish, and salmon.

**Delta Junction** (Mile 1422, KM 2288.4) Junction of Alaska and Richardson hwys. Turn south for Valdez. Visitor Center is at the junction (open June-September).

Motels, restaurants, stores, camping, car wash, bank, and other services. The route to Fairbanks is now part of the Richardson Highway.

**Delta State Campground** (Mile 1423.1, KM 2290.2) Picnic tables.

**Junction–Jack Warren Road** (Mile 1424.3, KM 2292.1) for Clearwater State Campground (10.5 miles, 16.9 KM). Picnic tables, boat launch, drinking water. Gas, store and lodge nearby on Remington Road.

**Turnoff–Tanana Loop Road** Connects with Jack Warren Road.

**Big Delta Historical Park** (Mile 1431.6, KM 2303.9) on Rika's Road. The park features a restored roadhouse, blacksmith's shop museum, and other buildings. Café.

**Turnoff–Quartz Lake Recreation Area** (Mile 1433.7, KM 2307.2) 2.8 miles (4.5 KM) to Lost Lake Campground, picnic tables.

**View of Alaska Range:** Mt. Hayes, Hess Mountain, and Mt. Deborah (Mile 1444, KM 2323.8).

**Highway Services** (Mile 1451, KM 2355) Gas, food.

**Highway Services** (Mile 1470, KM 2366.9) Café, bar, lodging.

**Harding Lake State Campground** Picnic park, boat ramp.

**Highway Services** (Mile 1478.2, KM 2378.9) Café, motel.

**Fairbanks** (Mile 1520, KM 2446.2) The end of the Alaska Hwy., a major city with full visitor services.

# Alaska Highway Travel Tips

Any kind of car or recreational vehicle can be used on the Alaska Highway drive, or for that matter, on any of the routes in this book. Because of frost heaving on stretches of the route, the presence of gravel on some sections, and summer bugs, some precautions are necessary, and some advance planning is required.

Twenty years ago, the large amount of gravel road surface caused tires to blow, and windshields were often shattered by rocks flying—mainly from trucks. Even five years ago I was driving too fast just north of Fort Nelson, and my windshield was broken by a flying stone. It was my own fault, because I knew that it pays to drive slowly, or even stop, when meeting large trucks. Cautious driving should help you avoid both smashed glass and blowouts.

Travelers should take an extra tire if theirs are not a standard size, particularly trailer tires. Vehicles with powerful motors and low gas-mileage rates should carry along at least a five-gallon gas container for security over the isolated sections. Mud flaps are worthwhile for people driving RVs; they help to stop gravel from flying back against the rear of your vehicle, which can look as if someone took aim at your RV with a shotgun. Bug screens help to keep mosquitoes and other flying critters from embedding themselves permanently on your hood.

While motels and lodges abound on the Alaska Highway, camping along the way is enjoyable and economical. Parking regulations along the route are liberal, and you can park in a scenic location off the highway during the off-season. Pulling an RV or pickup off the road to camp for the night beside a river or other scenic wonder adds spice to the trip. In the spring and fall months the government campgrounds are not open and any spot along the highway is fair game for a night's stay.

# The Alaska Highway
## *Destinations*

This chapter includes destinations along the Alaska Highway in British Columbia. Alaska Highway destinations and attractions in the Yukon Territory and Alaska are included in the Yukon and Alaska chapters. Unlike the listings in other chapters, the Alaska Highway destinations are shown in geographical progression, from south to north.

## Dawson Creek

Dawson Creek is a major business and transportation center, situated at the junction of the Hart Highway, the Alaska Highway, and Highway 2 (east), which leads to the province of Alberta and the city of Edmonton. Dawson Creek runs through the middle of the city. It was named after George Mercer Dawson, the federal government surveyor who explored and surveyed much of the Canadian northland.

The town is centrally located in the northeastern B.C. prairie, an area with substantial agricultural and forest industries. It's also an energy center, providing services for the oil and gas industry in the region, and supplying the huge coal-mining operation to the southwest of town, near Chetwynd.

Canola (rapeseed) is a major crop and this area supplies much of the seed processed in Alberta. The city is also served by railways. It's on the British Columbia Rail line and is the northwestern terminus of the Canadian National railroad. With the building of the Alaska Highway in 1942, Dawson Creek began to grow.

After the war the city became a destination for tourists wanting to drive the complete Alaska Highway route. The tradition continues to this day, with travelers coming to Dawson Creek from both southern B.C. and Alberta to tackle the rigors of the Alaska Highway—from end to end.

Dawson Creek is not really focused as a tourist destination, except for the fact that the Alaska Highway begins here. As a result, the town is a beginning instead of an "end," and suffers a decided lack of things to do, except for assembling Alaska Highway memorabilia. The "Mile 0" signpost is located in the middle of the intersection of 102nd Avenue and 10th Street. Nearby you will find gift shops where you can buy "I Drove the Alaska Highway" T-shirts. As part of the Infocentre and Museum complex on the Alaska Highway, a grain elevator has been converted into an art gallery. Several nearby parks provide interesting overnight accommodation and sightseeing. On the way to Kiskatinaw Provincial Park, east of town, is an original curved wooden bridge on an original section of the Alaska Highway. Monkman Provincial Park has no campsites but is a wilderness park, accessible by riverboat.

The town's Travel Infocentre is at 900 Alaska Avenue (off Highway 97, 604-782-5211). This visitor facility is located next door to the museum and art gallery complex, in the former railway station.

## Where to Eat

Dawson Creek has more than a dozen cafés plus several fast food chain restaurants. Among the best of the latter is **Boston Pizza**, at 1525 Alaska Avenue, serving family-style food such as pizza, ribs, pasta, steaks, and sandwiches. **Alaska Café and Dew Drop Inn**, beside the "Mile 0" milepost in the center of town, has good food with lots of atmosphere. The food operation is part of a bed and breakfast inn. **Lily's**, in the George Dawson Inn, 11705 8th Street, is a good hotel dining room with a wide variety of dishes. The hotel also has a coffee shop, **Ma's Stopping Place**. The **Stagecoach Restaurant**, 1725 Alaska Avenue, is a popular local café, with basic North American cuisine, in a central location.

# Fort Nelson

Like other towns in Northern B.C., Fort Nelson was founded in the early 1800s by fur traders. It's now a resource center for forest, oil and gas companies. The Fort Nelson plant of Northwest Energy is one of the largest natural-gas processing plants in North America, with more jobs created by a sawmill, veneer plant, plywood factory, and a factory that produces chopsticks from the abundant lodgepole pine.

The Alaska Highway brought modernity to Fort Nelson. Because it's a newer townsite than most highway communities, it offers modern hotels, shopping facilities, and community services.

The town Infocentre is located in the recreation center, on the Alaska Highway at the west end of town. The Heritage Museum is across the street from the Infocentre. In previous years, Fort Nelson has staged information evenings for travelers, providing material about the natural attractions of the area. For information on this Welcome Visitor Program, and Fort Nelson in general, call (604) 774-2541 (year-round).

North of Fort Nelson, the Liard Highway takes the truly adventurous to Fort Liard in the Yukon, to the Nahanni National Park area (Headless Falls), and on to Fort Simpson in the Northwest Territories. River tours and charter flights to prime fishing lakes are available in Fort Nelson, with information at the Infocentre.

Several modern RV parks provide hookups and recreational facilities. The town has a good supply of restaurants, deli stores—including the Northern Lights Deli in the Landmark Plaza—and camping supply outlets.

### Where to Eat

**Smitty's Delicatessen**, in the Landmark Plaza, features eat-in or take-out food, including submarine sandwiches, salads, cold meats, and cheeses. This is a good place to pick up picnic supplies. **Dan's Neighbourhood Pub**, on the Alaska Highway at the southeast end of town, serves standard pub fare in "The Bistro." The pub operates a cold beer and wine store. **Coach House Inn Restaurant**, at 4711 50th Avenue South, is one of several good hotel dining rooms in Fort Nelson, all of which serve cuisine suitable for families.

# Fort St. John

In 1793, fur traders led by explorer Alexander Mackenzie came along the Peace River and established the first of a series of forts which served the fur trade for more than a hundred years. Until 1943, Fort St. John was a sleepy village, but all that changed with the building of the Alaska Highway. The population grew from 30 to 2,000. The highway opened the area to ranching, and then the oil boom of 1947 made the town a center for oil and gas exploration. It's now called the "Energy Capital of B.C.," and has a population of 14,000.

There's an 18-hole golf course on Charlie Lake. The nearby community of Hudson's Hope is the site of a giant hydro-electric dam and an interesting museum exhibiting fossils and mammoth bones unearthed during dam construction. The town has a good selection of hotels and motels in the downtown area and along the Alaska Highway. The Totem Mall is located on the Alaska Highway.

The Fort St. John–North Peace Museum features displays with thousands of artifacts focusing on regional history, particularly the pioneer era during the 1800s. It is located in Centennial Park, on 100th Street.

Fish Creek Community Forest provides a fascinating stroll through a demonstration woodlot, next to Northern Lights College, on 100th Street (north). The forest contains three interpreted nature trails, with information on forest biology and management.

The town's Infocentre is at 10139 101st Avenue. For advance information, call (604) 785-4625.

## Where to Eat

**Mackenzie Room**, in the Alexander Mackenzie Inn, 9223 100 Street, serves up standard hotel dining room fare, with adjacent coffee shop and pub. The **Coachman Inn Restaurant**, on the Alaska Highway, is a popular spot which attracts travelers and locals, including oil and gas workers—thus the food is nourishing and plentiful. **Red Barn Pub**, 9.5 KM (6 miles) north of downtown on the Alaska Highway features rustic cooking in a rustic setting, with a selection of beers and filling dishes.

# Liard River

Liard River is one of those spots which epitomize the term "Alaska-Yukon adventures," although it is in neither Alaska nor the Yukon. Here, in the middle of the northern B.C. wilderness close to the Yukon border, is a unique and beautiful provincial park, featuring sparkling, natural hot spring pools surrounded by a distinctive ecosystem found nowhere else. The community has only a lodge with gas station, another café, and the park. Yet thousands of people stop here each year to walk through the trails in the hot springs park and to soak in the pools.

There are two pools left in a natural state, with outdoor changing houses. You enter the park and cross a boardwalk over a steaming marsh to reach the first pool. A second pool is located up the hill, a quarter of a mile past the first one. The first pool is hotter (43°C, 109°F). Each pool is surrounded by tall evergreen trees and a thick underbrush. The marsh areas, fed by the warmed water from the pools, harbor unusual semi-tropical plants.

Try the pools during the daytime and again after dark (the people at the lodge will loan you a flashlight). A nighttime soak is a wonderful experience, with mists swirling up from the pools and the quiet sounds of the forest. It's a good place to strike up conversations with other bathers, who come from around the world to visit this unique site. It's not to be missed!

The Liard River is impressive. It drains the Rocky Mountains in the area and flows across the plain, providing a natural route for engineers to situate the Alaska Highway. The river was used in the late 1700s and early 1800s for fur trading. The Liard flows northeast and empties into the Mackenzie River. **Liard River Lodge**, the neighboring hotel, is one of the famous and colorful Alaska Highway lodges. This log building was built during the construction of the highway in the 1940s. A more recent addition to the community is **Trapper Ray's Liard Hot Springs Lodge**, featuring an unusual staircase made of willow. The lodge has a café, rooms to stay in, a campground with showers, and a gas station with tire repair facilities. **Coal River Lodge** is a few miles north of Liard River, with a motel, RV park, and tent sites with showers, coffee shop, and gas station. New management took over the lodge in 1994.

### Where to Eat

The dining room in **Liard River Lodge** is recommended for its 1940s log decor, and friendly service by the lodge's owners. Their home-style breakfasts include cinnamon buns and full breakfast plates. The café in **Trapper Ray's Liard Hot Springs Lodge**, on the Alaska Highway, features freshly baked breads and desserts. Otherwise, picnicking is the order of the day at the provincial campsites and picnic parks along the Alaska Highway (see the Highway Log section for location of parks and picnic sites).

# Atlin

Although Atlin is accessible only via a road from the Yukon Territory, it is located in the northwest corner of British Columbia. This is lake country, in the midst of the Coast Mountains. Highway 7 (Atlin Road) runs south to Atlin from the Alaska Highway at Jake's Corner (a crossroads restaurant), 65 KM (40 miles) south of Whitehorse. The well-surfaced gravel road runs 95 KM (59 miles) to Atlin. Tucked into the mountains, Atlin started life during the Klondike Gold Rush period as a gold mining town. Many of the original turn-of-the-century buildings still exist, some of them restored and in use. Atlin Provincial Park curves around the southern third of Atlin Lake, the largest natural lake in the province, 90 miles (145 KM) long. Llewellyn Glacier dominates this beautiful park, which is often called the "Little Switzerland of Canada."

Things to do and see in Atlin include visiting the historic Native American cemetery, south of the town. The building housing the Atlin Historical Museum is the restored original Atlin schoolhouse. It contains gold mining displays and photos of the gold rush days.

The *MV Tarahne*, sitting next to the lake in the downtown area, is now a museum, but in its prime years this ship carried freight and passengers from Atlin to Scotia Bay—across the lake—until 1936. While the boat now sits on dry land, Atlin residents have been working to restore the hull and machinery so that the ship may be put back in the water for lake cruises.

The working gold mine at Spruce Creek, near Discovery, the original Atlin townsite, is also open for viewing. You reach this site by taking the Discovery Road, from the junction with Atlin Road, and then driving 5.83 KM (3.6 miles). Then turn south onto Spruce Creek Road, which leads first to a public gold panning area, to the active mining operation on Spruce Creek. The ghost town is located 8.7 KM (5.4 miles) from the Atlin Road junction. After crossing the creek on a narrow bridge, the road leads to Surprise Lake, a waterfowl viewing spot. The road crosses over the Surprise Lake Dam, with a turnout. The Surprise Lake Recreation Site is near the end of the road, offering several campsites (one near the main road and others along a very bumpy track). There are picnic tables, fireplaces, a boat launch, and fishing for grayling.

A working hydraulic mine is reached by taking Warm Bay Road, leading from Discovery Road. The Pine Creek Campground and Picnic Area is located 2.6 KM (1.6 miles) from the Atlin Road junction. There are two hiking trails off this road, at

3.7 KM (2.3 miles). Monarch Trail offers a three-mile (4.8 KM) hike starting in meadows and leading to a scenic overlook, at the summit of Monarch Mountain. Beach Trail is a short nature trail. The Palmer Lake Recreation Site is at 19 KM (12 miles), with free camping, fishing, and picnicking. The Warm Bay Recreation Site (on Atlin Lake) has free campsites, fishing, picnic area, and toilets. Another 3 kilometers (1.8 miles) south brings you to the Grotto Recreation Site, where you'll have a good view of Llewellyn Glacier, plus more campsites, picnic tables, firepits, and toilets.

The alpine lakes near Atlin are renowned for fishing, with fly-in opportunities for salmon, steelhead, and rainbow trout. Local bush place services are available. Atlin Lake provides lake trout and grayling. Fishing licenses are available from the government agent's office, or at the Atlin General Store.

The community has a hotel, bed and breakfast inns, and cottage complexes. Several restaurants serve basic, good food. Information on the town and nearby attractions is available from the Atlin Visitors Association, P.O. Box 365, Atlin, B.C. V0W 1A0. The Infocentre is located in the Atlin Historical Museum. For advance information, call (604) 651-7677.

## Where to Eat

The **Atlin Inn Restaurant** is located in the only full-service hotel in town. You can expect standard dishes in this licensed hotel dining room. The hotel also has a lounge. Three places offer camping food and other supplies. **Pine Tree Services**, on the road into Atlin, looks like a gas station, and is a gas station, but also has a licensed restaurant that specializes in family meals, including fresh pastries and fine pies. The **Atlin General Store** is the spot to purchase food for camping and picnics, as well as hardware and clothing. **Vi and Cor's Food Basket** is a specialized food and video store, providing campers with fresh produce and groceries, including eggs fresh from the farm.

# The Alaska Highway
## Places to Stay

### ATLIN

**Atlin Inn**
P.O. Box 39
Atlin, B.C. V0W 1A0
(604) 651-7546 or
fax: (604) 651-7700

Located on the lake, the Atlin Inn is a full-service hotel with restaurant and lounge. Don't let the exterior look of the place fool you; the rooms are large and well appointed. The building has been here for quite a while, but it has been completely renovated during the past ten years. ($$)

**Kirkwood Cottages**
P.O. Box 39
Atlin, B.C. V0W 1A0
(604) 651-7500 or
fax: (604) 651-7546

This complex of lakeside log cottages contains 2-bedroom housekeeping units, all with private bath. It is operated by the same people who run the Atlin Inn, thus the same mailing address. The cottages appeal to families and those, including anglers, who wish to do their own cooking while staying in Atlin. ($$)

**The Noland House**
P.O. Box 135
Atlin, B.C. V0W 1A0
(604) 651-7585

This superior bed and breakfast has revitalized a historic home. The owners and hosts live next door. The rooms feature private baths and sitting rooms. Complimentary wine and snacks are available, and there is a fully equipped kitchen. Open from May through October. ($$)

**Norseman Adventures**
P.O. Box 184
Atlin, B.C. V0W 1A0
(604) 651-7535

This RV park and campground is located on Atlin Lake, with water and electrical hookups for trailers and RVs. The operation arranges fishing charters, and also rents power boats and houseboats. Fishing licenses are available from the office.

## BUCKINGHORSE RIVER

**Buckinghorse River Lodge**
Mile 175 Alaska Highway
Profile River, B.C.
V0C 2B0
(604) 773-6468

Situated exactly halfway between Fort St. John and Fort Nelson, this long-time motel and café sits next to another fishing stream. Camping here is free, with showers. There's also a gas station on-site. ($)

## DAWSON CREEK

**George Dawson Inn**
11705 8th Street
Dawson Creek, B.C.
V1G 4N9
(604) 782-9151

This long-time downtown hotel has standard rooms and a few suites, plus a dining room, lounge, and pub. ($$)

**Inn Margaree**
933 111th Avenue
Dawson Creek, B.C.
V1G 2X4
(604) 782-4319

This small bed and breakfast inn is located close to the downtown shopping area. The rooms have king or queen beds, and a hearty breakfast features freshly baked bread, rolls, scones, or muffins. ($$)

**Mile "0" Campsite**
900 Alaska Avenue
Dawson Creek, B.C.
VIG 4T6
Summer only: (604) 782-7144 or (604) 782-2590
Winter only: (604) 782-9595

This city campground, on the Alaska Highway one kilometer west of the Highway 97 junction, has treed sites, electrical hookups, showers, laundry, and dump station. It is more suitable for tenting than for RVs. The campground is lo-

cated next to the Walter Wright Pioneer
Village and a small man-made lake

**Northern Lights RV Park**
P.O. Box 2476
Dawson Creek, B.C.
V1G 4T9
(604) 782-9433

This modern RV and trailer park is located on Highway 97 South, 2.4 KM (1.5
miles) from the Alaska Highway junction. The park features pull-through sites
with full or partial hookups, picnic tables, showers, and firepits. The operation
has an RV wash, plus a service station
which does lube jobs and minor repairs
to cars and RVs.

**Peace Villa Motel**
1641 Alaska Avenue
Dawson Creek, B.C.
V1G 1Z9
(604) 782-8175

Two blocks east of the junction of the
Alaska Highway and Highway 97, this
motel has large rooms at a reasonable
price, with bed sizes ranging from twin
doubles to king. All rooms have private
bath with tub and shower. The motel has
a sauna, laundry, and in-room coffee. ($)

**Trail Inn**
1748 Alaska Avenue
Dawson Creek, B.C.
V1G 4H7
(604) 782-8595

This modern motel, at the Alaska Highway and Highway 97 junction, features
standard rooms and several suites, with
king and queen beds, and even though
it's on several levels, all rooms are accessible by car. There is in-room coffee, and
free continental breakfast is served. ($$
to $$$)

**Tubby's RV Park**
1913 Hart Highway
Compartment 29,
1725 Alaska Avenue
Dawson Creek, B.C.
V1G 1P5
(604) 782-2584

This large RV park has full hookups,
pull-through sites, tenting sites, picnic
tables, ice, free showers, laundry, and
dump station, plus a service station with
a car wash and lube service.

# FORT NELSON

**Blue Bell Motel and Campground**
P.O. Box 931
3907 50th Avenue South
Fort Nelson, B.C.
V0C 1R0
(604) 774-6961 or fax
(604) 774-6983

Almost hidden behind a Petro Canada gas station, this modern motel has standard rooms, plus units with kitchenettes. Rooms have mini refrigerators, and tub/shower combinations. The motel has winter plug-ins, a convenience store, and there's gasoline at the door. ($ to $$) The adjacent campground has full hookups, showers, and dump station.

**Coach House Inn**
4711 50th Avenue South
P.O. Box 27
Fort Nelson, B.C.
V0C 1R0
(604) 774-3911

This is a full-service hotel with licensed dining room, lounge, winter plug-ins, saunas, and whirlpool. It's downtown, close to the shopping area and visitor center. ($ to $$)

**Husky Fifth Wheel RV Park**
Rural Route #1
Fort Nelson, B.C.
V0C 1R0
(604) 774-7270

Located next to a truck stop with restaurant, this RV park has full hookups, a convenience store, showers, laundry, and a recreation hall, plus a gas station with propane service and ice.

**Provincial Motel**
P.O. Box 690
Fort Nelson, B.C.
V0C 1R0
(604) 774-6901

For those on a budget, this is a modest, standard motel, located at the south end of town. It has regular rooms, plus some units with kitchenettes, and a few with extra-long beds for the very tall. ($)

**Sikanni River RV Park**
Mile 162 Alaska Highway
Fort Nelson, B.C.
V0C 2B0
(604) 774-7628

Located beside a fine fishing stream, the Sikanni Chief River, this campground has partial and full hookups, tenting sites, fire rings, showers, and laundry. A convenience store with gas and propane service is on-site, with a few cabins available for overnight stays. It is located 181 KM (112 miles) north of Fort St. John. ($)

**Westend RV Campground**
P.O. Box 398
Fort Nelson, B.C.
V0C 1R0
(604) 774-2340

This is a large RV and trailer park with full hookups, also with grassy tenting sites, showers, playground, picnic tables, fire pits, free firewood, laundry, and dump station. It's located on the Alaska Highway, next to the museum at the north side of town.

## FORT ST. JOHN

**Alexander Mackenzie Inn**
9223 100 Street
Fort St. John, B.C.
V1J 3X3
(604) 785-8364

This full-service hotel in the downtown area has large rooms, a pool which may or may not be open for use (it has been under repair), dining room, cocktail lounge, and bar. ($$)

**Coachman Inn**
8540 Alaska Road
Fort St. John, B.C.
V1J 5L6
(604) 787-0651

This Alaska Highway motor hotel has a popular licensed dining room and coffee shop, serving large, hearty meals. The motel has a sauna and whirlpool. ($)

**Pioneer Inn**
9830 100th Avenue
Fort St. John, B.C.
V1J 1Y5
(604) 787-0521 or
800-663-8312

This full-service hotel, in the downtown area, has standard and executive rooms, indoor pool, sauna, whirlpool, coffee shop and dining room, and a lounge which features entertainment. The hotel provides free RV parking and plug-ins. ($$)

**Ron's Tent and Trailer Park**
Mile 52 Alaska Highway
P.O. Box 55
Charlie Lake, B.C.
V0C 1H0
(604) 787-1569

This campground has treed tenting sites, full hookups for trailers and RVs, flush toilets, showers, picnic tables, fireplaces, wood, laundry, and a playground.

**Rotary RV Park**
Mile 511 Alaska Highway
P.O. Box 6306
Fort St. John, B.C.
V1J 4H8
(604) 785-1700

While it has a Fort St. John mailing address, this modern RV park is located in Charlie Lake. The park has full and partial hookups, showers, laundry, dump station, a boat ramp, dock, and picnic tables. The operation is located next to the Red Barn Pub and a convenience store.

## LIARD RIVER

**Coal River Lodge**
Mile 533 Alaska Highway
Alaska Highway, B.C.
V1G 4J8
(604) 776-7306

Located at the junction of the Coal and Liard rivers, this long-time tourist operation, was taken over by new owners in 1994. It includes an RV park and motel, and features a coffee shop, laundry, showers, full hookups for RVs, a dump station, and gasoline. ($ to $$)

**Lower Liard River Lodge**
Mile 496 Alaska Highway
P.O. Box 9
Muncho Lake, B.C.
V0C 1Z0
(604) 776-7341

This historic log lodge is located across the Alaska Highway from Liard Hot Springs Provincial Park, just north of the Liard River Bridge, at Mile 496. Rooms are in the lodge building, with private and shared baths. The log-sided dining room is open for three meals a day. Other facilities include a store selling groceries and camping supplies, laundry, dump station, and gasoline. ($ to $$)

**Trapper Ray's Liard Hot Springs Lodge**
Mile 497 Alaska Highway
Alaska Highway, B.C.
V1G 4J8
(604) 776-7349

A recent addition to Lower Liard, this operation includes a lodge with modern rooms, a campground, RV park, and a hot spring. The lodge is both rustic and modern, with a European alpine flair. All rooms have private baths. The building includes a café serving freshly baked breads and pastries. ($$) The campground has pull-through sites and tenting sites, showers, and dump station, plus gas, tire, and propane service.

## MUNCHO LAKE

**Highland Glen Lodge**
Mile 462 Alaska Highway
P.O. Box 8
Muncho Lake, B.C.
V0C 1Z0
(604) 776-3481

This motel, with a campground, is open year round, and is one of the traditional overnight stopping places in this beautiful part of the B.C. Rockies. Accommodations include motel and chalet-style units. The lodge has a licensed dining room and bakery. ($ to $$) The campground has sites with full hookups, plus tenting sites and a laundry.

**Muncho Lake Lodge**
Mile 463 Alaska Highway
Muncho Lake, B.C.
V0C 1Z0
(604) 776-3456

Another long-time seasonal roadside operation, the lodge and adjacent campground are open from May to October, with standard rooms and housekeeping units ($), RV and trailer sites with full hookups, toilets, showers, and a gas station.

## PINK MOUNTAIN

**Mae's Kitchen and Ed's Garage**
Mile 147 Alaska Highway
Pink Mountain, B.C.
V0C 2B0
(604) 772-3215

This place seems to have been here forever. It's more of a rustic eating place than it is a place to stay, but it does have a small motel, with very inexpensive rooms. The restaurant is an old-fashioned spot, serving basic roadside diner food and fresh pies. The full-service garage is open year-round. ($)

**Pink Mountain Campsite and RV Park**
Mile 143 Alaska Highway
Pink Mountain, B.C.
V0C 2B0
(604) 774-1033

Approximately halfway between Fort St. John and Fort Nelson, Pink Mountain offers a break in this long wilderness stretch. This campground has shaded campsites for tents and sites with full and partial (electrical) hookups for trailers and RVs, a laundry, and showers. There's a gas station, store, liquor outlet, and post office at the same location.

**Pink Mountain Motor Inn**
Mile 143 Alaska Highway
Pink Mountain, B.C.
V0C 2B0
(604) 772-3234

One of the more welcome roadhouses along the southern part of the Alaska Highway, this motel has standard but comfortable rooms ($ to $$), a licensed restaurant (famous for its butter tarts), grocery store, treed campsites with picnic tables, RV hookups, laundry, dump station, drinking water, and hot showers. There's also a gas station on the same side of the highway.

## SUMMIT LAKE AREA

**Rocky Mountain Lodge**
Mile 397 Alaska Highway
Summit Lake, B.C.
V1G 4J8
(604) 232-7000

This motel, constructed of cedar, is also in the Stone Mountain Provincial Park area, with a gas and service station, campground, and a store which has deli food for take-out. This is one of several places to put a calorific focus on cinnamon buns. ($ to $$)

**Summit Lodge**
Mile 392 Alaska Highway
Summit Lake, B.C.
V1G 4J8
(604) 232-7573

Located in the Stone Mountain Provincial Park area, close to Summit Lake and wildlife, the lodge is at the highest point along the Alaska Highway. The operation includes motel rooms with TV, a restaurant and gift shop, and a restaurant. The "Grizzly Burger" is one of their favorites. ($ to $$) The Lodge operates a campground, some sites with hookups, tenting sites, and showers. There's a gas station on-site.

## TOAD RIVER

**Poplars Campground and Café**
Mile 426 Alaska Highway
P.O. Box 30
Toad River, B.C.
V0C 2X0
(604) 232-5465

This campground is a few miles north of Toad River, offering campsites and a few inexpensive cabins. The campground has pull-through sites for trailers and RVs with electrical hookups, tenting sites, showers, and dump station. The operation includes a small café featuring foot-long hot dogs, and fresh baked goods. The gas station sells propane, and has a tire repair service. ($)

**Toad River Lodge**
Mile 422 Alaska Highway
Toad River, B.C.
V0C 2X0
(604) 232-5401

One of the older, atmospheric Alaska Highway lodges, this one is located 193 KM (120 miles) north of Fort Nelson, in the village of Toad River. Open year-round, with a café festooned with caps across the ceiling, the lodge offers rooms and cabins, propane, and tire service. ($)

# Alaska

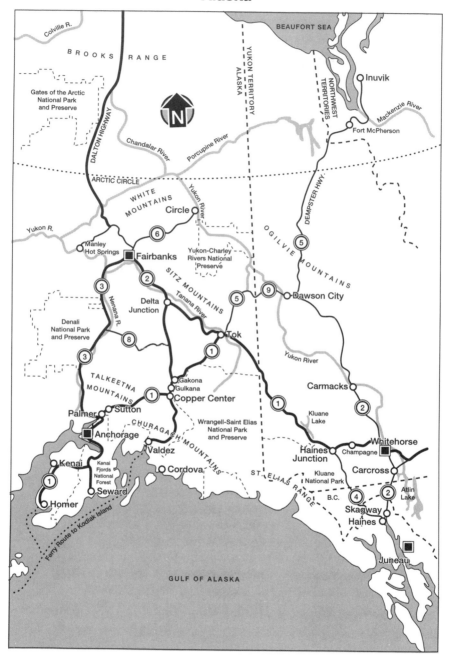

# *Alaska*
## *Drives*

With Alaska the most sparsely populated state in the U.S., one would expect it to be almost devoid of highways. Fortunately for you and me, such is not the case. The Alaskan interior and south-central Alaska are well served with highway routes which lead to all but the most remote areas: islands, the inland wilderness, and the remote Arctic and Bering coasts. The highways work their way around the two major mountain ranges, the Brooks and the Alaska.

Fairbanks is the main population center of the interior region, serviced by the Alaska Highway. The **George Parks Highway** runs south between Fairbanks and Anchorage, passing Denali National Park and the park's chief attraction, Mount McKinley (Denali). The **Taylor Highway**, joining the Alaska Highway near Tok (sounds like *poke*), leads to gold mining country along the Fortymile River and ends at the remote community of Eagle. The **Steese Highway** leaves Fairbanks, providing a route to two hot springs (Chena and Arctic Circle) and to Circle City, on the banks of the Yukon River. The **Dalton Highway** leads north from Fairbanks and stretches to the Arctic Ocean at Prudhoe Bay.

South-central Alaska centers around Anchorage, reaching from the Gulf of Alaska coast to the Alaska Range. The **Glenn Highway** leads diagonally across the region, joining Tok to Anchorage, providing super views of the Wrangell and Chugach mountains. The **Richardson Highway** runs in a north/south direction, linking Delta Junction to the port town of Valdez. The **Seward** and **Sterling** highways lead south from Anchorage to the Kenai Peninsula, providing access to Portage Glacier, Seward,

Kenai, and Soldotna. At the end of the Kenai Peninsula route is Homer, the most westerly town in North America connected to the rest of the continent by road.

To the north and west is Northwest Alaska, reached only by air or ship. The region includes Katmai National Park and Preserve, near King Salmon—a brown bear habitat, and a magnificent reminder of the earth's volcanic history. Katmai's fumaroles were created by the great volcanic eruption of Novarupta in 1912.

# Glenn Highway/Tok Cutoff Drive

### Tok to Anchorage

This major route joins the Alaska Highway, at Tok, to Anchorage, in south-central Alaska. It provides the fastest way to Anchorage if you are driving north from the Yukon along the Alaska Highway. To pay full homage to the many attractions along the drive, we have divided this spectacular journey into two highway logs.

The drive is half of a grand circle tour, starting and ending at Tok, with stops in Anchorage, then doing the Kenai Peninsula, and visiting Denali National Park and Fairbanks on the return to the Alaska Highway. Doing the grand tour in the opposite direction, you continue along the Alaska Highway to Fairbanks, and then take the George Parks Highway to Denali and continue south to Anchorage. If you choose to do the tour in a counterclockwise direction, the following logs will serve you well, but read from bottom to top.

For the sake of this introduction to the drive, I'll presume you're doing the tour in a clockwise direction, driving north to south between Tok and Anchorage. You'll cross two mountain ranges and an expansive section of the Alaskan interior. The route offers an opportunity to make a sidetrip to Valdez and Prince William Sound. This complete day's drive of 326 miles offers possibilities for satisfying sightseeing, including leisurely stops at several notable sites and a detour to Wrangell–St. Elias National Park.

The Tok Cutoff ends at Gulkana Junction. On the last 16 miles before reaching Glennallen, the Glenn and Richardson highways share the same route.

## Along the Way

**Mentasta Mountains**   The drive is only 12 miles old when you get your first good mountain views. Passing through the Tanana Valley State Forest, the route begins the climb toward Mentasta Summit. The highway crosses the Tok River and curves to follow the course of the Little Tok River, continuing to climb past Mineral Lakes, and reaching the summit and Mentasta Lake, at 2,434 feet. As the ascent progresses you'll have increasing opportunities for wildlife viewing: bears, moose, and Dall sheep. Rest areas in this section provide picnic tables with views. The summit is 45 miles from Tok. The descent provides more than a dozen river and creek crossings, with wonderful views of the Wrangell Mountains to the southwest.

**Fishing Opportunities**   A dedicated angler could spend several weeks exploring the streams and lakes along this route, without ever reaching Anchorage. Beginning with the Tok and Little Tok Rivers, and on to Mentasta Lake, the Slana River (flowing into and out of Mentasta Lake and into the Copper River), tiny Grizzly Lake (about 30 miles past the summit), Caribou Creek and Jack Creek (via a backroad running southwest from Slana), and the Copper River, after descending the west flank of the Mentasta Mountains, the fishing opportunities are almost endless. The road follows and crosses major fishing streams all the way to Anchorage. Grayling and Dolly Varden are the major catches in Caribou and Jack creeks. Salmon run in Slana Slough in August, and in the Indian River in late June and most of July. Many lakes in the Glennallen area are stocked with rainbow trout and coho salmon.

**Wrangell–St. Elias National Park and Preserve**   Glennallen is headquarters for America's largest national park, located southwest of the highway. Flightseeing tours of the park are available, showing the huge glaciated areas and striking mountain peaks.

# HIGHWAY LOG
## Tok to Glennallen
### 141 miles—3 hours

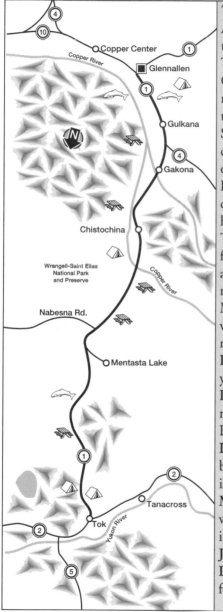

**Tok** Located at the junction of the Alaska and Glenn hwys. For those traveling the Alaska Hwy. and the Taylor Hwy. route from Dawson City, the Glenn Hwy. is the short route to Anchorage. Tok has motels, gas stations, cafés, and stores.

**Sourdough Campground** Private campground located 2 miles south of the junction.

**Eagle State Recreation Site** A campground with picnic areas and hiking trail, 15.7 miles from Tok.

**Tok River Bridge** Located 21 miles from Tok, there is a boat launch on a sideroad to the north. The hwy. now continues southwest to the Mentasta Summit. This is prime wildlife viewing country with moose and Dall sheep often seen.

**Picnic Area** Found 20 miles beyond the Tok River Bridge.

**Picnic Area** Beside a turnout, three miles beyond the Little Tok River Bridge.

**Little Tok River Crossing** Another bridge with a turnout. The fishing is good here (grayling).

**Mineral Lakes** Watch for moose and waterbirds in these sloughs. Fishing for grayling and northern pike.

**Junction–Sideroad to Mentasta Lake** A Native American village is found here.

Mentasta Summit (el. 2,434 feet) Dall sheep are often seen on the mountain slopes.
Mentasta Lodge Located 47 miles from Tok. Gas, motel, café, store, laundry, overnight parking.
Picnic Area At the Slana River Bridge, 49.5 miles from Tok.
State Recreation Site Near the Porcupine Creek Bridge. Camping, picnic tables, drinking water, toilets.
Viewpoint Find this 62 miles from Tok, with historic marker and fine views of the Wrangell Range. There are views of Noyes Mt. from the top of the hill.
Duffy's Roadhouse Just beyond the marker at mile 62.7 with a café, gas, bar, and store.
Ahtell Creek Bridge Fishing access from the parking area at east end of the bridge.
Junction–Nabesna Road Leads southwest for 45 miles to the mining community of Nabesna. There is good fishing along the road with several primitive campsites.
Picnic Area At the Indian River Bridge. Tables, fire pits, toilets. Salmon spawn here in late June and July.
Chistochina Trailhead At Chistochina River Bridge #1. The river originates in a glacier on Mt. Kimball.
Sinona Creek Campground Near the Native American village of Chistochina, with full hookups and tentsites.

Chistochina Lodge and Trading Post Gas, café, saloon, store. Found 92.8 miles from Tok.
Picnic Area To south of road with tables, fire pits, and toilets. Trails lead to the Copper River.
Buster Gene Trailhead Three miles beyond the picnic area.
Tulsona Creek Bridge Good fishing for grayling.
Gakona Found 122.3 miles from Tok. Gas, private campground, restaurant. Gakona Lodge is one of the original roadhouses, built in 1877.
Picnic Area To south of hwy. at the Gakona River Bridge.
Junction–Highway 4 This is the north junction with the Richardson Hwy. (to Delta Junction). From here, both hwys share the road south for 14 miles. We continue southwest on the combined hwys. toward Anchorage.
Junction–Richardson Highway (Hwy. 4) This is the south junction. Hwy. 4 leads south to Valdez. We continue toward Anchorage on Hwy. 1.
Glennallen A small town in the Copper River Valley, 141 miles from Tok. Information center in the log cabin at the junction. Gas, motels, private campgrounds, cafés, stores. Lake Louise, 27 miles west, offers excellent grayling and trout fishing as do Tolsona and Little Junction Lake.

# HIGHWAY LOG
## *Glennallen to Anchorage*
### 187 miles—4 hours

**Glennallen** The Copper River Valley town has full services for tourists (see previous log).
**Tolsona Wilderness Campground** Fourteen miles from Glennallen, with sites beside the creek, hookups, dump station, and laundry. Good fishing for grayling in the creek and for rainbow in Tolsona and Moose lakes.
**Ranch House Lodge** Restaurant, bar, and camping.
**Tolsona Creek Recreation Site** Camping, picnic tables, no drinking water.
**Tolsona Lake** Fishing for grayling. The Tolsona Lake Resort offers motel rooms, café, and lounge.
**West Lake Trailhead** At a turnout, 1 mile from lodge.
**Lost Cabin Lake Trailhead** From the paved turnout, a 2-mile hike to the lake.
**Junction–Lake Louise Road** Located 27 miles from Glennallen, this 19.3-mile long drive takes you to the Lake Louise Recreation Area with camping, fishing, and glacier views.
**Little Junction Lake** Fishing for rainbow and grayling to the south.
**Tazlina Glacier Lodge** A log lodge with rustic cabins. There are views of the glacier to the east of the highway.

**Arizona Lake** To the south, fishing for burbot and grayling.

**Little Nelchina Recreation Site** Four miles past Nelchina Lodge. Camping, picnic tables, water, fire pits.

**Old Man Creek Trailhead** A 2-mile hike to Old Man Creek and 9 miles to Crooked Creek. These are part of the Chickaloon-Knik-Nelchina trail network.

**Eureka Summit** (el. 3,322 feet) The highest point on the Glenn Hwy. To the northwest is the Talkeetna Range. The Chugach Mts. lie to the south.

**Eureka Lodge** A motel with café and gas, just beyond the summit. The original (and first) Glenn Hwy. Lodge is next to the newer building.

**Belanger Creek–Nelchina River Trailhead** Near a turnout to the south. Eureka Creek Trail: 1.5 miles, Goober Lake Trail: 8 miles, Nelchina River Trail: 9 miles.

**Sheep Mountain Lodge** Café, bar, store, gas, cabins, RV hookups, camping, hot tub, sauna. Located 73.5 miles from Glennallen. The highway now descends into the valley of the Matanuska River, with some of the best scenery in the state, including views of the Matanuska Glacier.

**Long Rifle Lodge** A restaurant overlooking the glacier, plus gas and showers. Another 102 miles to Anchorage.

**Matanuska Recreation Site** Campsites, picnic tables, glacier views, hiking trails.

**Long Lake** A popular fishing spot in a canyon. Long Lake State Recreation Site has campsites and picnic tables.

**Old Chickaloon Road** Leads beside river from Chickaloon River Bridge to picnic areas and a defunct coal mine.

**King Mountain Lodge** Café, bar, accommodations.

**Sutton** Found 61 miles from Anchorage, this village has a store and gas stations.

**Junction–Jonesville Road** Access to Coyote Lake State Recreation Area (camping, picnicking, trails, swimming).

**Musk-Ox Farm** The world's only domestic musk-ox farm. Summer tours are available.

**Palmer** Located 42 miles from Anchorage, this town of 3,000 people is the service center for the Matanuska Valley, a rich farming area. The town has all visitor services including excellent restaurants and hotels. The visitor center is on South Valley Way at East Fireweed Avenue. For Palmer details, see page 134.

**Junction–Palmer-Wasilla Highway** The Glenn Hwy. continues southwest for another 42 miles to Anchorage. For Anchorage details, see page 104.

# George Parks Highway Drive

## Fairbanks to Anchorage

Many visitors to Alaska make Denali National Park their major destination, and this route takes you there quickly, as well as farther south to Anchorage. This drive is the latest in the network of Alaskan highways, having opened in the early 1970s. If you intend to make the grand tour through Anchorage and back to the Alaska Highway, this is the first route on the counterclockwise drive which begins on the Alaska Highway in Fairbanks and heads to Denali and Anchorage, through the Kenai Peninsula, and then returns to the Alaska Highway at Tok via the Glenn Highway.

## Along the Way

**Nenana and Tanana Rivers**    Leaving Fairbanks, heading south, the Parks Highway passes through rolling hill country covered with spruce and birch. After 53 miles you'll reach Nenana at the confluence of the Tanana and Nenana rivers. The town is home to a sizable tug and barge fleet, which services Alaskan villages located along the Tanana and Yukon rivers. The docks are located to the left side of the highway (southbound). A historic tug, the *Taku Chief,* sits behind the town's information center. The barges move down the river as soon as the ice is gone, taking enough supplies to outfit the villages for the next year. Moving down the river, they travel at about 12 miles per hour. On the way back, fighting the current, they slow to about five or six mph. The Nenana Ice Classic celebrates the moment each year when enough ice disappears to move a metal tripod set over the river, connected with a cable to a clock. The best guesser wins close to $200,000 for the most accurate prediction. The ice leaves sometime between mid-April and mid-May.

**Alaska Range–North Slope**    After leaving Nenana and passing the turnoff to the small coal-mining town of Healy (Spur Road), the route begins to climb across the Alaska Range. Only 109 miles from Fairbanks, Healy is just 15 minutes north of the entrance to

Denali National Park. There are several places to stay in the town, including the historic Healy Hotel. Before reaching Denali, the highway crosses a deep canyon carved out by the Nenana River. You'll find a turnout on the south side of the bridge for gorge-viewing and picture-taking.

**Denali National Park**   The boundary of the park is at the north end of Crabb's Crossing Bridge, the second bridge over the Nenana River. The highway runs through the park for another 6.8 miles before coming to the main entrance road. As you get closer to the entrance road, you'll encounter more lodges and restaurants. The turnoff to the main park road is 120.7 miles from Fairbanks.

The park visitor center is a half-mile along the entrance road. Campsites in the park are allocated on a first-come, first-served basis, with sign-up forms available at the visitor center. For details on park attractions, see page 113.

Past the park road, another few miles of rustic motels, cabins, restaurants, RV parks, and assorted tourist traps assail the traveler. Because accommodations within the park are limited, you may choose to stay in one of these highway places.

**Broad Pass and Salmon Country**   After leaving the Denali area, the Parks Highway continues to climb to the unsigned summit at Broad Pass, a beautiful mountain valley with fine vistas. The pass sits in the divide between the Cook Inlet and Yukon River watersheds. Rest areas with picnic tables are located at East Fork (52 miles from the park road), where a half-mile loop road leads to the picnic area and overnight parking lot, and also at the Hurricane Gulch Bridge, eight miles past East Fork. The highway then drops out of the Alaska Range into the broad Matanuska/Susitna Valley. In this area are found the most impressive salmon runs accessible by car. When the salmon aren't in the streams, anglers set their hooks for rainbow trout.

# HIGHWAY LOG
## *Fairbanks to Anchorage*
### 358 miles—6 hours, 30 minutes

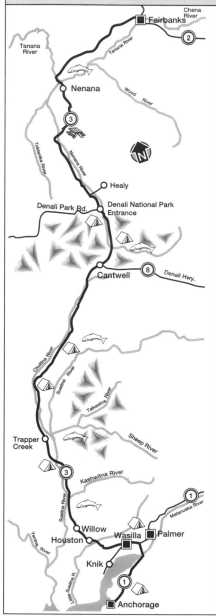

**Fairbanks** Junction of Airport Way and Parks Hwy.

**Viewpoint** (Mile 39.2) The Tanana River is seen on both sides of the road.

**Nenana** (Mile 53.5) Village with river port facilities for tugs and barges. The Visitor Center is in front of an old tugboat called the *Taku Chief.* Gas, café, stores, bank, and motel, with picnic area at *Taku Chief.*

**Turnoff–Anderson** (Mile 74.5) Village, 6 miles from the highway. Nearby Clear is a military installation.

**Highway Services** (Mile 82) Campground, hookups, store.

**Rest Area** (Mile 89) Picnic park on June Creek.

**Panquinque Creek Bridge** (Mile 105.5) Fishing for grayling.

**Healy** (Mile 109.3) Village with gas, store, cafés, motel, private campground.

**Highway Services** (Mile 119.1) This is the beginning of a string of motels, restaurants and campgrounds north and south of the entrance to Denali National Park.

**Denali Park Road** (Mile 120.7) Denali National Park entrance. See page 113.

**Turnout** (Mile 141.7) for view of Panorama Mountain.
**Highway Services** (Mile 147.6) Gas, campground, hookups.
**Junction–Denali Highway (Hwy. 8)** (Mile 148.1) Turn west for Cantwell: Gas, lodging, store, café and bar, private campground, hookups.
**Broad Pass Summit** (Mile 156.7) Divide of the Cook Inlet and Yukon River watersheds.
**Rest Area** (Mile 172.4) Picnic tables, toilets, drinking water.
**Rest Area** (Mile 184) Picnic tables at bridge. A short trail offers views of Hurricane Gulch.
**Turnoff** (Mile 194.2) To Coal Creek parking area. Trail and fishing for grayling, rainbow trout, and salmon.
**Highway Services** (Mile 201) Gas, café, lodging. This is the last gas for 32 miles.
**Picnic Area** (Mile 210.8) Memorial on loop road.
**Byers Lake Campground** (Mile 211) Picnic park, trail.
**Troublesome Creek** (Mile 220.3) Trail and fishing for grayling, rainbow trout, and salmon.
**Turnout** (Mile 222.8) Display and views of Mt. McKinley.
**Turnout** (Mile 223.3) Piped spring water.
**Chulitna River Bridge** (Mile 225.2) Fishing for rainbow trout and grayling.
**Rest Area** (Mile 236.5) Picnic tables.

**Trapper Creek** (Mile 243.5) Village with gas, café, store, lodging, RV hookups.
**Highway Services** (Mile 253.7) Gas, café, motel.
**Junction–Talkeetna Spur Road** (Mile 259.3) Turn east for the village of Talkeetna (14.5 miles).
**Montana Creek Campground** (Mile 261.5) Trails, no tables. Private campground on north side of creek.
**RV Park and Campground** (Mile 286.5)
**Junction–Hatcher Pass Road** (Mile 286.8) Willow Creek state campground and picnic area (1.2 miles). Independence Mine Historical State Park is 31.8 miles from the junction.
**Willow** (Mile 287) Village with gas, store, café.
**Turnoff** (Mile 290.8) To Nancy Lake Recreation Area. Trails, picnic tables, canoe launch.
**Houston** (Mile 300.5) Village with gas, café, store, lodging, camping.
**Wasilla** (Mile 315.8) Town located between Lucille and Wasilla lakes in the Susitna Valley. Visitor Center at museum on Main Street, just off the hwy. (see page 148 for details).
**Junction–Glenn Highway** (Mile 323) This is Alaska Route 1 to Anchorage. Downtown Anchorage: 35 miles.

# Steese Highway Drive

## Fairbanks to Circle

Although this trip could be managed as a one-day sightseeing and hot spring–soaking jaunt, it is better done with an overnight stop at the hot springs resort in Circle, or in the community of Central. The entire one-way trip is 162 miles. Completed in 1927, the route starts as a paved road for 44 miles, and continues over a good gravel roadway to Central, narrowing for the rest of the drive to Circle.

## Along the Way

**Chena Hot Springs Road**   Less than five miles from the start of the drive, this route leads northeast beside the Chena River for 56.5 miles. Chena Hot Springs, at the end, is a private hot springs resort, open daily year-round. With hotel rooms, a spring-fed hot pool, whirlpools, hot tub, and an expansive deck, the resort offers just about anything you could wish for in a re-laxing Alaskan resort. Rustic cabins and RV sites are also available, along with bicycles and horses for trail rides. Winter activities include cross-country skiing and snowshoeing. But the resort is only one of many attractions along this scenic road. The Chena River Recreation Area offers prime fishing (grayling), hiking trails to several outstanding rock formations, picnic areas, campsites, and canoeing from several access points.

**Gold Dredge Number 8**   This area northeast of Fairbanks was a prime gold field, and to some extent remains one. The 127 miles between Fairbanks and Central is littered with the ruins of former gold operations. There are more reminders of what used to be, though, than actual gold workings, although a few still exist. The old dredge, a "National Historic Mechanical Engineering Landmark" (whew!), is located on the Old Steese Highway (exit at mile 9.5). It worked its last pile of rock in 1959.

**Cleary Summit**   Less than 21 miles from Fairbanks, the route climbs to the first of three summits. From the top, at 2,233 feet, you are able to see the Chatanika River Valley and the White Mountains to the north, and the Tanana Valley and Mount McKinley to the south.

**Chatanika Gold Camp**   The road climbs for a short spell, reaching this historic and privately owned rustic resort. On the site of an early gold operation, the camp has a bunkhouse and cabins, a dining room that serves a sourdough breakfast buffet every Sunday, dogsled rides in winter, snowmobile rides, and gold panning. The Chatanika Lodge is to the east, with rooms and meals (halibut and catfish fry on Fridays, fried chicken on Sundays). If you can't see the frequent aurora borealis in the sky, you can watch borealis videos in the lodge.

**Twelvemile Summit**   Situated on the divide between the Yukon and Tanana river drainage basins, this summit at 2,982 feet offers views and a spectacular explosion of wildflower colors in the late spring and early summer. Before you reach the summit, you will encounter a water pipeline and a backroad leading west to Nome Creek. This six-mile route takes you to recreational gold panning, and also to some of the best grayling fishing spots in the Fairbanks area. The road is not suitable for low-slung vehicles or large RVs and trailers.

**Eagle Summit**   This is the highest of the three summits at 3,624 feet. The narrow and steep sideroad leading to the summit is said to be the best wildflower viewing area along any road in Alaska (alpine azalea, rock jasmine, mountain avens, gentian, lousewort, and many more). Fairbanks people come here on June 21st to observe the summer solstice, when the sun shines through the night at this high point.

**Circle Hot Springs**   Early prospectors enjoyed the hot springs at Circle, using tent bathhouses to protect themselves during the harsh winter months. It's far more comfortable now, with an indoor Olympic-size pool and other resort comforts, including an old hotel, hostel, cabins, restaurant, and saloon.

# HIGHWAY LOG
## *Fairbanks to Circle*
### 162 miles—3 hours, 20 minutes

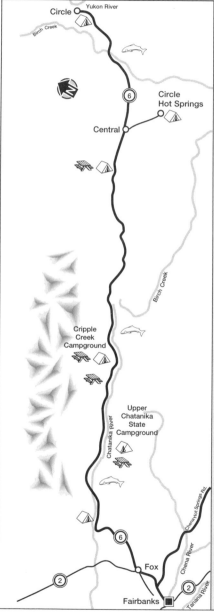

The Steese Hwy. was completed in 1927 and used mainly for mining camp transportation until the end of the Second World War and the opening of the Alaska Hwy. It is paved for the first 44 miles (71 KM) and then becomes a gravel road leading to the town of Central. Over the 35 miles (56 KM) between Central and Circle, the road is narrow and winding. Chena Hot Springs Road, 5 miles (8 KM) from Fairbanks, offers year-round recreation areas with picnicking, canoeing, hiking trails, and campgrounds as well as the hot spring resort at the end of the road.

**Downtown Fairbanks** The drive starts at the junction of Airport Way and Steese Expressway (Hwy. 2).
**College Road** Exit to west for access to Bentley Mall and the University of Alaska.
**Turnoff** (Mile 2.8) To Birch Hill Recreation Area (2.3 miles), a ski area, hiking trails, and picnic tables.
**Junction–Chena Hot Springs Road and Old Steese Highway** (Mile 4.6) Gas and store to the west, on Old Steese Hwy.
**Turnoff** (Mile 6.3) To the left, with a scenic view of the city.

Viewpoint (Mile 7) A good view of the Trans-Alaska Pipeline. Turnoff (Mile 8.4) Pipeline display and viewpoint.
Goldstream Road (Mile 9.5) Exit to Old Steese Hwy. for Gold Dredge #8. Tours, admission fee.
Permafrost Tunnel (Mile 10.4) Turn off to see one of the few places in Alaska with exposed permafrost. North Country Inn nearby.
End of Steese Expressway (Mile 11) Turn east for Steese Hwy. (Hwy. 6) to Circle. Continue straight for the Elliott Hwy. Turn west for Fox and Old Steese Hwy.
Cleary Summit (Mile 20.6) Viewpoint at 2,233 feet.
Turnout (Mile 20.9) Mining operation and view of valley and ghost town of Cleary.
Chatanika (Mile 27.9) Turn right (up the hill) for an old gold camp founded in 1925 and closed in 1957. The highway now parallels the Chatanika River for 30 miles. Good fishing for whitefish, grayling, northern pike.
Upper Chatanika River State Campground (Mile 39) Picnic tables, access to canoe trail, fishing.
Highway Services (Mile 41.8) Gas and store.
Turnoff (Mile 47) for canoe trail access (quarter mile).
U.S. Creek (Mile 57.5) Picnic tables.

Cripple Creek Campground (Mile 60) Picnic tables, trail, toilets, access to Bureau of Land Management cabin and canoe trail.
Highway Services (Mile 65.7) Gas, store, cabins.
Turnout (Mile 85.6) Access to Pinnell Mountain National Recreational Trail (also parking at mile 107.1). This 24-mile trail runs along ridge tops with views of the White Mts., and the Brooks and Alaska ranges.
Turnoff (Mile 94) On sideroad to Birch Creek. Canoe trail access. Undeveloped campsites. Fishing for grayling.
Pinnell Mountain Trail (Mile 107.1) Access point.
Eagle Summit (Mile 108) Viewpoint at 3,624 feet.
Turnoff (Mile 119.2) Bedrock Creek Campground, picnic tables. Take left fork.
Central House Roadhouse (Mile 127.5) Built in 1894 and rebuilt after a fire in 1926, this is a national historic site. Gas, motel, store, post office, cafés, bar in the village.
Junction–Circle Hot Springs Road (Mile 127.8) Gas, store, café. The resort is located at the end of this road (8.3 miles).
Circle (Mile 162) On the banks of the Yukon River. Gas, stores, café, motel, campground, pioneer cemetery. See page 110 for details.

# Richardson Highway Drive

## Delta Junction to Valdez

The 266-mile drive to the Pacific Coast begins 98 miles from Fairbanks, at the Richardson Highway's junction with the Alaska Highway. Crossing the Chugach Mountains and the Alaska Range, this route provides the most scenic drive in the state, past spectacular glaciers, through green spruce forests, and across meadows. The Richardson follows the route of the oldest trail in Alaska, as it was the state's first road. Gold prospectors used the rough trail between Valdez and Eagle (on the Yukon River), and on to Dawson City, during the gold rush of 1898. The trail was again used during the Fairbanks Gold Rush in 1902. It was expanded to a wagon road in 1910, and paved in 1957.

## Along the Way

**Mountain Views**   As well as providing a number of outstanding fishing locations (try Meadows Road or Coal Mine Road, both for four-wheel-drive vehicles) and wildflowers, the early stretch of the highway provides magnificent views of the Alaska Range from a paved turnout 22 miles from Delta Junction. Three of the range's highest peaks are seen: Mount Deborah, Hess Mountain, and Mount Hayes.

**Isabel Pass**   A monument to General Wilds P. Richardson marks the summit of Isabel Pass, the highest summit on the highway at 3,000 feet. While serving as the head of the Alaska Road Commission, Richardson negotiated with Congress on the need for roads to be built in the state. Before the pass you get a fine view of Gulkana Glacier, just past the turnoff to Fielding Lake Campground (1.5 miles). The pass often has snow long after other parts of the route are in spring bloom. Winds are sometimes fierce at the summit.

**Copper River Valley**   The roadway through part of the valley serves both the Richardson and Glenn highways. The Copper

Valley Visitors Center is located at the south junction of the two highways, at Glennallen, with a valley historical display beyond the junction. Copper Center is the next town, with a loop road connecting the highway with both ends of the village. Both communities were founded with the establishment of roadhouses on the trail from Valdez. The visitor center for Wrangell–St. Elias National Park is found 12.5 miles before reaching Copper Center. Access to this huge wilderness area is via the Edgerton Highway and McCarthy Road. The center is open daily from 9 A.M. to 6 P.M. from Memorial Day to Labor Day, and from 8 A.M. to 5 P.M. weekdays in winter. There is a full-service hotel at Gakona Junction, where the Tok Cutoff joins the Richardson Highway.

**Thompson Pass**    A gentle climb follows from Copper Center to the Thompson Pass Summit, at 2678 feet. The tundra near the pass is a prime viewing location for wildflower fans (yellow heather, bluebell). Before reaching the pass, you'll have among the best chances in the state to touch a glacier from a roadside location. Worthington Glacier flows down Girl's Mountain, and is accessed via a short sideroad. It's possible to drive almost to the toe of the glacier, where visitors can walk to the ice. Twenty-seven-mile Glacier is seen just west of the Worthington Recreation Site.

**Keystone Canyon**    Approaching Valdez, the road passes this deep chasm, with three waterfalls cascading into the canyon within the space of a mile. The first is Horsetail Falls, seen from a paved turnout to the west. Bridal Veil Falls, the most spectacular of the three, is discovered a few hundred yards south, with Riddleston Falls visible from the last of the three bridges in the canyon.

**Valdez**    In recent times, this seaport gained notoriety during the Exxon Valdez grounding in 1989. The town and surrounding shoreline were untouched by the oil spill, as was much of the sound. The prime attraction in the area is the Columbia Glacier, with charter boats touring the waters of the glacier on a daily basis during the tourist season. Cordova, a small fishing village on the sound, is accessible by ferry.

# HIGHWAY LOG
## *Delta Junction to Valdez*
### 266 miles—5 hours

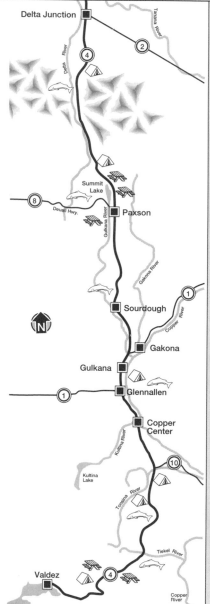

**Delta Junction** Services include motels, gas, cafés, and store. The Visitor Center is at the junction. **Meadows Road** (Mile 4.5) Four-wheel-drive access only to fishing. **Picnic Area** (Mile 13.2) At view-point. **Donnelly Lake Trail** (Mile 21.7) To west, fishing for king and silver salmon, rainbow trout. Donnelly Dome is the name of the mountain nearby. **Viewpoint** (Mile 22) At pulloff, view of three high peaks: Deborah, Hess, and Hayes. **Coal Mine Road** Four-wheel-drive access. Fishing for lake trout, grayling, Arctic char. **Donnelly Creek Recreation Site** (Mile 28) Via loop road. Camping, picnicking. **Picnic Area** (Mile 40.6) At pull-out. Historical marker on Black Rapids Glacier and moraine. There are several pulloffs along the road to view the pipeline and mountain ranges, and a marker at mile 49.3, at Lower Miller Creek. **Picnic Area** (Mile 59.6) There are additional picnic tables located at turnouts for the next 100 miles. **Spring Water** (Mile 62)

**Fielding Lake Campground** (Mile 65.6) To the west (1.5 miles). Picnic tables, toilets, fishing.
**Summit Lake Turnout** (Mile 71) Seven miles long, this lake has good fishing for burbot, lake trout, red salmon, and grayling.
**Junction–Denali Highway** At the village of Paxson. To Denali National Park and the George Parks Hwy. Lodge, gas, store.
**Paxson Lake Wayside** (Mile 86.6) Picnic area.
**Paxson Lake Campground** (BLM) (Mile 91) On 1.5-mile road, 50 campsites, water, tables, fire pits, dump station, boat launch, fishing.
**Meier's Lake Roadhouse** (Mile 96) Gas, food, lodging, camping. Fishing for grayling. There are several BLM trails between here and Gulkana.
**Sourdough Roadhouse** (Mile 118.3) An original—with café, cabins, bunkhouse, gas, grocery, saloon. BLM campground is nearby.
**Junction–Richardson and Glenn Highways** (Mile 137.4) The Glenn leads east to Tok. Both hwys. lead south toward Anchorage. Gas, store.
**Gulkana** Via access road, a small village on the river. Camping beside the bridge.
**Dry Creek Recreation Site** (Mile 148) Camping, tables.
**Glennallen** (Mile 151) Town at the south junction of Richardson and Glenn hwys.

**Historical Marker** (Mile 153.4) About transportation in Alaska, with views of Wrangell Mts.
**Copper Center Loop Road** The new hwy. bypasses Copper Center, a historic village on the old hwy. Lodge, trading post, gas, cafés, store. National Park Info Center for the Wrangell–St. Elias National Park and Preserve. Ranger on duty, video, maps, and publications.
**Junction–Edgerton Highway (Hwy. 10)** (Mile 183.4) This road leads east to McCarthy, in the national park and preserve.
**Squirrel Creek State Campground** (Mile 186.4) Creekside sites.
**Tonsina Recreation Site** (Mile 201) Campsites, water, fire pits. Fishing for Dolly Varden.
**Tiekel River Lodge** (Mile 210) Café, lodging, gas. Located 56 miles from Valdez.
**Picnic Area** (Mile 411) By Tiekel River with covered tables.
**Worthington Glacier Recreation Site** (Mile 237.4) Picnic tables, viewing site, displays.
**Blueberry Recreation Site** Via 1-mile loop road. Camping, picnicking.
**Keystone Canyon** The highway passes through the canyon with waterfalls, turnouts, and historic markers.
**Old Valdez Townsite** (Mile 266) The mileposts begin and end here (it's four miles to Valdez).

# Kenai Peninsula

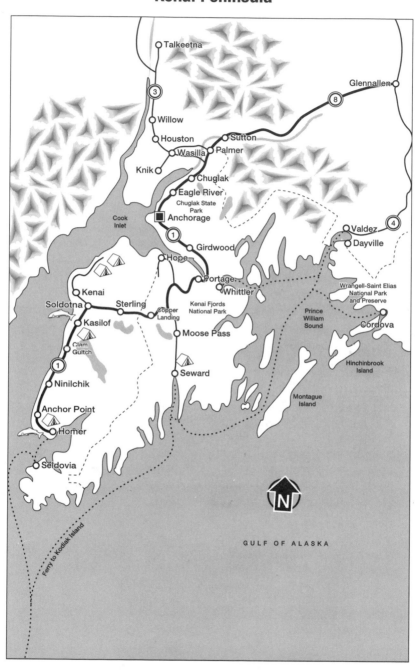

# Kenai Peninsula Drive

## Anchorage to Homer

Captain Cook explored the waters around the Kenai Peninsula when looking for the northwest passage. He reached Turnagain Sound, the inlet south of Anchorage, and legend has it that he named it by telling his crew to "turn again" as they looked for the passage. The peninsula is a rugged, highly scenic area capped with tall white mountain peaks, meadows full of mountain sheep, and high seas.

The Seward Highway leads south from downtown Anchorage past historic Girdwood and the old Crow Creek Mine, beside Turnagain Sound and Portage Glacier, one of the most accessible glaciers in North America. Portage Lake fans out from the toe of the glacier, with icebergs constantly calving from the icefield. There's an information center, nearby camping, and a lodge within the glacier park. The route ends in the coastal town of Seward, the terminus of the Alaska Railroad.

The Sterling Highway runs from the Seward/Sterling junction to the lower portion of the Kenai Peninsula, near the town of Kenai (an old whaling station), and through Soldotna. The route continues south along the shoreline of Cook Inlet, past Ninilchik and Anchor Point. The literal end of the road is at the picturesque town of Homer.

At Homer, a nine-mile spit juts into Kachemak Bay, a magnet for salmon and halibut anglers. The halibut caught off Homer often weigh over 200 pounds. The town is a charming community of art galleries, craft shops, restaurants, raucous saloons, and genteel bed and breakfast homes. Kenai National Wildlife Refuge offers streams, lakes, trails, and campgrounds. Moose, wolves, and bear are seen in their natural habitat. Off the mainland, reached by ferry or plane, Kodiak Island is Alaska's oldest community. Explored by Russian fur traders, it now has a thriving commercial fishing industry. For anyone visiting Homer, the logical thing to do is to take the ferry to Kodiak—beyond the "end of the road."

# HIGHWAY LOG
## *Anchorage to Homer*
### 256 miles—5 hours

**Anchorage** The drive begins downtown on Gambell Street at 10th Avenue. At 1.8 miles, the road becomes a freeway which leads toward Turnagain Arm.

**Potter Marsh** (Mile 9.6) A wildlife preserve with boardwalks and views of waterfowl including trumpeter swans, Canada geese, ducks, and more.

**Junction–Old Seward Highway** This road provides access to the Johnson Pass Trail, which leads to Johnson Summit (el. 2450 feet) and on to Crescent Lake.

**Chugach State Park** (Mile 11.7) Visitor Center and Railroad Museum. Potter Creek trailhead to the west.

**McHugh State Wayside Park** (Mile 15.2) Picnic tables, stream, and waterfall.

**Viewpoint** (Mile 16.7) Beluga Point, views of Turnagain Arm.

**Bird Creek Recreation Area** (Mile 25.8) Camping and picnic tables, drinking water, bike trail. Gas, store, and bar beyond park.

**Junction–Alyeska Road** Three-mile road to old Crow Creek Mine, Girdwood, and the Alyeska Resort (skiing and summer fun). Gas, café, and store at junction.

**Twentymile River Bridge** (Mile 46.3) Water flows from Twentymile Glacier, which can be seen to the northeast.

**Alaska Railroad Loading** (Mile 46.7) One of two loading points for loading cars and passengers for the trip to the ferry and the town of Whittier. The former town of Portage was destroyed in the 1964 earthquake.

**Junction–Portage Glacier Road** (Mile 48) Just 5.5 miles to the glacier viewing area and visitor center, plus campgrounds, a café, summer boat tours of the lake, and trails.

**Turnagain Pass Recreation Area** (Mile 58.9) A snowmobile and cross-country ski area, rest rooms.

**Johnson Pass North Trailhead** (Mile 63.2) A 23-mile hike to Bench and Johnson lakes (rainbow trout).

**Granite Creek Campground** (Mile 64) Picnic tables.

**Picnic Area** (Mile 70.2) Small wayside park with tables, toilets, and litter barrels.

**Junction–Hope Highway** (Mile 70.3) Leads right to historic mining community (28 miles). Old townsite, campgrounds, Resurrection Pass trailhead, Bear Creek Lodge, motel.

**Tenderfoot Creek Campground** (Mile 81) Located 0.6 mile from hwy., picnic tables, boat launch.

**Summit Lake Lodge** (Mile 81.2) This huge log lodge in the Chugach National Forest has a good restaurant and motel.

**Devil's Pass Trailhead** (Mile 87.6) To west of hwy. Climbs from 1,000 ft. to 2,400 feet. Hike takes about 5.5 hours.

**Junction–Sterling Highway** (Mile 90) Continue on Seward Hwy., if your destination is Seward, on Prince William Sound. Take the Seward Highway for another 37.7 miles to reach the port town.

For the Kenai Peninsula Drive, take the Sterling Hwy. to Kenai, Soldotna, and Homer, beginning at Tern Lake Junction (Mile 90). A USFS campground is two miles past the junction.

**Quartz Creek Recreation Area** (Mile 98) Via sideroad. Campground (three miles). Trail to Crescent Lake.

**Cooper Landing** (Mile 101.4) Small community with motel, café, gas, store, camping.

**Skilak Loop Road** (Mile 111) This 19.1-mile road leads to the Skilak Wildlife Recreation Area (four campgrounds, fishing, trails, and boating).

**Swanson River Road** (Mile 136.4) A good gravel road leading 30 miles to campsites, fishing, and Swan River Canoe Route.

**Soldotna** (Mile 148.2) Town stretches along the Sterling and Kenai Spur highways. Motels, B & Bs, cafés, stores, gas. The Kenai National Wildlife Refuge is at the top of Ski Hill Road (nature trail, visitor center). The Kenai Spur Highway leads to the historic town of Kenai (39.6 miles).

**Kalifornsky Beach Road** (Mile 149.1) Loops 22 miles, and f ollows the shore of Cook Inlet to Kasilof. Camping, beaches, picnicking, beaver dam, café, viewpoints.

**Kasilof** Stretched-out community 13 miles south of Soldotna. RV park, lodge, store, gas.

**Clam Gulch** (Mile 171.2) Village with lodge, café, bar, store, RV park.

**Ninilchik** (Mile 188.1) Village with RV parking, campsites, motel, beach, historic Russian church, state campground.

**Anchor Point** (Mile 209.7) Small town with store, café, and gas. The North Fork Road offers an alternate route back to the Sterling Hwy. The Anchor River Beach Road leads 1.6 miles to inns, state campground, and an RV park.

**Homer** (Mile 225.8) A town on Kachemak Bay with motels, B & B homes, the Pratt Museum, and attractions on the famous Homer Spit.

# Dalton Highway Drive

## Fairbanks to Deadhorse

Formerly this highway was called the North Slope Haul Road, a private road used for transporting supplies to the oil fields of Prudhoe Bay. The complete drive became accessible to the public in December 1994. Before then, the gravel road was open only for 175 miles. Now, after driving 414 miles, you arrive in Deadhorse, the small town developed to service the oil fields. The town is several miles distant from the Arctic shoreline. Permission is required from the oil consortium and signing up for a guided tour in Deadhorse or Fairbanks is necessary to travel the final few miles to the ocean. The summer road provides a spectacular way to see prime northern Alaska wilderness, on a route that has opportunities for fishing, mountain viewing, wildlife, berry picking, and feeling the spell of the North.

## Along the Way

**Trans-Alaska Pipeline**   Construction of the 48-inch pipeline took place between 1974 and 1977. More than half of the line is above ground, with ten pumping stations controlling the flow. The road passes four of these stations, the first (#6) seen just before reaching the Yukon River crossing.

**Fishing Possibilities**   Anglers just have to bring their gear for this trip. Fishing for Arctic grayling is particularly rewarding along rivers accessible from the highway. It's necessary to walk only a few hundred yards from the road to reach prime fishing spots all along the way. Burbot, salmon, whitefish, and northern pike are caught in the larger rivers, including the Kanuti, Jim, Koyukuk, Dietrich, Sagavanirktok. You'll find Dolly Varden in high country, in the northern half of the drive.

**Patton Bridge and Services**   This wood-decked bridge, 2,290 feet long, is the only bridge across the Yukon River in Alaska. It is named for E. L. Patton, the late president of the Alyeska Pipeline Service Company. Located 56 miles from the Elliott junction, this is the beginning of the wildlands managed by the Bureau of Land Management. A BLM information station here is open seven days a week. Alyeska also has an interpretive display here, with information on the river and pipeline construction. A camping area is east of the road. You'll also find Northern Ventures Alaska, with a gas station, the first of several tire-repair places (does that tell you anything about this road?), a café, motel, and telephone.

**Arctic Circle** After 115 miles the road comes to the Arctic Circle, and a little park with picnic tables, rest rooms, and an interpretive display. A large "Arctic Circle" sign provides a fun photo backdrop. A short sideroad leads to a primitive campsite.

**Coldfoot and Wiseman** Shortly after passing Twelvemile Mountain and Cathedral Mountain (both to the north), you'll arrive in Coldfoot, formerly the end of the public road. It's now a little less than halfway to Deadhorse. This is the site of a historic mining camp, on the east bank of the Middle Fork Koyukuk River, at the mouth of Slate Creek. Coldfoot Services provides three motels, a restaurant (open 24 hours), general store, gift shop, coin laundry, and a gas station (tire repair). You'll also find an RV park with hookups and dump station. The Parks Service maintains an information center for the nearby Gates of the Arctic National Park. Thirteen miles beyond Coldfoot is the turnoff to the old mining village of Wiseman. This is still an active mining area, although only two dozen souls live hear year-round. Wiseman has a general store, museum, and campground.

**Atigun Pass** Seventy miles past Coldfoot, the route climbs to the highest highway pass in the state. Atigun Pass marks the Continental Divide, at an elevation of 4,800 feet. James Dalton Mountain is seen to the west, and Phillip Smith Mountain lies to the east.

**Deadhorse** From the pass, the highway descends to the North Slope. A service station offers gas and tire repairs.

# HIGHWAY LOG
## Fairbanks to Deadhorse
477 miles—10 hours

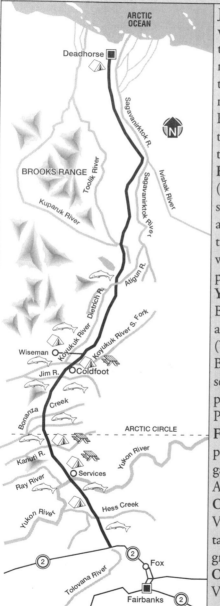

Junction–Elliott and Dalton Highways To reach the start of the Dalton Hwy., take the Steese Hwy. north from Fairbanks. Turn onto the Elliott Hwy. at Fox, 11 miles north of Fairbanks. Drive along the Elliott for another 62 miles (paved, then gravel surface) until reaching the Dalton Hwy. junction.

**Hess Creek Bridge and Campsite** (Mile 23.8) Hess Creek is a sizable stream, with grayling and whitefish available. The campsite is in the treed area. The short road leading west gives access to the pond and parking space.

**Yukon River Crossing** (Mile 55.6) Beyond the long bridge you'll find a motel, café, and service station (Yukon Ventures Alaska), plus a BLM information center, open seven days a week, and an interpretive display by the Alyeska Pipeline.

**Five Mile Airstrip** (Mile 60.8) Be prepared to stop when control gates are closed. Operated by Alyeska Pipeline.

**Overlook–Ray River** (Mile 70) Viewpoint showing Ray Mountains to the west. Fishing for grayling, burbot, and pike.

**Overlook–Pinnacles** (Mile 86.5) Viewpoint is one mile west, with views of tall pinnacles, locally called tors. The pillars extend from the tundra, a result of erosion. The Yukon Flats Wildlife Refuge is to the east.

**Above the Tree Line** (Mile 96) Berries are plentiful in the area of tundra. Look for low-bush cranberries and blueberries. Wildflowers are also present.

**Viewpoint–Kanuti River Valley** (Mile 98.2) Kanuti Flats is seen ahead, with Caribou Mountain to the northwest.

**Arctic Circle** (Mile 115.3) A photo-op and rest stop at the imaginary line.

**Backroad to Prospect Camp and Pond** (Mile 135.7) The old camp is to the left, and the half-mile road leads to Claja Pond (beaver engineering).

**Jim River Bridge** (Mile 144) Fishing for chinook (king) salmon, pike, grayling, whitefish. There are two more bridges over the Jim, with equally good fishing at all.

**Grayling Lake Turnout** (Mile 150.8) The lake is well named.

**South Fork Koyukuk River Bridge** (Mile 156) We're now in the Brooks Range foothills. Fishing for chinook salmon, whitefish, grayling.

**Coldfoot** (Mile 175) An oasis in the wilderness, with three motels, a restaurant, service station, RV park, dump station, and the "farthest north saloon in North Amer-ica." The saloon has "readable walls." Guided fishing and hunting trips are available here.

**Marion Creek Campground** (Mile 179.9) A large campground (for this part of Alaska),with RV parking, tentsites, picnic tables, toilets, water, fire pits, and Marion Creek Trail.

**Middle Fork Koyukuk River Bridge** (Mile 188.5) Another fishing spot, with Dolly Varden, whitefish, grayling.

**Road to Wiseman** (Mile 188.6) A fairly level drive to this old gold mining town, with museum, store, telephone, and campground.

Following the Wiseman turn-off, the highway offers views of Sukakpak Mt., to the north, Wiehl Mt., east of Sukakpak Mt., and then a view of the braided middle fork of the Koyukuk River.

**Dietrich River Bridge** (Mile 207) Turnout to west of bridge, fishing for burbot, grayling, whitefish, Dolly Varden.

**Tree Line** (Mile 235.3) The end of the spruce zone is just beyond the turnoff. From here, it's tundra.

**Pingo View** (Mile 376) The large hill to the west is a "pingo," an upraised mound caused by water freezing on former lake beds, often rising to several hundred feet.

**Deadhorse** (Mile 414) Several miles from the ocean and the end of the road for tourists.

# Alaska
## *Destinations*

## Anchorage

More than half of Alaska's population lives in the south-central region, and Anchorage is the area's major city with 245,000 people. South-central has a wide range of geography and scenic attractions, from the fertile farming area of the Matanuska and Susitna river valleys to the fishing villages of Prince William Sound and the Kenai Peninsula. Its cities and towns are scattered along the seashore, warmed by the Japan current and enjoying a surprisingly moderate climate compared to the dry, frigid environment of the Alaskan interior.

The Kenai Peninsula is a popular area for visitors to the region. The Seward Highway takes you south to the port town of Seward, nearby Kenai Fjords National Park, and flightseeing trips to beautiful Resurrection Bay. Kenai, the original oil center of the state, is home to unique historic buildings from the Russian era. Soldotna is a favorite location for river chinook (king) salmon fishing. Homer, an artists' colony and fishing village, is located on the tip of the peninsula, as is the Kenai National Wildlife Range, home to 9,000 protected moose.

The Wrangell Mountains, part of the Coast Range, offer a back-country recreational paradise. The Wrangell–St. Elias National Park and Preserve is located off the scenic Edgerton Highway. A gravel road takes you to the old mining towns of McCarthy and Kennicott, now designated as national historic landmarks.

As in other parts of Alaska, glaciers provide scenic excitement. Tustumena Glacier in the Kenai Mountains is a favorite hikers' destination. Matanuska Glacier abuts the Glenn Highway.

Exit Glacier is found on the Kenai Peninsula at the edge of the Harding Icefield. Close to Anchorage, Portage Glacier lies at the head of Turnagain Arm. Here, at this accessible glacier, large icebergs fall off the toe and bob around Portage Lake. A viewing center overlooks the lake and glacier, and a tour boat provides daily cruises from mid-May to mid-September.

Prince William Sound has gained worldwide notoriety because of the 1989 oil spill. Some of the rocky beaches of the sound have been scrubbed, eliminating a little of the detritus from the spill, but nature will take a long time to recover fully from the disaster. Sports fishing remains excellent, however, and the towns around the sound don't seem to have suffered much from the effects of the spill. The fishing village of Cordova is as charming as ever, although its economy is suffering from low salmon prices. The Alaska ferry, which departs from Whittier for Valdez and Cordova, takes you for a close-in view of the Columbia Glacier.

The people of Anchorage enjoy a modern lifestyle and big-city recreational opportunities, including skiing at the Mount Alyeska ski area. Anchorage boasts a zoo. The Potter Point State Game Refuge is home to 130 species of wildfowl. Chugach State Park, on the Eagle River, has hundreds of miles of hiking trails, camping, and kayaking and rafting on the river.

Anchorage is the urban part of Alaska: a busy, bustling city of almost 250,000 which in many ways doesn't seem part of the Alaska that we dream about. Anchorage is the commercial and transportation capital of the state, with one of the busiest international airports in the world. It suffers from urban blight, as do most other large cities, yet Anchorage definitely remains an "Alaskan" city worth exploring. The city has a moderate rainfall, about 20 inches a year. The winter temperatures hover around the zero mark, with the coldest days around 10 below.

Eighty-five years ago the townsite was pure wilderness. Anchorage was first developed as the main construction camp of the Alaska Railroad. The railroad workers came to what was then called Ship Creek in 1915. By 1917, with the oil boom on the Kenai

Peninsula, the town became a center for corporate offices. The population rose to around 3,000 before the Second World War, when army and air force bases were constructed outside of town.

Much of Anchorage was destroyed by the devastating earthquake of March 27, 1964, which registered 8.6 on the Richter scale. The city was rebuilt, with new office towers giving it a modern look. The business community brought high-rise hotels, restaurants, and nightlife, offering a more cosmopolitan lifestyle than other Alaskan cities. Close to many natural attractions, Anchorage is a good place to base a visit to south-central Alaska.

## Practical Information

The Log Cabin Visitor Information Center is located at West 4th Avenue, at F Street (907) 274-3531. Maps and brochures on Anchorage attractions are available here. One special hot line bears noting: the All About Anchorage Line, (907) 276-3200, which lists daily happenings.

The Alaska Public Lands Information Center is located in the Old Federal Building on 4th Avenue, between F and G streets (907) 271-2737, providing information on national and state parks and other remote areas, plus exhibits and an interactive video display.

The Post Office is located at West 4th Avenue and C Street, in the lower level of the downtown shopping mall (907) 277-6568. The station for the Alaska Railroad is at 2nd Avenue near Ship Creek (907) 265-2494, with daily service to Seward, Whittier, Denali Park, and Fairbanks.

Alaska Marine Highway (ferry) offices are at 333 West 4th Street (907) 272-4482, in the Post Office Mall, for tickets and ferry reservations.

Anchorage International Airport is located a few miles southwest of the downtown area via International Airport Road. Take the People Mover Bus or the airport limousine (907) 694-6484.

## Things to See and Do

The Anchorage Museum of History and Art is at 121 West 7th Avenue, (907) 264-4326. This should be your first stop after settling in. To get a historical perspective, go to the second floor and visit the Alaska Gallery, with dioramas showing Alaska's progression, from prehistoric archaeology to the pipeline era. Other galleries include historical art, featuring paintings by the famed Alaskan artist Sydney Laurence. The Cook Inlet collection is another highlight.

The Heritage Library Museum is located in the Bank of Alaska offices, at Northern Lights Boulevard and C Street (907) 365-2834. This free museum presents a cornucopia of Alaskan artifacts, books, newspapers from the early 1900s, and gold rush scenes on the original glass photographic plates. You will find more Sydney Laurence paintings as well as collections of Native American parkas and rare maps. A browser could spend at least a day here.

Alaska Experience Center, at 705 West 6th Avenue, (907) 276-3730, a 40-minute audio-visual show projected on the inside of a dome, features panoramic vistas with earth-shaking sound and music. The attraction also features an earthquake exhibit.

The Alaska Wilderness Museum (West 5th Avenue and I Street) and the Alaska Wildlife and Natural History Museum (West 4th Avenue and E Street) both feature stuffed bears and other Alaskan animals.

A self-guided walking tour starts at the Log Cabin Visitor Center where you get your map. A guided tour is available from Historic Anchorage, 542 West 4th Avenue, on the second floor of City Hall, (907) 562-6100. Tours depart Monday through Friday at 10 A.M.

The Alaska Zoo is on O'Malley Road, (907) 346-3242. This park features the animals of Alaska as well as a few elephants and big cats. Although the six types of owls are impressive, caged Alaskan animals provide a sad, silent commentary. The kids will enjoy the zoo, but why not visit the national and state parks, and see the animals in the wild?

The Potter State Game Refuge hosts more than 130 species of waterfowl that visit or reside year-round at this outstanding nature reserve. A boardwalk runs over the large marsh. Find it south of Anchorage on the Seward Highway, the route to Portage Glacier and the Kenai Peninsula.

Chugach State Park, a superb alpine wilderness, lies north of town, with impressive high meadows and peaks.

An unusual day trip to Whittier has you driving south along the Seward Highway (beside Turnagain Arm), and then putting your car on an Alaska Railroad flatcar for a 30-minute trip to Whittier, on Prince William Sound. From Whittier, you can take a ferry to Valdez and view a constellation of glaciers, including the Columbia.

If you're traveling along the Glenn Highway, you'll see a large glacier across a valley. Viewing the Matanuska Glacier provides a good day-trip from Anchorage, with the additional benefits of visiting the towns in the Matanuska and Susitna Valleys.

A 50-mile day trip offers an exciting drive over Hatcher Pass to Independence Mine Historic State Park. Drive from Anchorage on State Route 1 (Glenn Highway) to the junction of the George Parks Highway (Highway 3). Take Highway 3 northwest to the junction of the Fishhook and Willow roads (just past Willow), and turn right (east). The historic mine is on this road beyond Hatcher Pass (el. 3,886 feet). After visiting the mine, drive to Palmer and return to Anchorage on the Glenn Highway for the second half of a fine loop drive.

Craftwork from across Alaska is available at several shops, including Alaska Native Arts and Crafts Showroom, 333 West 4th Avenue; Gingham House, a Native American crafts workshop and store at K Street and West 6th Avenue; and Bering Sea Originals at two locations, Diamond Mall, 800 East Diamond Boulevard, and Northway Mall, 3101 Penland Parkway. All offer weaving, baskets, carvings, and jewelry ($10 and up).

To obtain information on wilderness adventures, visit the Log Cabin Visitor Center. You'll find brochures on several companies that offer white-water trips and wilderness experiences in the area.

Several special events are held during the long Anchorage winter. Fur Rendezvous, held in the second week of February, includes trapper games, the world dogsled championships, and snowshoe softball. The start of the Iditarod dogsled race brings excitement to the city during the first week of March.

## Where to Eat

**Downtown Deli**, 525 West 4th Avenue, is a deluxe deli across the street from the Log Cabin Visitor Center. **Sack's Café**, 625 West 5th Avenue, serves sandwiches, salads, and some larger meals, including seafood dishes. This modern, trendy place specializes in mixing foreign cuisines. Brunch is served all day on Sundays.

**Simon & Seafort's Saloon and Grill**, at 420 L Street, provides seafood and pasta specialties with a good view of Cook Inlet. Lighter meals and chowders are available in the salon (not saloon—this place is of a higher class). Simon and Seafort's is a popular after-work gathering spot, and reservations are often necessary, (907) 274-3502.

**Old Anchorage Salmon Bake**, at 251 K Street, occupies a picturesque location in the original Anchorage townsite. Lunch and dinner are served. It's expensive, but you get large helpings of grilled salmon, halibut, reindeer, or crab legs, plus baked beans and a salad bar.

Chain restaurants include **Sea Galley**, on C Street between 36th and Tudor. Several **Skippers** locations provide probably the best family bargains in seafood, including all-you-can-eat fish and shellfish meals. The most interesting place to take the kids is **Sourdough Mining Company** (Juneau Street and International Airport Road, via the Old Seward Highway). This large restaurant replicates the mess hall of an old mining camp. People sit "family-style," with long tables set end-to-end. Dishes tend toward ribs and chicken (i.e., food you can pick up with your fingers). Reservations are accepted (907) 563-2272.

The **Double Musky Restaurant** is located south of town via the Seward Highway, near the Erikson's Mine historic site, on Crow Creek Road. A beacon for knowledgeable visitors, the restaurant is also highly regarded by Anchorage residents. The quality of the cooking and service is more than worth the 40-mile drive to Girdwood and then down the Seward Highway toward the Alyeska Resort. Cajun cuisine is featured, although other styles are served, including steaks and seafood. Open for dinner only and closed Mondays. For reservations, call (907) 783-2822.

# Circle and Chena Hot Springs

Before gold fever hit the Klondike, Circle was the largest town on the Yukon River. Gold was discovered on Birch Creek in 1893 and the town grew as a supply point, servicing the new diggings with modern buildings and services.

Circle is 50 miles south of the Arctic Circle, and was erroneously named by miners who thought it was far closer. Situated 162 miles from Fairbanks via the Steese Highway (state routes 2 and 6), Circle provides a scenic overnight sidetrip with the opportunity to enjoy two hot springs resorts and to stand beside the impressive Yukon River. Along the highway you'll encounter old mining camps, several excellent spots for viewing northern wildflowers, picnic areas, and campgrounds (see the Highway Log pages). You'll meet the Yukon River at the tiny village of Circle, set at the very end of the road. Most residents do not live in the village, but along the river, coming to town by boat to pick up supplies. The Yukon Trading Post houses the restaurant, saloon, post office, a gas station, and liquor store. The H.C. Company Store also has gas, and sells groceries and snacks. To get a feel for the founding of Circle during the 1893 gold rush, walk through the small Pioneer Cemetery with its old markers. You get there by walking upriver on a gravel road, past a barricade, and to a trail that is reached by crossing a private front yard. Please respect this privately owned access.

Camping spots are found at the end of the road, beside the Yukon. There is a parking area, picnic tables, and toilets.

The hot springs near Circle were discovered by prospector William Greats in 1893. Many miners spent their winters at the springs, using tents for bathhouses, when the creeks were too frozen to work. The Circle Hot Springs Road junction is located 128 miles from the start of the Steese Highway. A sideroad runs for 8.3 miles to the Circle Hot Springs Resort. The resort is built around the Olympic-sized pool, and a historic hotel that offers rooms, cabins, a hostel on the fourth floor, and dining. A campground is located two miles before you reach the resort.

Chena Hot Springs Resort is accessible via Chena Hot Springs Road. Turn off the Steese Highway at mile 4.6 and drive for 56.5 miles. This easy day trip from Fairbanks leads you to a relaxing time in the large, enclosed thermal pool, a 2,800-square-foot redwood deck, and a 10-person whirlpool. There is a dining room and overnight accommodations, including hotel rooms, cabins, and camping. The resort has an RV park with electrical hookups and dump station. Winter activities include cross-country skiing, guided snowmobile rides, and warm soaking with piles of snow outside.

## Where to Eat

**Central Motor Inn Restaurant**, in Central, mile 127, is a handy eating spot along the route. The **Yukon Trading Post Café**, in Circle, (907) 773-1217, is a restaurant at the end of the road, with "home cooking" and fresh pies. **Circle Hot Springs**, eight miles off the road to Circle, has a dining room in the historic hotel building dating from 1930.

**Chena Hot Springs Restaurant**, at mile 56.5 of the Chena Hot Springs Road, has a dining room and lounge in the remodeled lodge building. Standard American cuisine is served here at moderate prices.

Food for picnics and camping is available at the Yukon Trading Post general store and the H.C. Company Store in Circle, and at Parson's General Store at Circle Hot Springs Resort.

# Cordova

For a completely different view of life on Prince William Sound, take the 5.5-hour ferry ride from Valdez to Cordova. You'll discover a small fishing town that does not have road connections, marches to its own drummer, and lives according to its own schedule. Originally a copper town founded by prospectors in 1884, Cordova now relies on fishing and canning to provide employment for just about all of its residents. Many of the town's buildings were built in the 1908 copper boom. A good place to start your walking tour of Cordova is the Cordova Historical Museum, in the Centennial Building at First and Adams. The Chamber of Commerce Visitor Center is on 1st Street next to the National Bank, (907) 424-7260.

An unforgettable day trip experience involves driving the 50-mile Copper River Highway, leading from Cordova along a former route to the Kennicott Copper Mine. The absolutely spectacular scenery includes mountains, glaciers, rushing streams, and river delta. At mile 48 the Million Dollar Bridge overlooks Childs Glacier and provides other breathtaking vistas, including a view of Miles Glacier and the iceberg-covered Miles Lake.

## Where to Eat

The **Reluctant Fisherman Inn** is a very good dining room, at 407 Railroad Avenue, and a fine place from which to watch the fishing fleet in Cordova Harbor. Not a rustic operation, this surprisingly sophisticated restaurant serves local fresh salmon and halibut along with other dishes.

The **Powder House**, a bar and restaurant at mile 2.1 of the Copper River Highway, is a more likely place to meet local residents than is the Reluctant Fisherman. This informal place specializes in soup, sandwiches, seafood (in season), summer barbecues, and even sushi. Bluegrass and country music is often heard in the evenings. A deck places you above Eyak Lake. This is the site of the old Copper River Railroad's powder house, built for railroad construction about 1906.

# Deadhorse

Like the smaller Eagle Plains in the northern Yukon, Deadhorse is the Alaskan version of a company town. Its only reason for being, situated as it is above the Arctic Circle, is to service the busy oil operations of Prudhoe Bay. Deadhorse is the end of the Dalton Highway, a rough and ready drive from Fairbanks, through some of the finest scenery in Alaska (see the Dalton Highway Drive, starting on page 100).

There are two places to stay in this town of anywhere from 3,500 to 8,000 (depending on how busy the oil operations are at the time): the Prudhoe Bay Hotel and the North Slope Borough Camp. Both places serve meals. A service station in town offers gas and tire service. Scheduled airline flights are available, connecting this Arctic outpost to Fairbanks and Anchorage.

Deadhorse is several miles from the Arctic Ocean. An oil company road leads north from town, but permits are required to travel on the road. The best thing to do is to sign up for a guided tour of the oilfields and the Arctic Coast. Sign up in Deadhorse after you arrive. Tours can be booked in Fairbanks, with Northern Alaska Tour Company, P.O. Box 82991, Fairbanks, AK 99708, or call (907) 474-8600. These tours start from Fairbanks and are limited to 10 participants. Tours cover the oilfield operations and the pipeline, and feature wildlife viewing along the coast.

# Denali National Park

Denali National Park and Preserve is the most popular tourist attraction in Alaska. Its central feature is the tallest mountain peak in North America: Mount McKinley. For centuries, Alaska's Native Americans have called this mountain Denali—The Great

One. The mountain rises 20,320 feet above the low-lying sub-alpine tundra of the park. At the lower levels, the tundra holds many ponds and low shrubs including willow, blueberry, and dwarf birch. The wildflowers of the park provide a spectacular carpet of many colors.

The geology of Denali is fascinating. Eight long glacial troughs radiate from the Cathedral Spires, many of them with headwalls more than a mile deep. The Denali Fault, a long fault system stretching for 1300 miles across Alaska, runs through the park. Granite domes look down on wide plains.

The ecosystem supports a wide range of wildlife, including moose, caribou, wolves, grizzly bears, Dall sheep, wolverines, and more than 150 species of birds, many of them waterfowl. The negative effects of too much traffic on the park road leading to the major camping and resort area has caused the National Park Service to limit traffic through the park. Shuttle buses provide the preferred form of transport through the park areas, and visitors are required to park their vehicles in one spot and leave them there.

Mountain climbers have challenged Mount McKinley since 1903. The mountain is shrouded by clouds and mist two days out of three during the summer months. The best times of the day to see the summit from the lowlands are in the early morning or late evening. Late September and October provide the best times for consistent views.

The Riley Creek Information Center, just inside the park on Park Road, is the place to obtain information on the park and campground reservations. There are seven campgrounds within the park, located along Park Road, an 87-mile drive ending at Wonder Lake. The first 14 miles of the road are paved. The park headquarters area contains a resort hotel and lodge, and private hotels and campgrounds are located outside the park along George Parks Highway (see Places to Stay). Three lodges are located 100 miles inside the park at the end of Park Road. People planning to visit the park are urged to reserve their hotel accommodations well in advance to avoid disappointment. The park campgrounds are filled on a first-come basis and lineups for sites start to form before 9 A.M.

For information on the park, write Denali National Park and Preserve, P.O. Box 9, Denali Park, Alaska 99755 or call (907) 683-2294. Bus passes and campsites may be reserved by contacting Denali's reservation service in Anchorage at 800-622-7275 or (907) 278-7275.

The Visitor Infocenter is three miles past the park entrance, on Denali Park Road. Enter from the George Parks Highway. All visitors stop here for an orientation.

### Where to Eat

Other than the hotel dining rooms, few restaurant choices exist inside the park. Outside, there are more than two dozen restaurants and food stores along George Parks Highway. These include the **Overlook Bar and Grill**, at the Crow's Nest Cabins, providing an exceptionally fine view of the Denali Park area. This summer operation is located right across the George Parks Highway from the park gate. For reservations call (907) 683-2723.

**Denali Princess Lodge**, a joint operation of Princess Cruises and Alaska Airlines, features two restaurants (including the Summit Room) plus lounges. Located on the George Parks Highway, the resort is open from mid-May to mid-September.

With a fine location beside Carlo Creek, 134 miles from Fairbanks on the George Parks Highway, **The Perch** is a restaurant and bar sitting on a hill near Healy, serving seafood, steaks, and other dishes. Cinnamon rolls are a popular morning take-out item at The Perch. The restaurant is part of a small resort operation with cabins. For information and reservations call (907) 683-2523.

**McKinley-Denali Salmon Bake** is housed in a rustic building located 1 mile north of the Denali Park entrance on George Parks Highway. Salmon, steaks, burgers, and chicken dishes constitute the main fare. The restaurant runs a shuttle bus service to and from several Denali area hotels.

# Fairbanks

Born of the gold rush, Fairbanks is Alaska's second largest city, the home of the main campus of the University of Alaska. The Log Cabin Visitor Information Center is located at 500 1st Avenue. The Alaska Public Lands Information Center at 3rd and Cushman gives out information on state and federal parks and forest and wildlife preserves. Downtown Fairbanks is situated on the banks of the Chena River, which winds through the city. To the south of the city is the Alaska Mountain Range. Denali National Park is a three-hour drive to the south.

The city is well equipped with visitor services, including hotels, motels, good restaurants, shopping, and several museums. The University of Alaska is worth a lengthy visit. The museum there features displays on prehistoric Alaska. The riverboat *Discovery* provides an excellent day trip along the Chena and Tanana rivers, twice each day. To reach it, drive along Airport Road and turn right at Dale Road. The boat stops at a trapper's camp recreation, complete with fish wheel and smokehouse.

The fall scenes outside of Fairbanks are amazing, as the birch forests that cover the region turn to gold in September. Summer temperatures average 63°F. In June and July, the sunlight averages 21 hours and golf is played 24 hours a day.

## Early Days

The founding of Fairbanks is a classic gold rush story. In August 1901, merchant E.T. Barnette was riding up the Tanana River aboard the *Lavelle Young*. He had a boatload of supplies bound for a gold rush trail near Tanacross. Captain Charles Adams, unable to get the riverboat past the rapids, turned into the Chena River and ran aground on sandbars. Adams lightened the boat by dumping all of Barnette's merchandise on the riverbank. Barnette was furious and his wife was in tears, but it turned out to be a lucky break.

Prospector Felix Pedro had recently found flecks of gold in several of the nearby creeks and desperately needed supplies for the winter to continue prospecting. He convinced Barnette to sell him the needed supplies. Shortly after, Felix Pedro hit pay dirt and the merchant set up shop in what is now downtown Fairbanks. Miners headed to the Chena region from the Klondike and Nome. Barnette founded the Washington-Alaska Bank to survive the mining industry, but it failed in 1911.

Hounded by the bankruptcy, Barnette left Fairbanks and never returned. Several books, available in Fairbanks bookstores, tell his fascinating story. The city was named by Barnette's friend, Judge James Wickersham, to honor Indiana senator Charles Fairbanks, who later became Theodore Roosevelt's vice-president.

In 1923, the Alaska Railroad reached Fairbanks from Seward and Anchorage, promoting large-scale mechanized mining. Huge dredges were used to pull the gold from the depths of the permafrost. Over the years, more than $200 million was taken from the frozen muck. The building of the Alaska Highway in 1942 brought new income and prosperity to the city. Fort Wainright (formerly Ladd Field) was established during the war and remains today as an important part of the city's economy.

The 1968 Prudhoe Bay oil strike propelled Fairbanks into a new era. A boom developed for three years as the Trans-Alaska Pipeline was built. Twenty-two thousand pipeline workers were hired, and at one point so many job seekers arrived in Fairbanks that the city fathers took out ads in southern newspapers urging people to stay away.

Fairbanks now has a stable economy, with the University of Alaska campus, air force and army bases, and its role as the communications and transportation center for the Alaskan interior. It's a modern city with shopping plazas, excellent restaurants, and a busy cultural scene.

Fairbanks lies in the wooded Tanana River valley, surrounded by low-lying hills covered with white spruce and birch. Majestic Mount McKinley can be seen from a distance. The best views of the area are from the campus of the University of Alaska.

## Practical Information

The city's travel information center is in the Convention and Visitors bureaus and Log Cabin Visitor Center, at 550-Q 1st Avenue in the downtown area, (907) 456-5774. Free one-hour walking tours of the city start here.

The Alaska Public Lands Information Center is at 201 1st Avenue for maps and information on remote areas including Alaska's parks.

Local Transit is based at 6th Avenue and Cushman Streets (907) 456-3279. Routes run through downtown and outlying areas, including a bus to North Pole. Schedules are available here and at the Visitors Bureau cabin.

The Alaska Railroad is located at 280 Cushman Street, with service to Denali National Park and Anchorage (907) 456-4155. Fairbanks International Airport is located 6 miles southwest of downtown via Airport Road. Several charter airlines provide sightseeing flights. Scheduled service is provided by Mark Air, Alaska Airlines, United Airlines, and Air North.

## Things to See and Do

The University of Alaska campus is worth visiting, particularly the UOA Museum at 907 Yukon Drive. There is an eclectic range of exhibits such as Russian era artifacts and Native American crafts. Another interesting activity at the university is visiting the Agricultural Research Station to gaze at the gigantic vegetables that grow in the 20-hour sunlight. Free public tours of the campus operate during summer months. Call (907) 474-7581 for information and schedules.

The Trans-Alaska Pipeline can be seen on the Steese Highway north of Fairbanks. This elevated pipeline is insulated from the ground to protect the tender permafrost.

Alaskaland, the city's frontier-style theme park, features authentic pioneer homes, replicas of Native American dwellings, an amusement park with rides, the sternwheeler *Nenana,* cancan dancers, a salmon bake, and gift shops. It's open daily, with no general admission charge.

The Dog Musher's Museum, four miles down Farmer's Loop Road, offers live dogsled demonstrations, narrated slide-audio programs, and exhibits. It's located in a picturesque log building. Call (907) 457-MUSH. The museum stages several special event days during the summer season.

### Special Events

One of the most unusual sports events in the world takes place in Fairbanks each summer. The Midnight Sun Baseball Game is played late at night on the June solstice, when perpetual light (at least for a few days) enables people to play ball, and golf, throughout the nighttime hours.

Golden Days are held in mid-July, as Fairbanks residents dress in turn-of-the-century costumes and celebrate the gold rush with pancake breakfasts, canoe and raft races, and the Felix Pedro Parade honoring the discoverer of gold in the Tanana hills. The Fairbanks Summer Arts Festival is held in late July, with classical and jazz music, dance, theater, and visual art exhibitions.

Fairbanks alternates starting and finish lines with Whitehorse for the Yukon Quest, a noted dogsled race. The race started in Fairbanks in 1990. For information on the race, call (907) 457-MUSH.

### Where to Eat

The **Pump House Restaurant** is an exceptional place, at the former location of a large pumping station that moved water from the Chena River to mining operations. While the food and service are excellent, the Pump House has a relaxed atmosphere, in the dining room and especially on the large outdoor deck area beside the river. Food is appealingly presented, particularly at the superb Sunday buffet. The restaurant is at mile 1.3 of Chena Pump Road. For reservations call (907) 479-8452.

**Pike's Landing** is another fine restaurant beside the Chena River, at 4438 Airport Way. A large deck overlooks the river, with a fine dining room inside and a neighboring sports bar for those who really want a noisier ambiance. For reservations call (907) 479-7113.

The **Salmon Bake**, inside Alaskaland at Airport Way and Peger Road, serves up barbecued salmon, halibut, and ribs, in the gold rush atmosphere of the theme and amusement park. The restaurant is open from May to September.

The **Bunkhouse**, at Cripple Creek Resort in Ester, eight miles south of downtown, offers old-style grub with a gold camp ambiance. The all-you-can-eat buffet includes reindeer (caribou) stew, fried chicken, baked halibut, and hot biscuits, plus side dishes including corn-on-the-cob, baked beans, and an apple crisp dessert. For information and reservations call (907) 479-7274.

Also reached by taking a short drive from Fairbanks, the historic **Fox Roadhouse** (2195 Old Steese Highway, near the junction of the Steese and Elliott highways) provides Alaska seafood, including lobster, steaks, ribs and such, plus fine desserts. The intentionally rowdy lounge features pool, darts, and dancing.

# *Haines*

Haines lies alongside the Lynn Canal, between Chilkoot and Chilkat inlets. The town is framed by the Cathedral Peaks (el. 6,500 feet) and the rain forest. It has a rich Native American culture from the two Tlingit tribes that settled the area. The Chilkat are famous for their crafts, including striking goat-wool blankets.

The Chilkat lived in this area and had it to themselves before John Muir and S. H. Young established a mission here in 1879. Salmon canneries followed, and during the Klondike Gold Rush, Haines was the southern end of the Dalton Trail, a toll route to the Yukon Territory, on the way to Dawson City.

Possible activities here include exploring Fort Seward, formerly the army barracks. Here is a replica of a Tlingit longhouse and a trapper's cabin. Alaskan Indian Arts hosts a cultural center at Fort Seward, featuring silversmithing and woodcarving. The Wild Iris Chilkat Dancers perform in the Chilkat Center for the Arts.

## Practical Information

Haines' visitor information center is on 2nd Avenue, near Willard Street. This is the place to start a visit to this picturesque town. Material on nearby state parks, including hiking maps, is available. For advance information call (907) 766-2234. The State Park Office is located at 259 Main Street, above Helen's shop, (907) 766-2292.

The Alaska Ferries terminal is located on Lutak Highway; call (907) 766-2111. White Pass Bus Lines has service from Haines to Whitehorse and Fairbanks. The bus depot is on 2nd Avenue, across from the town information center. For schedule information call (907) 766-2030.

## Where to Eat

The Catalyst, on Main Street, (907) 766-2670, has well-prepared seafood, salads, soups, and desserts, all at moderate cost.

Hotel Hälsingland Restaurant is in the hotel (formerly army housing) on the Fort Seward parade square, south of downtown. Seafood is a specialty in this fine dining room, with moderate to expensive pricing. A wine bar with a view is also a hotel feature. For reservations call (907) 766-2000.

Port Chilkoot Potlatch is part of the Fort Seward Tribal House. The famous salmon bake is a "must" experience. This is an all-you-can-eat operation, open daily from 5 to 8 P.M., between June and late August. The Tribal House is located across the parade square from the Hotel Hälsingland.

# Homer

See Kenai Peninsula, page 129.

# Juneau

Juneau is built on a thin strip of land flanked by mountains on one side and Gastineau Channel on the other. Originally a gold camp, Juneau became the state capital in 1906. Many hold that Juneau is the most beautiful capital city in the U.S. It's hard to argue when you're in this world of rugged beauty, visited each year by more than 200,000 tourists, most of them arriving on cruise ships. The city was named for Joe Juneau, a prospector who arrived here in October 1880 and led a notoriously riotous life.

Glacier Bay National Park is a short flight from Juneau. The Admiralty Island National Monument is nearby. The Mendenhall Glacier is Juneau's drive-up glacier, located 15 miles northwest of town on the Glacier Highway. The glacier is 1.5 miles wide at its base and has been receding for at least 250 years. It is now several miles shorter than it was when Russian explorers came to the area.

The Alaska State Museum is valuable to first-time visitors (907) 465-2901. Open daily, it has an excellent collection of Native American artifacts, including fascinating exhibits of Yupik Eskimo masks and Siberian and Alaskan kayaks. A large upstairs area is devoted to the early Russian period. An art gallery in the museum features the works of contemporary Alaskan artists. Other places to visit include the House of Wickersham, a state historical site, (907) 586-9001, St. Nicholas Orthodox Church at 5th and Gold streets, and the State Office Building on Willoughby Avenue. Go to the eighth floor, which has a panoramic view of the area, a 19th-century totem pole, and a restored 1926 Kimball pipe organ. There's a walking tour map available from hotels and from the info kiosk at Marine Park. The tour leads you around downtown Juneau to all of the principal buildings and sights.

## Practical Information

Log cabins seem to be the *de rigeur* structure for visitor centers in Alaska, and Juneau is no exception. The Davis Log Cabin is found at 134 3rd Street downtown. This is your best source for walking tour maps and other information on the area. To contact the cabin call (907) 586-2284. A visitor kiosk is open sometimes, when cruise ships are in town, at Marine Park next to the cruise ship dock. There's also a local events hot line with hot tips on upcoming and current activity, at (907) 586-5800. The Juneau-area Weather Line is at (907) 586-3997, and the local Fishing Line is at (907) 465-4116.

The U.S. Forest Service is located at 101 Egan Drive, with exhibits and audio-visual programs on southeast Alaska forests and wildlife. Reservations for forest cabins are made here. Information is available by telephone at (907) 586-8751.

The Alaska Marine Highway's Auke Bay Terminal is on Glacier Highway, with ferry service to Prince Rupert, Bellingham, Ketchikan, Sitka, and other southeast Alaska towns. For schedule information, call (907) 465-3941 or 800-642-0066.

Capital Transit, (907) 789-6901, services Juneau, Douglas, and Auke Bay. For busses to the airport and ferry terminal, phone Mendenhall Glacier Transport at (907) 780-8687.

## Night Life

Several Alaskan cities, including Fairbanks, Skagway, and Juneau, offer atmospheric entertainment places, where you may behave just how you might imagine a prospector from the 1800s would. This is all good fun and adds greatly to a visit to the more remote areas of North America. The **Red Dog Saloon**, on South Franklin Street, is an authentic Alaskan saloon, with sawdust on the floor and Chinook (an Alaskan microbrew) on draft. The joint jumps when cruise ships are in town. Music is featured nightly, (907) 463-3777.

The **Lady Lou Revue** is performed in the Elks Hall on Franklin Street, (907) 586-3686. This is a lusty musical revival of the early gold rush days in Juneau. For something different, take in **Marine Park Music**, heard on Friday evenings at Marine Park, near the cruise ship terminal. This series of free music concerts is presented every week during the summer months.

## Where to Eat

**Fiddlehead Restaurant and Bakery**, at 429 Willoughby Avenue near the Alaska State Museum, features fresh Alaskan sourdough bread, soups, salads, seafood, and tasty desserts, all at moderate prices.

The **Channel Bowl Café**, at 608 Willoughby Avenue, is in a bowling alley. Don't let the location and the decor fool you; this is honest-to-goodness comfort food, and is very popular with local residents for breakfast and lunch.

**The Silverbow Inn**, at 120 2nd Street downtown, boasts a popular dining room. The eatery is furnished in an eclectic style, favoring the early Juneau days, with furniture (parlor and dining chairs) and decor from the pioneer era. The building, originally a large bakery, was built in 1912. The present dining room features country French fare along with American cuisine (fresh fish, Cajun dishes) served in a country-inn ambiance. For reservations call (907) 586-4146.

Juneau has its own very good salmon bake. The Gold Creek Salmon Bake is located in a scenic wooded spot at the end of Basin Road. Better than driving yourself, the free shuttle from in front of the downtown Baranof Hotel takes you right to the action. You'll eat fresh salmon, cooked over alderwood, and usually supplemented with ribs. Baked beans are also part of the meal. The place offers gold panning in Salmon Creek, with pans available for free, and you can keep any gold you find. There's an old mine (the A. J.) sitting above the restaurant. As with most other places of this type, the price of the dinner is steep (more than $20), but offers a unique Alaskan experience.

The Foodland Supermarket, downtown at 615 Willoughby Avenue, is the most central place to pick up picnic supplies.

# Katmai National Park and Preserve

The Alaska Peninsula extends 400 miles into the Pacific Ocean, jutting toward the Aleutian island chain. At the head of the peninsula is Lake Clark National Park and Preserve, a spectacular setting of mountains, high glaciers, and an extremely rugged seacoast. The communities of Dillingham, King Salmon, and Iliamma are serviced by airlines from Anchorage. In the midst of great fishing steams and lakes, the area around these three villages offers a number of fly-in fishing lodges.

King Salmon is the headquarters for and the nearest community to the splendid Katmai National Park and Preserve, a wild, primitive landscape. Here one of the century's most violent volcanic eruptions took place—in 1912—with serious effects for Mount Katmai. The eruption began on June 5th of that year, with shuddering and black ash rising from the 9,000-foot peak, and then the volcanic vent called Novarupta blew open the next day with a blast heard in Juneau—750 miles away. The ash traveled so far that some of it fell in Vancouver, B.C. All of North America was affected by the clouds of ash which cooled temperatures considerably that summer. Mount Katmai collapsed into itself, and 2,000 feet of mountain disappeared. Ash devastated the area in every direction, and thousands of fumaroles vented sulfurous steam.

This is an elemental landscape, where thousands of fumaroles belched steam and smoke (now just steam)—the remnants of the Novarupta explosion. The fumarole valley, a prime place to visit and to hike, is named the Valley of the Ten Thousand Smokes. Other features of the park include hundreds of glaciers, snowfields clinging to the many mountain peaks, and lakes (Lake Nanek, the fourth largest lake in Alaska, has been called an "inland sea"). You can walk through birch groves at the lower levels of the park, and up to alpine tundra and the edge of icefields. There are many species of birds in the park, and campers get very excited when hearing the fervent calls that Alaskan birds seem to give.

The Park Service visitor center in the area organizes guided walks of the "Valley of the Ten Thousand Smokes," or you can take a hiking tour on your own with guidance from the staff of the visitor center.

Brooks Camp is the famed place to watch brown bears catching salmon in the rushing stream and waterfall. Brooks Lodge, with overnight accommodation and food service plus a campground, is located at Brooks Camp. You may also wish to fly to other lodges in the interior of the park. Some of the best sockeye salmon fishing in the world is experienced at Brooks Camp and on interior streams of Katmai National Park.

### How to Get There

Visitors to the park usually fly by scheduled aircraft to King Salmon, and then take an air taxi operated by Peninsula Airways to Brooks River, where there is a National Park ranger station. Some people charter their own planes to get into Katmai. For information on the park, write the National Parks Service, P.O. Box 7, King Salmon, AK 99613, or phone (907) 246-3305.

# Kenai Peninsula

If you could visit only one part of Alaska by car or RV, we'd suggest a tour of the Kenai Peninsula. Kenai provides most of the scenic features of Alaska: fjords, glaciers, and icefields, large rivers filled with fish, sparkling lakes, fishing villages, port towns, and off-shore islands.

The Kenai Peninsula is the most popular recreation area for Alaskans, close to Anchorage and easily accessible by high-quality paved roads. The Kenai Mountains form the backbone of the peninsula. The gigantic Harding Icefield dominates the southern region. Most of the peninsula is federal government nature preserve, including the Kenai National Wildlife Refuge, Chugach National Forest, and Kenai Fjords National Park.

Originally inhabited by the Kenai, the area was settled by Russians, who built a fort near Kasilof in 1786 and another fort at Kenai seven years later. Gold was discovered on Turnagain Arm, bringing the Alaska Railroad to the area in the 1920s. Oil was found off the west coast in 1957. Today, some 40,000 people are engaged in fishing, transportation, and tourist services.

The roads of the Kenai Peninsula beckon travelers to this unspoiled wilderness. The 127-mile Seward Highway linking Anchorage and Seward is a designated National Forest Scenic Byway. The Seward follows the north shore of Turnagain Arm, leading through Chugach State Park and the Chugach National Forest. Pods of beluga whales are often seen in the Arm. This long, narrow inlet has a extremely high tide that causes a tidal bore from time to time. The wall of water flooding into the Arm can be as high as 6 feet. The tidal bore is best seen between miles 32 and 37 on the Seward Highway, $2^1/4$ hours after low tide in Anchorage.

The Sterling Highway connects the southwestern communities on the peninsula with the Seward Highway, passing through the Kenai National Wildlife Refuge and the Chugach National Forest. Throughout the route you'll encounter forest recreation sites, including many campsites within a mile or two of the highway, plus canoeing rivers, marshes, and wildlife sanctuaries. There are three larger communities along the Sterling drive: Soldotna, neighboring Kenai, and Homer—at the end of the drive. From Soldotna south, the highway follows the west coast of the peninsula along the shore of Cook Inlet. Along the way several small fishing villages and overlooks offer great views (on sunny days) of the volcanic mountain peaks on the Alaska Peninsula across Cook Inlet.

Several sideroads lead off the two main highways to interesting old villages and fine scenery. The Alyeska access road provides access to Crow Creek Road and the historic Crow Creek Mine, which is open to visitors daily. This national historic site in the middle of the Chugach National Forest includes a campground, ponds, and gardens. Visitors can walk on the old Iditarod Trail, which has its head at the end of this backroad at Milk Creek. Also along the Alyeska access road is the community of Girdwood, an old mining camp. At the end of the road is the Alyeska Resort, Alaska's most popular ski and summer resort. The chairlift takes you above 3,000 feet for wonderful views of Turnagain Arm and several glaciers.

Another sideroad drive takes you to Portage Glacier at mile 48.1 of the Seward Highway. We've mentioned the glacier before, and only need to remind you that this is one of the most accessible glaciers in the state.

A 17-mile sideroad leads northwest from the Seward Highway (at mile 70.3) to the village of Hope (population 224). This historic mining community was founded in 1896 by prospectors who found gold on Resurrection Creek and several smaller creeks. This is a popular cottage area for Anchorage residents. Hope offers good fishing near the ocean, and has a café, store, and motel. Just beyond the present-day community is the original Hope townsite. Part of the town was destroyed in the 1964 earthquake.

### Kenai

Kenai has been settled longer than any other community on the peninsula. The old town near Cook Inlet is a fascinating blend of Russian, early American, and modern development. The Kenai Historical Museum, housed in a replica of Fort Kenai, features artifacts from the town's eras, including Russian icons, early photographs, and stone tools.

A walking tour of the old town starts from the Visitors Center, in John "Moosemeat" Hedburg's Cabin at Main Street and Kenai Spur Road, (907) 283-7989. Next to the museum stands Holy Assumption Russian Orthodox Church, built in 1896. A good view of the mountains is seen from viewpoints on the bluff, via Mission Road. The Captain Cook State Recreation Area is a half-hour drive, at the end of Kenai Spur Road, with swimming, picnicking, canoeing, and fishing.

### Soldotna

At this most noted fishing spot in the area, record-sized salmon are caught in the Kenai River. The visitor center on the Sterling Highway, (907) 262-1337, has information and displays. The Kenai National Wildlife Refuge is a huge nature preserve (197 million acres), home to moose, Dall sheep, and other wildlife.

There's a short nature trail near the visitor center, on Funny Lake Road, off Ski Hill Road. Several canoe routes thread through the forest, and free maps of them are available at the visitor center.

## Homer

Lying beside a long sand spit at the end of the Sterling Highway, Homer boasts a mild climate and gorgeous scenery, with the dramatic Kenai Mountains across beautiful Kachemak Bay. Huge halibut regularly run to over 200 pounds. Homer is home to many artists and craftspeople, and the town features several small galleries and craft shops.

A small gold rush at nearby Sunrise and Hope brought settlers to the area in the 1890s. One of the most colorful prospectors, Homer Pennock, gave his name to the town. Gold ran out quickly but fishermen and homesteaders settled the area during the 1920s, encouraged partly by the rich veins of exposed coal, some of it lying right on the beach. The highway connected Homer with the rest of Alaska in the early 1950s. Some 4,000 people live here, engaged in fish processing, transportation, and tourism. The four-mile spit has a small boat harbor, boardwalks, restaurants, a motel at the end of the spit, and the unique ambiance of the Sawlty Dawg Saloon in a former lighthouse that looks like it's going to fall down at any time. The structure is sturdy, however, and even the loud bands that play here in the evening can't shake the boards loose.

The Chamber of Commerce provides information in its office on Pioneer Avenue, (907) 235-7740. Pick up the walking tour brochure and the visitors guide. Brochures on hotels, fishing charters, and tours are also available here. The Pratt Museum, 3779 Bartlett Street, (907) 235-8635, also offers information as well as an outstanding collection of Alaskan plant specimens. The Marine Gallery features a whale skeleton and displays of fish, shellfish, shorebirds, otters, and Native American history dioramas.

The U.S. Fish and Wildlife Alaska Maritime National Wildlife Refuge has an office and visitor information center in

Homer. The center is open daily during the summer and on weekdays during winter months. There are displays, video presentations, and a shop that sells books and pamphlets on refuge wildlife.

Skyline Drive offers a drive along the top of the bluffs that rise over Homer. East Hill Road and West Hill Road lead to this area. You'll see masses of fireweed and other wildflowers, including lupines, roses, paintbrush, and wild geraniums.

Homer is one of the best fishing centers in the state, with huge halibut caught regularly, as well as salmon. The annual halibut derby is held from May 1 through Labor Day. More than $35,000 in cash prizes are awarded each year for the biggest fish and tagged halibut. Catches are often over 200 pounds. Derby tickets can be obtained at the little information kiosk and charter fishing offices on the Homer Spit. Many charter boats are available for fishing cruises. To obtain advance information on these charters, write to the Homer Charter Association, P.O. Box 148, Homer, AK 99603.

A "must" sidetrip is a short boat cruise to Halibut Cove, a picturesque village of 50 people. This is a beautiful spot, with boardwalks, art galleries, and dining on a ship, the *Saltry*. For a fishing-boat cruise (day cruise or evening dinner cruise), call Halibut Cove Experiences at (907) 235-8110.

### Where to Eat

**Wallace's Café,** on Lack Street near Pioneer Avenue, serves burgers, soup, and sandwiches. It's an inexpensive place for breakfast or lunch.

**Boardwalk Fish & Chips,** on the Cannery Row Boardwalk, serves local halibut at moderate prices.

**The Fresh Sourdough Express Bakery and Restaurant** is a far cry from its origins as a van selling fresh baked goods. Fish omelets are a specialty, with the local halibut a standout. More exotic dishes include reindeer creations. This fine café is at 1316 Ocean Drive, at the entrance to the Homer Spit. For reservations call (907) 235-7571.

The **Saltry** is a restaurant at Halibut Cove, with a deck overlooking the boat dock. It specializes in fresh seafood dishes and a fine selection of imported and microbrewery beers on draft.

While the **Sawlty Dawg Saloon**, on Homer Spit, is less a restaurant and more a raucous bar with music at night, you can also get a filling meal in an unforgettable ambiance.

# Ketchikan

Ketchikan is Alaska's southernmost city, and its wettest! The locals receive 162 inches of rain a year. Nothing in Ketchikan stops for the rain. The city hugs the steep hillside of the Tongass Narrows on Revillagigedo Island, just 60 miles north of Prince Rupert. Two canneries, two fish cold-storage plants, and a pulp mill provide employment for the 15,000 people who live here.

Creek Street, the best-known boardwalk in Alaska, has wooden houses built on pilings over Ketchikan Creek. The street once was the town's red light district. Now it's a center for tourist shops. Dolly Arthur's House is a "museum of ill repute."

Ketchikan has Alaska's best collection of totem poles and they are everywhere. Visit the Totem Heritage Center, up the hill on Deermont Street, and Totem Bight State Park (eight miles northwest of the ferry terminal), with 15 Tlingit and Haida totem poles and a replica of a Haida clan house. Saxman Totem Park is 2.5 miles south of Ketchikan, with a cultural center, carving shed, and performances by the Cape Fox Dancers.

### Practical Information

Tourists obtain information on current happenings at the Ketchikan Visitor's Bureau, 131 Front Street, across from the cruise ship dock, downtown. For advance information call (907) 225-6166.

The U.S. Forest Service is found in the Federal Building, at Steadman and Mill streets. For advance information on national forest cabins and hiking trails, call (907) 747-6671.

The Alaska Marine Highway terminal is on North Tongass Highway, call (907) 225-6181.

Air Service to Ketchikan is provided by Alaska Airlines (907) 225-2141. The airport is across the narrows via a small ferry from the ferry terminal.

### Where to Eat

**Pete's Sourdough Inn**, at 834 Water Street downtown near the tunnel, offers large-sized breakfasts and soup and sandwiches for lunch at reasonable prices.

**Kay's Kitchen**, at 2813 Tongass Avenue near the ferry, serves lunch only. Try the patio if it's not raining.

**George Inlet Lodge**, 12 miles south of town, (907) 225-6077, has a unique logging camp ambiance and good food. Prices are higher here than in most other area restaurants.

# Kodiak Island and Kodiak

Kodiak is Alaska's largest island and the second largest in the U.S.: 6,000 square miles of fjords, spruce forests, and alpine tundra with cool, wet weather. The town of Kodiak receives 75 inches of rain a year.

Russian fur traders landed on Kodiak Island in 1763. The sea otter trade flourished after Alexander Baranof arrived in 1764 to manage the Russian American Company and the colony on Kodiak. By 1800, the sea otter population had been decimated. The 8,000 Native American inhabitants were reduced to fewer than 4,000 through disease and massacres by the Russians. The 1912 eruption of Novarupta on the mainland covered the island with ash and foul air, necessitating the removal of the population in a dramatic rescue.

During the Second World War, the island was a first line of defense for the U.S. military, with submarine bases, gun emplacements, and other fortifications. King crab took over the economy after the war. Then another natural disaster devastated

Kodiak: The 1964 Good Friday earthquake flooded the town with several tidal waves, sweeping half the town from its foundations. The town was rebuilt, and fishing—for salmon, halibut, shrimp, herring, cod, and other species—has become the prime industry.

### How to Get to Kodiak
Kodiak Island is the only easily accessible part of southwest Alaska. The island is 250 air miles from Anchorage, and 84 nautical miles from Homer on the Kenai Peninsula. Ferries run to Kodiak from Homer three times a week. For the drive from Anchorage to Homer, see page 98. It is possible to take a ferry to Dutch Harbor in the Aleutians every three weeks. Daily airline flights connect Kodiak with Anchorage.

### Practical Information
The visitor infocenter is at Center Street and Marine Way, at the ferry dock (907) 486-4070. It's open year-round, 8 A.M. to 5 P.M. weekdays, and 10 A.M. to 3 P.M. weekends. The center provides a self-guided tour map, along with information on local busses and charters, as well as hunting and fishing opportunities.

The Alaska Marine Highway office is in downtown Kodiak, (907) 486-3800, with ferry service to and from Homer and Seward. The cruise from Homer takes about 10 hours, and the ride from Seward takes 13 hours. You can also reach the ferry system by calling 800-526-6731 (U.S.).

The Kodiak Driver Express runs busses hourly to the airport, and to Fort Abercrombie State Park.

### Where to Eat
The **Fox Inn**, in the Shelikof Lodge at 211 Thorsheim in downtown Kodiak, dishes up nourishing food with large servings, ranging from burgers to seafood, at moderate prices.

**Kodiak Café**, 203 Marine Way downtown, specializes in large breakfasts, plus lunches and dinners with fresh halibut and other seafood. This is a popular spot with local residents, and prices range from inexpensive to moderate.

**El Chicano** is on the second floor of the Center Street Plaza. This is fine, reasonably priced Mexican food where you don't expect it.

Two food stores are suggested for picnic and camping food: **Safeway**, two miles from downtown on Mill Bay Road, and **City Market** on Lower Mill Bay Road downtown.

# Manley Hot Springs

Located at the end of the Elliott Highway, this small hot springs resort is located beside Hot Springs Slough. In 1907, Frank Manley built a resort hotel at what was then called Baker Hot Springs. The name was changed in 1957. The community of about 90 people includes a roadhouse, trading post, and the resort. The Manley Roadhouse has a restaurant, bar, and some accommodations. The restaurant specializes in cinnamon rolls (a must for any self-respecting northern café), fresh-baked pies, and an informal atmosphere. There's a public campground near the bridge, with fees paid at the Roadhouse. A picnic area is located beside the slough, near the campground.

The resort is open year-round, with a hot pool, restaurant, bar, and rooms, plus an RV park with facilities that include showers and a laundry. Gasoline is available here as well as at the Trading Post. Slough fishing is a popular activity for visitors, with large pike as the main attraction from May to September. You may also want to fish in the Tanana River, located 2.5 miles from town via a gravel road leading from the old Northern Commercial Company store. Salmon are here in abundance from mid-June to the end of September (chinook, silver, and coho).

# Palmer

Due north of Anchorage lies the Matanuska Valley, a fertile farming area settled by 200 Scandinavian-American farm families who were drawn to the valley from the Midwest states during the 1930s Depression and FDR's New Deal. The story is well told in James Michener's novel *Alaska*. Living first in cabins with tent-tops, the colonists cleared the land, built their houses and farm buildings, and planted vegetables. Within five years, large harvests were realized and Palmer had become a growing town. Best known are the incredibly large vegetables grown in the almost constant summer sunlight, like 75-pound cabbages, 10-pound onions, and 125-pound pumpkins. Roadside stands have fresh produce in season.

To reach Palmer, take the Glenn Highway, which runs north from Anchorage to Tok. The Palmer Information Center provides all the information you need to see the valley, including a listing of farms, other attractions, and tours of the Matanuska Valley.

The Agricultural Research Station in Palmer has greenhouses and an arboretum. A mile south of town stand the Alaska State Fairgrounds. The annual fair started as a harvest celebration during the early years of valley farming. It's now a major event, held during the last week of August through Labor Day. Thrill-rides take visitors on airboats traveling up the Knik River to Knik Glacier. Two companies offer three-hour tours. The local visitors center, across the railroad tracks at South Valley Way and East Fireweed Avenue, has information on all local attractions and special events.

### Where to Eat

The **Gold Miners Hotel**, in downtown Palmer at 918 South Colony Way, serves three meals a day and has an adjoining lounge. Like most restaurants in Palmer, this one offers basic cuisine, mostly standard American dishes. The restaurant at the **Fairview Motel** offers what it calls fine dining, and it is for this part of the country, at mile 40.5 of the Glenn Highway across from the State Fairgrounds. The **Valley Hotel**, an aging institution at 606 South Alaska Street, has a 24-hour coffee shop, along with a lounge and liquor store. The restaurant here is basic and inexpensive, as are the accommodations.

# Petersburg

The fish canning center of the southeast, Petersburg has a delightful Norwegian flavor. It's a "picture postcard" town unaffected by cruise ship tourism. Rosemaling decoration is found on many of the town's buildings. Petersburg is close to the LeConte Glacier, accessible by plane, (907) 772-9258, and the southern-most glacier on the continent to calve icebergs into the sea. Thingit villages are found at Kake, on Kupreanof Island, and at Angoon. There are three fish canneries in town.

The Clausen Memorial Museum (2nd Avenue and Fram Street) has displays on fishing history and techniques, as well as Native American artifacts. The Heintzleman Tree Nursery, (907) 772-3841, and Crystal Lake Fish Hatchery are open to the public. In mid-May, Petersburg holds its Little Norway Festival, commemorating Norwegian independence.

## Practical Information

The Ketchikan Visitors Bureau is found in the office of the Chamber of Commerce, in the Harbormasters Building on the downtown dock, (907) 772-3646.

The U.S. Forest Service operates a visitor information center in the Federal Building (post office), at Haugen Street and Nordic Drive. The office is open seven days a week from 8 A.M. to 4:30 P.M. Ketchikan is headquarters for Misty Fjords National Monument and the Ketchikan Ranger District of Tongass National Forest. For advance information call (907) 225-3101. The ranger station is located at 3031 Tongass Avenue, open on weekdays from 8 A.M. to 5 P.M.

The Alaska Marine Highway terminal is 1 mile from downtown, on Mitkof Highway. The ferry system has service to and from Bellingham, Washington, as well as runs to all of the southeast Alaska mainline cities, including Sitka, Wrangell, and Juneau, and also to Prince Rupert, B.C.

The airport is 1 mile from downtown via Haugen Drive (907) 225-6800.

## Where to Eat

**Homestead Café**, Nordic Drive at Excel, serves good burgers for lunch, and seafood and other dishes for dinner, all at moderate prices.

**The Petersburg Fish Co.**, a restaurant at the fish plant, is noted for fresh and tasty seafood, and the ambiance is certainly different from anything you'll experience in the lower 48 states. Be prepared to lay out a good amount of money for a meal here.

**Annabelle's Keg and Chowder House** is located in the Gilmore Hotel, and is divided into two parts. The larger part (Keg & Chowder House) serves pasta and seafood, and includes an espresso bar. The more refined Annabelle's Parlor has more than basic seafood dishes, which are prepared with finesse. The parlor also has excellent service. The prices range from moderate to expensive.

The large dining room restaurant at **Salmon Falls Resort** is well worth the drive. A half hour from downtown at mile 17 of the North Tongass Highway, it is constructed of pine logs and specializes in fresh seafood. The views of Clover Passage from this octagonal dining room are spectacular. For reservations call (907) 225-6009.

For those who can get by on lesser amounts of food than the above places (noted for their trencherman's servings), you might like to stop in at **Kay's Kitchen**, at 2813 Tongass Avenue. This informal spot serves great soup and sandwiches that are sizable but not completely intimidating.

# Seward

A port town in the Kenai Mountains, Seward is situated on a beautiful bay and is the only large town on the east side of the peninsula. The town is served by ferries from Seward, and the Alaska Railroad terminates here. Nearby is Kenai Fjords National Park. This rugged area includes the Harding Icefield (36 glaciers) and is as scenic as the better-known Glacier Bay. Baranof's Russian shipyard was established here in the 1790s. The small downtown area looks out on Resurrection Bay, with views of Mount Alice and Mount Marathon.

The Information Cache, a visitor information service, is in the Seward Rail Car, at 3rd and Jefferson Streets, (907) 224-3094. Pick up a map of the self-guided walking tour. The National Park Service Visitor Center, (907) 224-2874, is at the Small Boat Harbor on 4th Avenue. This is the place to get maps and other information on Kenai Fjords Park. The Chugach National Forest Ranger Station, at 334 4th Avenue, has hiking trail information and maps of the National Forest.

### Where to Eat

**The Depot** is really a fast-food restaurant but is not part of the usual chains. It serves a variety of food, ranging from burgers to seafood to barbecue. It's at mile 1 of the Seward Highway.

**Harbor Dinner Club and Lounge** is your best bet for fresh local seafood. The restaurant has a homey, informal atmosphere, with service to match. The menu includes full lunch and dinner dishes, and burgers (including a great halibut burger). Prices are low to moderate.

For those with a bent toward continental cuisine, a call to **Le Barn Appétit** is in order. This is a bed-and-breakfast inn with a restaurant attached. The nice feature of dining in Alaska is that even for the fussiest meals, you don't have to dress up. For reservations call (907) 224-8706.

# Sitka

Sitka is a picturesque harbor town, situated on Baranof Island. Mount Edgecumbe on Kruzof Island (el. 3,000 feet) hovers over the town.

Sitka was the Russian capital of Alaska, established in 1799 by Alexander Baranof of the Russian American Company. At one time Sitka had a larger population than San Francisco or Seattle. The town is steeped in history from the Russian era, with sites such as Saint Michael's Cathedral and Castle Hill providing reminders of the town's origins. Also evident are the rough relations between the Russians and the Tlingit people, who fought the Russian invaders to the teeth on several occasions and wound up isolated from the town by a stockade. Visit the reconstructed blockhouse of the stockade that kept the Tlingit restricted to a walled area. East of the blockhouse is the Alaska Pioneers Home. A Russian Orthodox cemetery, with graves going back to 1848, is at the end of Observatory Street.

## Practical Information

Visitor information is available at the Isabel Miller Museum in the Centennial Building at 330 Harbor Drive, beside the Small Boat Harbor. You may also wish to contact the Sitka Convention and Visitors Bureau, at P.O. Box 1226, Sitka, AK 99835, or call (907) 747-5940.

The Forest Service office is also located in the Centennial Building, (907) 747-6671, or write to Sitka Ranger District, 201 Katlian, Suite 109, Sitka, AK 99835.

Alaska Ferries arrive and depart from the Alaska Marine Highway terminal, 7 miles from downtown on Halibut Road, with service to Ketchikan, Juneau, and other southeast towns, (907) 747-8737.

The airport is located on Japonski Island, with service by Alaska Airlines, (907) 966-2266. The airline offers scheduled flights to Seattle, Anchorage, Juneau, and Ketchikan.

Sitka Tours operates a shuttle bus from the ferry terminal, as well as local tours, (907) 747-8443.

## Things to See and Do

Three museums warrant attention: the Isabel Miller Museum, in the Centennial Building, contains artifacts from the early Russian days (907-747-6455); the Sheldon Jackson Museum is an excellent museum of Native American history offering collections of masks, baskets, boxes, dogsleds, and kayaks; the Bishop's House is the restored house of the Russian bishop, displaying artifacts from the 1800s.

Sitka National Historic Park is located at the end of Totem Street (907) 747-6281. A Tlingit fort and restored totem poles accompany audio-visual shows and craft demonstrations by Native American artisans.

The New Archangel Russian Dancers perform regularly in the Centennial Building during the summer cruise-ship season.

The Sitka Summer Music Festival is one of Alaska's most popular festivals, with chamber music artists coming to Sitka in June from around the world. The main concerts are held in the Centennial Building. Ticket reservations are recommended. Contact the Visitor Infocenter or call (907) 747-6774, summer, or (907) 688-0880, winter.

Castle Hill, located behind the old post office building, is the former site of Baranof's castle. The viewpoint has historical information and offers a fine view of Mount Edgecumbe, a snow-capped inactive volcano that dominates the town.

The Sitka Forest Service has good information on more than 40 miles of good local walking trails. The easiest to reach is the Indian River Trail, leading to an 80-foot waterfall (5.5 miles). The Gaven Hill Trail (three miles) climbs to 2,500 feet and offers great alpine vistas. Kids will enjoy the Japonski Island Trail, which explores World War II gun emplacements and other military sites near the airport. Access is by boat or by special escort at the airport, (907) 966-2960.

### Where to Eat

The **Channel Club**, at 2906 Halibut Road, is three miles from downtown (907) 747-9916. It's a popular local café, specializing in salads and other light food, at reasonable prices. Seafood (of course) is the specialty, but steaks are also on the regular menu. The seasoned steaks are a special treat for red-meat lovers. Halibut cheeks are also on the menu.

**Revard's,** at 324 Lincoln Street downtown, is an informal eatery and a good place for breakfast.

For the best view in town, and maybe the best food preparation, try the **Raven Room** in the Westmark Shee Atiká Hotel. Seafood, steaks, and pasta are the mainstays here, and the setting is superb, between the views and the hotel's wonderful decor in a southeastern Alaskan Native American theme. Considering the wonderful atmosphere, the prices are remarkably reasonable, in the moderate range. For reservations call (907) 747-6241.

**Sea Mart,** 1867 Halibut Point Road, is a store with fresh meat and groceries, deli foods, and a bakery. It's about the best place to pick up picnic supplies.

# Skagway

During the Klondike Gold Rush, Skagway (first spelled Skaguay) was the gateway to Canada and the Yukon River system for most of the adventurers who traveled north to seek their fortunes. The town still capitalizes on the 1898 stampede, but now as a tourist center with an outstanding heritage restoration.

Skagway is reached by road and from the sea. Alaska State ferries and cruise ships arrive daily during the summer months, augmenting the population by thousands of cruise ship passengers who disembark for a few hours to walk around the town and to shop.

Some highway travelers arrive by the car ferries. Other visitors arrive on the Klondike Highway, coming from Whitehorse or points south via the Alaska Highway. A special feature of the summer season in Skagway is the scenic railway ride up the White Pass, on the original Klondike Gold Rush route.

Because Skagway is a slim piece of flat land squeezed between high mountains and the Lynn Canal, there are very few miles of road. The longest drive in the area is down the road to the site of

Dyea (pronounced *dye-ee*), the town that disappeared. Here at the mouth of the rushing Taiya River is the start of the historic Chilkoot Trail and the Chilkoot Slide Cemetery. Skagway's visitor center is the office of the Klondike National Historic Park, on Broadway, a short walk from the ferry terminal and all motels.

## White Pass Trail

The Klondike Highway follows one of the two main routes from the port of Skagway to the Klondike gold fields, taken by thousands of prospectors and adventurers during the Klondike Gold Rush, beginning in the winter of 1897/98.

The White Pass was the trail of choice for the more prosperous prospectors who had the financial resources to buy horses for the trip up the slope. Horses were a great help in transporting the ton of goods required for each prospector by the Royal Canadian Mounted Police for entry into Canada. The trail was so rough and so deadly that most of the 3,000 horses that worked the trail perished on the steep slopes. Some died from exertion, others fell off the narrow trail into the canyon below.

The White Pass & Yukon Route replaced the trail when it was constructed and opened in 1900. Much of the blasting was accomplished by men hanging by ropes from the rock ledges. The scenic summer railway trip takes tourists along this historic route, although the year-round railway service between Skagway and Whitehorse ended more than a decade ago.

## Chilkoot Trail

The other "poor-man's" route was the Chilkoot Trail, which began at the town of Dyea at the head of Taiya Inlet. This trail followed an old Native American passage from tidewater to Lindeman and Bennett lakes: the headwaters of the Yukon River. The first part of the trail was wet, running through swamps and bogs. The tree line ended near Sheep Camp, with snow visible throughout the year. Pictures taken during the stampede show hundreds of men struggling up the ice steps of the Chilkoot Pass, carrying their supplies—over and over again—to get their ton of goods up to the Canadian border.

A snow slide in March of 1898 killed more than 100 stampeders as they struggled up the pass. The slide cemetery at Dyea is a memorial to these prospectors who never realized their Klondike dreams.

The Chilkoot Trail was replaced by the White Pass & Yukon Route railway in 1900. By the end of the year Dyea ceased to exist. The wood from the buildings was taken away to construct another town.

Today, the trail is a mecca for hikers from around the world and a living museum of the Gold Rush era. Thousands of people walk the trail each year to experience a scenic and historical adventure. Transportation is available from the Canadian end of the trail, for the return trip to Skagway.

A narrow wedge of land pushes from the Lynn Canal into the mountains, leading to the White Pass. Skagway was the transition point for over 20,000 gold rush stampeders in 1897 and 1898, and it was the most uncontrolled and lawless town in North America. The prospectors were held hostage by Jefferson "Soapy" Smith and his band of rogues, cutthroats, crooked gamblers, thieves, and murderers, as they took advantage of Skagway's location as the gateway to the Klondike.

A notorious con man from Colorado, Soapy Smith was shot and killed by Frank Reid, the surveyor who laid out the Skagway townsite. Their graves are in the Gold Rush Cemetery. Soapy Smith's grave is marked by a simple wooden slab.

The rowdy town was the jumping-off point for the two preferred trails to the Klondike: the White Pass and Chilkoot trails. After the main stampede of 1897 and 1898, the White Pass & Yukon Route was blasted up the White Pass, linking Skagway on tidewater with Whitehorse on the Yukon River. While the railroad ceased operations in 1982, a special summer tourist train began operating in 1988 and is a highlight of many visits to Skagway.

Most visitors to Skagway arrive on cruise ships which stop here during summer months. Others come to hike the Chilkoot Trail, a 32-mile walk along the historic route of the gold rush stampeders. This three- to five-day hike attracts thousands of people each summer. It's possibly the best way to relive the days of the Trail of '98, following the path that starts in the Dyea forest, climbing up through the Chilkoot Pass, and hiking above the tree line to Lindeman and Bennett lakes and the launching spots for thousands of boats and rafts in the spring of 1898. Visitors can easily spend two or three days in Skagway, reliving the history of the Trail of '98, visiting the restored buildings of the Gold Rush era, and hiking on several local trails. An excellent way to experience the 1898 ambiance is to see the show "Skaguay in the Days of '98," performed nightly in the downtown dance hall at 6th and Broadway. It's been running for more than 60 years.

## Practical Information

The visitor center for the Klondike Gold Rush National Historical Park, and also for the town of Skagway, is at Broadway and 2nd Avenue downtown. Walking tours leave here daily at 11 A.M. and 3 P.M. There's a lecture on the Chilkoot Trail at 4 P.M. and ranger talks at 10 A.M. An excellent 30-minute film narrated by Hal Holbrook, with tinted photos from the Gold Rush, is shown on the hour during summer months.

The Alaska Marine Highway ferry terminal is at the foot of Broadway, within sight of the National Park visitor center. For schedule information call (907) 983-2941. The Bus Depot is at 3rd Avenue and Spring Street, in the Westmark Inn, (907) 983-2241. White Pass bus service includes runs to Whitehorse, and via Haines Junction and Fairbanks and Anchorage.

## Things to See and Do

Klondike Gold Rush National Historic Park offers walking tours of the historic downtown district centered around Broadway. Included on the tour are several significant buildings such as the

Arctic Brotherhood Hall, the Mascot Saloon, one of 80 saloons and breweries that opened to quench stampeders' thirsts, and Captain William Moore's Cabin, Skagway's original house (1888).

Dyea, Skagway's sister town on Taiya Inlet, a few miles from downtown, is now an empty space with only memories of its role in the stampede. The Slide Cemetery at Dyea is an impressive memorial to the 60 victims of the spring avalanche in 1898 that covered the Chilkoot Trail.

The Trail of '98 Museum on the second floor of City Hall, with artifacts of the Gold Rush, should be an essential part of your visit.

The White Pass & Yukon Route offers an unforgettable scenic train trip over the White Pass. The track parallels the trail used by thousands of stampede adventurers, and it's easy to see while climbing the steep mountainside how hundreds of horses and men lost their lives trying to make the ascent. The train leaves the downtown depot daily at 9 A.M. and 1:30 P.M. during the summer visitor season.

### Where to Eat

Siding 21, a restaurant in a replica of an old-time railroad station, is located next to the Wind Valley Lodge, on the Klondike Highway (State Street) between 21st and 22nd avenues. It is family operated and geared to family dining. Prices are moderate for this summertime tourist destination. Reservations are rarely needed.

My favorite place to eat—and stay—in Skagway is the **Golden North Hotel** on Broadway. This is the oldest hotel in Alaska, built in 1898 in the middle of the gold stampede. The dining room here evokes those days, and you can imagine the life in this room during that tumultuous period. Along with the rest of the hotel, the dining room has been faithfully restored to its 1898 style. Three meals a day are served, with the evening menu focusing on salmon and other seafood. Meals here are not expensive.

The **Prospector's Sourdough Restaurant** is popular with visitors and locals alike, with sourdough pancakes and omelets for breakfast, and seafood in the evenings. Meals here are in the inexpensive range.

If a grand-luxe hotel had been built in Skagway in 1898, and if it had had a dining room, it would have been what you'll experience in the **Chilkoot Room** of the Westmark Inn, on 3rd Avenue near Broadway. This summer operation offers a much grander ambiance than ever existed in early Skagway, with what we imagine as bordello-style decor and meals that range from steaks to seafood, including family-style service of salmon and crab dishes. For reservations call (907) 983-6000.

# Valdez

What does one say about Prince William Sound? First, the 1989 oil spill has made this beautiful area notorious around the world. Second, the sound continues to be a beautiful, supremely scenic area. The oil has left the sound and has hardly impacted tourism in the area, although there will be largely unseen effects of the spill for years to come.

Cordova is a short ferry ride from Valdez and Whittier. The area is home to thousands of sea otters, bald eagles, sea lions, and killer whales. Whittier is the ferry and railroad terminus that serves the area as its transportation center. The Portage Glacier is nearby, and a hiking trail starting near the train tunnel leads to a great view of Passage Channel and onward to a view of the glacier. The Alaska Railroad provides a short ride three times a day to Portage, winding through wildlife areas. Information on Whittier is available in the Visitor Center, in the old railway car near the harbor.

Named for Spanish naval captain Antonio Valdes, Valdez (pronounced *val-deez*) was founded by a few prospectors looking for an easier way to reach the Klondike gold fields. The Valdez Glacier proved an insurmountable barrier. Copper was discovered in the Wrangell mountains in the early 1900s, and the town revived. The earthquake of 1964 devastated Valdez with tidal waves, and the government ordered the town moved four miles away from the original townsite.

Modern Valdez lives on the oil boom that resulted in the building of the Trans-Alaska Pipeline, bringing oil from the north slope oilfields to the terminal in Valdez. Fishing is important to the economy as well. The oil terminal houses 18 large storage tanks that hold the oil until it can be pumped into tanker ships. A guided tour of the terminal leaves from the Westmark Hotel, (907) 835-2357.

The Valdez Heritage Center, a museum, concentrates on the 1964 earthquake and the impact of the pipeline. Displays show early Native American history and maps from the Russian period. Two spectacular waterfalls, Bridal Veil and Horsetail, are found 13 miles up the Richardson Highway. Mineral Creek Road provides a scenic drive with alpine views.

The gem of Prince William Sound is the Columbia Glacier, which once filled the entire sound. Now covering about 440 square miles, the glacier rises to 300 feet above the water. Many travelers take the ferry from Valdez to Whittier to view the glacier from a distance of two miles. Several cruises are available for a close-up look at the gigantic piece of ice, which plunges 4,000 feet below the surface of the sea. Walk around the small harbor to investigate tour times and prices.

## Where to Eat

You will not be able to relax over a three-hour meal, dining on continental cuisine, in Valdez. As befits an oil port town, the food served here is basic. If you're prepared for standard but nourishing dishes, you might wish to try the following two places:

The **Totem Inn** is decorated in the style of Old-Town Valdez and serves three meals a day, beginning at 5 A.M. There's an adjacent lounge, and fresh seafood occupies a good part of the menu, along with burgers and other comfort food.

**Mike's Palace** is not a palace by a long mile, but this semi-Greek café with Italian decor serves fresh seafood and a few Greek dishes. You'll find a lot of local residents eating here. Mike's Palace is located on the Valdez Harbor, along North Harbor Drive.

## Wasilla

Wasilla and the Susitna Valley are close to Anchorage, via the George Parks Highway, or to Palmer on the Palmer-Wasilla Road. Wasilla ("breath of air") is a newer agricultural center, developed since 1977.

A visitor center is found on Main Street, north of the Parks Highway, in the same building as the Dorothy G. Page Museum. The historical museum is open year-round, and is filled with odd artifacts of local settlement. Behind the museum (and included in the entry price) is Old Wasilla Town Site Park, with a collection of old buildings including the town's first schoolhouse, a bunkhouse exhibit, and a steambath.

Wasilla is the headquarters for the Iditarod dogsled race that runs each winter from Anchorage to Nome. The Iditarod Museum and Visitor Center are found at mile 2.2 of Knik Road. Summer hours are from 8 A.M. to 5 P.M. (daily), and Monday through Friday for the same hours during the off-season.

### Where to Eat

The restaurant at the **Mat-Su Resort** offers basic American dishes (it isn't fancy enough to call cuisine), at 1850 Bogart Road. Seafood and steak are the standard menu entries. The restaurant does have a lengthy wine list, and the room has fine views. Prices are in the moderate range.

Another room with a pleasant view is the dining room in the **Lake Lucille Inn**, at 1300 West Lake Lucille Drive. Along with being a good place to stay, only a 45-minute drive from Anchorage, the inn's restaurant is better than most at serving up the standard steak and seafood fare common to this part of the state. But, after all, there is some logic to seafood and steak, for there are plenty of fish in the nearby sea, and what they call the Mat-Su Valley is the agricultural headquarters for the state.

# Wrangell

At the northern end of Wrangell Island, this town of 2,400 people is a scenic microcosm of the Alaskan Panhandle. The town has a mixture of fishing and logging to support its economy and a strong Native American heritage. For many centuries the Tlingit people lived along the Stikine, catching salmon for eating and for trading with other tribes. Russians began trading on the Stikine in 1811. Wrangell was rebuilt twice, after fires devastated the town in 1906 and 1952. Today it's a perfect place for a two-day visit or for a week if you're here for the fishing.

The Wrangell Museum at 122 2nd Street is open in the afternoons, offering a very good collection of local relics including petroglyphs, Tlingit artifacts, and old photographs.

For a living, out-of-doors display of petroglyphs (which, after all, are just early graffiti) walk along Evergreen Avenue to Petroglyph Beach, where at low tide, among other revealed rocks, you'll find several dozen large stones with designs chiseled out by unknown artists from an earlier age. Rock rubbings here are discouraged, but you may obtain duplicates (made with a rubber stamp) at the museum or on the cruise dock.

There's good hiking on the Rainbow Falls Trail, across the road from Shoemaker Bay Campground.

## Practical Information

The local travel infocenter is the Chamber of Commerce, at Outer Drive and Brueger Street, (907) 874-3901. This A-frame building is set near a large totem pole and City Hall, in the docks area. The Wrangell Convention and Visitors Bureau, located in the City Museum at 122 2nd Street, is open during summer months when ferries and cruise ships are in port, between 1 and 4 P.M., Monday through Saturday.

The U.S. Forest Service office is on Bennett Street, past 2nd Avenue toward the airport, (907) 874-2323. The staff has helpful information on Stikine River journeys, and more than 20 recreation cabins available for overnight stays. The cabins can be booked here, although advance application is recommended.

The airport is located off Bennett Street, one mile from downtown. Wrangell Air Service can be reached at (907) 874-2369.

The terminal for Alaska Marine Highway ferries is located in the downtown area, at the end of 2nd Street, also known as Zimovia Highway. For information on ferry schedules, call (907) 874-3711.

## Where to Eat

The **Dockside Restaurant**, in the Stikine Inn on Stikine Avenue, has a good view of the waterfront, with standard meals, including a full salad bar, in the moderate to expensive range. For reservations, call (907) 874-3388. A lounge and liquor store are also located in the hotel building.

**Roadhouse Lodge** is a little way out of town, but offers more than just food. Located at mile 4 of Zimovia Highway, the decor focuses on early Alaskan history, with the walls full of marvelous pictures and artifacts. Try the Indian frybread (deep-fried to a turn), and the great variety of seafood dishes made of the local catch. For reservations call (907) 874-2335.

For fast food, try **J&W's** and the **Snack Shack**, both on Front Street. They sell burgers and other fast food, and like all costs in this part of Alaska, food prices are high. **Benjamin's Supermarket**, 223 Brueger Street, is the place to go for picnic essentials.

# Alaska
## Places to Stay

**ALYESKA**

**Alyeska Resort Hotel**
P.O. Box 249
1000 Arlbury
Girdwood, AK 99587
(907) 754-1111 or
800-880-3880

*For Alyeska Accommodations call (907) 783-2000 or write to P.O. Box 1196, Girdwood, AK 99587.*

Although this ski and summer resort is located 40 miles south of Anchorage (where most visitors stay), the scenery here is wonderful and the amenities are worth the commute. It's actually a very good place to base a vacation that includes a tour of the Kenai Peninsula. The resort has restaurants, lounges, and a chair lift to high scenic panoramas. ($$ to $$$) An option available at the resort is to stay in a privately owned condo or cabin, fully equipped with bedding and kitchen utensils.

**ANCHORAGE**

*Anchorage boasts a wide selection of hotels and motels. At the high end of the price scale are the large chain hotels including Westmark (800-544-0970), Sheraton (800-325-3535), and Holiday Inn (800-465-4329). Below are listed some of the less expensive and/or more interesting places to stay. As in other Alaskan cities and towns,*

151

*motels and B & B homes often provide freezer space for storing those large fish you are likely to catch in the vicinity.*

**Anchorage Hotel**
330 E Street
Anchorage, AK 99501
(907) 272-4553 or
800-544-0988

This small downtown hotel is a historic landmark, lovingly restored to its 1916 roots. Located close to shopping and restaurants, this charming, cozy hotel is a delight to stay in. A continental breakfast of coffee and pastries is served each morning in the lobby. (**$$ to $$$**)

**Anchorage International Hostel**
700 H Street
Anchorage, AK 99501
(907) 276-3635

As with other hostels, this one in downtown Anchorage has spartan accommodations at a low price, with a shared kitchen and chores required. Reservations are taken for the hostel's three double rooms that offer privacy, unlike the dorm accommodations. A six-bed room is suitable for families to share. Facilities include a laundry and storage area. ($)

**Atherton Road Bed & Breakfast**
12441 Atherton Road
Anchorage, AK 99516
(907) 345-5015

Sitting on a hillside, this B & B offers rooms with private bath and a full breakfast, in a quiet, secluded location. Children are welcome. There's a large deck to sit on during the warm summer evenings. ($$)

**Black Angus Inn**
1430 Gambell Street
Anchorage, AK 99501
(907) 272-7503 or
800-770-0707

This large motor hotel is located at the south end of the business district, close to the Sullivan Sports Arena. The rooms are large but basic. Suites are available. This relaxed place is popular with Alaskans visiting the city. ($$)

**Days Inn**
321 East 5th Avenue
Anchorage, AK 99501
(907) 276-7226 or
800-325-2525

A convenient member of the large chain operation, this hotel is situated at the corner of 5th and Cordova. The lobby may be small but the rooms are quite large. Facilities include a restaurant, room service, and a courtesy van providing local transportation. ($$$)

**Golden Nugget Camper Park**
4100 DeBarr Road
Anchorage, AK 99504
(907) 333-2012

This RV park welcomes children, and has a playground for their use. Other facilities include full hookups, picnic tables, laundry, and free showers. It's a few blocks south of the Glenn Highway via South Bragaw Street or Boniface Parkway.

**Hotel Captain Cook**
5th and K Streets
Anchorage, AK 99501
(907) 276-6000

The first major building to be constructed after the earthquake of 1964, this is probably Anchorage's finest hotel. It provides a range of accommodations including rooms of moderate price, but tend to be quite small. The more expensive rooms have teak furniture and deluxe decor. Facilities include four restaurants, a pool, and a fitness center including sauna, steam rooms, and racquetball courts. ($$ to $$$+)

**John's RV Park**
3543 Mountain View Drive
Anchorage, AK 99508
(907) 277-4332 or
800-478-4332

This is an adult-only RV park with concrete pads, full hookups, showers, laundry, dump station, and a gift shop. It's 2.5 miles from downtown. From the north, turn onto Bragaw Street and turn left at the next light. From the south, take 5th Avenue East and turn left on Mountain View Drive.

**Two Morrow's Place**
1325 O Street
Anchorage, AK 99501
(907) 277-9939

This friendly B & B home is operated by Margo and Dave Morrow. They offer private or shared baths, and a full breakfast. It's in downtown Anchorage, close to restaurants and shopping. ($$)

**Voyager Hotel**
501 K Street
Anchorage, AK 99501
(907) 277-9501

This small hotel, popular with the business crowd, sits across the street from the Hotel Captain Cook. The rooms have kitchens, queen beds, and a double sofa-bed. The view rooms are on the west side. Facilities include a restaurant, open for dinner only. This is a popular place and reservations are almost always required. ($$ to $$$)

*There are more than 20 B & B homes in Anchorage. Contact these reservation services for information on homes in Anchorage and the Kenai Peninsula: Accommodations in Alaska (907) 345-4761; Alaska Private Lodgings B & B (907) 258-1717; and Sourdough Bed and Breakfast Association (907) 563-6244. These services represent B & B homes with prices ranging from $35 to $85.*

## CHENA AND CIRCLE HOT SPRINGS

**Central Motor Inn and Campground**
Central, AK 99730
(907) 520-5228

If you're on a driving tour ending at Circle, you may wish to stay along the Steese Highway. The village of Central is located at mile 127. The motel has a restaurant, lounge, laundry, RV spaces, and tentsites. It's open year-round. ($)

**Chena Hot Springs Resort**
P.O. Box 73440
Fairbanks, AK 99707
(907) 452-7867

The resort is situated at the end of a 60-mile spur road off the Steese Highway. The resort hotel features rooms, suites, and cabins, with the main attraction a hot springs pool. A restaurant and lounge are located on the property, as is a campground with basic sites. ($ to $$)

**Circle Hot Springs Resort**
P.O. Box 254
Central, AK 99730
(907) 520-5113

Located on Hot Springs Road, this modest resort hotel has an Olympic-sized hot springs pool, dining room, lounge, store, and RV parking. The original hotel has been restored and offers rooms plus a hostel on the fourth floor. The resort is eight miles off the Steese Highway. ($ to $$)

**Yukon Trading Post**
18 Front Street
Circle, AK 99733
(907) 773-1217

At the end of the Steese Highway, beside the Yukon River, the Yukon Trading Post has several basic hotel rooms, as well as a restaurant (great pies), a saloon, and a grocery store. ($ to $$)

## CORDOVA

**Cordova Rose Lodge**
1315 Whitshed Road
P.O. Box 1494
Cordova, AK 99574
(907) 424-7673

A B & B on a barge by a large mudflat makes an unusual place to stay. Near the barge sits an old lighthouse, maintained by the B & B's owners, the Glein family. A full breakfast is served. The Copper River Delta, of which the Hartney Bay mudflats are a part, attracts millions of migratory shorebirds each year, and the jetty is close by for walking. ($$)

**Municipal Campground**
c/o City Hall
P.O. Box 1210
Cordova, AK 99574
(907) 424-6200

The city campground, with showers, is one mile from town on Whitshed Road. Facilities include RV and tenting sites.

**Oystercatcher Bed & Breakfast**
P.O. Box 1735
Cordova, AK 99574
(907) 424-5154

One of several B & B homes in Cordova, this one is two blocks from town. A full breakfast is served. For reservations call late in the day. The owner is a teacher. ($$)

**Reluctant Fisherman Inn**
407 Railroad Avenue
P.O. Box 150
Cordova, AK 99574
(407) 424-3272

This modern, well-equipped and well-staffed hotel sits on a bluff above the small harbor. Ask for a room overlooking the waterfront. The lobby contains Native American art and artifacts, and the decor in the bar needs to be checked out. ($$ to $$$)

## DENALI NATIONAL PARK

**Camp Denali**
P.O. Box 67
Denali Park, AK 99755
(907) 688-2290 (summer)
(603) 675-2248 (winter)

This outpost resort, located at the end of the national park road in the heart of Denali Park, is considered by many the finest place to really get to know the mountain and the park. This is a compound of log buildings, with a spacious dining room, and a laundry and bath facility with hot showers (the rustic cabins do not have electricity or running water). Wallace and Jerri Cole own and operate the resort, and also operate the nearby **Northface Lodge**, which does have baths in its rooms. The resort and lodge share the nature interpretation programs. Hiking, canoeing, rafting, fishing, and mountain biking are available. All meals are supplied. ($$ to $$$)

**Denali Crow's Nest Cabins**
P.O. Box 70
Denali Park, AK 99755
(907) 683-2723

This aerie on Sugarloaf Mountain has a fine overlook of the Nenana River and Horseshoe Lake. Located one mile north of the park entrance, at mile 238.5 of George Parks Highway, the log cabins all have private baths. Facilities include hot tubs, and a bar and grill. The Overlook Restaurant is well known for its salmon and halibut dishes, with a good selection of beers and wines. The operation provides free shuttle service to the park and other locations in the area. ($$ to $$$)

**Denali National Hotel & McKinley Chalet Resort**
Denali Park Hotels
P.O. Box 78
Denali Park, AK 99755
(907) 276-7234 or
800-276-7234

The hotel is the "official," inside-the-park hotel operation, located 1.5 miles beyond the entrance to the park. McKinley Chalet Resort, also operated by the park concessionaire, is outside the gate. Both offer full facilities including restaurants, lounges, and gift shops. Reservations are absolutely essential during the busy summer period. ($$$ to $$$+)

**Denali Park Campgrounds**
c/o Denali National Park
Denali Park, AK 99755
800-622-7275

Seven campgrounds are located in the park, with sites available for RV, trailer, and tent camping. Three are accessed via shuttle and are for tenters only. All campgrounds are found along Park Road.

**Igloo Creek Campground**, at mile 34, reached by shuttle bus, or by car with permit, has river water and pit toilets.

**Morino Creek Campground**, at mile 2.4, is a hike-in site with drinking water a short walk away and pit toilets.

**Riley Creek Campground** (one-quarter mile down the road) has flush toilets and piped water.

**Sanctuary River Campground**, at mile 22, is accessible by shuttle or with a vehicle permit. Facilities include river water and pit toilets.

**Savage River Campground**, at mile 12, requires car permits. The sites have flush toilets and drinking water.

**Teklanika River Campground**, at mile 29, is accessed via shuttle bus, or by car with a permit. The sites have piped water and pit toilets.

**Wonder Lake Campground**, at mile 85, is the preferred destination for park campers, because of the flush toilets,

**Denali Park Campgrounds**
*(continued)*

piped water, and great views of the mountain. Shuttle bus access, no vehicles allowed, and tent camping only.

**Denali Princess Lodge**
Denali Park, AK 99755
(907) 683-2283 or
800-426-0500

This could be called the Love Lodge. It's operated by Princess Cruises, which runs a joint program with Alaska Airlines. This modern hotel overlooks the Nenana River, off George Parks Highway, near the park entrance. The rooms are large and the resort has full facilities including restaurants, lounge, a café, outdoor whirlpools, and a gift shop. They provide a free shuttle service to the park and train depot. ($$ to $$$)

**Denali RV Park and Motel**
P.O. Box 155
Denali Park, AK 99755
(907) 683-1511 or
800-478-1501 (in Alaska)

Located eight miles north of the park road, the motel has more than a dozen budget rooms. ($ to $$) The RV park has full and partial hookups, pull-through sites, showers, and dump station.

**Denali Wilderness Lodge**
P.O. Box 50
Denali Park, AK 99755
(907) 683-1287 or
800-541-9779

This superb rustic inn lies 15 minutes' flying time from the park airstrip. The complex is made up of more than 25 buildings, including guest cabins, a sauna, a barn, and the main lodge. There are free dining flights from the airport, and overnight packages offer nature and photographic walks, and horseback rides. The grub is great, and birders will have a fine time identifying northern residents. ($$$)

**McKinley KOA Kampground**
P.O. Box 340
Healy, AK 99743
(907) 683-2379

This full-service RV park and campground is found north of the park at mile 248.4 of the Parks Highway. Facilities include full hookups, tenting sites, showers, ice, propane, a grocery store, laundry, tables, and fire pits.

## FAIRBANKS

**Alaskan Iris
Bed and Breakfast**
P.O. Box 58483
Fairbanks, AK 99711
(907) 488-2308 or
800-IRIS-BNB

This B & B inn is set on 20 acres of countryside, and is open year-round. Facilities include a phone and TV in each room, and a guest laundry. Full breakfast is served. (**$ to $$**)

**Applesauce Inn
Bed & Breakfast**
119 Gruening Way
Fairbanks, AK 99712
(907) 457-3392 or
800-764-3392 (in Alaska)

This fascinating home on stilts is located a few minutes' drive from downtown Fairbanks, in the woods. The rooms are fairly large, with private or shared bath. You can grill your dinner in the screened gazebo, and applesauce is available among the other breakfast items. Christine and Corbett Upton are the owners. (**$$**)

**Cedar Creek Inn**
P.O. Box 10355
Fairbanks, AK 99710
(907) 457-3392 or
800-764-3392 (in Alaska)

Christine and Corbett Upton own this inn as well as the Applesauce Inn Bed & Breakfast. Located on two wooded acres seven miles from Fairbanks, the house has two bedrooms, washer and dryer, and a kitchen stocked for breakfast. The deck has a barbecue. (**$$**)

**Ester Gold Camp**
P.O. Box 109
Ester, AK 99725
(907) 479-2500 or
800-676-6925

The hotel is located in Ester, a historic mining camp eight miles south of downtown off the George Parks Highway. It is part of a gold camp resort, with old-style saloon, restaurant, and RV parking with showers and dump station (no hookups). The Malamute Saloon features evening performances including dancing, stories, and Robert Service poetry. The Bunkhouse is a large buffet restaurant, serving a bounty of halibut, reindeer stew, Alaska crab, chicken, biscuits, beans, apple crisp, and other dishes of a certain era. The hotel rooms are modest but comfortable, with semi-private bathrooms. (**$ to $$**)

**Fairbanks Princess Hotel**
4477 Pike's Landing Road
Fairbanks, AK 99709
(907) 455-4477 or
800-426-0500

Located on the banks of the Chena River, this sparkling new hotel's fine decor includes Alaskan art in all of the rooms. Facilities include three restaurants, lounge, health club, and gift shop. (**$$$ to $$$+**)

**Golden North Motel**
4888 Old Airport Way
Fairbanks, AK 99709
(907) 479-6201 or
800-447-1910

Located near the airport, this reasonably priced modern motel has private baths, TV, free continental breakfast, and eating places nearby. It's close to shopping, and room prices are about the most reasonable in town. (**$ to $$**)

**Regency Fairbanks Hotel**
95 10th Avenue
Fairbanks, AK 99901
(907) 452-3200

A newer, modern hotel near the downtown area, its lobby is done up in Victorian style. Some rooms with kitchenettes, with other features including a dining room, lounge, laundry, and whirlpool. (**$$ to $$$**)

**River's Edge RV Park**
**and Campground**
4140 Boat Street
Fairbanks, AK 99709
(907) 474-0286 or
800-770-3343 (Alaska)

This large RV park has full and partial hookups, tenting sites, free showers, laundry, dump station, and gift shop, and also provides a free shuttle to Alaskaland. The management also arranges tours to Denali Park, Barrow, and the Arctic Circle.

**Sophie Station Hotel**
1717 University Avenue
Fairbanks, AK 99709
(907) 479-3650

One of the best places to stay in the region, with high quality rooms and service, the Sophie Station is located near Fairbanks International Airport. All units are suites with kitchenettes, and the hotel has a restaurant, lounge, and gift shop. (**$$$**)

**Westmark Fairbanks Hotel**
820 Noble Street
Fairbanks, AK 99901
(907) 456-7722

One of the Alaska/Yukon chain of Westmark hotels, this large modern hotel includes a restaurant, lounge, coffee shop, and guest laundry. The hotel is built around a courtyard, ensuring a quiet stay. Some rooms have fitness equipment. ($$$)

## HAINES

**Captain's Choice Motel**
P.O. Box 392
Haines, AK 99827
(907) 766-3111
or 800-247-7153
or 800-478-2345 (in
Alaska, Yukon, and B.C.)

The prices at this standard motel in downtown Haines are very reasonable, and facilities include cable TV and private baths. Several large suites are available, along with the basic motel rooms. (**$ to $$**)

**Eagle Camper RV Park**
755 Union Street
P.O. Box 28
Haines, AK 99827
(907) 766-2335

This campground accommodates RVs, trailers, and tenters, with a circular driveway leading to all sites. Facilities include full hookups, showers, propane, barbecues, and picnic tables. It's a seasonal operation.

**Haines Hitch-up RV Park**
P.O. Box 383
Haines, AK 99827
(907) 766-2882

To reach this medium-sized RV park and campground, you drive a half-mile west of Main Street. With five acres, the park offers pull-through sites with full hookups, level grass for tents, showers, laundry, propane, and a gift shop.

**Hälsingland Hotel**
P.O. Box 1589
Haines, AK 99827
(907) 766-2000 or 800-
542-6363 (in Alaska)
or 800-478-2525 (in
Yukon and B.C.)

A national historic site, this hotel is a fine place to stay, located on the Fort Seward parade grounds overlooking the Lynn Canal, south of downtown. The building is the former officers' quarters for the army post. The hotel has a renowned dining room, with an adjacent lounge including a wine bar. Some rooms have fireplaces. (**$$ to $$$**)

**Officer's Inn**
P.O. Box 1589
Haines, AK 99827
(907) 766-2000 or
800-542-6363 (in Alaska)
or 800-478-2525
(in Yukon and B.C.)

Under the same ownership and management as the Hälsingland Hotel, this B & B inn is located in another Fort Seward building. Some of the rooms have good views and fireplaces, and you have a choice of private or shared bath. (**$$ to $$$**)

**Summer Inn Bed & Breakfast**
1117 Second Avenue N
P.O. Box 1198
Haines, AK 99827

This historic home has a fine view of the Lynn Canal, and provides a full breakfast. The B & B is open year-round. Winter rates are lower than summer rates. (**$$**)

## HOMER

**Bay View Inn**
2851 Sterling Highway
P.O. Box 804
Homer, AK 99603
(907) 235-8485 or
800-478-8485 (in Alaska)

Sitting on top of a hill, the Bay View provides wonderful views of Kachemak Bay and the Kenai Mountains. Rooms have private baths. Kitchenettes are available, as is a suite with fireplace. The Inn also has a secluded "Honeymoon Cottage." Morning coffee is available. (**$$**)

**Beeson's Bed and Breakfast**
1393 Bay Avenue
Homer, AK 99603
(907) 235-3757

Beeson's has a convenient location, close to the water, eating, and shopping in town. The beachfront location in a spruce forest offers a secluded stay. Rooms have private baths, TV, and phone. Open year-round. (**$$**)

**Driftwood Inn**
135 Bunnell Avenue
Homer, AK 99603
(907) 235-8019

A hotel/motel and B & B inn, the Driftwood is a historic beachside property, with individual rooms, free coffee and tea, and continental breakfast available. The common areas include a library, fireplace room, fish-cleaning area, and a shellfish cooker. There's space to park your RV. This homey family operation is situated in what was Homer's first schoolhouse. (**$$**)

**Heritage Hotel Lodge**
147 East Pioneer Avenue
Homer, AK 99603
(907) 235-7787

The log building has relatively modern units including one suite. There's a restaurant on the premises and the hotel provides free coffee. Open year-round. ($$)

**Homer Spit Campground**
P.O. Box 1196
Homer, AK 99603
(907) 235-8206

This private campground is located at the end of the Homer Spit, close to restaurants, the Sawlty Dawg, Land's End Resort, and the boardwalk shops. The operation has hot showers, rest rooms, electrical hookups, and dump station. Halibut charters are available. The campground operates a 60-foot boat called the *MV Endeavor*, which takes visitors out on puffin-viewing tours.

**Land's End Resort**
4786 Homor Spit Road
P.O. Box 273
Homer, AK 99603
(907) 235-2500

This gray jumble of a hotel is found at the end of the Homer Spit. The motel rooms offer harbor views, with oceanside decks overlooking the bay, and a restaurant specializing in seafood. It's open year round. ($$ to $$$) The resort has RV parking at the end of the spit, with electrical hookups, showers, laundry, and ice.

## JUNEAU

**Airport Travelodge**
9200 Glacier Highway
Juneau, AK 99801
(907) 789-9700

Located next door to a Mexican restaurant (Fernando's), this ersatz Mexican hacienda is quite out of place in southeast Alaska, yet it has some attractions, including an indoor pool and whirlpool, and Fernando's tempting burritos. The units are standard motel-style as per any Travelodge. ($$ to $$$)

**Alaskan Hotel and Bar**
167 South Franklin Street
Juneau, AK 99801
(907) 586-1000 or
800-327-9347

A historic site, worth staying in for the atmosphere, the Alaskan Hotel has been in downtown Juneau since 1913. You'll want to hold up the antique bar for awhile, and then soak in one of the hot tubs. Some rooms have kitchenettes, and some have shared bathrooms. ($)

**Baranof Hotel**
127 North Franklin Street
Juneau, AK 99801
(907) 562-2660 or
800-544-0970

This venerable hotel, one of the oldest in this part of the state, is now operated by the Westmark chain. It has been a long-time haunt of Alaskan legislators, lobbyists, and business people. Located in the midst of everything, it is extremely handy for forays into the historic downtown area, to local museums, and to the Juneau waterfront. The hotel has a dining room, lounge, and some rooms have kitchens. ($$$ to $$$+)

**Pearson's Pond Inn**
4541 Sawa Circle
Juneau, AK 99801
(907) 789-3772

This luxury B & B inn features suites, with a self-serve breakfast. The inn is close to the ferry landing and shopping, offering a rowboat, bicycles, and a health club. There's a two-night summer minimum, and the inn is open year-round. ($$ to $$$)

**The Prospector**
375 Whittier Street
Juneau, AK 99801
(907) 586-3737

Its location next to the Alaska State Museum is enough to recommend a stay here. The museum is the first place anybody arriving in Juneau should visit. But The Prospector has other benefits, including large comfortable rooms with spiffy decor. There's a very good dining room, with lounge. Steaks and seafood are the prime entrées. ($$$)

**Silverbow Inn**
**120 2nd Street**
**Juneau, AK 99801**
**(907) 586-4146**

This is the site of a large bakery that dated from 1890. It is a very small hotel, with only a half-dozen rooms, but the period atmosphere is quaint and those who are history buffs may wish to stay here, if you haven't already booked in at the Alaskan Hotel and Bar. The inn has a respected restaurant.

## KATMAI NATIONAL PARK AND PRESERVE

**Brooks Lodge**
**4550 Aircraft Drive**
**Anchorage, AK 99502**
**(907) 243-5448 or**
**800-544-0551**

Katmailand Inc. operates Brooks Lodge, Grosvenor Camp, and Kulic Lodge. All are summer operations, accessible by air—normally from the town of King Salmon, a 280-mile flight from Anchorage. Bush planes will take you into the park and Brooks Camp. Brooks Lodge is famous for its bear-watching and fishing. People usually take the two-night, three-day package, which includes air transportation from Anchorage. Grosvenor Camp and Kulic Lodge are the places for really dedicated anglers to stay, located next to some of the best salmon fishing streams in the world.

## KENAI AND SOLDOTNA

**Beluga Lookout RV Park**
**929 Mission Avenue**
**Kenai, AK 99611**
**(907) 283-5999 or**
**800-745-5999**

With great views of Cook Inlet and the Kenai River, this RV park offers full hookups, pull-through sites, cable TV, picnic tables, barbecue pits, showers, and laundry. The operation also has a fish cleaning station, freezers, and smokers.

**Katmai Hotel**
10800 Kenai Spur
Highway (at Main)
Kenai, AK 99611
(907) 283-6101

The hotel has been here for more than a few years, and has been recently refurbished. The rooms are basic motel-style, and a 24-hour restaurant and lounge are located on the premises. The hotel is within walking distance to downtown Kenai. (**$ to $$**)

**Kenai Princess Lodge**
P.O. Box 676
Cooper Landing, AK 99572
800-426-0500

Undoubtedly the finest place to stay on the Kenai Peninsula, the lodge is operated by Princess Cruises and offers deluxe rooms and suites, plus a dining room and lounge, gift shop, outdoor hot tubs, and an exercise room. The lodge is located before you get to Soldotna, at mile 47.7 of the Sterling Highway (at Bean Creek Road). (**$$$**) The resort also has an RV park, with RVers enjoying privileges at the lodge. Regional tours are available through the lodge tour desk.

**Kenai River Lodge**
393 Riverside Drive
Soldotna, AK 99669
(907) 262-4292

This huge motel is situated at the Kenai River crossing. The place is favored by anglers who find good fishing right at the door. The lodge has private docking facilities, and offers guided fishing trips. (**$$ to $$$**)

**Overland RV Park**
Mile 11.5 Kenai Spur Highway
Kenai, AK 99611
(907) 283-4512 (summer) or
(907) 283-4117 (winter)

Located in downtown Kenai, the Overland has level sites with pull-throughs, full hookups, rest rooms, showers, laundry, and dump station. There's a gift shop in the office.

**Posey's Kenai River Hideaway**
P.O. Box 4094
Soldotna, AK 99669
(907) 262-7430

This B & B inn is located on the bank of the Kenai River, and is open year-round. Their country breakfasts will fill you up before you continue on a road tour or take off early in the morning for a fishing experience. Hosts are Ray and June Posey. (**$$ to $$$**)

**Soldotna Bed & Breakfast**
399 Lovers Lane
Soldotna, AK 99669
(907) 262-4479 or
800-869-9428 (packages)

This fine B & B inn is like something you'd find in the Irish or French countryside. It's a large home, beautifully decorated, on the Kenai River. From early September to late May, you must reserve your breakfast in advance. Lodging and guides are available in a package, or separately. Northstar, the tour operator, offers full fishing packages including king and silver salmon, halibut, and trout. Fly-in trips are available. ($$$)

**Soldotna Inn**
35041 Kenai Spur Highway
Soldotna, AK 99669
(907) 262-9169

Located at the Soldotna "Y" (a three-sided intersection) at the turnoff to Kenai, this motel offers modern rooms, some with kitchenettes, plus cable TV and Mykel's Restaurant on-site. ($$)

## KETCHIKAN

**Best Western Landing Hotel**
3434 Tongass
P.O. Box 6814
Ketchikan, AK 99901
(907) 225-5166

Located across from the ferry terminal, near the airport, the hotel has rooms and mini-suites, a restaurant, and lounge. It is open year-round. ($$ to $$$)

**Clover Pass Resort**
P.O. Box 7322
Ketchikan, AK 99901
(907) 247-2234

Located at mile 15 on North Tongass Highway, the resort offers lodge rooms and cabins on the waterfront, plus sites for RVs and campers. It is open from April through October. ($$)

**Ingersoll Hotel**
303 Mission Street
Ketchikan, AK 99901
(907) 225-2124 or
800-478-2124

Ketchikan accommodations are on the basic side, with one exception—and this isn't it. This hotel has been on the waterfront in the downtown area for a long time, offering basic rooms, but it is close to shops and restaurants. ($$)

PLACES TO STAY 167

**Ketchikan Youth Hostel**
First United
Methodist Church
Grand and Main streets
P.O. Box 8515
Ketchikan, AK 99901
(907) 225-3319

This summer operation is located in the local Methodist Church. Even more so than other hostels, the accommodations are very basic. ($)

**Westmark Cape Fox Lodge**
800 Venetia Way
Ketchikan, AK 99901-6561
(907) 225-8001 or
800-544-0970
or 800-999-2570 (in
Canada)

The deluxe Northwest-style lodge is perched on a high point overlooking Tongass Narrows and the town, with luxurious rooms and suites. There's a restaurant and lounge, gift shop, and a scenic tram ride that descends 130 feet to the downtown waterfront area. The restaurant specializes in fresh seafood. ($$$)

## KODIAK

**Buskin River Inn**
1395 Airport Way
Kodiak, AK 99615
(907) 487-2700

A modern lodge, three miles from the downtown area and located near the Kodiak airport, the inn offers large rooms—some with a view. The river runs in front of the hotel, offering good fishing opportunities. ($$ to $$$)

**Shelikof Lodge**
211 Thorsheim Avenue
Kodiak, AK 99615
(907) 486-4141

This is one of the town's several downtown hotels, offering modern rooms overlooking Kodiak Harbor. The hotel has a restaurant and lounge, and offers free airport and ferry pickup. Information for anglers and hunters is available. ($$)

**Westmark Kodiak**
236 Rezanof Street West
Kodiak, AK 99615
(907) 486-5712 or
800-544-0970

The restaurant and some of the hotel's rooms overlook the harbor. This is the priciest hotel on the island, but it offers modern rooms and excellent service. The restaurant serves local seafood as well as a fairly standard American cuisine (primarily steaks, pasta, and salads). ($$ to $$$)

# PALMER

**Gold Miner's Hotel**
918 South Colony Way
Palmer, AK 99645
(907) 745-6160 or
800-725-2752

This basic hotel is located in the historic section of downtown Palmer, offering standard units at a reasonable price. ($ to $$) You might also wish to stay in the **Motherlode Lodge**, operated by the same management. The country lodge is located at mile 14 of the Palmer-Fishhook Road, close to the Independence Mine and the Musk Ox Farm. Both hotels have a restaurant and lounge. ($$ to $$$)

**Homestead RV Park**
Mile 36 Glenn Highway
P.O. Box 354
Palmer, AK 99645
(907) 745-6005

Located six miles south of Palmer on the Glenn Highway, this woodsy campground offers water and electrical hookups, tentsites, showers, laundry, and dump station. Look for the rustic log cabin office at the junction of the Glenn and Parks highways.

**Mountain View RV Park**
P.O. Box 2521
Palmer, AK 99645
(907) 745-5747 or
800-264-4582

Located off the Old Glenn Highway at milepost 75, on Smith Road, this large operation provides full hookups, pull-through sites, modern rest rooms, showers, dump station, and a laundry. The park offers fine views of the Matanuska Mountains.

**Valley Hotel**
606 South Alaska Street
Palmer, AK 99645
(907) 745-3330

If you're on a budget and don't mind somewhat faded decor, this is the place for you. The hotel has been here since the 1940s, but the rooms are large, all units have baths, and the staff is helpful. Facilities include a coffee shop, liquor store, and lounge. ($)

## PETERSBURG

**Leconte RV Park**
P.O. Box 1534
Petersburg, AK 99833
(907) 772-4680

This campground, with facilities for RVs, trailers, and tenters, is located at 4th Street and Haugen Drive, one mile from the ferry terminal. It's within walking distance of downtown. There are hookups, showers, and a laundry.

**Scandia House**
P.O. Box 689
Petersburg, AK 99833
(907) 772-4281 or
800-722-5006

Located downtown close to the waterfront, this historic inn was renovated several years ago, with comfortable rooms (some with shared baths) and free continental breakfast. Skiff rentals are available, as are rental cars. ($ to $$)

**Tides Inn**
307 North First Street
P.O. Box 1048
Petersburg, AK 99833
(907) 772-4288

This two-storied motel is located at First and Dolphin streets, in the downtown area. Aside from the standard rooms, the motel offers free continental breakfast. ($$)

## SEWARD

**Hotel Seward**
P.O. Box 670
Seward, AK 99664
(907) 224-2378 or
fax (907) 224-3112

This Best Western operation is located on 5th Avenue downtown, decorated in the gold-rush style, and offering large, modern rooms with queen-size beds. Some of the rooms overlook the bay. The hotel offers a free shuttle service to the harbor. ($$$)

**Kenai Fjords RV Park**
P.O. Box 2772
Seward, AK 99664
(907) 224-8779

Located at 4th Avenue and D Street, this RV park offers electrical hookups, and is otherwise a basic RV and camping facility.

**Kenai Fjords Wilderness Lodge**
P.O. Box 695
Seward, AK 99664
(907) 224-5271

This island lodge is in a remote wilderness region, overlooking Kenai Fjords National Park. The lodge management specializes in offering wildlife tours, including guided tours into the fjords, where you'll see whales, sea otters, puffins by the hundreds, and many other sea- and shorebirds. Canoeing, sea kayaking, and photography attract visitors to this beautiful area. ($$$)

**Le Barn Bed and Breakfast**
P.O. Box 601
Seward, AK 99664
(907) 224-8706 or
(907) 224-3462

At mile 3.7 of the Seward Highway, just outside of town, Le Barn is not only a B & B in the country, but also has a fine dining room specializing in continental cuisine, especially seafood dishes, as well as crepes and omelets. This is one B & B where children are welcomed, with a petting park on-site. ($$ to $$$)

**New Seward Hotel and Saloon**
217 5th Avenue
P.O. Box 670
Seward, AK 99664
(907) 224-8001

Located in downtown Seward, this old hotel is close to restaurants and shopping. Standard rooms and units with kitchenettes are available. The hotel is open year-round. ($$)

**Van Gilder Hotel**
307 Adams Street
P.O. Box 2
Seward, AK 99664
(907) 224-3079

An ancient and restored national historic site, the hotel has authentic period charm, including a stylish old-time bar. Many of the rooms are furnished with antiques. Private and shared baths are available. Some rooms have a view of the harbor. ($$ to $$$)

## SITKA

**Alaska View Bed and Breakfast**
1101 Edgecumbe Drive
Sitka, AK 99835
(907) 747-8310

This cozy B & B home serves a full breakfast, and offers rooms with private baths and a whirlpool on the patio. It is a non-smoking facility. ($$)

**Helga's Bed and Breakfast**
2827 Halibut Point Road
P.O. Box 1885
Sitka, AK 99835
(907) 747-5497

This small B & B operation is located on the beach, with a fine view of the sound. ($$)

**Potlatch House**
713 Katlian Street
Sitka, AK 99835
(907) 747-8611 or
800-354-6017

This modest motel has rooms and suites, with daily and weekly rates, and laundry facilities. There is a restaurant and some rooms have good views. ($$)

**Sitka Youth Hostel**
303 Kimsham Street
P.O. Box 2645
Sitka, AK 99835
(907) 747-8356

The hostel is one of several in southeastern Alaska offering basic accommodations, particularly helpful for young people and older folks traveling on a budget and not needing cozy rooms. There are no kitchen facilities in this hostel, open from June 1st to August 31st. ($)

**Westmark Shee Atiká**
330 Seward Street
Sitka, AK 99835
(907) 747-6241 or
800-544-0970

Close to the historic area and the boat harbor, the hotel has comfortable rooms and suites, and a very good restaurant, however pricey. There's also a lounge, and the hotel has room service, a luxury not available in most panhandle places. ($$ to $$$)

## SKAGWAY

**Golden North Hotel**
P.O. Box 343
Skagway, AK 99840
(907) 983-2451 or
(907) 983-2294

This is the oldest, continuously operating hotel in Alaska, a remnant of the Klondike Gold Rush built in 1898. The rooms are wonderfully furnished in period antiques, and the hotel has a dining room and saloon. If you're a history buff and prefer staying in historic places, this hotel is a must! It's open year-round, and reservations are recommended. ($ to $$)

**Skagway Inn**
P.O. Box 500
Skagway, AK 99840
(907) 983-2289 or
800-478-2290 (in Alaska only)

Another historic place, this inn was built in 1897 but not operated continuously as a hotel. This B & B inn is located at Seventh Street and Broadway, close to downtown, with Victorian decor, substantial breakfasts, and helpful advice from innkeepers Sioux and Don Plummer on what to do and see in Skagway. ($$)

**Skagway RV and Camping Parks**
P.O. Box 324
Skagway, AK 99840
(907) 983-2768

These two campgrounds in Skagway are parts of the same operation. Pullen Creek RV Park is next to the Alaska State Ferry dock and the city's Pullen Creek Park, a short walk from the Klondike National Historic Park office and the downtown area. It has electrical and water hookups, showers, and a dump station. Hanousek Park, located on Broadway, is also within walking distance of downtown, with electrical and water hookups, wooded RV and tenting sites, showers, fire pits, and dump station.

**Wind Valley Lodge**
P.O. Box 354
Skagway, AK 99840
(907) 983-2236

All rooms in this modern motel have private baths. There are no-smoking rooms and a guest laundry. The Siding 21 Restaurant is located next door. ($ to $$)

## VALDEZ

**Bear Paw RV Park**
P.O. Box 93
Valdez, AK 99686
(907) 835-2530

The RV facility is right on the small harbor in downtown Valdez. Facilities include full and partial hookups, level sites, rest rooms, showers, laundry, and dump station. The park is the ticket agent for Stan Stephen's Cruises, which offers Columbia Glacier cruises and fishing charters.

**Casa de LaBellezza**
P.O. Box 294
Valdez, AK 99686
(907) 835-4489

This is a B & B inn with high standards, offering an Italian ambiance, queen or twin beds, and private or shared bath. Families are welcomed with special rates. ($$)

**Downtown B & B Inn**
113 Galena Drive
P.O. Box 184
Valdez, AK 99686
(907) 835-2791 or
800-478-2791

Located near the harbor, this is either a three-storied motel or a B & B, depending on how you see it. Families are welcomed and breakfast is served daily. Facilities include a guest laundry and in-room phones. ($$)

**Westmark Valdez Hotel**
100 Fidalgo Drive
Valdez, AK 99686
(907) 835-4391 or
800-544-0970

Another of the hotels in the Alaska/Yukon chain, the Westmark Valdez is located beside the small harbor, offering modern rooms with good views. A dining room and lounge are located in the hotel, along with full room service and rates lower than in most of its sister hotels around the state. ($$)

## WASILLA

**Lake Lucille Inn**
1300 West Lake
Lucille Drive
Wasilla, AK 99654
(907) 373-1776

One of the best features about this modern Best Western operation is its popular dining room, a particular favorite with local residents for its sumptuous Sunday buffets. There are standard rooms and suites with whirlpool baths, plus an athletic facility with a whirlpool and sauna, a floatplane dock, and paddleboat rentals. ($$ to $$$)

**Mat-Su Resort**
1850 Bogard Road
Wasilla, AK 99654
(907) 376-3228

Located on Wasilla Lake, a spawning ground for silver salmon, this lodge-style resort has lakeshore units and more standard motel units, plus several suites. Some units have kitchenettes. Overall, the rooms are large and comfortable. The resort's dining room is open for lunch and dinner. The grounds include two covered picnic areas, a floatplane dock, swimming, fishing, and row boats. (**$$ to $$$**)

## WRANGELL

**Harding's Old Sourdough Lodge**
P.O. Box 1062
Wrangell, AK 99929
(907) 874-3613

This is a very different type of B & B operation, open year-round. The lodge's restaurant, serving home-style meals, is like the dining room of an old-fashioned boarding house. Breakfast and lunch have a standard price. The operation has rooms (with private baths) furnished with either a king bed or twin beds. Facilities include a cocktail lounge, sauna, steam bath, whirlpool, and laundry. Lodge staff arrange fishing charters as well as other kinds of activities including eagle-watching excursions and photography outings. (**$ to $$**)

**Stikine Inn**
P.O. Box 990
Wrangell, AK 99929
(907) 874-3388

This large building looks more like a cannery than a hotel, but it has a handy downtown location and offers rooms with baths, TV, and phones. The Dock Side Restaurant, a lounge, a liquor store, and the rest of the hotel facilities are all located beside the water, one block from the ferry terminal. (**$ to $$**)

# Yukon and Northwest Territories

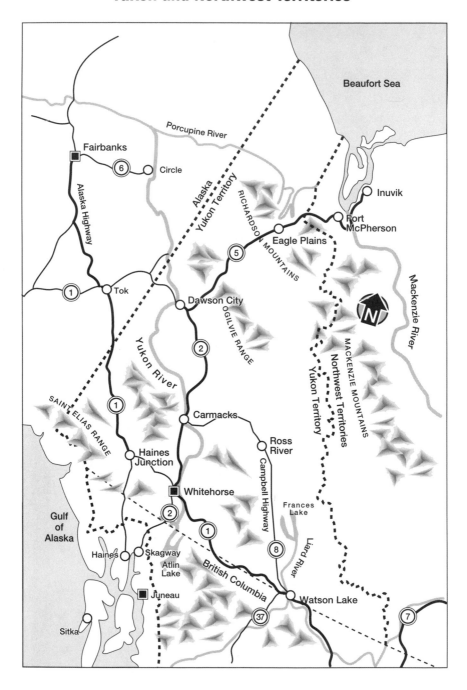

# Yukon
## Drives

For such a far-northern territory, the roads of the Canadian North are surprisingly driveable. In the Yukon, the Alaska and Klondike highways are totally paved. Even the Dempster Highway, although unpaved, offers comfortable driving across the Arctic Circle. Only the Campbell Highway and its offshoot, the Canol Road, require warnings of rough rides ahead.

The major north/south Yukon road is the **Alaska Highway**, linking Watson Lake and the rest of the world with Whitehorse and Alaska. Actually, this road leads in a northwest/southeast direction. An alternative to the Alaska Highway, if you're driving between Watson Lake and Dawson City, is the more rugged **Robert Campbell Highway**.

The **Klondike Highway** links tidewater at Skagway, Alaska, to Whitehorse in the central Yukon, and then heads northwest to the fabled gold rush town of Dawson City. From Skagway it climbs to the top of White Pass, across Tormented Valley, and then passes through some great scenery to Carcross. It doubles with the Alaska Highway for a while on the trip to Whitehorse. It parts again from the Alaska Highway just north of Whitehorse, near Takhini Hot Springs, and passes the "marge of Lake Laberge," the celebrated place where fictitious Sam McGee was cremated in the Robert Service poem. The lake, however, is real—it's a widening of the Yukon River. Approaching Dawson, the highway shadows the Klondike River, and you can almost see the miners with their pans. What you do see are the snaking piles of tailings left from the huge dredges that plied the river and nearby creeks after the gold rush ended in the 1890s.

# Klondike Highway Drives

## Skagway to Whitehorse

The drive on Highway 2 between Skagway, Alaska, and White-horse provides a look at one of the most historic and fascinating parts of northern Canada and Alaska—a route that partially re-traces the journey taken by gold stampeders in 1898 on their way to Dawson City and the imagined riches of the Klondike. A few years later, the White Pass and Yukon Railroad built a narrow-gauge line between the two pioneer towns. With the railroad closed since 1988, the highway now provides the only year-round link be-tween the communities, although a summer excursion train takes tourists on a short run from Skagway to Lake Bennett. Our high-way log for this route runs from south to north. For those starting the tour in Whitehorse, please read the log from bottom to top.

## Along the Way

**Klondike Gold Rush National Historic Park**   Before you leave Skagway, be sure to visit the former railroad station, located downtown near the waterfront. Much of Skagway's restored downtown area, centered around Broadway, has been designated as part of the park. The other major part is the Chilkoot Trail, protecting the route of the gold seekers of 1898, between the nearby Dyea townsite and Lake Bennett.

**Historical Marker**   Almost three miles into the drive along Highway 2, you'll see a plaque to the east. The marker honors the men and women of the Klondike Gold Rush. Nearby is a scenic area along the Skagway River.

**Ascent to White Pass**   After the marker, the highway begins a steep climb from sea level to White Pass, at an elevation of 3,290 feet (1,003 meters). Carved out by glaciers during the most re-cent ice age, this narrow valley has sheer sides, making the White Pass Trail (an alternative route to the Chilkoot Trail) a treacher-ous adventure.

**Summit Lake and Tormented Valley**  The highway winds past Summit Lake, one of several lakes in this high area north of White Pass. The Canada Customs station, open 24 hours, is at Fraser. Just beyond the station is the beautiful dark green Bernard Lake. At 26 miles (42 KM) the road enters Tormented Valley, a wild, phantasmagorical landscape of stunted trees and shrubs and weird rock formations.

**Tutshi and Tagish Lakes**  The area around this seven-mile-long lake was the scene of gold and silver mining which lasted until the Venus mine closed in 1981. This is a perfect area for canoeing, and also for picnicking along Highway 2. A picnic table is in a scenic location situated next to Windy Arm, an extension of Tagish Lake. Three hundred people lived near here in a little town named Conrad when the mining operation was at its early peak around 1905. Lime Mountain (5,225 feet, 1,593 meters) lies to the east beyond Bove Island.

**Carcross**  This was a bustling little town for the first quarter of the 20th century, starting with the Klondike Gold Rush. Originally known as Caribou Crossing because of the migratory caribou herds that traveled between Nares and Bennett lakes, the town became a stop on the White Pass & Yukon Route railway line in 1900. Stern-wheelers took train passengers on to other destinations.

**Sand Dunes**  The Carcross desert is one of the anomalies of the north. This group of sand dunes along the highway (between kilometer-posts 108 and 110) is certified to be the world's smallest desert. The sand was once on the bottom of a long-ago glacial lake. The small shrub that survives on the sand is called kinnikinnick. A few lodgepole pines have also taken root on the dunes.

**Emerald Lake**  Also called Rainbow Lake, this startling blue-green lake is seen from a turnout to the west of the highway. The vivid color is produced by sunshine reflecting off the lake's white bottom, a mixture of decomposed seashell fragments and light clay.

# HIGHWAY LOG
## *Skagway to Whitehorse*
### 177 KM (109.8 miles)—2 hours

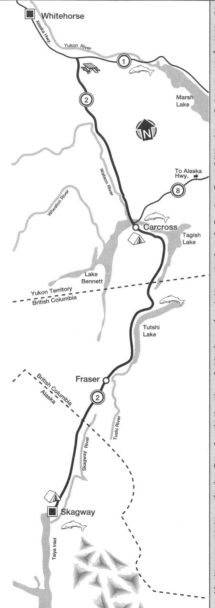

**Skagway** Downtown at the ferry terminal.

**Junction–Dyea Road** (KM 3.7, mile 2.3) This road leads 12.4 KM (7.7 miles) to the site of Dyea, Skagway's sister gold rush town. Take this road to the end for the Slide Cemetery and the starting point of the Chilkoot Trail.

**Turnout** (KM 8, mile 5) To the east, with views of the White Pass & Yukon Route tracks across the canyon.

**Turnout** (KM 8.8, mile 5.5) To the west with historical signs.

**U.S. Customs Station** (KM 9.8, mile 6.1) All traffic entering the U.S. must stop here.

**Viewpoint** (KM 12.4, mile 7.7) A look at Pitchfork Falls, flowing from Goat Lake.

**Turnout** (KM 14.6, mile 9.1) To the east with historical signs about the White Pass gold rush trail. View of canyon to Esk Glacier.

**Turnout** (KM 18.7, mile 11.6) Captain William Moore Bridge, view of Skagway River waterfalls.

**White Pass Summit** (KM 23.2, mile 14.4) Turnout to the west.

**U.S./Canada border** (KM 24, mile 14.9) Turnout to the west. Monument to the east. There is a time zone change to Pacific time;

driving north, set your watch forward one hour. The road now leads beside Summit Lake. **Canada Customs Station** (KM 36.2, mile 22.5) At Fraser. All travelers entering Canada must stop here. This is the turnaround on the White Pass train ride. **Bernard Lake** (KM 36.4, mile 26.6) To the east.
**Turnout** (KM 42.8, mile 26.6) Views of Tormented Valley, filled with small lakes and stunted trees. **Historic Site** (KM 43.9, mile 27.3) The highway crosses the White Pass & Yukon Route tracks at the former site of Log Cabin, an old RCMP station. **Tutshi** (pronounced *too-shy*) **Lake** (KM 50, mile 31.1) Good fishing for grayling and lake trout in the spring. **Turnoff** (KM 64.5, mile 40.1) To picnic area on Tutshi Lake. **Old Venus Mine Concentrator** (KM 75.1, mile 46.4) Low silver prices closed the mine in 1981. **Turnout** (KM 81, mile 50.2) with picnic table overlooking Windy Arm, an extension of Tagish Lake. **Turnout** (KM 83.5, mile 51.9) To the east with picnic table and sign about the old Venus Mine. **Turnout** (KM 95.8, mile 59.5) With information on Bove Island. Good view of Windy Arm. **Turnoff** (KM 105.1, mile 65.3) Sideroad to Native American community of Carcross and Carcross

Cemetery. Buried here are Klondike gold discoverers Skookum Jim and Tagish Charlie. **Carcross** (KM 106.5, mile 66.2) Turn west for the village. Caribou Mountain can be seen to the east. **Junction–Yukon Highway 8** (KM 107, mile 66.5) To Tagish, the Atlin Road, and the Alaska Hwy. at Jake's Corner. **Carcross Desert** (KM 108.3, mile 67.3) The world's smallest desert. **Game Park** (Museum of Yukon Natural History Inc.) (KM 108.6, mile 67.9) Animals in their native habitat (admission charge). **Highway Services** (KM 115, mile 72.1) Gas, café, lodging, camping, road to park on Spirit Lake. **Junction–Annie Lake Road** (KM 139.4, mile 87.5)West to McConnell and Annie lakes, and golf course. **Turnoff** (KM 154.2, mile 95.5) Kookatsoon Lake Picnic Park, swimming, boat launch. **Junction–Alaska Highway** (KM 157.1, mile 98.8) Whitehorse is 20.6 KM (12.8 miles) from the junction. Turn northwest for Whitehorse. Turn southeast for Watson Lake. **Wolf Creek Campground** (KM 161, mile 100) Picnic tables, fishing for grayling (1.3 KM off hwy.). **Whitehorse–North Access Road** (KM 177.7, mile 110.4) Two-Mile Hill. For Whitehorse details, see page 241.

## Whitehorse to Dawson City

This first part of the highly recommended Klondike Loop Tour begins in Whitehorse, proceeds north on the Alaska Highway for only a few miles, and then leads to Dawson City. The distance between Whitehorse and Dawson City is 526 KM (327 miles).

The second part of the tour involves crossing the Yukon River from downtown Dawson City, and driving the 105-KM (65-mile) Top of the World Highway into the wilds of Alaska, and then completing the loop via the Taylor Highway (another 175 KM, 109 miles) to meet the Alaska Highway south of Tok. If you don't intend to come to the Yukon again for many years, don't miss the fascinating region made famous by the 1898 Klondike Gold Rush, and other Alaskan gold stampedes. The second part of the loop, past Dawson City, is described in the next drive on page 184.

## Along the Way

**Takhini Hot Springs**    Six miles off the highway, via a side road, the Takhini Hot Springs Resort offers hot bathing in an enclosed concrete pool, and camping, with bed-and-breakfast homes nearby. Native Americans in the Yukon used the springs in times past, as did trappers who arrived in the area in the 1800s.

**Lake Laberge**    To the east of the highway is this 64 KM/40-mile-long lake, a widening of the Yukon River. Imagine the old river steamers, with huge paddle wheels, chugging up and down the lake. Two of the remaining boats are in dry dock in Whitehorse and Dawson City. This was the lake made internationally famous by Robert W. Service, in his poem "The Cremation of Sam McGee."

**Fox Lake and Braeburn Lodge**    This is a particularly lovely lake, lying east of the Miners Range. There is fine fishing in Fox Creek (grayling in June and July), and a public campground is located on the lake, with a kitchen shelter and drinking water. The lake offers grayling year-round, while burbot and lake trout may be taken from the shore.

People fly to the airstrip at Braeburn Lodge, a roadside café and lodge at Braeburn Lake. The major attraction for aviators and road warriors is the tasty batch of cinnamon buns baked each day at the lodge: a culinary oddity that has achieved legendary status in the Yukon. The lodge has other food, as well as a gas station.

**Montague House**  What used to be a roadhouse on the wagon trail to Dawson City is now a crumbling log structure beside the highway. This was one of more than 50 such places spaced along the stagecoach route.

**Carmacks**  This is the only community of any size between Whitehorse and Dawson, with about 400 residents. Visitor services include a motel, restaurant, store, laundry, and gas station, and Native American crafts are usually for sale at the visitor info tent. Boat tours of the famed Five Finger Rapids are available here.

**The Great Rivers**  A bridge crosses the Yukon River at Carmacks, and there are more river crossings between Carmacks and Dawson. But the only way to see the historic site of Fort Selkirk is to take a boat tour from either Carmacks or Minto Resort. This old Hudson's Bay Company post was occupied until the 1950s. It still remains much as it was in 1900. The demise of the river boats, because of bridge construction, brought an end to the old fort. Other rivers crossed include the Pelly and the Stewart. Both crossings have small communities. Pelly Crossing is a Native American village. Stewart Crossing facilities include a gas station, campsites, meals, and lodging.

**Midnight Dome**  A trip to the top of Midnight Dome is a "must" experience for visitors to Dawson. Here, where the sun bobs on top of mountain peaks in late June, are panoramic views of the Yukon River valley and the gold fields. Drive out of town on the Klondike Highway and turn left on Dome Road. The old cemeteries are at KM 1, including a small resting place for the early RCMP officers.

# HIGHWAY LOG
## *Whitehorse to Dawson City*
### 542 KM (337 miles)—6 hours

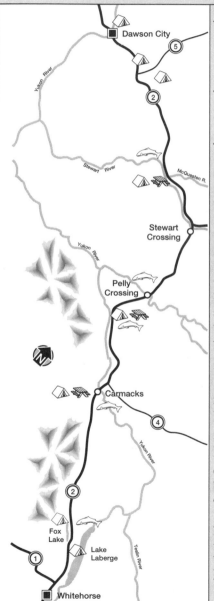

Dawson City

Yukon River

Stewart River

McQuesten R.

Stewart Crossing

Yukon River

Pelly Crossing

Carmacks

Yukon River

Fox Lake

Lake Laberge

Teslin River

Whitehorse

**Junction–Alaska Highway** (KM 177.5, mile 110.2) At the north access road to Whitehorse. Drive northwest for Dawson City.
**Junction–Klondike Highway** (KM 192, mile 119.3) Turn north for Dawson City.
**Junction–Takhini Hot Springs Road** (KM 198, mile 123) The hot springs and campground are 9.6 KM (6 miles) from the hwy.
**Northern Splendour Reindeer Farm** (KM 208, mile 139.8) Open to the public (admission charge).
**Lake Laberge Campground** (KM 225, mile 139.8) Boat launch, fishing for lake trout, grayling, and northern pike.
**Turnout** (KM 239, mile 148.5) View of Fox Lake.
**Fox Lake Campground** (KM 248, mile 154.1) Picnic tables. Fishing for lake trout and grayling.
**Highway Services** (KM 281. 5, mile 175) Gas, food, lodging. Braeburn Lodge is noted for its cinnamon buns. Fishing in Braeburn Lake.
**Twin Lakes Campground** (KM 308, mile 191.4) Picnic tables. Fishing for pike, grayling, and trout.
**Rest Area** (KM 355, mile 220.5)

**Carmacks** (KM 356, mile 221.2) Historic village with motel, café, gas, stores, post office. Campground (located on the Yukon River), tables, and boat launch. **Junction–Robert Campbell Highway (Hwy. 4)** (KM 360, mile 223.7) Turn west for Faro, Ross River, and Watson Lake. **Sideroad** (KM 361, mile 224.3) To Tantalus Butte coal mine. **Tatchun Creek Campground** (KM 383, mile 238) Picnic tables. **Tatchun Lake Campground** (KM 384, mile 238.6) Sideroad to campsites (7 KM, 4.3 mi.) Picnic tables, fishing (northern pike). **Viewpoint** (KM 396, mile 246) "Gardens of the Yukon" (islands in the Yukon River). **Loop Road to Minto** (KM 431, mile 267.8) To site of old settlement. Campground, picnic tables, boat launch. **Pelly Crossing** (KM 464.5, mile 288.6) Small Native American village with gas, café, and store. **Viewpoint** (KM 467, mile 290.2) Pelly Crossing, historical marker. **Turnout** (KM 488.5, mile 303.5) To west, view of Willow Creek. **Sideroad to Jackfish Lake** (KM 491, mile 305) **Crooked Creek** (KM 524.5, mile 325.9) Fishing—pike and grayling. **Sideroad** (KM 526.5, mile 327.1) To Ethel Lake campground (26.7 KM, 16 miles), narrow road, boat launch, fishing.

**Stewart Crossing** (KM 537.5, mile 340) Gas, café, lodging. **Stewart River Bridge** (KM 538.2, mile 334.4) Junction with Silver Trail (Hwy. 11) to Mayo, Elsa, and Keno. **Turnoff** (KM 554, mile 344.2) Beside Stewart River. River access to west. Historical marker. **Highway Services** (KM 561.9, mile 349) Gas, café, Moose Creek Lodge. **Moose Creek Campground** (KM 562, mile 349.2) Picnic area, toilets. **McQuesten River** (KM 583.5, mile 362.6) **Beaver Dam Creek** (KM 617, mile 383.4) **Klondike River** (KM 668.5, mile 425.4) From here, the road parallels the Klondike to its mouth at Dawson City (47.5 KM, 29.5 miles). **Turnoff** (KM 671.5, mile 417.2) Historical sign about the Klondike. **Junction–Dempster Highway (Hwy. 5)** (KM 678, mile 421.3) Gas, motel, café. The Dempster runs north for 724 KM (448 miles) crossing the Arctic Circle and ending at Inuvik (see page 194). **Klondike River Campground** (KM 700, mile 435) Picnic tables. **Downtown Dawson City** (KM 719.3, mile 447) The information center is at the corner of King and Front streets (see page 218).

# Top of the World/Taylor Highway Drive

## Dawson City to Alaska Highway

The alpine views from the Top of the World Highway are spectacular, whether you take the road on a day trip or if you choose to continue on the Taylor Highway to join the Alaska Highway at Tetlin Junction, south of Tok. This route takes you through present-day gold mining country and the rustic wilderness of the North Yukon and Alaskan interior. The distance from Dawson City to Tetlin Junction is 280 KM (174 miles).

## Along the Way

**Yukon Ferry Crossing**   You begin the trip with the crossing of the Yukon River on a ferry from downtown Dawson City. This free ferry is often crowded during summer, and you are advised to either get to the ferry landing early in the morning or be prepared to leave your car in the lineup for an hour or two. Another option is to make the crossing in the afternoon and spend the night at the public campground on the other side of the river. The Top of the World route is not a normal highway. The average speed for the road is between 40 and 55 KM per hour (25 to 35 mph). Yukon law requires that you drive with your headlights on.

**Backroad to Clinton Creek Ghost Town**   Fifty-nine kilometers (37 miles) from Dawson, a backroad leads to the ghost town of Clinton Creek, a former asbestos-mining community. The confluence of the Fortymile and Yukon rivers is 4.8 KM (3 miles) below the remains of the town. The Fortymile is the top canoeing river in this part of Alaska—more on that later. You also have good fishing prospects in the Yukon River, for king salmon (July and August) and chum salmon (August).

**Canada/U.S. Border**   The border is 105 KM (65 miles) from Dawson. The Canadian station is open daily from 9 A.M. to 9 P.M. (Pacific time) from about May 15th to September 15th. The U.S. border station is open 8 A.M. to 8 P.M. (Alaska time). The stations, and the road, are closed in winter.

**Jack Wade Junction**  This major highway junction is 127 KM (79 miles) from Dawson. This is where you meet the Taylor Highway, (Route 5) which runs north for 104 KM (65 miles) to the isolated community of Eagle, on the Yukon River, and south for 154 KM (96 miles) to Tetlin Junction on the Alaska Highway.

**Sidetrip to Eagle, Alaska**  The historic town of Eagle provides a wonderful chance to immerse yourself in the history of early Alaska and the Yukon. There is so much to see here, including several museums, that it takes about three hours to cover the walking tour of the picturesque town. Guided tours are provided daily by the local historical society at 9 A.M., Memorial Day through Labor Day. A National Parks visitor center provides information on the Yukon–Charley Lakes National Preserve. Visitor hours are 8 A.M. to 5 P.M. Old Fort Egbert, restored by the Bureau of Land Management, is on display with an interpretive center. A popular float trip down the Yukon, through the national preserve to Circle, is available throughout the summer.

**Chicken, Alaska**  Chicken has to be seen to be believed. This old mining community still manages to survive—and with much gusto—in this remote region. The original town has been abandoned, but the new town provides a variety of visitor services to highway travelers. Drive off the main road into town, and you'll come across the Chicken Mercantile Emporium, Chicken Creek Café, Chicken Saloon, and Chicken Gas. The Goldpanner offers gas, souvenirs, and gold panning. Although the road to the original Chicken townsite is blocked off, guided walking tours are available. Ask at the Chicken Café. Overnight RV parking is available at the Goldpanner.

**Fortymile River**  Just past Chicken on the Taylor Highway is the bridge over the Mosquito Fork of the Fortymile River. A picnic area sits beside the bridge, and river access offers canoeists one of the finest river trips in the state. This is one of several access points for the Fortymile Wild and Scenic River System.

# HIGHWAY LOG
## Dawson City to Tetlin Junction
### 281 KM (174 miles)—4 hours

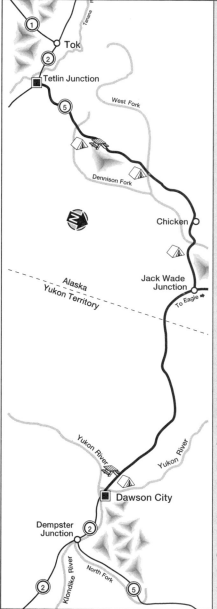

**Dawson City** At the ferry landing downtown.

**Yukon River Campground** (KM 0.3, mile 0.2) On the riverbank across from Dawson City. Picnic tables, shelters, playground.

**Viewpoint** (KM 5, mile 3.2) with view of the Yukon Valley.

**Rest Area** (KM 14.5, mile 9) with picnic tables, toilets. The highway now climbs above the tree line, to run across several high ridges.

**Turnout** (KM 53, mile 33) To south with good view. The Castle Rock formations are seen at this point.

**Sideroad** (KM 60.3, mile 37.5) To Clinton Creek, a former settlement at an asbestos mine that closed in 1979. The road (64 KM or 40 miles) is not maintained. There is access to the junction of the Yukon and Fortymile Rivers 4.8 KM (3 miles) from the townsite.

**Turnoff** (KM 87.3, mile 54) This road leads west to a mine at Sixtymile.

**Canada/U.S. Border Stations** (KM 107.8, mile 67) The customs offices are open from approx. May 15th to September 15th during daytime hours only. There is a time change here. We now switch to miles, followed by kilometers.

**Boundary** (Mile 69.2, KM 111.4) The lodge at Boundary was one of the earliest roadhouses in Alaska. Gas, café. The only gas station between here and the Alaska Hwy. is in Chicken (mile 108).

**Turnoff** (Mile 78, KM 125.6) for viewpoint and map.

**Jack Wade Junction** (Mile 78.8, KM 126.9) The Taylor Hwy. (Route 5) runs north to Eagle on the Yukon River. Keep left (southwest) for Tetlin Junction and the Alaska Hwy.

**Turnout** (Mile 82.6, KM 133) **Old Jack Wade Mining Camp** (Mile 86.5, KM 139.2) There is still mining in this area.

**Old Dredge** (Mile 88.4, KM 142.3) From the Jack Wade operation in the creek next to the road. Turnout to the east.

**Campground** (Mile 92.4, KM 148.7) Next to the Walker Fork Bridge, an access point for the Fortymile River Canoe Trail, a popular wilderness adventure for experienced canoeists. The road descends with views of the Fortymile valley (mile 96, KM 154.5).

**Turnout** (Mile 97.7, KM 157.2) View of oxbow lakes.

**Day-use Area** (Mile 99.2, KM 159.6) At the South Fork bridge, canoeing.

**Lost Chicken Creek** (Mile 105.6, KM 170) Mining began here in 1895 after several gold strikes over the previous nine years along the Fortymile River.

**Old Townsite of Chicken** (Mile 107.2, KM 172.5) Ghost town and old gold dredge to the northwest.

**Access Road–Chicken** (Mile 108, KM 173.9) Gas, café, stores, bar, RV parking, post office.

**Day-use Area** (Mile 110, KM 177) At north end of Mosquito Fork Bridge. Picnic table, canoe access.

**Taylor Creek** (Mile 124.3, KM 200) **Loop Road** (Mile 125.5, KM 202) To BLM campground with picnic tables, fire pits, water, canoe access.

**Cabin Creek Bridge** (Mile 131.5, KM 211.6) Turnout at west end of bridge, creek access via sideroad.

**Turnout** (Mile 135.4, KM 217.9) To the west.

**Turnout** (Mile 146.2, KM 235.3) To the west, good views.

**Turnout** (Mile 168.5, KM 271.2) To east with rest area. Spring water should be boiled.

**Turnout** (Mile 170, KM 273.6) To the east. Access via trail to Fourmile Lake (rainbow trout).

**Tetlin Junction** (Mile 174, KM 280.8) Alaska Highway. Village with gas, cafés, store, lodging, camping, hookups. The town of Tok is located 12.5 miles (20 KM) north of Tetlin Junction with additional accommodations, restaurants, and stores. Tok is at the junction of the Alaska Highway and the Tok Cutoff to the Glenn Highway.

# Campbell Highway Drive

## Carmacks to Watson Lake

This backroad route—running to the east of the Alaska High-way—was named for Robert Campbell, the first European explorer of what is now the Yukon Territory. This highway is charted in a northwest to southeast direction, to provide an alternate route to the Klondike and Alaska highways for those driving south from Alaska or Dawson City.

The route runs through prime Yukon wilderness, with several convenient camping locations along the way. Accommodations and gas are available in Carmacks, Faro, Ross River, and Watson Lake.

This route also provides access to the CANOL Road, built during World War II, and the difficult but scenic Nahanni Range Road, which leads from Miner's Junction northeast for 201 KM (125 miles). Anglers will find this route a special treat.

## Along the Way

**Eagles Nest Bluff**   Seventeen miles after leaving the Klondike Highway junction, and after passing the Tantalus Butte coal mine, you'll encounter a turnout to a viewpoint overlooking the bluff formerly called Eagle Rock. This was a long-time marker for Yukon River travelers, and the scene of a major riverboat tragedy. The *Columbian,* a paddle wheeler, exploded and burned when a crewman accidentally fired a gunshot into the cargo, which was mainly gunpowder.

**Four Scenic Campgrounds**   The first Yukon government campground along the route is accessed about 41.4 KM (25.7 miles) from the junction. A sideroad leads 8 KM (4.9 miles) north of the highway to Frenchman Lake and Nunatak Campground (just beyond the first campsites). The last part of the road, past Frenchman Lake, is rough. Fishing for grayling, pike, and trout.

Little Salmon Lake Campground is located off the highway at 83 KM (51.6 miles). Facilities include boat launch, picnic tables, kitchen shelter, fire pits, and pit toilets. The narrow access road is steep and winding.

Drury Creek Campground is reached via a short access road, at the 117.3-KM (73.7-mile) mark. This public campground sits at the east end of Little Salmon Lake. Lena's Place, with food and overnight accommodations, is nearby.

Johnson Lake Campground is 41.8 KM (3 miles) south of the town of Faro, with several pull-through sites, picnic shelter, firewood, pit toilets, boat launch, and drinking water.

**Faro**   One of two towns along the Campbell Highway, Faro lies along the Pelly River, 9 KM (5.6 miles) off the highway. In 1969, Cypress-Anvil, a mining company, opened a lead-zinc-silver operation here. It was active until 1982 when low prices forced its closure. The mine was reactivated in 1986 and closed again soon after. Again reopened in 1995, the mine is the western world's largest producer of lead and zinc concentrates. Through the years, the little town has hung on by its fingernails. At last visiting, there were two restaurants, both with motels attached, plus a service station. The municipal campground offers RV and tent sites. Four miles from town is a wildlife observation station, built in 1994. For advance information on accommodations and special events, call 800-910-FARO.

**Ross River**   After passing a government campground (Lapie Canyon), you'll meet the access road to the community of Ross River. After driving the 11.2 KM (7 miles) from the highway, you'll find the town named in 1843 for Donald Ross, chief trader for the Hudson's Bay Company. Later, from about 1903, Tom Smith founded Nahanni House, a trading post largely servicing the Native American people of the region, located where the Ross River joins the Pelly. The CANOL Pipeline service road was constructed through here during World War II, and the town was firmly connected to the outside world by road in 1964 with the construction of the Campbell Highway. The community has gas stations, a grocery store, and two motels with cafés (including the Welcome Inn).

# HIGHWAY LOG
## *Carmacks to Watson Lake*
### 591 KM (367 miles)—7.5 hours

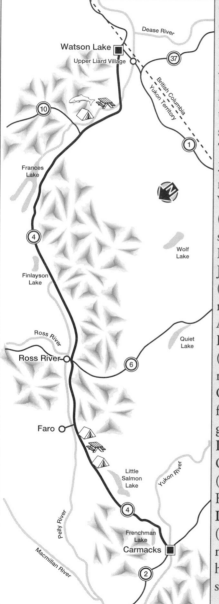

**Carmacks** The junction of the Campbell Hwy. with the Alaska Hwy. is two miles north of Carmacks, a small village beside the Yukon River. See the Alaska Hwy. logs for the drive from Whitehorse to Carmacks or from Fairbanks south to the junction.

**Tantalus Butte Coal Mine** (KM 3.7, mile 2.3) The mine is to the north near the junction.

**Viewpoint–Marker** Found 27 KM (16.8 miles) from the junction showing the Yukon River and Eagles Nest Bluff.

**Junction–Road to Salmon River** (KM 37.8, mile 23.5) The 1-mile road leads south to a small Native American village.

**Frenchman Lake Campground** (KM 41.4, mile 25.7) Via access road leading 8 KM (5 miles) north. Campsites, picnic tables. Good fishing for pike, trout, and grayling.

**Picnic Area** (KM 47, mile 29.2) On Little Salmon River, 46 KM (28.8 miles) from the Alaska Hwy. junction.

**Little Salmon Lake Campground** (KM 83, mile 51.6) Reached by a narrow road leading south from hwy. Campsites, boat launch, shelter, fishing.

**Drury Creek Campground** (KM 117.3, mile 72.9) On creek at east end of Little Salmon lake. Campsites, picnic tables, shelter, fishing for northern pike, whitefish, grayling, and lake trout.

**Johnson Lake Campground** (KM 168.3, mile 104.6) Picnic tables, firewood, shelter, boat launch (168 KM or 104 miles from Alaska Hwy. Junction).

**Junction–Road to Faro** (KM 173, mile 107.5) The access road leads 9 KM (5.6 miles) to the town, and the Cyprus-Anvil lead-zinc operation. Gas, hotel, motel, cafés, stores, and RV park.

**Lapie Campground** Located 51 KM (31.8 miles) from Faro Road. Picnic tables, shelter, water (needs to be boiled), canyon trails.

**Junction–Road to Ross River** (KM 226.4, mile 140.7) The village is 7 miles off the hwy. on the southwest bank of the Pelly River, with gas, store, motels, and cafés. From Ross River, the Canol Road leads 232 KM (144 miles) to the Northwest Territories border (see page 198).

**Coffee Lake** (KM 238.5, mile 148.2) South of the hwy. Fishing for cutthroat trout. Swimming.

**Hoole Canyon Bridge** Located 60.6 KM (37.7 miles) from Ross River Junction, a temporary wooden bridge called a Bailey bridge with turnout to the north.

**Frances Lake Campground** (KM 425, mile 264.1) Via access road that leads 1 KM (0.6 mile) to campsites, boat launch, shelter, water (should be boiled). The peak between the two arms of the lake, Simpson Tower, is named for a governor of the Hudson's Bay Company, Sir George Simpson. Fishing for grayling, northern pike, and lake trout.

**Junction–Nahanni Range Road** (KM 490, mile 304.5) Rough road leads 201 KM (125 miles) northeast to Tungsten, a former mining town. The last 43 miles of the road are not maintained and not recommended for driving except by four-wheel-drive vehicles. Great fishing in the Hyland River for grayling. A campground is at KM 84 (mile 52.2).

**Simpson Lake Campground** Via access road west for 1 mile. Picnic tables, boat launch, shelter, swimming, water (must be boiled), and good fishing for grayling, pike, and trout.

**Picnic Area** At the Frances River Bridge (58 KM or 36 miles from Watson Lake).

**Junction–Alaska Highway** At the town of Watson Lake, near the Yukon/British Columbia border. Watson Lake has a full complement of motels and stores, a car wash (important), and cafés.

# Dempster Highway Drive

## Dawson City to Inuvik

In all of North America, across the vast wilderness which makes up northern Canada and Alaska, only one public highway crosses the Arctic Circle. Today the trail has become a well-maintained gravel roadway, leading to an unparalleled scenic wilderness. Surprisingly, at the northern end of the highway there is civilization—in Inuvik, the modern Arctic service center founded in the mid-1950s. Inuvik offers a startling contrast to the virgin wilderness of the Dempster Highway.

Government campgrounds (and a most unusual hotel "oasis") provide overnight accommodation, allowing visitors as much time as is needed to explore this great wilderness route. The Dempster Highway provides road-explorers of the Canadian northland with the ultimate northern adventure.

Highway kilometer-posts have been replaced and repositioned, providing more accurate mileages than in previous years.

The Dempster drive is unforgettable, for its crossing of the mountain ranges, for the alpine tundra on Eagle Plains, the wildlife-filled marshes of the Mackenzie Delta, and the crossing of the Arctic Circle. Before reaching Eagle Plains, the highway traverses three major regions.

**North Klondike River**   The north branch of the Klondike has its source in the southern Ogilvie Mountains and flows with the southern branch through the Klondike gold fields into the Yukon River at Dawson. Starting at its junction with the Klondike Highway, the Dempster Highway follows the North Klondike through the Tintina Trench and boreal forest. The most northerly stand of pine trees in Canada can be seen at KM 8 (mile 5). At 915 meters (3,000 feet), timber gives way to shrub tundra with willow and alder shrubs.

The Klondike Region was not glaciated during the most recent ice age. This factor made possible the slow erosion of the area, leading to the exposure of gold in the gravel of the Klondike creek beds.

**Southern Ogilvie Mountains**   The North Fork Pass, beginning at KM 75.5 (mile 47), is at the divide between the Yukon River watershed, which drains into the Pacific, and the Peel River drainage area, which feeds the Arctic Ocean via the Mackenzie River. This region lies primarily above the tree line. The road continues through the East Blackstone River valley.

Unlike the other mountain regions along the Dempster, the southern Ogilvies were heavily glaciated, with many signs of glacial rubble and cirques shaped by the ice. The permafrost here supports only tundra vegetation on the higher slopes. There are many small lakes and ponds, another sign of the presence of glaciers.

Tombstone Mountain is seen at KM 75.5 (mile 45). This wedge-shaped peak looks over the North Klondike River valley. Further on, from KM 87 (mile 54), the Blackstone uplands is an excellent area for bird-watching, especially for birds of prey such as short-eared owls, bald eagles, peregrine falcons, and gyrfalcons. Chapman Lake, at KM 122 (mile 76), is the largest lake in the region. This serves as a crossing area for barren-ground caribou that appear in October.

**Northern Ogilvies**   These rolling hills and mountains, quite different from the southern Ogilvies, are composed mainly of sedimentary rock, including shale and limestone. The summits are bare of vegetation with many of the hills covered with rock rubble. Past KM 160 (mile 99.4), some of the ridges are castellated, having been carved into towers by erosion. Timberline is at 914 M (3,000 feet) and the forest consists of cottonwood and white spruce. At the higher levels, there is the typical black spruce tundra. Beavers, Dall sheep, grizzly, and black bears live in this region.

# HIGHWAY LOG
## Dawson City to Eagle Plains
363.5 KM (232.3 miles)—5 hours, 30 minutes

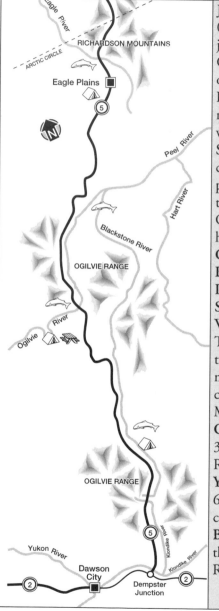

Junction–Klondike Highway (KM 0, mile 0) Gas, lodging, café. This junction also known as Dempster Corner is 40.2 KM (25 miles) east of Dawson City.

Klondike River Bridge (KM 0.3, mile 0.2) This is a one-lane, wooden-planked bridge.

Sideroad (KM 6.4, mile 4) Now closed, it leads to an old dam and power house built to supply power to the gold dredges and Dawson City. The road provides a scenic hike.

Glacier Creek (KM 24.5, mile 15.4)

Benson Creek (KM 29, mile 18.1)

Pea Soup Creek (KM 41, mile 25.6)

Scout Car Creek (KM 51, mile 31.7)

Wolf Creek (KM 48, mile 29.8) There is a trapper's cabin beside the road. The hwy. follows the north fork of the Klondike River, climbing into the Tombstone Mountain range.

Grizzly Creek (KM 58.9, mile 36.6) Look to the right for Mt. Robert Service.

Yukon Government Road (KM 65.8, mile 41) To a maintenance camp.

Bridge (KM 67.3, mile 41.8) Over the north fork of the Klondike River. The Dempster climbs above the tree line with views of the Tombstone Range.

**Tombstone Mountain Campground** (KM 72.6, mile 45.1) Picnic tables, shelter, fireplaces, toilets. An interpretive center operates from a trailer during summer months. Several hikes are possible from this campsite. There is a good valley access route following Wolf Creek.

**Viewpoint** (KM 73.5, mile 45.7) Tombstone Mountain (southwest) and North Fork Pass. The Blackstone River is ahead, flanked by the Ogilvie Mountains.

**Bridge** (KM 87.9, mile 54.6) The east fork of the Blackstone. Bridge (KM 117.4, mile 72.9) over the west fork of the Blackstone. Fishing for grayling—down the river at the fork.

**Marker** (KM 118, mile 73.3) Commemorates the Northwest Mounted Police dog sled patrols, with a view of Chapman Lake.

**Yukon Government Airstrip** (KM 125.3, mile 77.9) One of several airstrips that use the roadway as part of the landing area. Watch for aircraft at these points. At KM 154.5 (mile 96), the Dempster passes through a hilly, desolate area called Windy Pass.

**Creek** (KM 169.7, mile 106) Notable for a sulfurous smell, and red color from iron oxide in the hills.

**Engineer Creek** (KM 173.9, mile 108) Showing the iron oxide color.

**Engineer Creek Campground** (KM 195.8, mile 121.7) Picnic tables, shelter, fireplaces, toilets. Sapper Hill, above the campground, has unique castellated ridges formed by erosion.

**Bridge** (KM 196, mile 121.9) Over the Ogilvie River. This bridge was built by Canadian Forces engineers as a training exercise. They passed! The Yukon government road maintenance camp is on the north side of the river that parallels the highway for the next 40 KM (25 miles).

**View** (KM 212, mile 132) Castellated mountain ridges.

**Elephant Rock** (KM 226, mile 140) To the right side of the road (northbound). Fishing for grayling in the Ogilvie River. The Dempster now climbs away from the Ogilvie River and approaches the plateau known as Eagle Plains. As you travel across the ridges, you will see seismic cut lines heading across the tundra.

**Airstrip on Road** (KM 329, mile 204.4)

**Eagle Plains Hotel** (KM 363.5, mile 232.3) This oasis on the Dempster is a welcome sight. There is a motel, lounge, restaurant, gas station, and great views of the Richardson Mountains (see page 215).

# HIGHWAY LOG
## *Eagle Plains to Inuvik*
### 368 KM (228.7 miles)—5 hours, 30 minutes

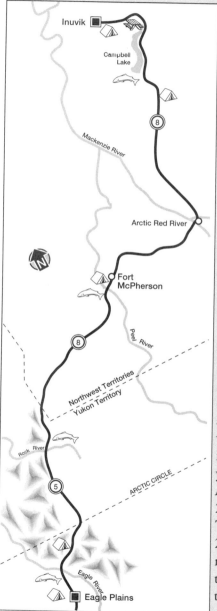

The drive through the Richardson Mountains from Eagle Plains is truly inspiring. From KM 450 (mile 280), the highway is above the tree line, crossing alpine tundra. Small willows, shrubs, and stunted pines are found only along the streams. The color of the tundra ranges from a pastel green in the spring to soft reds and browns in autumn months.

**Eagle River Bridge** (KM 373.5, mile 232) A short sideroad just south of the bridge leads to a picnic site and marker about the "Mad Trapper of Rat River," Albert Johnston, who was killed near here in a shoot-out with Mounties in February 1932. The road climbs through the Richardson Mountains, named for Dr. John Richardson, a member of the Franklin expedition. These unusually smooth and rounded mountains were not glaciated during the last ice age. Erosion over millions of years has shaped the range.

**Airstrip on Road** (KM 394, mile 254.7)

**The Arctic Circle** (KM 410, mile 255) with parking area and signs marking the crossing. You'll want to have your camera ready for this shot, and you may be lucky enough to meet the "Keeper of the Arctic Circle."

**Cornwall River Campground** (KM 450, mile 280)

**Turnout** (KM 468, mile 291) Overnight RV parking is permitted on the wider turnouts.

**Wright Pass** (KM 470, mile 292) Historical marker about Al Wright, the engineer who charted the route of the Dempster Hwy. Yukon/Northwest Territories border (KM 471, mile 293). The time zone changes here to Mountain Time. Set timepieces ahead one hour when going north.

**James Creek Maintenance Camp** (KM 485.2, mile 301.5) Fishing, overnight parking for RVs.

**Wright Pass Summit** (KM 494.6, mile 307.4) The road soon descends to the Peel River Plateau.

**Airstrip on Road** (KM 520.5, mile 323.5) There is a good view of Fort McPherson in the distance, and the Peel River valley. Look for planes as well as scenery.

**Peel River Crossing** (KM 545.5, mile 339) This ferry crossing is a free government service, operating 15 hours daily during summer months. The ferry does not operate after freeze-up but vehicles use an ice bridge after the river freezes. Phone 800-661-0752 for ferry information. The ferry landing is 12.8 KM (8 miles) from Fort McPherson.

**Nutuiluie Campground** (KM 547. 3, mile 340.1) An information center is open daily during summer months.

**Turnoff** (KM 557, mile 346.1) Sideroad to Fort McPherson. This Dene village has two stores, cafés, two gas stations, and shopping for crafts including Kutchin (Loucheux) beadwork and hide clothing.

**Frog Creek** (KM 594.5, mile 346.4) Picnic area on road to north. Fishing for northern pike, grayling.

**Mackenzie River Crossing** (KM 614.7, mile 382) Take the ferry to a landing at Arctic Red River and/or across the river to the Dempster Hwy. landing.

**Arctic Red River** A small Native American settlement with gas and store (limited hours).

**Rengling River** (KM 649.3, mile 403.5) Fishing for grayling.

**Caribou Creek Campground** (KM 692.5, mile 430.4) Picnic site.

**Campbell Lake** (KM 701.5, mile 436) The escarpment ahead is known as a good spot for viewing peregrine falcons.

**Cabin Creek** (KM 716, mile 445) Picnic site, toilets.

**Picnic Area** (KM 719.3, mile 447) Fishing for whitefish and pike. Boat launch with access to Campbell Lake.

**Chuk Park Campground** (KM 730.6, mile 454) At the edge of Inuvik.

# Liard/Mackenzie Loop Drive

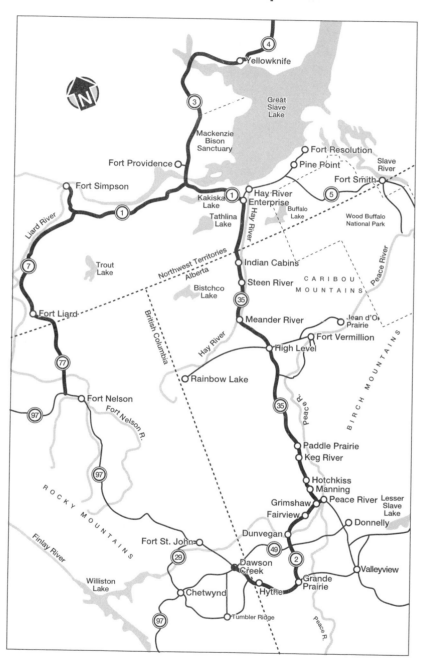

# Liard/Mackenzie Loop Drive

Although this tour of Canada's northland is in neither Alaska nor the Yukon, its northern location and the awesome landscape seen along the routes make it an important consideration for vacation planning. It is offered here—as a bonus—to be savored as a special adventure—which it is.

The tour uses two routes to adventure in the Northwest Territories, and they are organized as a loop drive instead of being shown as two different routes to the north. The logic is that if you drive north, you have to drive south again. Should you wish to drive these highways in a different direction, be my guest! The logs will work for you in either direction.

Let's face it, unless you're devoting your whole summer to traveling the northland, one cannot drive through Alaska and the Canadian Arctic in one trip. Traveling these long distances takes time, and visitors should not spend a lot of money driving thousands of miles without pausing along the way to enjoy the natural attractions. So I urge you to take your time, plan well in advance, and enjoy your tour of this largely undiscovered part of the world.

This loop tour begins with the Liard Highway, a gravel road that runs 393 KM (244 miles) from its junction with the Alaska Highway, just north of the town of Fort Nelson. In British Columbia it is called Route 77, and in the Northwest Territories it is Route 7. The Liard (also called the Fort Simpson Highway) ends at its junction with the Mackenzie Highway, which will then take you west to Fort Simpson, an old Hudson's Bay Company fur trading settlement.

The Liard Highway passes through vast rolling plains of boreal forest and muskeg. You'll see plenty of fireweed along the roadsides, and even more black and white spruce, trembling aspen, and balsam (poplar). The word Liard means "black poplar." Wildlife to be seen along the route includes wood bison, black bear, moose, and many species of birds, including red-tailed hawks and grouse. As with other northern roads in the dry summer, the

Liard (and the Mackenzie) can be quite dusty, and very muddy after a rainfall. The road runs parallel to but not immediately beside the Liard River. The best place to stop for river access is at Blackstone Territorial Park, a campground where the Blackstone joins the Liard (at KM 284, mile 179).

The Mackenzie Highway, named for explorer Alexander Mackenzie, is a long route that crosses the sub-Arctic muskeg, with its western end at Fort Simpson. Leading southeast into Alberta, all the way to Edmonton, it gives travelers access to Yellowknife, the capital city of the Northwest Territories located on the northern shore of Great Slave Lake. This is a drive to be done at leisure. The road is unpaved, and if not dusty it is bound to be somewhat muddy. Ferries are used to cross the wide Mackenzie River at several points, and there is much unusual scenery to experience. The distances are enormous: the route from Fort Simpson to Yellowknife is 632 KM (393 miles). But the trip's rewards are as great as the distance covered.

## Along the Way

**Liard River Valley**   For most of the route between the Alaska and Mackenzie highways, the Liard Highway passes north through the valley of the Liard River. The two-lane paved road leads through boreal forest made up of black spruce (*liard* in French), white spruce, balsam (poplar), and quaking aspen. Few places are available to provide access to the Liard. Blackstone Territorial Park, near the confluence of the Blackstone and Liard rivers, offers river access as well as camping and picnicking facilities.

The first part of the drive will be uneventful, except in the case of recent rains, when the road will be muddy. Otherwise, flying dust will be your one concern. Kilometer-posts are found in both the British Columbia and Northwest Territories parts of the drive. The first river crossing is over the Fort Nelson River, 42.5 KM (26.4 miles) from the Alaska Highway junction. This is the largest Bailey bridge in the world. The second major crossing is at KM 133.2 (mile 82.8), where the Petitot River offers fishing and a canoe route to the town of Fort Liard. Here the Petitot (locally called the Black) joins the Liard.

A sideroad leads 6.4 KM (4 miles) to Fort Liard, with gas available to the junction. This Native American community takes advantage of its position along the route and its closeness to Nahanni National Park, focusing on tourism for its economic benefit. The fishing is excellent (pike, goldeneye, pickerel, grayling), and air charters fly visitors to Virginia Falls in the national park.

**Nahanni National Park and Fort Simpson**   The huge wild park lies west of Fort Liard and south of Fort Simpson. There is no road into the park, and visitors must charter a flight from Deh Cho Air in Fort Liard, from Blackstone Aviation on the Liard Highway at the Blackstone River, or in Fort Simpson.

This town is another former Hudson's Bay Company post, situated on the wide Mackenzie River. This grand river is still provides the major means of transportation for the entire region, with summer tugs and barges transporting a year's worth of supplies from Hay River to the river's mouth on the Arctic Ocean. Dating from 1804, this town is home to the Slavey people, who offer their crafts and art at several stores. Services include a hotel, motel, several restaurants, gas stations, grocery stores, department and hardware stores, a bank, and a laundry. A boat launch is located at the government wharf, offering access to the Mackenzie.

**Yellowknife and Great Slave Lake**   The Mackenzie Highway leads in a general west-to-east direction, while the Yellowknife Highway runs north from the Mackenzie Highway, ending in Yellowknife. This small city, on the shore of Great Slave Lake, is the administrative center for the Northwest Territories, a vast region that spans the top of Canada. It is largely occupied by Native Americans (now called Dene) and Inuit (formerly called Eskimo). Yellowknife's stability and size results from its civil service activity, but tourism plays a large role in its summer activity.

# HIGHWAY LOG
## *Alaska Highway to Fort Simpson*
### 457 KM (284 miles)—7 hours, 30 minutes

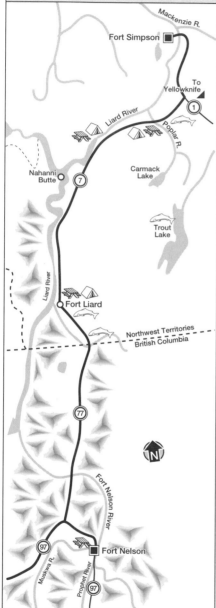

The Liard Highway runs through the Liard River Valley, linking the Alaska Hwy. near Fort Nelson to the Mackenzie Hwy., 64 KM (39.8 miles) south of Fort Simpson. This is a good summer route, with gas available only at Fort Liard, and at the Mackenzie Hwy. junction.

The two-lane gravel road begins in a mixed forest and moves above the tree line into muskeg. There are facilities for travelers in Fort Liard and at the Mackenzie Highway junction. We then continue on a portion of the Mackenzie Highway to Fort Simpson. There is a ferry crossing near Fort Simpson.

**Junction–Alaska Highway (Hwy. 97) and Liard Highway (Hwy. 77)** (27 KM, 16.5 miles) North of Fort Nelson.

**Picnic Area** (KM 10.2, mile 6.3) Beside Beaver Lake, via a short sideroad. Tables, firewood, toilet, trail to creek and dock.

**Fort Nelson River** (KM 42.5, mile 26.4) The bridge here is a single-lane crossing and it's the longest Bailey bridge in the world.

**Picnic Area** At north end of bridge.

**Tsinhia Creek** (KM 64, mile 39.7) Spring fishing for grayling.

**Tsinhia Lake Sideroad** Rough road leads 3 KM (1.8 miles) to the lake. Not for trailers or long RVs.

**Maxhamish Lake Sideroad** (KM 115, mile 71.5) Very rough road for 13 KM (8 miles)—for four-wheel-drive vehicles only.

**Beaver Pond** (KM 119, mile 74) Beaver and other wildlife may be seen where a small creek empties into Emile Creek (to the east).

**Petitot Bridge** (KM 133.2, mile 82.8) Canoe launch site and good fishing for pickerel, pike, and grayling.

**B.C./Northwest Territories Border** (KM 136.8, mile 85) Going north, set watches ahead one hour to Mountain time.

**Junction–Fort Liard Road** (KM 174.8, mile 108.6) The sideroad leads 6.5 KM (4 miles) to the small town (see page 228). Gas available at the junction. Fort Liard Hotel and stores in town. Campground with picnic tables, toilets, and river access off the sideroad.

**Muskeg River** (KM 182.4, mile 113.3) Turnoff at north end of the bridge. Fishing for pike and pickerel plus freshwater clamming and swimming.

**Turnout** (KM 214, mile 133) With a good view of nearby mountains to the west of road.

**Turnout** (KM 222, mile 136.7) A short trail, an old access road, leads to the Liard River. Wildlife in the area includes wood bison.

**Road to Liard River** (KM 227, mile 141.2) A rough road to Whissel Landing.

**Winter Road** (KM 267, mile 165.9) To Nahanni Butte, to the west. No summer access.

**Upper Blackstone River** (KM 283.7, mile 176.3) Picnic site on the river with tables and firewood.

**Blackstone Territorial Park** (KM 288.3, mile 179.1) Campground with tables, fireplaces, wood, toilets, and drinking water. The dock is unusable during spring months. Visitor center open May to September.

**Lindberg Landing** (KM 291.2, mile 180.9) A rustic B & B home.

**Airstrip on Road** (KM 310.3, mile 192.8) Watch for planes.

**Road to the Liard River** (KM 358.5, mile 222.8) Leads west for 6.4 KM (4 miles), for four-wheel-drive vehicles. Beach, bird-watching, and other wildlife may be seen.

**Junction–Mackenzie Highway (Hwy. 1)** (KM 393.4, mile 244.5). Turn left (north) on Hwy. 1 for Fort Simpson. Gas, store at junction. For Yellowknife, turn south.

**Ferry Crossing** Free ferry across the Liard River, operates daily May to October, from 8 A.M. to 11.30 P.M. An overnight campground is near the ferry crossing with tables, fireplaces, and toilets.

**Fort Simpson** (KM 457.4, mile 184.2) Town with motels, cafés, stores, gas, propane, and campground.

# HIGHWAY LOG
## Fort Simpson to Yellowknife
631 KM (392 miles)—8 hours

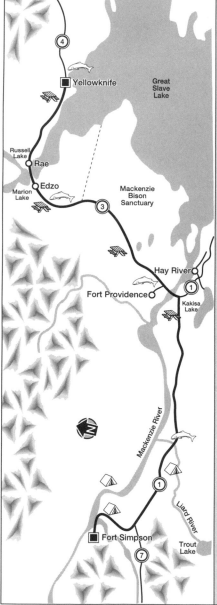

This route makes a very long day on gravel roads with two ferry crossings. We suggest that you take two days to travel from Fort Simpson to Yellowknife, stopping overnight in Fort Providence or a campground.

**Fort Simpson** Town with gas, hotels, motels, stores, and Nahanni National Park headquarters and info center.

**Junction–Mackenzie Highway** (KM 3.8, mile 2.3). Turn left (south) for Yellowknife and Hay River.

**Ferry Crossing** Over the Liard River. Operates daily (no charge) May through October. An ice bridge services light vehicles from late November, with heavy vehicles allowed after full freeze-up.

**Overnight Campground** Near ferry landing.

**Turnout** (KM 43.1, mile 26.7) Emergency cabin and toilet.

**Junction–Liard Highway** For Fort Liard and Fort Nelson, turn right (west). We continue on the Mackenzie Hwy. to Yellowknife.

**Turnout** (KM 96.5, mile 60) Emergency cabin and toilet.

**Turnout** (KM 145, mile 90.1) Emergency cabin and toilet.

**Whittaker Falls Territorial Park** (KM 152, mile 94.5) with campground overlooking Trout River,

tables, firewood, toilets, and string fishing for grayling. Another campground is located at the east end of the Trout River Bridge.
**Turnout** (KM 198.3, mile 123.2) Emergency cabin.
**Passing Zone** (KM 215.8, mile 134.1)
**Turnout** (KM 244.7, mile 152) Emergency cabin and toilet.
**Junction–Highway 3** (KM 289, mile 179.5) To Yellowknife, turn left.
**Picnic Area** At Dory Point (KM 310.2, mile 192.7) Tables, kitchen shelter.
**Ferry Crossing** (KM 313.3, mile 194.7) A free ferry crosses the Mackenzie River, operating from May to November from 6 A.M. to midnight. For ferry information phone Zenith 2010 or (403) 873-7799.
**Highway Services** (KM 320.2, mile 199) Motel, gas, café, phone.
**Junction–Road to Fort Providence** This small town is 4.5 KM (2.8 miles) off the hwy., with gas, motels, café, and store. Boat rentals and river fishing nearby. A territorial campground is one KM (0.6 mile) west of the junction on the access road (tables, kitchen shelter, toilets, and dump station).
**Mackenzie Wood Bison Sanctuary** (KM 324.6, mile 195.5) The wood bison are not always seen but wildlife is plentiful, including grouse, ptarmigan, and sandhill cranes.
**Passing Zone** Look for passing zones over the next 242 KM (150 miles).

**Turnout** (KM 357.1, mile 221.9) To the east of the road.
**Passing Zone** (KM 389.8)
**Picnic Area by Chan Lake** (KM 410.6, mile 255.1) Tables, shelter, fireplaces, and wood.
**Passing Zone** (KM 443.7, mile 275.5)
**Turnout** (KM 450, mile 279.6) To the east of the road.
**Passing Zone** (KM 465.7, mile 289.4)
**Turnout** (KM 497.8, mile 309.3) To the east of the road.
**Turnout** (KM 514.7, mile 319.8) To the east of the road.
**Mosquito Creek Bridge** (KM 516.3, mile 320.8) Spring fishing for pickerel and whitefish.
**Picnic Area** (KM 521, mile 323.7) Tables, shelter, fireplaces, wood, toilets. Bears may be present, beware!
**Junction–Road to Edzo** (KM 528, mile 328)
**Junction–Road to Rae** (KM 534, mile 331.8) Rae has visitor services, 11.2 KM (7 miles) from the hwy. Gas, store, café, phones.
**Fred Henne Recreational Park** (KM 627, mile 389.6) Campground and picnic area on Long Lake, just west of Yellowknife.
**Old Airport Road** Access to Yellowknife. There is a picnic area near a commemorative plaque, and historic Bristol aircraft.
**Yellowknife** (KM 631, mile 392) Northwest Territories' capital city with gas, hotels, motels, restaurants, and stores.

# HIGHWAY LOG
## Yellowknife to Hay River
483 KM (300 miles) 8 hours

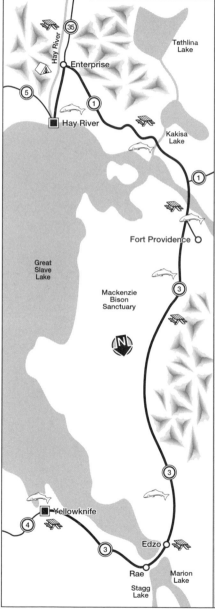

The first 342 KM (212.6 miles) retraces the Yellowknife Highway to its junction with the Mackenzie Highway (Hwy. 1). The trip then proceeds southeast along the Mackenzie Highway to Enterprise and on to Hay River.

As with other gravel roads in the north, dust can be a problem. Travelers frequently meet highway crews grading the roads and applying dust treatments. We have marked passing zones that should be dust-free. For information on road conditions, phone Zenith 2018 placed through the operator.

There is good fishing along this part of the circle route: at the Mosquito Creek Bridge at KM 114.7; at Fort Providence where boats and guides are available; and at other fishing spots along the Mackenzie Highway, including the Kakisa River Bridge and nearby in Kakisa Lake.

**Yellowknife** The drive begins in downtown Yellowknife, via Airport Road.
**Junction–Yellowknife Highway** (KM 1.3, mile 0.8) Nearby is a picnic park and a commemorative site with a historic Wardair Bristol aircraft on display.

**Fred Henne Recreational Park** (KM 4, mile 2.2) Campground and picnic park.

**Stagg River Bridge** (KM 84.8, mile 52.7)

**Junction–Road to Rae** (KM 97, mile 60.3) The sideroad leads 11.2 KM (7 miles) to gas, stores, a café, and phones.

**Junction–Road to Edzo** (KM 103, mile 64) To small Native American village, no services.

**North Arm Territorial Park** (KM 110, mile 68.3) Tables, campsites, shelter, fireplaces, wood, and toilets.

**Mosquito Creek Bridge** (KM 114.7, mile 71.2) Fishing for whitefish and pickerel.

**Junction–Road to Fort Providence** (KM 310.4, mile 192.9) A territorial campground is 1 KM (0.6 miles) west of the hwy. Small town has services including motels, gas, store, and boat rentals. Fishing guides are available in town.

**Highway Services** (KM 310.8, mile 193) Motel, gas, restaurant, phone.

**Ferry Crossing** Free ferry across the Mackenzie River, operated daily May to November from 6 A.M. to midnight. For ferry information phone Zenith 2010 with operator assistance or (403) 873-7799.

**Picnic Area** (KM 320.8, mile 199.3) At Dory Point. Tables with shelter.

**Junction–Mackenzie Highway** (Hwy. 1) (KM 342, mile 212.5) Turn left (east) for Hay River. Turn right (west) for Fort Simpson and the Liard Hwy.

**Highway Services** (KM 346.4, mile 215) Gas and café.

**Kakisa River Bridge** Picnic park with tables, fireplaces, and wood at KM 359.8 (mile 223.6). A hiking trail leads to Lady Evelyn Falls from an access road that leads south for 7.2 KM (4.5 miles). A campground offers picnic tables, fireplaces, wood, and shelter.

**Picnic Area and Fire Tower** (KM 400.2, mile 248.7) Reached by an access road. A trail leads to an ancient coral reef with panoramic views of the surrounding area including Great Slave Lake and the Mackenzie River.

**Turnout** (KM 408.9, mile 254.1) View of McNalley Creek Falls.

**Enterprise** (KM 408.9, mile 254.1) A small village at the junction of the road to Hay River (Hwy. 2). There is gas, a café, motel, and phone at the junction. Turn left (north) for Hay River.

**Campground and RV Park** (KM 460.7, mile 286.3) Private.

**Junction–Highway 5** (KM 479.1, mile 297.7) To Fort Smith.

**Hay River** (482.8, mile 300) Town with gas, hotels, motels, cafés, stores.

# HIGHWAY LOG
## Hay River to High Level (Alberta)
313 KM (195 miles)—4 hours, 30 minutes

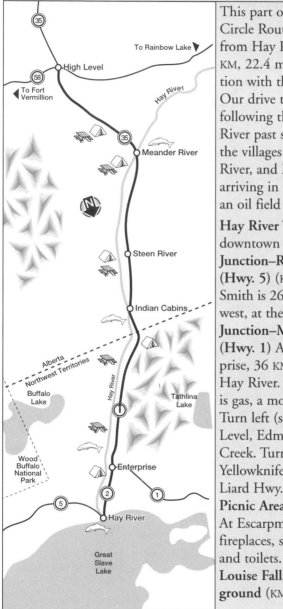

This part of the Liard/Mackenzie Circle Route retraces the road from Hay River to Enterprise (36 KM, 22.4 miles), reaching the junction with the Mackenzie Highway. Our drive then heads southwest, following the route of the Hay River past several waterfalls and the villages of Indian Cabins, Steen River, and Meander River, before arriving in High Level, Alberta—an oil field and agricultural town.

**Hay River** The drive begins in downtown Hay River.

**Junction–Road to Fort Smith (Hwy. 5)** (KM 5.7, mile 3.6) Fort Smith is 267 KM (166 miles) southwest, at the end of the highway.

**Junction–Mackenzie Highway (Hwy. 1)** At the village of Enterprise, 36 KM (22.4 miles) from Hay River. At the junction there is gas, a motel, café, and phone. Turn left (southwest) for High Level, Edmonton, and Dawson Creek. Turn right (northwest) for Yellowknife, Fort Simpson, and the Liard Hwy.

**Picnic Area** (KM 42.3, mile 26.3) At Escarpment Creek, with tables, fireplaces, shelter, drinking water, and toilets.

**Louise Falls Territorial Campground** (KM 44.9, mile 27.9)

Campsites, picnic tables, shelters, toilets, fireplaces, wood, and drinking water. Trails lead to Louise Falls and Alexandra Falls. **Alexandra Falls** (KM 47.2, mile 29.3) A trail leads from the parking area to the viewpoint above the falls. Here the Hay River plunges 33 meters (109 feet). **Grumbler Rapids** (KM 79.9, mile 49.6) To the east of the highway. During low-water periods in the summer and fall months, the rapids make what some think is a "grumbling" sound. **Reindeer Creek** (KM 116.9, mile 72.6) **Campground** (KM 119.8, mile 74.4) Campsites, a picnic area with tables, shelter, drinking water, canoe launching area, and dump station. **Northwest Territories/Alberta Border** (KM 119.8, mile 74.4) The visitor center is open from May 15th to September 15th for issuing fishing licenses and camping permits. Maps and brochures are also available here with information on fishing and road conditions. The highway now becomes Alberta Route 35. **Indian Cabins** (KM 135.5, mile 84) Small village to the east, with gas, store, and phone, an historic log church and spirit cemetery. The original "Indian Cabins" have disappeared.

**Steen River** (KM 163.3, mile 101.5) Village to the east. Gas, café, and phone. **Steen River Campground** (KM 169.1, mile 105.1) Picnic tables, shelter, fireplaces, wood, toilets and drinking water. **Junction–Road to Zama** (KM 225.4, mile 140) This access road leads 63 KM (39 miles) to a pipeline and oil field village. **Railway Bridge** (KM 226.3, 140 miles) A view of the bridge to the east. **Meander River Campground** (KM 232.4, mile 144.4) Picnic tables, shelter, fireplaces, wood, drinking water, and toilets. **Meander River** (KM 239.6, mile 148.9) Village with gas, store, and phone. **Hutch Lake Campground** (KM 277, mile 172) With picnic tables, fireplaces, toilets, and trail to the lake. **High Level Golf Club** (KM 309, mile 192) Nine holes. **Junction–Highway 58** (KM 312.5, mile 194.2) Hwy. 58 leads east toward Jean D'or Prairie and to Fort Vermilion. **High Level** (KM 313.2, mile 194.6) This prairie town has hotels, motels, gas stations, stores, and cafés. A private campground is located at the south edge of town. The municipal campground is located on Hwy. 58, east of the downtown area.

# HIGHWAY LOG
## High Level to Dawson Creek
480 KM (298 miles)—6 hours

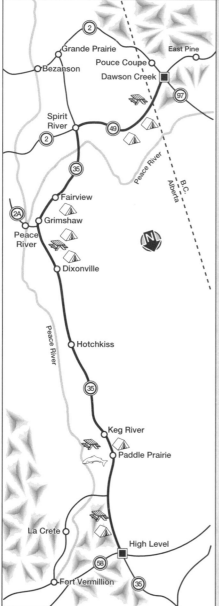

**High Level** An agricultural center with hotels, motels, gas, cafés, campgrounds, and stores.

**Junction–Highway 58** (KM 0, mile 0) In High Level, leading east to Jean D'or Prairie and west to Fort Vermilion (78 km, 48.5 miles).

**Junction–Highway 697** (KM 60.8, mile 37.8) Leads east to the small town of La Crete (85 km, 53 miles) and on to Fort Vermilion (125 km, 78 miles).

**Boyer River Provincial Campground** (KM 61.9, mile 38.4) To the east, with picnic tables, shelter, fire pits, wood, toilets, and drinking water.

**Paddle Prairie** (KM 71.6, mile 44.5) Small village of the Metis.

**Keg River** (KM 98.5, mile 61.2) Small community just north of the Keg River has gas, a café, cabins, and phone.

**Junction–Sideroad to Carcajou** (KM 101, mile 62.8) This gravel road leads 38 km (24 miles) to a Native American village on the Peace River.

**Twin Lakes Campground** (KM 137, mile 85) To the east of the road with picnic tables, shelter, fireplaces, firewood, drinking water, toilets, beach, and boat launch (no motors permitted). Good fishing for rainbow trout.

**Twin Lakes Lodge** (KM 137, mile 85) To the east of the road with accommodations, food, gas, and phone.

**Notikewin Provincial Park** Junction at KM 159.8 (mile 99.3) Off the hwy., 30 KM (18.6 miles) east via Hwy. 692. Camping, picnic areas, toilets, boat launch, and fishing.

**Hotchkiss** (KM 180.7, mile 112) Small community with gas, café, phone, nine-hole golf course, and store. Hotchkiss Provincial Park is located to the east of the hwy. one mile south of town, with camping, picnic tables, shelter, fire pits, fishing, and toilets.

**Manning** (KM 198, mile 123) Town with gas, restaurants, motels, drug store, golf course, and Battle River Pioneer Museum.

**Grimshaw Provincial Campsite** (KM 277, mile 172) To the west of the road with picnic tables, shelter, fire pits, wood, toilets, and drinking water. Free camping.

**Queen Elizabeth Provincial Park** (KM 277.5, mile 172.4) Found 5 KM west, on Lac Cardinal, with campsites, picnic tables, and swimming.

**Dixonville** (KM 239, mile 148.5) Small village with gas station. Sulphur Lake Provincial Campground is located 55 km (34 miles) west of town on Road 689 (gravel).

**Grimshaw** (KM 279.4, mile 173.6) Town with full visitor services.

"Mile 0" of the Mackenzie Hwy. Just south of town, we turn onto Hwy. 2, leading southwest. Dawson Creek is 195 KM (120 miles) from Grimshaw.

**Fairview** (KM 337, mile 209.6) Town located 58 KM (36 miles) west of Grimshaw. Gas, cafés, store, and campground.

**Provincial Campground** (KM 349.4, mile 217) Just north of the Peace River Bridge, with picnic tables, fire pits, toilets, and drinking water.

**Rycroft** (KM 369.4, mile 229.5) Small town with gas, café, store. We turn onto Hwy. 49 in Spirit River, and head west toward Dawson Creek.

**Spirit River** (377.4, mile 234.5) Village with gas, café, store, campground.

**Moonshine Lake Provincial Park** (KM 404.4, mile 251.3) Camping, reached by Road 725 leading north from the hwy. Picnic tables, fire pits, shelter, wood, and drinking water.

**Alberta/B.C. Border** (KM 457.4, mile 284.2)

**Dawson Creek** (KM 480, mile 298) The start of the Alaska Hwy., and a town with full visitor services. For Prince George and Vancouver, B.C., take Hwy. 97 south (the Hart Hwy.). For Edmonton, Alberta, take Hwy. 2 southeast, toward Grande Prairie.

# Yukon
## *Destinations*

## Dawson City

In 1897, a steamer with Klondike prospectors aboard landed in Seattle. The ship carried almost three tons of gold and word of the Klondike spread immediately to all corners of the globe.

Thousands of adventurers tried to reach the junction of the Klondike and Yukon rivers during the next three years. They came from around the world—driven by a passion for gold and the untold riches that the Klondike promised. But the real challenge was not mining the gold; it was getting to Dawson City. Most of the adventurers left from Seattle and made their way north by steamship. Some journeyed all the way to Dawson on the water: by steamer to the mouth of the Yukon on the Bering Sea, and on smaller boats up the river to the Klondike. Most began their overland journey in Skagway, Alaska. Here they were met by the most incredible collection of thugs and con men ever assembled in one place. Those who escaped the clutches of Skagway had to climb the ice steps of the Chilkoot Pass over and over again, carrying a ton of supplies and crossing into Canada, where they had to build boats and rafts to take them down the Yukon River system, passing through treacherous rapids and swift canyons, to Dawson City.

Those who made it to Dawson found the prime spots on the creeks already claimed. Many turned around and returned home. Some stayed to take advantage of the Klondike Gold Rush by setting up businesses, hotels, restaurants, theaters, dance halls, and all of the other amenities which made Dawson known as the

"Paris of the North" during the four years when 30,000 people lived in the frontier city.

Dawson City was the largest city north of San Francisco. The successful gold miners spent fortunes on grand living in the hotels, dance halls, saloons, and other establishments, including those that offered the services of young ladies who were specially imported to the gold rush capital.

Most accouterments of civilization were available in Dawson, such as local daily newspapers. Arizona Charlie Meadows built the Palace Grand Theatre, which offered high-class entertainment by world famous artists. "Fresh" eggs were rafted down the Yukon. Champagne flowed in the Eldorado Hotel and boatloads of whiskey arrived before freeze-up each year.

By 1903, more than $96 million in gold had been taken out of the creeks. Ten years after the discovery of gold, the rush was over. There were a few millionaires and many who left with unfulfilled dreams.

The Klondike Gold Rush is remembered as the greatest adventure of them all. It was a brief, exciting period of history that continues to live through memory and existing reminders of the gold rush period in Dawson City, Whitehorse, Skagway, and places in between.

The history of the Yukon since the end of the Klondike Gold Rush in 1903 is a story of ups and downs, decline and revival. The miners of Dawson City continued to take gold out of the Klondike gold field, switching to hydraulic mining, which washed earth down from the hillsides. Then huge dredges traveled along the creek beds, sweeping all in their paths, extracting what gold remained after the gold rush was over. These dredges, operated mainly by the Consolidated Gold Company, created the long tailing piles that remain today. Gold dredging was finally concluded in the 1960s when gold prices dropped and dredging became uneconomical. The population of Dawson City declined over the years. By 1960, there were 350 permanent residents.

Other kinds of minerals supported the economy of the Yukon. Silver mines at Elsa, near Mayo, were an important factor. Later, the lead-zinc mine at Faro added to the importance of Whitehorse as the commercial center of the Yukon.

However, it was the Second World War that brought new people and money to the Yukon with the construction of the Alaska Highway in 1942. Thousands of army engineers and construction workers flooded through the Yukon to build and maintain the highway as a military roadway to Alaska. Whitehorse quickly eclipsed Dawson City as the Yukon's major city, and the Yukon territorial government moved there in 1953. Whitehorse became the trading and transportation center of the territory, with Canadian army and air force bases and the train connection with Skagway, Alaska. While the military bases are no longer there, Whitehorse has expanded over the years and is now a modern, bustling commercial and government center.

Following the end of the war, the Alaska Highway was opened for public traffic and brought the first highway tourists to the Yukon. By the early 1960s, tourism had become a growing focus for Yukoners. The Yukon and Canadian governments realized that Dawson City provided a priceless heritage that should be preserved. With its decline in population, Dawson's original buildings had been abandoned and left to deteriorate. While some buildings remained from the gold rush era, several fires had swept through the community, and quick action was required to preserve the surviving structures.

The Palace Grand Theatre was restored to its original glory in 1962. The paddle-wheeler SS *Keno* was moved down the river from Whitehorse to become a historical museum on the banks of the Yukon. Dawson was declared a National Historic Site and the National Parks Service was placed in charge of the restoration of significant Dawson buildings and gold mining sites. Virtually the whole town and several places outside of Dawson are historic sites, and the work continues today.

Your car or RV will be useful in getting around the historic gold rush areas close to Dawson City. Aside from the downtown area, the most fascinating sights are slightly out of town, around Bonanza, Hunker, and Bear creeks. These old mining camps and the large dredge on Bonanza Creek (where it all began) take you back to the "Days of '98" and the most incredible and last great gold rush on earth.

The best place to go, as soon as you arrive, is the Visitor Information Centre on Front Street. This office has the answers for all of the questions you may have, from hotel rates to guided tours of the gold fields and the departure times of the daily river cruises. Here you'll find a useful map of the downtown area.

There are guided walking tours leaving from the information center each day. Other guided tours take you by mini-bus to the historic gold fields. Panning for gold (helped by a bit of friendly cheating) is a popular activity.

One of several walking trails leads to the old Native American community of Moosehide, downstream from Dawson. Should you visit this abandoned village, please respect private property. Another trail leads up the Midnight Dome for spectacular views of Dawson City, the Yukon Valley, and the gold fields.

Dawson City is a one-of-a-kind experience. Located 286 KM (165 miles) south of the Arctic Circle at the confluence of the Klondike and Yukon rivers, Dawson remains a living reminder of the greatest gold rush of all time: the 1898 Klondike Stampede.

For an immersion in history, Dawson (its official name) has no equal with its dusty, sometimes muddy streets, boardwalks, sagging gold rush–era buildings, restored national historic sites, authentic 1890s gambling casino, working gold claims on the historic creeks, and the more recently constructed hotels, stores, and restaurants with false fronts. Over the past 30 years, Dawson City has been carefully preserved and restored and is, for our money, the outstanding tourist destination of the north. To catch the full excitement and romance of Dawson City, you should read Pierre

Berton's book *Klondike*, published by McLelland and Stewart, the definitive book on the Klondike Gold Rush. It's available at bookstores in Dawson and Whitehorse and throughout the U.S. and Canada.

As viewed from the Midnight Dome—the round mountain which rises behind Dawson City—the townsite is a large, orderly grid. It was surveyed by William Ogilvie to accommodate the 30,000 people who lived here during the short gold rush period. Today, 1,600 people live in or near Dawson City, some of them mining for gold more than 90 years after the discovery. Dawson City was declared a national historic site in the early 1960s and significant buildings and gold mining sites have been restored. These locations are open for public viewing from June through mid-September. Accommodations and food are expensive in Dawson City, and visitors should plan ahead for the higher-than-average costs of a stay in Dawson.

## Practical Information

The city's Visitor's Reception Centre is operated by the Klondike Visitors Association, a community group. The center is located at Front and King streets, downtown. This building is a re-creation of an old Northern Commercial Company store. This is the location for complete information on the Klondike area, and the starting point for walking tours. The office is open daily from mid-May to mid-September. For advance information, call (403) 993-5566.

The Dempster Highway and Northwest Territories Information Centre is found in the British Yukon Navigation (B.Y.N.) Building, across Front Street from the town visitor center. The building was the former home of the British Yukon Navigation Company. The infocentre is open daily from 9 A.M. to 9 P.M. from June to September.

Dawson City Airport is located south of town on the Klondike Highway. The government ferry crosses the Yukon River from Front Street, connecting with the Top of the World

Highway. This is a free ferry, operating daily through the summer months. The highway is closed after snow falls.

## Things to See and Do

A minimum stay of two days is necessary to capture the full Dawson experience. After coming this far, visitors should relax and stay long enough to see the important sites and, especially, to soak up the incredible historical scene that Dawson City provides.

A walking tour through the downtown area leaves the town Infocentre at 10:30 A.M., 1 P.M., and 4:30 P.M. Guided mini-bus tours of the city and the gold fields are available from Gold City Tours, (403) 993-5175. Tours can include gold panning on an original gold rush claim site.

Parks Canada, the national parks service, has restored several historic sites including: Harrington's Store, where an excellent photography exhibit shows the work of early photographers who worked here during the gold rush; the Robert W. Service Cabin on 8th Avenue, home of the "Bard of the Yukon," the poet who wrote the classics "The Cremation of Sam McGee" and "The Shooting of Dan McGrew"; SS *Keno*, the river steamer on the riverfront, one of more than 200 sternwheelers that plied the Yukon River until the 1950s, and the last to sail down the river from Whitehorse; the Bear Creek Gold Camp, outside of town, with gold-mining buildings that provided support for gold dredging by the Yukon Consolidated Gold Company; the 1901 Post Office, still operating at 3rd Avenue and King Street. "Gaslight Follies" is performed nightly (except Tuesday) in the restored Palace Grand Theatre on King Street.

Diamond Tooth Gertie's celebrates its coup of being the first modern licensed gambling casino in Canada, with blackjack, roulette, and crown and anchor at the tables plus three floor shows a night by Gertie and the cancan dancers.

The Gold Room is a historic memento of the Klondike Gold Rush, located on the second floor of the original Bank of Commerce building on the waterfront. Miners brought their pokes to be weighed in the gold room, which is now open daily from 10 A.M. to 6 P.M. during the summer.

The Dawson City Museum is located in the former Territorial Administration Building on 5th Avenue, featuring many exhibits on the history of the Klondike. Silent films of the period, unearthed during a restoration project in 1978, are shown in the museum, along with a slide-audio program on the Dempster Highway. There's a coffee and gift shop. The museum is open daily, 10 A.M. to 6 P.M., from early June through Labor Day.

Jack London's Cabin is an interpretive center devoted to the author of *Call of the Wild* and other classics of the north. The cabin was moved to Dawson City from a more southerly location, and contains exhibits and readings from London's works.

If you're shopping for moccasins, mukluks, beadwork, parkas, and other handmade goods, go to Yukon Native Products, at Front and Princess. This is a cooperative of Native American groups and artisans from around the Yukon.

### Klondike Outdoors

Claim 33 is an original Bonanza Creek claim, open to the public for gold panning. Gold is guaranteed! (403) 993-5303. Guggieville, a combination RV park and gold rush theme park, offers panning on the original Guggenheim family mining camp at the junction of Bonanza Creek Road and the Klondike Highway. The sand here is also salted, to guarantee you a pay day. For information call (403) 993-5008.

Hunker Creek is the site of Klondike International Gold Mining Tours, which are offered 10 KM (6.5 miles) up Hunker Creek Road. Visitors work the gravel with shovels, wheelbarrows, shaker boxes, and pans, (403) 993-5428.

Dredge #4: This huge dredge is 13 KM (8 miles) south of Dawson City on Bonanza Creek Road (off the Klondike Hwy.). These dredges floated in their own ponds, scooping up creek gravel and gold. This is the largest wooden-hulled dredge ever built. Open daily, 9 A.M. to 5 P.M.

The Yukon River provides opportunities for cruising and sightseeing. The *Yukon Queen*, operated by Westmark Tours, takes tourists for cruises on the Yukon River, covering the 174 KM (108 miles) from Dawson to Eagle, Alaska. Departure time is 8 A.M. The cruise includes two meals and a stop in Eagle. Check at the tour desk in the Westmark Inn for times and cost. For advance information call (403) 993-5599.

Yukon Lou, a small river boat, features a 1.5-hour cruise down the Yukon, passing a steamboat graveyard, the Native American community of Moosehide, and other historic sites. The luncheon cruise to a salmon barbecue on "Pleasure Island" departs daily at 1 P.M. Dinner cruises are offered and reservations are required. For information call (403) 993-5482 or drop into the Birch Cabin Gift Shop on Front Street.

Midnight Dome is the hill that overlooks Dawson City and the gold creeks. You can drive to the top of the Dome to walk around it, viewing the historic landscape. A midnight celebration is held on the Dome by locals on June 21st, when the sun pops behind the tops of the Ogilvie Mountains for just a few seconds. It's a thrilling sight available on several evenings each June. The original RCMP cemetery is along this road.

As with other areas of the Yukon, the Klondike region offers many outdoor activities, including canoeing, fishing, and hunting. Outfitters in Whitehorse offer canoe trips down the Yukon River to Dawson. The North Klondike River provides good canoe tripping, with the Dempster Highway available to take you to a launching point. For hunting possibilities, contact a local guide. The town information center has names of registered hunting and fishing guides. Winter provides other possibilities for outdoor recreation. The most exciting cold-weather activity is dogsledding. Excursions are available from Dawson through Yukon Dog Voyageurs, (403) 993-5256. While the daytime temperatures may be in the frigid range, accommodations in Dawson hotels and cabins along the way provide creature comforts. These dogsled trips operate from November through March.

## Where to Eat

The best places to eat in Dawson City are the dining rooms and restaurants of the half-dozen downtown hotels. My favorite is the Jack London Grill and Sourdough Saloon in the **Downtown Hotel** at 2nd and Queen. This modern, comfortable room serves a variety of seafood and meat dishes, and the best Caesar salad I've had in years, made at the table like they used to do in the worry-free days when a fresh egg was an essential ingredient.

The **Westmark Inn**, at 5th and Harper, is a summer operation with dining room and lounge. The specialty here is what the Westmark calls the "Famous Klondike Barbecue." **Klondike Kate's Restaurant** is part of a cabin operation at 3rd Avenue and King Street, with three meals a day.

**Marinas** is a small restaurant on 5th Avenue, across the road from the Westmark Inn. With inexpensive meals including fresh pizza, soups, salads, and comfort foods like lasagna, this is a popular place with local residents and tourists alike.

For those planning to picnic or eat at their campsite, there's a supermarket on Front Street, with ice and camping supplies. **Smiley's Ice Cream and Deli** (Front Street) has a selection of deli meats and cheese, and provides lunches made to order.

# Dempster Country

Before the arrival of European fur traders and explorers, the Dempster Highway region north of Dawson City was inhabited by Kutchin people, part of the Athabaskan family. There were about 1,500 Kutchin, spread throughout the Porcupine, Arctic Red, and Peel river valleys. They hunted caribou and moose and fished in the rivers to provide their winter food. Europeans came to this harsh country with the fur trade and established Fort McPherson as a Hudson's Bay Company outpost. With the traders came the Northwest Mounted Police.

The Mounties sent a yearly dogsled patrol along the trail between Dawson and Fort McPherson. In 1911, four men and fifteen dogs set out for the winter patrol from Fort McPherson, to be swallowed up by the bitter cold, deep snow, and raging winds. After enduring 53 days of hardship on the trail, the members of the "Lost Patrol" were found dead only 40 kilometers from their starting point.

After the Klondike Gold Rush, prospectors looked for pay dirt in the Ogilvie Mountains, but weather and travel difficulties hampered prospecting. In the 1950s a potential for oil was discovered on the Eagle Plains, and the first exploration well was dug in 1954. Prime Minister John Diefenbaker's government (1957) developed a policy of "roads to resources" as part of its northern vision. Surveying of the road through the Ogilvies to the Eagle Plains was begun in 1958. By 1961, 116 kilometers (72 miles) of roadway had been constructed, but work was halted because of a poor showing in the oil exploration. Construction did not resume for 10 years until oil was discovered in the Beaufort Sea and an all-weather road was required to service exploration there. The Dempster Highway was opened to the public in 1979.

The Dempster drive is unforgettable, for its crossing of the mountain ranges, for the alpine tundra on Eagle Plains, the wildlife-filled marshes of the Mackenzie Delta, and the crossing of the Arctic Circle.

### North to Eagle Plains

The southern part of the region is the valley of the North Klondike River, which flows out of the Ogilvie Range. Within a few miles, the road meets the tree line, and Arctic tundra landscape is seen from here to the end of the highway, with some exceptions when the road dips into a few valleys.

The highway crosses the southern Ogilvies, and then the northern Ogilvies, reaching black spruce tundra with the stunted spruce clinging drunkenly to the surface of the tundra.

### Eagle Plains and Richardson Mountains

Eagle Plains is the hilly region that rolls between the Ogilvie and Richardson mountain ranges. The Dempster follows the high ridges of the land, with dramatic views of the expanse of sub-alpine tundra. In several places along the road, the scrubby trees lean in all directions, caused by frost heaving in the permafrost tundra. The Eagle Plains Hotel at KM 364 (mile 226) is a unique, self-contained oasis on a high ridge just 39 KM (24 miles) south of the Arctic Circle. From Eagle Plains, the Richardson Mountains provide an incredibly beautiful sight, forming a narrow north-south line of softly sculpted ridges. They are thought to be the most northerly range of the Rockies. The Arctic Circle is located at KM 403 (mile 250.4).

## Peel–Mackenzie Lowlands

The Dempster descends from the Richardsons into the Peel River plateau. This broad upland leads to the Peel River, the edge of the area covered by glaciers during the most recent ice age. There are many lakes and ponds on the plateau, with tundra and scattered areas of tamarack and black spruce. Ducks and other waterbirds nest here during the summer.

After crossing the Peel River by ferry, you'll come to Fort McPherson, an early Hudson's Bay Company post and now a Kutchin community of 800 people. The wide Mackenzie River is crossed by ferry at KM 613 (mile 381). You have the option of stopping at the small Native American community of Arctic Red River. The Dempster leads on through the Mackenzie delta, arriving in the town of Inuvik at KM 740 (mile 460).

## Hiking Possibilities

For mountain hikers, the three southern Dempster regions provide a hiking paradise. Several routes lead hikers into the Tombstone Range in the Northern Klondike region. Hikers may spend as little as 4 hours or as long as 8 to 10 days hiking through this range.

The southern Ogilvies provide several ridges for easy or strenuous hiking in the area of the Blackstone River valley, following creeks or walking across the brush and/or tundra, taking between three and eight hours. The northern Ogilvie ridges provide many opportunities for hiking from the Dempster roadside.

Canoeing down the Blackstone River provides hikers with access to more remote wilderness. The Richardson Mountains offer several hikes that are even more exciting during the midnight sun period. For the best listing of Dempster hikes, read *Along the Dempster* by Walter Lanz, published by Oak House Publishing, available at bookstores in the Yukon and in some major centers, including Vancouver, B.C.

## Dempster Wildlife

One of the largest herds of barren-ground caribou, the Porcupine herd, lives in the northern part of the Yukon. This herd of more than 130,000 lives in a 100,000-square-mile range, some of it crossed by the Dempster Highway. The migration routes of the caribou cross the Dempster in the Ogilvie ranges and in the Richardsons. By early July the entire herd moves into the northeastern Richardson mountains. The fall migration begins after the first snowfall. Some years see no caribou along the Dempster. In other years caribou winter near the highway in the southern Ogilvies. Some caribou of the Hart River herd stay in Dempster country year-round, moving up and down the mountains as the seasons change near the West Hart River.

Two types of bears, grizzly and black, live along the Dempster Highway route. The black bear is found in the forests along the Klondike, Ogilvie, and Eagle rivers. These are smaller than grizzlies and may be black or a cinnamon-brown color. Grizzly bears range over a wide area, mainly in the Ogilvies. A few grizzlies live in the Richardson range. Moose are seen at the lower levels.

Dall sheep are the white mountain sheep of Alaska and the Yukon. They may be seen along the Dempster as white spots moving along the mountain slopes. Lambs are born in late May and the sheep stay in family groups during the summer months. Although Dall sheep are prized as hunting trophies, no hunting is permitted within five miles of the Dempster Highway.

The southern stretches of the Dempster route are not known for fish, although Arctic grayling are found in the Blackstone and Ogilvie rivers. However, the Peel and Mackenzie areas make up for the lack of fish elsewhere. An important resource for the Native American population of the western Arctic, there are whitefish, Arctic char, trout, and burbot (freshwater ling).

Over 160 species of sub-Arctic birds have been sighted within five miles of the Dempster. The southern Ogilvies and the Blackstone uplands are prime birding areas. The Ogilvie Mountains provide a home for several birds of prey, including species of eagles, falcons, and owls. Ptarmigan are also seen here. Loons and many types of shorebirds inhabit the Peel plateau and the Mackenzie delta.

The various habitats along the Dempster provide visitors with an ever-changing view of wildflowers. From alpine flowers, including saxifrage, heather, and moss campion at the higher levels, to fireweed and forest plants below, there is a rich diversity of plant life. Two rare types of orchids grow in the northern Ogilvies. In July, the alpine meadows provide a carpet of many colors 24 hours a day. By early September the color of the Arctic tundra has turned to a light brown.

For details on Eagle Plains, see page 226; on Inuvik, see page 235.

# Eagle Plains

Eagle Plains is not a plain! This large, rolling region of hills nestles between the Ogilvie and Richardson mountain ranges. The area is at the alpine level and is mostly covered with stunted black spruce. Much of the ground has permafrost close to the surface and is covered with mosses, lichens, and short shrubs. The Eagle River, from which the area gets its name, wanders through the plains, fed by smaller creeks. Newcomers to the highway often consider Eagle Plains to be a boring, monotonous part of the trip. We would urge you to think otherwise.

The views from the Dempster throughout its crossing of Eagle Plains are awe-inspiring. The tundra requires close examination to see the delicate alpine vegetation. In late August and early September the land is ablaze with color as the alpine plants turn brilliant shades of crimson while the willows and birches along the creeks and the Eagle River turn a vivid yellow. Then the tundra turns brown as it waits for winter and the blowing snow to appear.

In all of our northern travels, one view remains the most memorable: the Richardson Mountains as seen from Eagle Plains. In late October the Richardsons were topped with fresh snow, enhancing the soft, sculptured look of the mountain peaks. A magnificent sunset bathed the mountains in buttery light, ending with subtle pinks as the sun went down. Some geologists say that the Richardsons are the northernmost peaks of the Rocky Mountains. The matter is still in scientific dispute.

There's an extensive border of fireweed along the highway at KM 364 (mile 226). The territorial flower flourishes throughout the Yukon. At KM 369 (mile 229) there's a good view of the Eagle River as it meanders through the plains. Several oxbow lakes created by the winding river can be seen from this point. Wildlife, including beavers, muskrats, and many birds, is abundant here.

Eagle Plains Hotel is a unique oasis in the middle of nowhere, and a logical place to stay overnight during your Dempster Highway trip. It is almost exactly halfway between Dawson City and Inuvik. This is a completely self-contained complex with electrical generator and water hauled by tanker truck from the Eagle River. The complex includes a gas station, government office, staff quarters, a campground, and a modern motel with dining room and lounge. For information and reservations, telephone (403) 979-4187, or write to Eagle Plains Hotel, Bag Service 2735, Whitehorse, Yukon Y1A 3V5. The hotel is open year-round.

Be sure to see several sets of historical photos on the walls of the hotel and lounge. These collections illustrating the stories of the Mad Trapper, the early RCMP dogsled patrols, and the great reindeer drive are well worth seeing for an understanding of the special history of the northern Yukon. If it is not possible to continue a drive along the Dempster to the Mackenzie Delta, then by all means drive the few miles to the Arctic Circle Crossing. You'll never forgive yourself if you don't.

## Where to Eat

There's only one place to eat at Eagle Plains: in the dining room of the **Eagle Plains Hotel.** One might think that being the only restaurant within hours of driving would tend to degrade the quality, but the food served here is very good. On my last visit I had a delicious plate of Hungarian cabbage rolls. And the food is mostly of the "comfort food" type, with big servings for the transport drivers who stay here on their trips to and from Inuvik.

# Fort Liard

Fort Liard is called the "Tropics of the Northwest Territories." It is famous for its benign climate with long, warm summer daylight hours, and for its tall trees and lush vegetation. There are several fine gardens in this little outpost village just north of the B.C. border on the Liard Highway. The community is located on a broad shelf where the Petitot River flows into the Liard. Wildlife including grizzly bears, caribou, and Dall sheep can be seen in the area.

The area is one of the oldest continually occupied sites in the Northwest Territories. The Small Knife culture lived here for about 9,000 years before the Slavey came to the area and remained here, still leading a traditional existence that includes trapping and hunting.

At an elevation of 213 meters (700 feet) Fort Liard sits above the majestic Liard River, which (at this location) is more than 426 meters (1,400 feet) wide. This is a settlement of log cabins and homes, set in a forest of spruce, poplar, and birch trees. Today's community was founded in 1805 when the Northwest Company established a trading post near the present site. The post was abandoned after a battle that saw a dozen white residents killed by Native Americans. The post was revived in 1820 and taken over the next year by the Hudson's Bay Company after the merger of the two companies.

The residents are famous for their handicrafts, particularly birch bark baskets and porcupine quill work. The baskets (a favorite souvenir item for visitors) are sewn together with spruce roots, which are prepared by boiling to soften the wood. The bark is peeled off and then split and trimmed for sewing. The porcupine quills that decorate the baskets are dyed brilliant colors, then threaded through the baskets with an awl. These craft works can be obtained at Acho-Dene Native Crafts, which is open Monday through Friday afternoons.

Nahanni National Park is accessible from Fort Liard, by aircraft from the small airstrip in the village. Deh Cho Air Company provides flights over the most dramatic parts of the park and also flies visitors to lakes for camping in the park. For information and reservations, phone (403) 770-4103.

Other recreation activities include fishing at the junction of the Petitot and Liard rivers, for pike, pickerel (walleye), and spring grayling. One can make a canoe trip to Trout Lake, Bovie Lake, and Fisherman's Lake.

# Fort McPherson

Leaving the Eagle Plains Hotel complex, the Dempster Highway descends into the valley of the Eagle River, crosses the river, and then heads upward into the Richardson Mountains.

At KM 414 (mile 257.2), travelers come upon the Arctic Circle crossing, marked with signs. This is a favorite stop for sightseeing and picture taking. Tour groups are often met by the somewhat eccentric "Keeper of the Arctic Circle," who is rumored to stay at the Eagle Plains Hotel and has been seen at the

Arctic Circle complete with formal attire and champagne glass in hand. Slightly onward, at KM 474.8 (mile 294.8) is the marker for the Continental Divide. West of here, water flows to the Pacific Ocean. East of this divide, water flows to the Arctic Ocean. There is a time zone change here; the Yukon observes Pacific time while the Northwest Territories uses Mountain time.

Aside from the people at the Eagle Plains Hotel, Fort McPherson is the first community north of Dawson City—some 570 KM (355 miles) away.

Fort McPherson is 12.8 KM (8 miles) from the Peel River ferry crossing. This cable ferry runs throughout the months when the river is open, from mid- to late June until mid-October. To phone ahead for information on ferry crossings, call (403) 979-3828 in Inuvik or Zenith 2022 (toll free from Yukon and NWT communities).

Native people from Fort McPherson have summer fishing camps along the Peel River. Racks of drying fish can often be seen near the ferry landing.

Originally situated 6.5 KM (4 miles) upstream from the present townsite, Fort McPherson was founded as a fur trading post in 1840 by the Hudson's Bay Company. Called Peel River Post, the name was changed in 1849 to honor Murdock McPherson, chief trader for the Mackenzie District.

Eight hundred people live in Fort McPherson, mostly Kutchin people, called Loucheux. The local economy is based on subsistence hunting and fishing, and trapping muskrat and mink. Handicrafts including Loucheux beadwork and hide clothing. A local canvas factory is open for tours during business hours.

Buried in the local cemetery are four members of the "Lost Patrol" of the RCMP who were frozen to death during a dogsled patrol in the winter of 1910–1911.

Services for visitors in Fort McPherson include two cafés and two general stores, one a Hudson's Bay store. The Native American co-op operates a combined hotel and café. There are two gas stations, one of which offers a tire-repair service.

# Fort Providence

One of the finest places to explore the Mackenzie River environment, Fort Providence was established in 1861 as a Roman Catholic mission.

A traditional trapping community, the village was earlier known for its Native American agriculture. The heritage of Alexander Mackenzie in exploring and settling the region is evident in the community. There are several historical markers that commemorate the roles of the church and of Mackenzie.

Fort Providence is located on the banks of this great river, 4.5 KM northwest of Highway 3, the Yellowknife Highway. The population is just over 600 and visitor services include two motels, cafés, and gas stations, with stores available for food, fishing gear, and other supplies. The village is serviced by air (Air Providence) and by Coachways bus lines. There is an air strip with emergency fuel only. The community is at the edge of the Mackenzie Bison Sanctuary.

The good fishing in the Mackenzie River brings hundreds of visitors to the village each summer. Local guides are available to assist with cabins and boat rentals booked through them. Fish species include northern pike, grayling, and pickerel—throughout the summer months and through September.

Prized memories of Fort Providence include spectacular sunsets over the wide Mackenzie. Dene culture is strong here. Fort Providence residents speak the Slavey language and the community is well known for its crafts, which are available in stores and include unique moosehair embroidery and porcupine quill crafts.

# Fort Simpson

The oldest continually occupied site on the Mackenzie River, Fort Simpson was founded when the Northwest Company moved into the western Arctic in 1804 and established what it called the "Fort on the Forks." The Hudson's Bay Company took over the trading post in 1821 and, at that time, the community was renamed Fort Simpson after the current governor of the company, George Simpson.

The town is set on a low island where the Liard joints the Mackenzie. Like Fort Liard, it is home to members of the Slavey people, many of whom live in camps outside the community.

Fort Simpson is the headquarters for Nahanni National Park, and the park Visitor Information Centre is located in here, outside of the park boundaries. Air transportation to the park can be arranged from town. Pope John Paul's visit to Fort Simpson was a celebrated event (and once-postponed because of inclement weather). The papal visit site commemorates the event and is a prime attraction for visitors. As in Fort Liard, the Slavey Indians exhibit and sell their quillwork, beading, and birch baskets. There is a craft shop in town.

Four smaller communities are just a short flight away from Fort Simpson. Jean Marie River is a Slavey community at the conjunction of the Jean Marie and Mackenzie rivers. The craftspeople here are famous for their moosehair tuftings and porcupine quillwork. Nahanni Butte, southwest of Fort Simpson, is a scenic spot where the Liard and South Nahanni rivers meet. One of the access points for Nahanni National Park, it is also close to Blackstone Territorial Park, located on the wide Liard and a popular canoeing destination. Trout Lake is south of Fort Simpson, where the fishing is fine and the Native Americans operate the Trout Lake Fishing Lodge. Wrigley is to the north, an old fur-trading post that moved around like most of the others and arrived at its present location in 1965. It's on a high ledge above the Mackenzie River, another good beginning for a canoe trip.

## Where to Eat

Food is basic in Fort Simpson. The coffee shop and dining room in the **Nahanni Inn** provides a broad selection of American cuisine, from pancakes for breakfast to steaks and seafood for dinner.

# Haines Junction

Haines Junction proper is a strip of motels, service stations, and restaurants at the junction of the Alaska Highway and Haines Road. What is notable is nearby Kluane National Park. Haines Junction was established with the construction of the Alaska Highway in 1942. The Haines Road now links the Yukon with the Alaska Marine Highway at Haines on the Lynn Canal. Kluane is the gem of Yukon parks and a national wilderness treasure. Mount Logan, located in the park, is the highest peak in Canada. Glaciers in the gigantic icefield fill several mountain valleys. They range in length from 10 KM (6 miles) to 100 KM (62 miles).

Park environments range from lush river valleys with aspen and spruce to alpine meadows filled with grasses and the higher reaches where moss campion, Arctic poppies, and other plants thrive on the alpine tundra. There is only one campground in the park, at Kathleen Lake—on the Haines Highway.

The village's Visitor Reception Centre is located off the Alaska Highway, a joint information desk for the Yukon government and Kluane National Park. Maps for canoe trips and hiking trails may be obtained from park staff. For park information call (403) 634-2345. Yukon Gold, the tourist radio service (96.1 FM), originates here. For advance information on Haines Junction events and facilities, call (403) 634-2291.

The village has several places to stay, all motels, plus RV parks, restaurants, and stores. The Village Bakery, a great place for campers and picnickers, is located next to the Kluane National Park visitor center. You should be able to buy sourdough bread in the original home of the sourdough, and this is the place! For groceries and other camping supplies, stop at Madley's General Store.

### Where to Eat
**Mackintosh Lodge**, located at historic mile 1022 of the Alaska Highway, has a large restaurant serving three meals a day. The lodge

has beer and liquor to go, plus RV and camping facilities including showers. The **Mountain View Motor Inn**, in town, has a licensed dining room, which means you can have beer or wine with your meal. The restaurant is part of a modern motel, with RV park.

# Hay River

Hay River is situated on the southern shore of Great Slave Lake, at the mouth of the Hay River. The town is built on the mainland and on Vale Island.

This is a transportation center, with commercial fishing and other businesses that service the regional economy. As the transportation terminal for the large barges that take goods from the highway and rail services on to Arctic communities down the Mackenzie River, Hay River plays an important role in supplying the whole Arctic and sub-Arctic region with basic supplies. The town was established as a Hudson's Bay Company post in 1868. The airstrip on Vale Island was constructed during World War II by the U.S. Army Corps of Engineers. Vale Island was the original townsite until floods in 1953 and 1963 forced the community to move to the mainland.

Hay River is a good overnight stopping point for through-travelers, and a good place to base a holiday of several days—for those who wish to explore the area fully, particularly the great fishing found here. There are 5 hotels and motels and 10 cafés, offering a good range of accommodations and food. You should reserve as far in advance as possible for a stay during the busy summer season.

Fishing is excellent in the Hay River area, with fishing camps set up on nearby lakes. Boat rentals are available in town, with northern pike, grayling, pickerel, and sheefish (inconnu) all caught here. The local Chamber of Commerce has a listing of fishing guides and fly-in charters available.

The Visitor Information Centre is located just east of the highway, open daily during the summer, (403) 874-3277. For advance information, write the Chamber of Commerce, Hay River, NWT X0E 0R0.

# Inuvik and the Mackenzie Delta

The Mackenzie River is crossed at KM 619.3 (mile 384.8) after traveling through the Peel wildlife preserve. Between the Peel and Mackenzie rivers lies a shallow lowland area, filled with muskeg and small lakes. The Mackenzie is the second longest river in North America and drains large parts of British Columbia, Alberta, Saskatchewan, and the Northwest Territories. Before the construction of the Dempster Highway, the Mackenzie River was the major transportation route to Canada's western Arctic area, with barges providing the only means of bulk transportation for towns such as Aklavik and Inuvik. In earlier days, the Mackenzie provided the transportation corridor that opened up the country for the Hudson's Bay Company.

Silt coming down the Mackenzie provides fertile land that supports forests of white birch, spruce, tamarack, and cottonwood. The spruces in particular are quite old and stunted. Some of them are over 500 years old but are very short. Waterfowl feed on the rich Mackenzie delta during their migratory flights. Moose are found in this northern lowland area, and small fur-bearing animals roam here in abundance.

Travelers taking the ferry across the Mackenzie have the option of stopping at Arctic Red River, a Native American village of 170 people, situated at the confluence of the Mackenzie and Arctic Red rivers. Tell the ferry attendant that you wish to stop at Arctic Red River. This is a picturesque Kutchin village established in 1868 as a trading post and mission. The residents hunt, fish, and trap. Groceries and gasoline are available in Arctic Red River during limited hours.

As with the Peel River crossing, the ferry operates from June through mid-September. No traffic crosses the river during the fall freeze-up period or the spring break-up period. During the winter, after sufficient ice has formed, vehicles drive on an ice bridge.

After crossing the Mackenzie River, the Dempster Highway follows a flat path across the river delta for 131 KM (81.4 miles) to the highway's end at Inuvik. The highway crosses the Rengling River at KM 654.3 (mile 406.6), where there is good fishing for Arctic grayling.

The Mackenzie Valley Reindeer Grazing Preserve is located at KM 676.5 (mile 420). In 1935 the Canadian government responded to the severe depletion by hunters of local caribou herds by organizing the importation of a 3,500 reindeer from western Alaska. It took more than five years to drive the herd the 5,000 kilometers to Aklavik, finally arriving in 1940; 2,400 animals survived the ordeal. Pictures of the drive are displayed on the walls of the Eagle Plains Hotel. Reindeer herding is now part of the local economy. Reindeer meat and hide garments are sold in Inuvik stores and some reindeer meat is available in local restaurants.

After a two-day drive along the wilderness route of the Dempster Highway, the city of Inuvik provides somewhat of a shock. Here is a modern community, with most big-city amenities, located north of the Arctic Circle in the middle of the immense wilderness of the Mackenzie River delta. Inuvik was founded by the Canadian government in 1954 as a model northern community. A city of 3,500 people, Inuvik is the administrative center for Canada's western Arctic region. The residents are Inuit, Dene, and Caucasian. Summers in Inuvik are influenced by the long days, when the sun rises on May 24th and doesn't set until July 24th. Visitors enjoy the Igloo Church, a round structure with lines painted to simulate the igloo look. Inside is an Inuit interpretation of the stations of the cross.

The community's tourist booth is located on Mackenzie Road, at the stoplight. Walking tour maps are available here. For advance information, call (403) 979-3111 or 800-661-0788, or write the Delta-Beaufort Tourism Association, P.O. Box 2759, Inuvik, NWT X0E 0T0.

The town's main airport is located off the Dempster Highway, outside Inuvik, with service to Whitehorse, Edmonton, and Yellowknife. A smaller in-town airport has charter services to western Arctic towns including Tuktoyaktuk (Antler Aviation, 403-979-2220).

### Where to Eat

Food in the smaller downtown cafés is quite basic. There are a couple of exceptions: **Anton's Dining Lounge**, at Finto's Motor Inn, Airport Road, is a dining room with European cuisine. This is the best place in Inuvik for quiet, romantic dinners. Prices range from moderate to expensive. **The Back Room**, behind The Roost on Mackenzie Road, is a small, cozy place with excellent food including local fish, and caribou burgers and steaks, along with several Italian dishes. Prices are moderate.

# Nahanni National Park

A one-of-a-kind wilderness preserve, Nahanni National Park was the first such park to be designated by UNESCO as a World Heritage Site. It is devoid of habitation and inaccessible by road. But in the late 1800s and early 1900s, prospectors roamed through the area looking for riches. They not only failed to find any but many lost their lives in the process. Their legacy is found in park names like Deadmen Valley and Headless Creek.

The park is truly exceptional. The South Nahanni River flows down the slopes of the Mackenzie Mountains, plunging over Virginia Falls which is twice the height of Niagara. Above the falls are 322 KM (193 miles) of wild, rushing river. Below the falls run an incredible 8 KM (5 miles) of high rapids that cause large waves as the river continues to roar down the mountainside.

The park has four notable canyons that go down as far as 1219 meters (4,000 feet) deep. There are several hot springs, including Rabbitkettle and Wildmint. Rabbitkettle Springs issues water which courses down terraces of tufa rock more than 24 meters (80 feet) high. The water is not really hot, about 68°F.

Because there is no road access, visitors to the park arrange to fly into various locations with charter air companies in either Fort Liard or Fort Simpson. You can also arrange for a flightseeing tour, which doesn't land but shows you the principal features of Nahanni, including Virginia Falls. Float plane tours can also be arranged from Fort Nelson, B.C., and Watson Lake, Yukon. If you're a casual tourist and not used to strenuous wilderness hiking and camping, it is best to arrange a stay in the park with a guided tour group. Thirteen species of fish abound in the park, including Dolly Varden and Arctic grayling. There are more than 40 species of animal wildlife, notably black bears, grizzly, wolves, caribou, and beaver, and at least 120 species of birds, such as golden eagles and trumpeter swans.

The closest lodge to the park is Nahanni Mountain Lodge, which is reached by flying from Fort Simpson. The lodge offers accommodations for eight people in two log cabins that have kitchen facilities and wood stoves. The resort is also equipped with boats, motors, canoes, and other equipment needed for a trip into the park. The lodge organizes three- to seven-day package stays from Fort Simpson at a rate of $500 to $1,000 per person for the package. The lodge is located on Little Doctor Lake. Nahanni River Adventures, based in Edmonton, Alberta, organizes Nahanni River trips that lead through the system of canyons in the park. For information, write P.O. Box 8368, Station F, Edmonton, Alberta T6H 4W6 (403) 439-1316.

For full information on the park, write Superintendent, Nahanni National Park, P.O. Box 348, Fort Simpson, NWT X0E 0N0, or call (403) 675-2310. You may also wish to obtain information on the region around the park by writing Nahanni-Ram Tourism Association, P.O. Box 177, Fort Simpson, NWT X0E 0N0, call (403) 695-3182.

# Teslin

Located 278 KM (173 miles) north of Watson Lake on the shores of Teslin Lake, Teslin is a picturesque lakeside community, its population of 450 primarily Teslin people. A small trading post was established here in 1903, mainly to serve the Tlingit. This nomadic people roamed throughout this area for centuries. The bridge here is the longest on the Alaska Highway. Teslin Lake was one of the waterways to the Yukon River and the Klondike during the gold rush of 1898. Steamers plied the waters of Teslin Lake until the 1940s.

The people of Teslin are involved in hunting, trapping, and fishing as well as providing services to tourists. This is a choice area for fishing. Charter trips are available from Coyote Air, (403) 390-2605, to remote lakes, or for wilderness trips down the Wolf River. Other facilities include houseboat charters at Morley Bay (Mobile Radio JR3 9305), and mountain bike rentals 11 KM south of Teslin at the Dawson Peaks Adventure Company, (403) 667-1103.

We recommend visiting the George Johnson Museum, named to honor a prominent local pioneer. It is operated by the Teslin Historical Society, open June to September, featuring the cultural history of the Tlingit, artifacts from pioneer days, and George Johnson's photographs.

## Where to Eat

For a small community, Teslin has a large number of places to eat, although the cuisine could be classed as basic with a few interesting quirks. **Shelly's Bakery**, right in Teslin, has fresh bread, donuts, and pastries. **Nisutlin Trading Post** is a general store in the village that stocks groceries and picnic supplies (closed Sundays). The **Yukon Motel** has a licensed café, with beer and liquor sales, on the shore of Nisutlin Bay, on the Alaska Highway.

**Halsteads**, a gas station, motel, and RV park on Teslin Lake, three miles west of the long bridge, has a café serving hamburgers, fried chicken, clams, and shrimp. Their specialty is rhubarb pie. This café, like others in the Yukon, makes an effort to outstrip competitors with the size and stickiness of its cinnamon buns. For the Yukon version of the Alaskan salmon bake, drive nine miles north of Teslin along the Alaska Highway, and enter **Mukluk Annie's**. Baked salmon is served from 11 A.M. to 9 P.M. daily. Alternatives include barbecue ribs, steaks, and chops, plus all-you-can-eat salad bar fixings. Mukluk Chuck's "Unique Yukon Breakfast" is served from 7 A.M. to 11 A.M. The hype at Annie's is as important as the food. A motel is located next to Annie's place.

# Watson Lake

Originally known as Fish Lake, Watson Lake developed quickly as a regional center during the Second World War and the building of the Alaska Highway. The community is an important commercial and transportation center for the southern Yukon area, with services for travelers, hunters, anglers, and trappers. During the war, servicemen and construction workers erected signposts from their hometowns. This custom was continued over the years by travelers, and today a forest of road signs from around the world stands beside the Alaska Highway. The Visitor Information Centre for the southern Yukon is located behind the sign forest. A nostalgic summer tent show focusing on the World War II years is staged next to the information center.

The Watson Lake Travel Infocentre is at the junction of the Alaska and Robert Campbell highways, behind the forest of signs. For advance information on local events and services, call (403) 536-7469. In the same building is the Alaska Highway Interpretation Centre, containing displays on the building of the highway in 1942. The Yukon Gold tourist radio service is broadcast from the Infocentre (96.1 FM).

### Where to Eat

**Nugget Restaurant** is a dining room and café serving moderately priced Chinese and western dishes. It usually closes on holidays.

The **Watson Lake Hotel Dining Room** is an excellent restaurant, serving steaks, seafood, and other meals. Prices are quite expensive, but after a long dusty day of driving, the good food and service found here are appreciated. For reservations call (403) 536-7781.

One of the newest facilities in town is the **Belvedere Motor Hotel**, located on the Alaska Highway. The hotel has both a coffee shop and a licensed dining room, plus a cocktail lounge. The food is comparable in quality to that served at the Watson Lake Hotel. The rooms and suites, being new, are better here but more expensive.

**Watson Lake Foods**, on the Alaska Highway, is a supermarket with bakery and deli foods, and a good bet for stocking up on picnic supplies.

# Whitehorse

Previously a quiet village of 500 people, Whitehorse boomed with the construction of the Alaska Highway in 1942. The village was originally established during the Klondike Gold Rush because of its location beside the forbidding Whitehorse Rapids on the Yukon River. Adventurers boating down the Yukon had to cope with Miles Canyon and the rapids. Enterprising entrepreneurs built log tramways and charged the stampeders to lift their boats, rafts, and supplies around the canyon and rapids. The gold rush and its aftermath created a major river port at Whitehorse, with paddle-wheelers plying the waters of the Yukon, taking supplies and passengers to Dawson and other mining towns.

With the war and the highway, Whitehorse became a city overnight with a wartime population of 10,000. Although the population declined somewhat after the war, Whitehorse became the Yukon's major trading and transportation center. The territorial government was moved to Whitehorse in 1953, replacing Dawson as the government center. The impressive government building is located on the bank of the Yukon River, next to Rotary Park. More than 60 percent of the Yukon's population lives in Whitehorse. The city limits encompass 421 square kilometers (162 square miles), including several suburbs spread along the Alaska Highway and the Riverdale subdivision on the east bank of the river.

The Whitehorse Visitor Information Centre is in the T.C. Richards Building, a large log cabin at 302 Steele Street downtown. Whitehorse attractions can be previewed from a laser disc. An audio-visual program is shown, and Yukon Gold broadcasts to tourists on 96.1 FM. For advance information call (403) 667-7545. The Parks Canada Information Centre is found next to the SS *Klondike* restoration at the end of 2nd Avenue downtown.

## Things to See and Do

Several days could be well spent in the Whitehorse area, visiting museums, taking river trips, shopping for Native American art and crafts, and visiting the special attractions that have been developed in recent years, including nighttime entertainment shows.

The Yukon Government Art Collection is on display in the territorial government building on 2nd Avenue downtown. Northern landscapes and people are shown in the works of prominent artists from the Yukon and other parts of Canada. It's open Monday to Friday, from 8:30 A.M. to 5 P.M. There's a gallery in the Whitehorse Public Library in the same complex.

Start your shopping for Native American crafts at Yukon Native Products and Northern Images, both on 4th Avenue. Yukon Native Products is a factory and store selling Yukon parkas, mukluks, and other northern clothing. Tours are available. Inuit and Native American art is sold at Northern Images. Other shopping is centered on Main Street and in the Quanlin Mall on 4th Avenue. Gold nugget jewelry is a specialty.

SS *Klondike,* the best remaining example of the Yukon River sternwheeler, is located on the bank of the river at Rotary Park at the end of 2nd Avenue. This is a National Historic Site, operated by Parks Canada. An interpretation center is located in the park.

The Old Log Church Museum, at 3rd Avenue and Elliot Street, was once the territory's Anglican Cathedral. It opened as a museum in 1962, and displays documents, artifacts, and photos of the early missionary days in the Yukon. The museum is open daily, June through August.

The Frantic Follies Vaudeville Revue is a 20-year staple of Whitehorse summer nightlife, staged in the Westmark Hotel downtown. Gold Rush songs, skits, Robert Service poems, and cancan dancing are highlights of this entertainment set in the Gold Rush days, (403) 668-3161. Another Gold Rush–era show is "Eldorado," a Gay '90s revue performed at the Pioneer Trailer Park Tuesday through Sunday at 8 P.M. Call (403) 668-6472.

The MacBride Museum, 1st Avenue and Wood Street, has a number of historical themes including natural history, Native American culture, the Gold Rush era, and the construction of the Alaska Highway. The museum is packed to the rafters with artifacts from the railway and other forms of early transportation in the area. Open daily May 15th to September 15th.

Yukon Gardens, on the Alaska Highway, is the only show garden in the northern territories. Here are large displays of wild plants as well as northern flowers, trees, and shrubs. Children will enjoy the petting farm and an international bird display. Open daily June to September.

Takhini Hot Springs, 9.6 KM (5.9 miles) off the Klondike Highway north of Whitehorse, is a memorable hot spring resort with a coffee shop and one of the best campgrounds in the north.

Northern Splendour Farm, a few kilometers farther along the Klondike Highway near Lake Laberge, is a reindeer farm open to the public. Visitors first watch a video on Canadian and Alaskan reindeer and then view and help feed the animals. Open daily May to mid-September.

### Tours and Walks

Walking tours are available through the Yukon Conservation Society, (403) 668-5678. These guided walks include tours to Miles Canyon, Grey Mountain, and Hidden Lake. They take from two to six hours.

Whitehorse Heritage Walks start from the Donnenworth House (3126 3rd Avenue) and lead through the downtown area. For information call (403) 667-4704.

The *MV Schwatka* offers daily tours of Miles Canyon on the Yukon River, (403) 668-3161. The *MV Anna Maria* makes four-day trips to Dawson as well as evening cruises at Whitehorse (403) 667-2873. This 65-foot ship has overnight berths and deck accommodation.

The biggest weathervane of them all! Drive to the Whitehorse airport, on the hill next to the Alaska Highway, and you'll see a DC3 aircraft rotating on a pedestal, pointing its nose to the wind. This historic aircraft flew for Yukon Airlines from 1946 until 1970. The Yukon Transportation Museum is also located at the airport.

The Dam and Fish Ladder along the Yukon River beyond the downtown area is worth visiting during spawning runs. This route to the ladder starts at the end of Nisutlin Drive in the Riverdale suburb, across the river from downtown. The fish ladder allows Chinook (king) salmon to migrate past the hydro dam to their spawning grounds upriver. August is the best time to see the migration. The fish ladder is open daily during July and August.

### Sidetrips from Whitehorse

The highway logs in this guidebook cover both ends of the Klondike Highway. The highway runs from Skagway, Alaska, at the south, to Dawson City and the Top of the World Highway, which links Dawson City to the Alaska Highway inside the state of Alaska. If time does not permit the highly interesting trip along these routes, we offer the following list of day trips that you can take while staying in Whitehorse.

**To Carmacks and Five Finger Rapids**  Drive north on the Alaska Highway from the Two-Mile Hill junction for 12 KM (7.4 miles), and turn onto the Klondike Highway (Hwy. 2). Passing the Takhini Hot Springs Road you approach Northern Splendour Farm, the Yukon's only reindeer farm. It is open to the public.

Lake Laberge, made famous by Robert W. Service in "The Cremation of Sam McGee," can be seen from viewpoints and from the Lake Laberge Yukon government campground 32.8 KM (20.4 miles) from the Alaska Highway junction.

Passing by Fox Lake and the small Twin Lakes, an old tumble-down log building revives memories of the early days of the Yukon. Montague House was a way-station on the rough wagon road to Dawson City.

Carmacks, a small community on the Yukon River, is located 165.3 KM (102.7 miles) from the junction of the Klondike and Alaska Highways. This was once a stop on the riverboat route to Dawson. Now, it has a hotel and café, plus a Yukon government campground with a picnic site.

189.1 KM (117.5 miles) from the junction is Five Finger Rapids, named by early prospectors for the 5 channels or "fingers" made by the rock pillars sticking out of the river. Riverboats had to be winched through the one navigable finger. There is an excellent viewpoint with steps leading down to a trail which gives a closer view of the rapids. 2 KM beyond the rapids is the road to Tatchum Creek Park.

**To Carcross and Atlin**   It makes a long day, but any visitor to Whitehorse should drive to the scenic village of Atlin, B.C., the historic gold rush town on Atlin Lake. Drive south along the Alaska Highway to the Klondike Highway junction and turn right towards Carcross. Carcross is a small village which was an important lake steamboat and rail center before the 1950s. The original Carcross Hotel is still in business with a café and lounge. The paddle-steamer *Tutshi* (Too-Shy) is beached here as a museum.

After visiting Carcross, turn northwest on Tagish Road (Hwy. 8) and drive to the junction with the Atlin Road, near Jake's Corner. The Atlin Road (Hwy. 7) provides a 93.3-KM (58-mile) drive along Little Atlin Lake and Atlin Lake. This area is called the "Switzerland of North America," for its high snow-clad peaks and hanging glacier.

Native tribes, descended from the early Athabaskans who traveled over the Bering Land Bridge—have been the primary residents of the Yukon for at least 10,000 years and probably as long as 30,000 years. Over the centuries, the Native people have survived the rigors of this harsh land, adapting to the changes brought first by the fur trade, then by gold discoveries, the Alaska Highway boom, and the recent mining and tourism development.

There are seven Native tongues used by Yukon tribes: Tlingit, Tagish, Kaska, and Southern Tutchone in the southern areas of the territory, Tutchone and Han in the central interior, Kutchin in the north. There are seven thousand Natives now living in the Yukon. A campaign has been waged to preserve the traditional languages, as well as the art of the Yukon groups, including leather crafts, beadwork, canoe-making, carving and parka-making. Many of these arts and crafts are exhibited for sale in crafts stores in the Yukon communities.

The Yukon Natives are deeply spiritual and have preserved this culture in the face of modern civilization. An outstanding experience for tourists is visiting the Native communities, exploring the local museums, and observing their ancient traditions.

### Yukon Outdoors

The vast Yukon Territory is an exciting land of mountains, rivers, plains, and northern muskeg. In most of the Yukon, permafrost is only a few feet under the surface of the ground. Canada's highest mountain is located in the southwest corner of the territory. The Dempster Highway, running north from Dawson City across the Arctic Circle, passes through the most northerly range of the Rocky Mountains, permitting tourists to see mountain tundra in the higher altitudes.

The Yukon provides a range for vast herds of caribou, seen as they migrate in the spring and fall. Throughout the Yukon there is an abundance of other wildlife: grizzly bears, Dall sheep, mountain goats, and fish including lake trout, northern pike, and Arctic grayling.

Outdoor recreation lies around every corner in the Yukon. Anyone who likes the outdoors will want to don a backpack and wander along the rivers, through mountain meadows, and on many trails found in the national and territorial parks. Kluane National Park is outstanding, with 250 KM (155 miles) of hiking trails, including trails for day hikes and others which take you to striking wilderness country and overnight camping. River trips are a popular pastime. Several outfitters in Whitehorse organize trips down the Yukon River and it's possible to canoe from Whitehorse to Dawson with a portage at the Five Finger Rapids. Other rivers offer white-water canoeing and rafting.

## Where to Eat

The dining room of the **Westmark Hotel** offers a sedate, sophisticated place to eat, year-round. Centrally located, at 2nd Avenue and Wood Street, the dining room menu includes a range of dishes from poached salmon to pork chops and tender steaks. No reservations are taken.

For something completely different, walk across the street from the Westmark, and drop into the **Klondike Rib and Salmon BBQ** (Second and State streets). Here you'll have a choice of "baked" salmon, Texas-style ribs, fish and chips, plus some Yukon specialties including musk-ox burgers. You may need a reservation: (403) 667-7554.

**Rosa's Cantina**, at 404 Wood Street in the downtown area, is an unlikely café for a town that is snowbound for about half the year. But Rosa's serves delicious Tex-Mex food, far from the Rio Grande, and even Mexican beer, at moderate prices.

**Bench and Gavel**, at 2141 2nd Avenue, downtown, is a modern restaurant and bar that takes its name from the nearby courthouse. The pleasant decor is accompanied by dishes such as steak, seafood, and pasta, at moderate to expensive prices.

**Swiftwater's**, 303 Jarvis Street, downtown, is a steak house with seafood dishes, and an extensive salad bar. There's a friendly atmosphere in this fancy saloon, named for Swiftwater Bill Gates, the notorious Klondike rogue. Swiftwater Bill's story is related on the menu. Prices are on the expensive side.

# Yellowknife

Situated on the north shore of Great Slave Lake, Yellowknife is the capital of the Northwest Territories. It is the largest community and the only city in the vast area of the territories.

With a population of close to 12,000, Yellowknife is growing as a tourist center. It was founded in 1934 when white settlers arrived to mine the gold of the area, with the first mine established by Cominco. A shanty town was built and the community slowly took shape over the ensuing 30 years. The first gold was shipped out in 1938. Mining was shut down during World War II and the mines reopened in 1948.

Bush planes were a vital part of the transportation system from the early days of the region's development. With the construction of the Yellowknife Highway in 1960, the city grew in population. It became the capital of the Northwest Territories in 1967.

Today, government is the main business of the city, with a strong presence from the federal and territorial governments. The two gold mines employ more than 800 people. More and more, tourism is playing a large part in the Yellowknife economy. There's clear air, clean water, and unlimited wilderness all around. Good hotels, motels, and restaurants service tourists as well as business travelers. The long days of summer make fishing a special experience. Air charters are available to take anglers to remote lakes throughout the region.

Highway drivers should be aware that road access to Yellowknife is not available during fall freeze-up and spring breakup periods, ranging from two to five weeks each season. An ice bridge crosses the Mackenzie River near Fort Providence during the winter months and there is a ferry service when the river is open— from May to November.

The major information center for the area is the Northern Frontier Regional Visitors Center, located at 4807 49th Street, featuring displays on the cultures and crafts of the area. The center is open year-round. Summer hours are 8 A.M. to 8 P.M. For advance information, call (403) 873-4262. For Northwest Territories Government tourism information, write Travel-Arctic, Dept. of Economic Development and Tourism, Yellowknife, Y.T. X1A 2L9, or call 800-661-0788. The Yellowknife Chamber of Commerce will send information. Also call (403) 920-4944.

## Things to See and Do

The history of Yellowknife and the Northwest Territories is well displayed around the community. The Prince of Wales Northern Heritage Centre is an informative museum, dedicated to the natural and cultural history of the north. The exhibits range from Inuit stone sculpture to photographic exhibitions, and a wide range of displays showing Dene and Inuit artifacts. The Centre is located on Frame Lake, on 48th Street. You can also get there through a pedestrian walkway behind the Yellowknife City Hall.

Local tour operators offer two- and three-hour guided tours of the city and the Nerco Gold Mine. A two-hour cruise on Great Slave Lake is available and a tour along Ingraham Trail winds along a scenic lakeside route.

Special local celebrations include the Yellowknife Fall Fair, held at the end of August, the fabled Midnight Sun Golf Tournament in June, and the Folk Music Festival in July. Winter events include the Caribou Carnival, held annually in March.

## Where to Eat

The **Mackenzie Dining Lounge**, in the Yellowknife Inn, downtown, is a modern dining room featuring northern specialties including Arctic char, musk ox, and caribou dishes, as well as more standard fare, with moderate to expensive prices. For reservations, call (403) 873-2600.

The **Office Restaurant**, 4915-50 Street, serves salads and vegetarian dishes for the vegan set, and smoked Arctic char and

ribs to others. There's a snack menu during afternoons and aft 9 P.M. Moderate prices.

**The Emporium**, at 4502 Franklin Avenue, is a large and somewhat boisterous place to have lunch or dinner. The full name of the place is "The Great Gold City Food and Beverage Emporium." It's an airy restaurant serving burgers, salads, and other dishes at reasonable cost.

# Places to Stay

## BEAVER CREEK

### Beaver Creek Motor Inn
Mile 1202, Alaska Highway
Beaver Creek, Y.T. Y0B 1A0
(403) 862-7600

Open year-round, this motel is the social center of town for local residents, with a licensed dining room, lounge, beer sales, and a gas station. The motel rooms have full baths and color TV. ($$)

### Ida's Motel and Restaurant
Mile 1202, Alaska Highway
Beaver Creek, Y.T. Y0B 1A0
(403) 862-7223 or
fax: (403) 862-7221

Ida's offers standard motel rooms with private bath and TV, plus free RV parking and tent spaces. The restaurant here is one of the better places to eat in Beaver Creek, with tasty soups, baked goods, and American cuisine, as well as a cocktail lounge. ($ to $$)

### Westmark Inn
Mile 1202, Alaska Highway
Beaver Creek, Y.T. Y0B 1A0
(403) 862-7501 or
800-544-0970 (in U.S.) or
800-999-2570 (in Canada)

Open during the summer travel season in this Yukon outpost town at the Canada/Alaska border, this large inn is a busy place, with hotel rooms, dining room and lounge, guest laundry, and gift shop. The Beaver Creek Rendezvous, staged in the inn, is a nightly barbecue feast and Klondike-style stage show. ($$ to $$$)

# CARCROSS

**Montana Services and RV Park**
P.O. Box 75
Carcross, Y.T. Y0B 1B0
(403) 821-3503 or
fax: (403) 821-3708

This gas station offers RV parking with electrical hookups, water, showers, propane, a café, and an RV wash. It's located at mile 75, at the Carcross turnoff.

# CARMACKS AND AREA

**Braeburn Lodge**
Mile 55
Klondike Highway, Y.T.
Y1A 4N1
Phone 0 Whithorse or
2M-3987, Fox Channel

This bed-and-breakfast place is better known for the size and taste of its cinnamon buns. Braeburn Lodge—about halfway between Whitehorse and Carmacks—has been a highway roadhouse for a long time. This is prime hunting and fishing country, and the lodge has an airstrip, plus canoe rentals and camping facilities. The café is licensed, and the cinnamon buns are freshly baked. ($)

**Hotel Carmacks**
P.O. Box 160
Carmacks, Y.T. Y0B 1C0
(403) 863-5221

For a little village that sits out of the Yukon countryside, it boasts a hotel/motel complex that is surprisingly modern. There are hotel- and motel-style units, a restaurant, cocktail lounge, and gas station. The store includes a small bakery, and the operation offers showers and a coin laundry. ($ to $$)

# DAWSON CITY

**Downtown Hotel**
P.O. Box 780
Dawson City, Y.T.
Y0B 1G0
(403) 993-5346 or 800-661-0514 (from the UK) or
800-764-GOLD (in Alaska)

This year-round hotel offers modern, comfortable rooms in its main two-storied structure, and additional rooms across the street in the hotel annex. The main building features a fine dining room and plush saloon. The annex has a whirlpool. ($$)

**Gold Rush Campground**
P.O. Box 198
Dawson City, Y.T.
Y0B 1G0
(403) 993-5247

This small private campground is at 5th Avenue and York Street, in downtown Dawson. Facilities include full and partial hookups, showers, laundry, store, car wash, and dump station. Open May through September.

**Guggieville**
P.O. Box 311
Dawson City, Y.T.
Y0B 1G0
(403) 993-5008

You'll see Guggieville signs as you approach Dawson City from the south. The campground and gold panning attraction are located on famed Bonanza Creek, and facilities include hookups, tent sites, showers, laundry, and a car wash.

**Klondike Kate's Cabins**
P.O. Box 417
Dawson City, Y.T.
Y0B 1G0
(403) 993-6527

This complex of cabins is found at 3rd Avenue and King Street, downtown. The operations includes a restaurant decorated in the 1898 style, and serving "down-home" comfort food. ($$)

**Klondike River Lodge**
Klondike and Dempster Highways
Dawson City, Y.T.
Y0B 1G0
(403) 993-6892

This motel and service station complex is operated by the Gwichin Tribal Council, and is perfectly situated for those planning a drive north on the Dempster Highway. Open year-round, the operation includes RV parking, a restaurant, grocery store, dump station, and car wash. The service station is open from 8 A.M. to midnight. ($ to $$)

**Triple-J Hotel**
P.O. Box 359
Dawson City, Y.T.
Y0B 1G0
(403) 993-5323 or
800-764-3555
800-661-0405 (in Yukon and B.C.)

This aggregation of tourist facilities includes a hotel, motel, and small ("bachelorette") cabins. All units have full baths. The main hotel building includes a restaurant and lounge. This is one of the few Dawson City hotels open year-round. ($$)

**Westmark Inn**
P.O. Box 420
Dawson City, Y.T.
Y0B 1G0
800-544-0970 (in U.S.)
800-999-2570 (in Canada)

This summer operation is one of the Westmark chain of hotels, focusing on the many tours that the company brings to Dawson. Done up in a false-fronted gold rush style, the inn is by far the largest hotel in town, and features a dining room, lounge, and gift shop. Barbecue is a dining room specialty. ($$ to $$$)

## DESTRUCTION BAY

**Talbot Arm Motel**
P.O. Box 40
Destruction Bay, Y.T.
Y0B 1H0
(403) 841-4461

Fronted by a Chevron service station, this popular place was remodeled in the late 1980s, resulting in more than two dozen modern rooms, with satellite TV and guest laundry. A cafeteria is open for overnight visitors, highway travelers, and bus tour groups. The complex also includes a licensed dining room, general store, and an RV park with partial hookups, propane, dump station, and showers. ($$)

## EAGLE PLAINS

**Eagle Plains Hotel**
Bag Service 2735
Whitehorse, Y.T.
Y1A 3V5
(403) 979-4187

This unique oasis, on the Arctic tundra of the Yukon's Eagle Plains, is a logical place to stay overnight during your Dempster Highway trip. It is almost exactly halfway between Dawson City and Inuvik. Located just 21 miles south of the Arctic Circle, this is a completely self-contained complex, with electrical generator, and water hauled by tanker truck from the Eagle River. The complex includes a gas station, government office, staff quarters, and a campground with showers and laundry. The industrial-style (but comfortable) modular motel has a dining room and lounge. The hotel is open year-round. ($$)

## FORT LIARD

**Liard Valley Motel**
General Delivery
Fort Liard, NWT
X0G 0A0
(403) 770-4441

The small motel is located in the Native American village, 6.4 km (4 miles) from the Liard Highway. Some rooms have kitchen facilities. The motel has a general store attached, with fishing and hunting licenses available in the store. ($)

**Pointed Mountain Motel**
Liard Highway # 77
Fort Liard, NWT X0G 0A0
(403) 770-4421 or
(403) 770-4441

This highway motel is located at the junction of the Liard Highway and the Fort Liard sideroad. As well as motel rooms, the complex includes a restaurant, laundry, public showers, and a service station with gas, diesel, and propane. ($ to $$)

## FORT SIMPSON

**Maroda Motel**
P.O. Box 67
Fort Simpson, NWT
X0E 0N0
(403) 695-2602

This medium-size motel has standard rooms and several units with kitchenettes. Plan to spend more money for lodgings in Fort Simpson than in more southern towns. However, for your money you get rooms equipped with two double beds, full bath, color TV, and air-conditioning. ($$$)

## HAINES JUNCTION

**Kluane Park Inn**
Mile 1016, Alaska Highway
Haines Junction, Y.T.
Y0B 1L0
(403) 634-2261

This medium-size motel has standard rooms, plus a cocktail lounge/bar, and light food including pizza available in the lounge. The motel office is open 24 hours during summer months. ($ to $$)

**Kluane RV Kampground**
P.O. Box 5496
Haines Junction, Y.T.
Y0B 1L0
(403) 634-2709

A large RV park and campground, Kluane RV has full hookups for RVs and trailers, pull-through sites, wooded tent campsites, showers, laundry, store, car wash, and dump station. It's located on the Alaska Highway, beside a gas station.

**Mackintosh Lodge**
Mile 1022 Alaska Highway
Alaska Highway, Y.T.
Y1A 3V4
(403) 634-2301

This friendly lodge and RV park is located 10.6 km (6.6 miles) northwest of Haines Junction. Starting out as a roadhouse after World War II, the lodge has become a favorite place to stay for those traveling the route regularly. The lodge complex includes a motel building, restaurant, lounge with fireplace, campground including pull-through sites and full hookups, a gift shop, and coin laundry. ($ to $$)

**Mountain View Motor Inn**
P.O. Box 5479
Haines Junction, Y.T.
Y0B 1L0
(403) 634-2646

This handy motel is located in town, with modern motel rooms (satellite TV), and a licensed dining room plus coffee shop. The adjacent RV park has full hookups for RVs and trailers, and showers. ($$)

## HAY RIVER

**Cedar Rest Motel**
938 Mackenzie Highway
P.O. Box 540
Hay River, NWT X0E 0R3
(403) 874-3732

On the Mackenzie Highway, this basic medium-size motel has suites, including some with kitchenettes. Other services include a store, gas pumps, and bus depot. ($)

**Hay River Hotel**
43035 Mackenzie
Highway
P.O. Box 487
Hay River, NWT X0E 0R9
(403) 874-6022

What you have here is plain old basic accommodation in this "old town" hotel on Vale Island, the original site of Hay River. Most of the town moved to the new townsite but the old hotel remained, offering budget rates. A convenience store is also located here. ($)

**Ptarmigan Inn**
10L Gagnier
Hay River, NWT
X0E 1G1
(403) 874-6781

A large modern hotel with comfortable rooms, dining room, bar, and coffee shop, the Ptarmigan is close to shopping and the town's swimming pool, part of a recreation complex. The hotel has a licensed restaurant and lounge. ($$ to $$$)

# INUVIK

**Finto's Motor Inn**
P.O. Box 1925
Inuvik, NWT X0E 0T0
(403) 979-2647

Located next to the Western Arctic Visitor Centre at the edge of town, this modern hotel offers large rooms, a few suites, some with kitchenettes, cable TV, guest laundry, and an excellent dining room with a sophisticated cocktail lounge. Reservations are advised. (\$\$ to \$\$\$)

**Mackenzie Hotel**
P.O. Box 1618
Inuvik, NWT X0E 0T0
(403) 979-2861

This is Inuvik's original hotel, renovated over the years, with a dining room, coffee shop, pub, and lounge (with nightly entertainment). Units include standard rooms and suites. (\$ to \$\$)

# TESLIN

**Halstead's Teslin Lake Resort**
General Delivery
Teslin, Y.T. Y0A 1B0
(403) 390-2608

This motel and campground are located three miles west of the Teslin Lake Bridge, north of the small town. The motel offers modern rooms with satellite TV, private baths, and refrigerators. Non-smoking rooms are available. (\$ to \$\$) The café is a long-time favorite with Alaska Highway travelers, with freshly baked bread, hamburgers, fried chicken, and seafood. The RV park has full hookups and pull-through sites, picnic tables, grills, and showers. The service station offers tire service, gas, and a dump station. Boat rentals and fishing guides are also available.

**Johnson's Crossing Campground**
General Delivery
Johnson's Crossing, Y.T. Y1A 9Z0
(403) 390-2607

Located along the Alaska Highway, across the Teslin River Bridge at mile 836 (km 1346), this is an RV park with full hookups, plus treed tent sites, showers, dump station, laundry, and grocery store selling campers supplies and baked goods, including cinnamon buns.

**Yukon Motel**
Mile 804 Alaska Highway
Teslin, Y.T. Y0A 1B0
(403) 390-2575

This standard motel, on the shore of Nisutlin Bay, has a licensed café, lounge, laundry, beer sales, and self-service gasoline. Their new RV park is now in operation. ($)

## WATSON LAKE

**Belvedere Hotel**
P.O. Box 288
Watson Lake, Y.T. Y0A 1C0
(403) 536-7712

One of the newest places to stay in Watson Lake, the Belvedere has both hotel and motel rooms, including a honeymoon suite, and rooms with water beds and whirlpool tubs. There are two places to eat: a licensed dining room and a coffee shop. ($$ to $$$)

**Campground Services**
P.O. Box 268
Watson Lake, Y.T. Y0A 1C0
(403) 536-7448

This campground, next to the Husky gas station, is located at Mile 632.5 of the Alaska Highway, with full and partial hookups, showers, laundry, and propane, plus a grocery store, car wash, and self-serve gas.

**Downtown RV Park**
P.O. Box 609
Watson Lake, Y.T. Y0A 1C0
(403) 536-2646 or
(403) 536-2224 (winter)

Located in the center of town, this medium-size operation has pull-through sites with full hookups, showers, laundry, and car wash. The park is open from May through September.

**Gateway Motor Inn**
P.O. Box 560
Watson Lake, Y.T. Y0A 1C0
(403) 536-7744

This red-clad motel sits on the Alaska Highway, with hotel rooms and motel units, and cabins open in the summer only. Some units have kitchens. The inn has a licensed restaurant and lounge, plus beer sales. ($$ to $$$)

**Watson Lake Hotel**
P.O. Box 370
Watson Lake, Y.T. Y0A 1C0
(403) 536-7781

Located in a prominent position along the Alaska Highway, not far from the signpost forest, this long-time fixture is a modern motor hotel with standard motel units, suites (some units with kitchens), plus one of the finest dining rooms along the highway, a lounge, laundry, and sauna. The hotel had a major renovation in 1992. ($$)

## WHITEHORSE

**High Country Inn**
4051 4th Avenue
Whitehorse, Y.T. Y1A 1H1
800-554-4471 or
fax: (403) 667-6457

One of the few high-rise buildings in Whitehorse (with five stories), this hotel has a variety of hotel rooms, and suites with kitchenettes. Most rooms include microwave ovens. The Malamute Saloon and Great North Pancake House are in the building, along with a guest laundry. A pool, sauna, gym, and whirlpool are located next door. ($$ to $$$)

**Klondike Inn**
2288 2nd Avenue
Whitehorse, Y.T. Y1A 1C8
800-544-0970 (in U.S.)
800-999-2570 (in Canada)

Another of the Westmark chain of hotels found throughout the Yukon and Alaska, the Klondike Inn is located near the northern entrance to town, at the bottom of Two-Mile Hill. Facilities include a dining room, coffee shop, lounge, beauty salon, and nightclub. This is a summer operation. ($$ to $$$)

**Mackenzie's RV Park**
301-922.5,
Alaska Highway
Whitehorse, Y.T. Y1A 3Y9
(403) 633-2337

Located six miles north of downtown, this park has RV and trailer sites with full hookups, plus tenting sites, showers, laundry, a grocery store, and an RV/car wash. Gold panning is a popular feature.

**Sourdough City RV Park**
411 Main Street
(mailing address)
Whitehorse, Y.T. Y1A 2B6
(403) 668-7938
800-661-0539
(in Yukon and B.C.)
800-764-7604 (in Alaska)

This large downtown RV park is located on 2nd Avenue, north of Ogilvie Street. The entry is at the 2nd Avenue Chevron. Facilities include RV and trailer sites with full hookups, additional sites with electrical hookups, tenting sites, showers, laundry, barbecue area, and a gift shop. This is the only camping park close to the downtown area. Open May 1st to October 1st.

**Stop In Family Hotel**
314 Ray Street
Whitehorse, Y.T. Y1A 5R3
(403) 668-5558

This new full-service hotel offers reasonable rates for its standard motel and hotel rooms. Other facilities include a restaurant, sauna, whirlpool, barbershop, and salon. (**$ to $$**)

**Takhini Hot Springs Campground**
Kilometer 10
Hot Springs Road
Rural Route 2, Site 19,
Compartment 4
Whitehorse, Y.T. Y1A 5A5
(403) 633-2706

This is arguably the best private campground in the Yukon, and a major attraction is the hot spring resort of which this is a part. It's located at the end of Takhini Hot Springs Road, off the Klondike Highway north of Whitehorse. Camping facilities include electrical hookups, showers, picnic tables, firewood, and laundry, and other resort features include a coffee shop, large outdoor hot spring pools, and guided trail rides. The resort is open year-round, with cross-country skiing and soaking in the steaming hot water.

**Westmark Whitehorse**
P.O. Box 4250
Whitehorse, Y.T. Y1A 3T3
800-544-0970 (in U.S.)
800-999-2570 (in Canada)

Situated in downtown Whitehorse, at 2nd and Wood streets, just behind Main Street, this year-round hotel attracts business people, government officials, and travelers during the tourist season. The modern hotel has a dining room and lounge, barber shop, and beauty salon. The hotel is the site of the Frantic Follies, a vaudeville revue now in its second quarter-century of delighting visitors with songs, cancan dancing, and other northern nonsense. The show is staged nightly from June to September. (**$$ to $$$**)

## YELLOWKNIFE

**Discovery Inn**
4701 Franklin Avenue
P.O. Box 784
Yellowknife, NWT
X1A 2N6
(403) 873-4151

This downtown hotel has clean, comfortable rooms (singles, doubles, or units with kitchenettes) at reasonable rates. You'll find a restaurant on the premises. (**$$**)

**Explorer Hotel**
Postal Service 7000
Yellowknife, NWT X1A 2R3
(403) 873-3531

Situated downtown at the corner of 48th Street and 49th Avenue, this modern, full-service hotel has standard rooms and suites, a dining room, and provides a complimentary continental breakfast. ($ to $$)

**Yellowknife Inn**
5010 49th Street
P.O. Box 490
Yellowknife, NWT X1A 2N4
(403) 873-2601

In a central location, this large hotel is in downtown Yellowknife, next to the Legislative Assembly Building. The modern hotel has rooms and suites, full room service, a licensed dining room, lounge, coffee shop, laundry, and several shops. ($$ to $$$)

**YWCA Bayview Apartment Hotel**
5004-54th Street
Yellowknife NWT X1A 2R6
(403) 873-9406 or
fax: (403) 873-4767

The "Y" offers coed accommodation in bachelor suites, some with kitchenettes. It's close to shopping and restaurants, and is a reasonably priced place to stay. ($ to $$)

# Access Routes

# Access Routes
## *Drives*

On the following pages you will find maps and log descriptions for the access routes leading from the U.S./Canada border points, and from southern British Columbia and Alberta, through the two western provinces to the Alaska Highway.

The first set of strip maps details the route that will lead you through the interior of B.C. and eventually to the Alaska Highway. This Fraser Canyon/Cariboo route starts in Vancouver, moves northward through the Fraser Canyon, and then through the historic Cariboo gold rush country to the city of Prince George, a major natural resource center located beside the Fraser River. The city is located along the Yellowhead Highway (Provincial Route 16), the major east/west route connecting Edmonton, Alberta, and Prince Rupert, the port city on B.C.'s north coast.

Your arrival in Prince George will present a choice in routes for travel to the Alaska Highway and the ultimate drive to the Yukon and Alaska. For those who wish to drive the complete Alaska Highway route, which includes some very spectacular Rocky Mountains scenery in northern British Columbia, take the Hart Highway (Highway 97) (page 274) to Dawson Creek and "Mile 0." The alternative route, to the west, begins at the junction of the Yellowhead Highway (Highway 16) and the Stewart/Cassiar Highway (Provincial Route 37). To access this route, described on page 278, drive west on Highway 16 for 493 kilometers (307 miles).

The second northward route begins with the Island Highway, running from Swartz Bay to Port Hardy, on Vancouver Island (page 276). This drive is included for those travelers wishing to visit Victoria and other Vancouver Island communities, and then take the scenic B.C. ferry trip through the Inside Passage to Prince Rupert. For those arriving in Prince Rupert by B.C. or Alaska ferry, or by cruise ship from Vancouver, the Stewart/Cassiar Highway provides the shortest route to the Alaska Highway, meeting it just north of Watson Lake in the Yukon.

The third major access route (page 288) leads from the Montana/Alberta border, through Calgary, and then Edmonton, ending at Mile "0" of the Alaska Highway: the real start of the journey to the Yukon and Alaska.

# Access Route 1

## Vancouver, B.C., to Dawson Creek

The first leg of the route through the British Columbia interior goes from Vancouver to Dawson Creek and the southern end of the Alaska Highway.

Leaving Vancouver, take Highway 1, the Trans-Canada route. The highway is accessed from downtown Vancouver via Hastings Street, or from 12th Avenue, which becomes Grandview Highway before it runs into Highway 1.

The Trans-Canada Highway is also accessible from the north shore communities of North and West Vancouver. In these cities, Highway 1 is the Upper Levels Highway that leads from the Horseshoe Bay ferry terminal and across the Second Narrows Bridge (crossing Burrard Inlet).

The highway leaves Vancouver, passing into Burnaby, a large suburban community with several exits. Take Willingdon Avenue for central Burnaby. Immediately south of the Port Mann Bridge is the exit to Coquitlam.

The highway then crosses the Fraser River and passes through the suburb of Surrey.

## Along the Way

**The Fraser Valley**   After leaving the built-up Vancouver area, the highway curves northward and runs through the wide valley of the Fraser River, one of the most productive farming regions in Canada. Soon you'll pass three valley towns, Abbotsford, Clearbrook, and Matsqui, all about 45 miles from downtown Vancouver.

**Hope**   This town is the center for recreational activity in the area known as Rainbow Country. The town has its Infocentre on Highway 1 downtown, along with several motels, gas stations, car wash, RV parks, restaurants, and stores. Thirty minutes east—along Highway 3—is Manning Provincial Park, a large, spectacular park in the Cascade Mountains. Closer to town is the Coquihalla River Canyon Recreation Area, featuring a wonderful historic trail on the roadbed of the former Kettle Valley Railway, including a walk through five tunnels cut into the rock in the Coquihalla River canyon.

**Cariboo Country**   British Columbia residents call it "The Cariboo." This is the enormous area between the Coast and Rocky mountain ranges north of the Fraser Valley, a historic region that saw much gold rush activity during the late 1800s. Today it is a region of large cattle ranches, superb fishing lakes, and a few reminders of the Cariboo Gold Rush days, particularly at the restored town (historical theme park) of Barkerville. Through this area, the highway traces the old wagon route used by the gold miners and early settlers. Several Cariboo towns bear numbered names, corresponding to their position along the highway.

   North of the Cariboo plain, the highway enters a more rugged area after passing through the town of Williams Lake. Here, the Cariboo Mountains lie to the immediate east of the route, with the Interior Plateau stretching to the west.

# HIGHWAY LOG
## *Vancouver to Hope*
### 150 KM (93 miles)—1 hour, 45 minutes

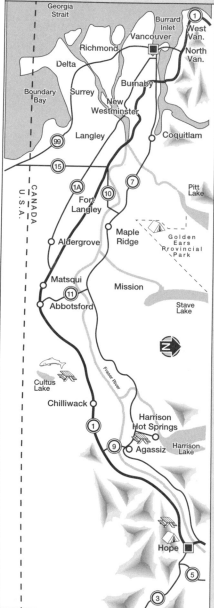

The drive begins on Highway 1, the Trans-Canada Highway, part of the federal route which runs from St. John's, Newfoundland, to the west coast of Vancouver Island. We're heading east and then north through the sprawling suburbs, collectively called the Lower Mainland. First, the highway passes through the city of Burnaby. The exit to the city of Coquitlam is found south of the Port Mann Bridge.

**Junction–Highway 15** Hwy. 15 leads south to Cloverdale and the U.S. border.

**Junction–152nd Street** This street leads south to central and south Surrey, the town of White Rock, and the main U.S. border crossing (to Blaine and Seattle, WA).

**Golden Ears Provincial Park** A popular park with a campground, lake swimming, and mountain trails, accessed via Hwy. 10 north and the Albion Ferry across the Fraser.

**Roads to Langley and Old Fort Langley** Take Hwy. 10 south to Langley. Turn onto Hwy. 10 north to Old Fort Langley, a restored Hudson's Bay Company fort, and the Albion Ferry to Maple Ridge and Highway 7. The Trans-Canada

Hwy. now curves northward and runs through the wide Fraser Valley, one of the most productive farming regions in Canada.

**Aldergrove** The Aldergrove exit leads south to the U.S. border.

**Exits to Abbotsford, Clearbrook, and Matsqui** The three Fraser Valley towns are located about 72 KM (45 miles) from downtown Vancouver, all offering gas stations, motels, restaurants, and stores. These are agricultural communities, part of the impressive "bread basket of B.C." where vegetables and fruit of almost every type are grown.

**Junction–Vedder Road** For Cultus Lake Provincial Park and Chilliwack Lake Provincial Park. Cultus Lake Park has four campgrounds plus picnic areas, swimming, boat launch, and hiking and bridle trails, as well as fishing for Dolly Varden and rainbow and cutthroat trout. Chilliwack River Provincial Park is nearby with picnic sites.

**Chilliwack** (KM 97.2, mile 60.3) Take the Yale Road exit for downtown Chilliwack. This agricultural city is at the north end of the Fraser Valley. A regional Infocentre is located at 44150 Luckaluck Way.

**Junction–Highway 9** (KM 111.8, mile 69.5) This road leads to the towns of Agassiz and Harrison Hot Springs. Harrison is a resort community with a public hot springs pool, large resort hotel, RV parks, and camping in Sasquatch Provincial Park. Hwy. 9 leads to a scenic riverside drive back to Vancouver via Hwy. 7.

**Viewpoint–Mount Cheam** (KM 119.8, mile 74.4) There are good views of Mt. Cheam (2107 meters, 6,912 feet) and Welch Peak (2,357 meters, 7,739 feet).

**Junction–Wahleach (Jones) Lake Road** (KM 130.2, mile 80.9) This logging road leads 5 KM (3.1 miles) to Jones Lake, a reservoir with fishing for rainbow and cutthroat trout, and kokanee.

**Rest Area** (KM 136.8, mile 85) Picnicking beside Hunter Creek.

**Junction–Silver Hope Road** (KM 145, mile 90) This road leads 61 KM (38 miles) through the Skagit Valley Provincial Recreation Area to campsites and the northern shore of Ross Lake reservoir.

**Hope** (KM 150, 93.2) This is the center for recreational activity in the area known as Rainbow Country. The town has an Infocentre on Hwy. 1 downtown, and has several motels, gas stations, RV parks, restaurants, stores, and a car wash.

**Suggested Sidetrip**

Manning Provincial Park is a 30-minute drive to the east, located in the Cascade Mountains and offering camping, swimming, canoeing, and hiking, with skiing (cross-country and downhill) during the winter months. Take Hwy. 3.

# HIGHWAY LOG
*Hope to Cache Creek*
193 KM (120 miles)—2 hours, 30 minutes

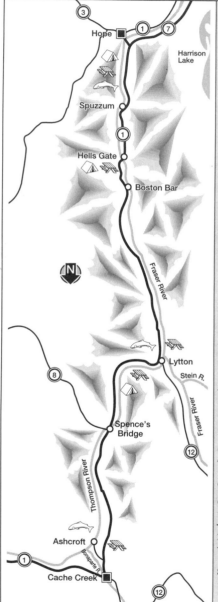

**Hope** Gas, cafés, motels, stores, pub. A scenic town beside the Fraser River to the south of Fraser Canyon. This is the junction point for the Coquihalla Hwy. (Hwy. 5), the toll road to Merritt, Kamloops, and the Okanagan Valley and Hwy. 3 (the Crow's Nest Hwy.). **Junction–Highway 7** At the west end of the Fraser River Bridge, to Agassiz and Harrison Hot Springs, and an alternate route to Mission and Vancouver.

**Rest Area** To the west, with swimming, picnic tables, fishing.

**Emery Creek Provincial Park** (KM 15, mile 9.3) Campsites, fishing, swimming, picnic tables. On the Fraser River, this park is on the original site of Emory City, which existed for a few exciting years during the gold rush period.

**Yale** (KM 23.5, mile 14.6) Gas, motels, stores, cafés. Historic town, 22 miles from Hope, the site of a Hudson's Bay Company post. The Spirit Cave Trail, 1 KM south of town, leads to views of the Cascades. The Yale Museum and St. John the Divine Church reflect the flavor of the gold rush era when Yale was the terminus for river steamboats.

**Spuzzum** Gas, café, store. Small village 20 KM (12.5 miles) from Yale.

**Alexandra Bridge Provincial Park** Turn to the east for campsites, and to the west for the picnic area. A trail to the west leads 10 minutes down the hill and across the railway tracks to a suspension bridge built in 1926 to replace an older bridge from 1863. The bridge affords a great view of the deep Fraser Canyon.

**Alexandra Lodge** A historic roadhouse built in 1862 and still operating with food and rooms.

**Hell's Gate** An airtram here takes visitors over Hell's Gate Rapids and a fish ladder. The fishway was built by the U.S. and Canada in 1946 to help more than 3 million salmon climb past the rapids each year.

**Hell's Gate Tunnel** One of seven tunnels in this section of the Fraser Canyon.

**Boston Bar** (KM 64.7, mile 40.2) Gas, motels, cafés. An old gold mining town, 41 KM (25.6 miles) north of Yale.

**Cog Harrington Bridge** The former North Bend cable ferry is on display on the east side of the river.

**Rest Area** Located 46 KM (28.5 miles) north of Boston Bar. Picnic tables beside Kanaka Bar, named for early Hawaiian settlers in B.C.

**Lytton** (KM 108.8, mile 67.6) Gas, motels, cafés, stores. Town 108 KM (68 miles) north of Hope. Info-centre at 400 Fraser Street. A cable ferry crosses the Fraser River to farms and the Stein River Valley.

**Sikhist Provincial Park** Just 6.4 KM (4 miles) north of Lytton. Campsites and picnic tables. This park beside the river offers views of the Thompson Canyon. There is a hiking trail on the old Cariboo Wagon Road.

**Goldpan Provincial Park** Located 23.4 KM (14.5 miles) north of Lytton. Campsites, picnic tables, swimming, and fall fishing for steelhead.

**Junction–Highway 8** Village of Spence's Bridge 37.5 KM (23.4 miles) north of Lytton. Gas, food, pub, store. This is a Thompson River rafting base.

**Red Hill Rest Area** Found 27.8 KM (17 miles) north of Spence's Bridge. Picnic tables.

**Ashcroft Manor** On the Trans-Canada Highway, an original roadhouse from the gold rush period, restored as a tea room and restaurant.

**Junction–Ashcroft Road (Highway 97C)** Found 11.3 KM (7 miles) south of Cache Creek, this sideroad leads to Ashcroft, a riverside agricultural town.

**Cache Creek** (KM 195.2, mile 121.3) Gas, motels, stores, restaurants, RV park.

# HIGHWAY LOG
## Cache Creek to Williams Lake
### 203 KM (126 miles)—2 hours, 15 minutes

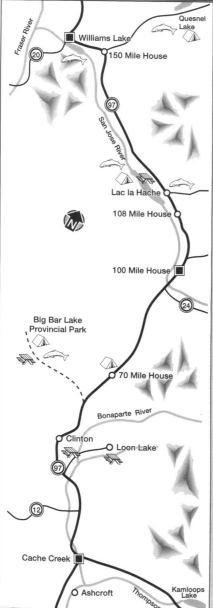

Cache Creek Town with gas, motels, restaurants, stores, RV park. Infocentre on Hwy. 97, two blocks north of Hwy. 1 junction (604) 457-9669. The Cariboo Hwy. bears the nickname "Gold Rush Trail." The road parallels the route of the historic Cariboo Wagon Road.

**Junction–Highway 12** (KM 10, mile 6.2) To Lillooet (75 KM, 46.6 miles).

**Junction–Loon Lake Road** (KM 21, mile 13) Turn east to Loon Lake, a resort and fishing area (20 KM, 12.4 miles). Loon Lake Provincial Park has campsites on the narrow 12 KM-long lake.

**Rest Area** (Carquille) (KM 26, mile 16.2) Picnic tables.

**Clinton** (KM 40, mile 25) Gas, cafés, motels, store. Some of the buildings are of historical interest, including the general store. The Infocentre, on the highway, is a former schoolhouse (604) 459-2442.

**Junction–Pavilion Mountain Road** (KM 40.2, mile 25) Runs southwest to Hwy. 12 (to Lillooet) and to Downing Provincial Park (15 KM). Campsites, swimming, picnic tables, fishing for rainbow. This is an extremely scenic backroad drive but be forewarned: The road may be hazardous during wet weather. It is closed during winter months. This is also an interesting route to access the road to Bralorne and Gold Bridge in the Chilcotin Mountain region.

**Rest Area** (KM 50, mile 31) Picnic tables with a view.

**Junction–Big Bar Road** (KM 60, mile 37) Runs west through sagebrush country to several guest ranches including the famous Gang Ranch and Big Bar Ranch. Also to Big Bar Lake Provincial Park (34 KM, 21 miles), with camping, swimming, picnic area, fishing, boating, wildlife.

**Junction–Chasm Provincial Park Road** (KM 65, mile 40.4) A day-use park, 4 KM east of the hwy., with a scenic chasm cut into lava.

**70 Mile House** (KM 69, mile 42.9) Gas, store, café. This village is a gateway to the south Cariboo lakes area. Campgrounds, resorts nearby.

**Junction–Highway 24** (KM 105.5, mile 65.6) To Lone Butte, Bridge Lake (41 KM, 25 miles) and the lakes district—with great fly fishing lakes.

**100 Mile House** (KM 115.9, mile 72) Gas, motels, restaurants, stores. Infocentre on the hwy. beside the gigantic skis (604) 395-5353. This thriving town is the market center for the central Cariboo district.

**Junction–Canim Lake Road** (KM 119, mile 74) Drive east to Canim Lake, a tiny village with lake activity and on to Mahood Falls (66 KM, 41 miles from the hwy.).

**108 Mile House Resort** (KM 131, mile 81.4) Ranch resort with golf course.

**Lac la Hache** (KM 140, mile 87) Gas, motels, cafés, pub, store. A prime fishing location. Infocentre is on Hwy. 97 (604) 396-7293.

**Junction–Timothy Lake Road** East from Lac La Hache to several fishing lakes. This gravel road leads to the villages of Likely and Horsefly and on to Barkerville.

**Lac La Hache Provincial Park** (KM 153, mile 95.1) Year-round camping, picnic area, beside the lake, beach, trails.

**Cariboo Provincial Nature Park** (KM 155, mile 96.3) A year-round nature study area on the San Jose River and Frog Lake.

**150 Mile House** (KM 190, mile 118) Gas, café, store, motel.

**Junction–Horsefly Road** Runs east from 150 Mile House to Quesnel Lake and village of Horsefly (56 KM, 34.8 miles). Horsefly Lake Provincial Park (69 KM, 43 miles) has campsites and lake activity.

**Williams Lake** (KM 203, mile 127.3) Gas, hotel, motels, restaurants, fast food places, stores. This is a fast-growing lumber, mining and ranching center.

# HIGHWAY LOG
## Williams Lake to Prince George
238 KM (148 miles)—2 hours, 40 minutes

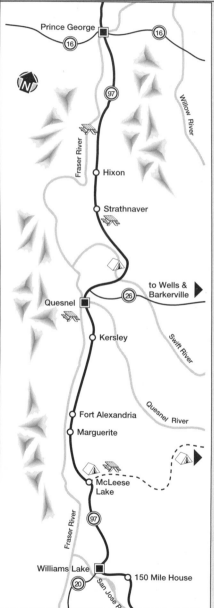

**Williams Lake** Gas, motels, hotel, stores, pub, restaurants. Infocentre on Hwy. 97 at south end of town.
**McLeese Lake** (KM 43, mile 26.7) Small village with gas, motels, campgrounds, café.
**Rest Area** (McLeese Lake) (KM 45, mile 28) At north end of the lake with picnic tables.
**Junction–Likely Road** (KM 45, mile 28) To Big Lake Ranch and the village of Likely, for resorts and campgrounds (open summer only). Infocentre: (604) 790-2422.
**Marguerite Ferry** (KM 63, mile 39.1) This aerial tram operates until freeze-up. Reaction power is supplied by the river. Free. By taking this car ferry across the Fraser River, you can take a scenic backroad route to Quesnel.
**Fort Alexandria** (KM 67, mile 41.6) Gas, store. A cairn marks the last post established in B.C. by the North West Company.
**Rest Area** (Australian) (KM 84, mile 52.2) Picnic tables.
**Kersley** (KM 98, mile 60.1) Gas, store, café.
**Junction–Quesnel-Hydraulic Road** (KM 114, mile 70.1) Runs beside the Quesnel River.
**Quesnel** (KM 120, mile 74.6) A lumbering, pulp mill and commer-

cial city, Quesnel offers gold panning for visitors (map at Gold Commissioner's office, 350 Barlow St., 604-992-4301). Infocentre on Hwy. 97 at south end of town opposite the rail station. Phone (604) 992-8716 (summer) or (604) 747-2444 (winter).

**Junction–Front Street** Leads west across the bridge and onto Nazko Rd. for Bouchie Lake, the village of Nazko and several access points for the Alexander Mackenzie Heritage Trail.

**Junction–Baker Drive** Leads west 8 KM (5 miles) to Pinnacles Provincial Park picnic area and hoodoos (erosion pillars).

**Cottonwood River Provincial Park** Take Old Prince George Road, west off Hwy. 97. at the north end of town. Camping, fishing, picnic area. The road cuts back to Hwy. 97 at Strathnaver.

**SUGGESTED SIDETRIP ON HIGHWAY 26**

For a fascinating trip into Cariboo history, take this road east to Wells, the Bowron Lakes, and Barkerville.

**Wells** A quaint, false-fronted village with gas, store, café, and a former gold-bearing quartz mine. Infocentre: (604) 994-3237.

**Bowron Lakes Provincial Park** (109 KM, 67.7 miles) has the province's most popular circle canoe route. There are six lakes with wilderness campsites, cooking shelters, and cabins. Lodges in the park area offer guided tours of the Bowron Lakes canoe route. Get information from the Ministry of Parks, Prince George (phone 604-565-6270), or at the Quesnel and Wells infocentres.

**Barkerville** (111 KM, 69 miles from Hwy. 97) is a restored gold rush town and a historical theme park.

**BACK ON HIGHWAY 97**

**Ten Mile Lake Provincial Park** (KM 131, mile 81.4) Camping, beach, boat ramp, trails.

**Rest Area** (Hush Lake) (KM 144, mile 89.5) Picnic tables, boat launch.

**Strathnaver** (KM 160, mile 99.4) Gas, store. Road to Cottonwood River Park (see above).

**Hixon** (KM 175, mile 113.1) Gas, café, store, pub.

**Viewpoint** (KM 182, mile 113) View of the valley to the west.

**Rest Area** (Woodpecker) (KM 185, mile 115) Picnic tables.

**Prince George** (KM 238, mile 149) Gas, hotels, motels, restaurants, pubs, stores. This is the major city of the northern B.C. interior, with large pulp mills and rail service. It is roughly the midpoint between Jasper and Prince Rupert on the Yellowhead Hwy. Prince George Infocentre: 1198 Victoria St. downtown; phone (604) 562-3700.

# HIGHWAY LOG
## Prince George to Dawson Creek
412 KM (256 miles)—4 hours, 30 minutes

Named for John Hart, a former B.C. premier, the Hart Highway is a scenic mountain road. Fifty kilometers from Prince George, the road parallels Summit Lake and then runs beside the Crooked River for 95 KM (59 miles). Here are some highlights: Crooked River, Whisker's Point, and Tudyah Lake provincial parks provide good picnic spots and campsites.

From the Parsnip River (KM 156.5, mile 97), the road begins climbing through two ranges of the Rocky Mountains. Carp Lake Provincial Park, with campsites, is off the highway near McLeod Lake. Highway 39 connects with the town of Mackenzie and Williston Lake, the largest man-made lake in the province. The Pine Pass viewpoint gives spectacular views. Powder King ski resort is 2 KM past the viewpoint. There is a time zone change here. Set your time one hour ahead as you travel north.

Highway 29 north is the shortcut to the Alaska Highway and the town of Hudson's Hope. Chetwynd, at KM 302 (mile 187.6), is a town with a variety of visitor services. Highway 29 South leads to the town of Tumbler Ridge and B.C.'s largest coal mine.

East Pine Provincial Park is a handy picnic stop beyond Chetwynd. Past Chetwynd, the road climbs for about 20 KM (12 miles) before descending to the flat prairie land of northeastern B.C. and the Alaska Highway.

**Turnoff to Giscome Portage Park** (KM 43.3, mile 26.9)
**Crooked River Provincial Park** (KM 70, mile 43.3) The first park north of Prince George is a large area (1016 hectares, 2510 acres) with campsites and fine sandy beaches on Bear Lake, plus swimming, non-power boating, and fishing for rainbow and brook trout, Dolly Varden, and grayling.
**Picnic Area** (KM 70.6, mile 44) In Crooked River Provincial Park.
**Bear Lake** (KM 72, mile 44.8) Small community with gas, motel, café.
**Highway Services** (KM 115.5, mile 71.8) Gas, café.
**Whisker's Point Provincial Park** (KM 125, mile 77.7) Turnoff to another good camping park with swimming and fishing.
**Fort McLeod** (KM 136, mile 84.5) Village with gas, store, motel, café. Monument to 1908 founders.
**Turnoff to Tudyak Lake Provincial Park** (KM 144.5, mile 90) Camping, picnic tables.
**Junction–Highway 39** (KM 154.8, mile 95.2) Gas, café, motel. The town of Mackenzie is accessed via

Hwy. 39. It's 29 KM (18 miles) from the junction where the Info-centre is located.
**Bijoux Falls Provincial Park** (KM 185.6, mile 115.2) A scenic picnic park on the hwy. A 40-meter (120-foot) waterfall plunges into the forest.
**Pine Pass** (KM 199, mile 119) Hart Hwy. summit. Stop at the viewpoint, two miles north of the summit, for a spectacular panoramic view of the Rockies and Azouzetta Lake.
**Powder King Ski Resort** (KM 192.2, mile 119.4) Downhill skiing, accommodations.
**Picnic Area** (KM 204.4, mile 127)
**Picnic Areas** (KM 263.3, mile 164) On both sides of road.
**Chetwynd** (KM 302, mile 187.6) This town has a good small museum, the Little Prairie Heritage Museum (on West Gate Road).
**Junction–Highway 29** Hwy. 29 south leads to the coal-mining town of Tumbler Ridge. Hwy. 29 north is the shortcut to the Alaska Hwy., via Hudson's Hope, a small town with cafés, motels, and stores, plus the huge hydro dam and museum.
**East Pine Provincial Park** (KM 335, mile 208) Picnic area, boating.
**Dawson Creek** (KM 412, mile 256) The town's Infocentre is located next to the museum and art gallery at 900 Alaska Avenue.

# Access Route 2

## Victoria, B.C., to Upper Liard, Y.T.

### Along the Way

**Victoria** British Columbia's capital city, and a major visiting place for tourists from around the world, Victoria offers much in the way of sightseeing and recreation. Its English heritage and ambiance are well known, as are its gardens. Founded by the Hudson's Bay Company, and playing a slight role in the War of 1912 (a local conflict involving the San Juan Islands, called the "Pig War"), Victoria is a combination of civil service town, retirement haven for genteel seniors, and a tourist trap of the best sort, with fine hotels and a host of bed-and-breakfast homes. The outlying areas are as fascinating as the city itself. The famed Butchart Gardens, north of the city, should be experienced. The Royal B.C. Museum, downtown, offers an overview of this fascinating province's history.

**Island Highway** From its southern tip to its north coast, the Island Highway runs along the eastern shore of Vancouver Island, connecting cities and towns, and taking visitors to island attractions. These include some of the best salmon fishing in the world, campsites in the island forests, and major recreation areas, including Strathcona Provincial Park and at least a dozen smaller parks along the eastern shoreline. The island connects placid resort and retirement communities in its southern half with the rugged fishing villages to the north.

This highway is the route taken to reach the Inside Passage ferry, *Queen of the North,* at its terminal in Port Hardy. The highway bears two numbers: It is called the 1 between Victoria and Nanaimo, and the 19 from Nanaimo to Port Hardy. Most visitors catch a ferry from the mainland, and arrive at Swartz Bay, near Victoria. Ferries are available from the Vancouver area to Nanaimo, 113 kilometers (70 miles) north of Victoria.

**North Island**   The character of the island landscape changes dramatically north of Campbell River. The highway turns inland, crossing several mountain ridges and running the length of deep valleys and beside lakes. Sideroads lead to several scenic communities, including Port McNeill (a fishing town with a ferry to Malcolm Island), and Telegraph Cove, a historic fishing port now famous for its restored buildings and whale-watching tours. At the end of the road is Port Hardy, with a busy fishing harbor and the B.C. ferries terminal. Ninety minutes' drive from town lies Cape Scott Provincial Park, containing a temperate rain forest, with a trail leading to the northwest coast of the island, an area that includes several long, isolated beaches.

**Inside Passage**   Two car ferries (*Queen of the North* and *Queen of Prince Rupert*) ply the waters of the Inside Passage between Port Hardy and the city of Prince Rupert on B.C.'s north coast. The ferries provide the essential connection for this access route as it continues from Prince Rupert and takes the Yellowhead and Stewart/Cassiar highways. In summer (from May 25th), northbound ferries depart from Port Hardy at 7:30 A.M. and arrive at Prince Rupert at 10:30 P.M. During June, July, and September, the ships depart on even-numbered days. In August the ferries leave Port Hardy on odd-numbered days. The scheduling is reversed for southbound travelers, with ferries leaving at 7:30 A.M. and arriving in Port Hardy at 10:30 P.M. This schedule is also followed during the last week of May. For more information, call (604) 386-3431, or visit the B.C. Ferries Internet site, http:// bcferries.bc.ca/ferries. Information is updated frequently and schedules for all B.C. ferry routes are available.

**Stewart/Cassiar Highway**   Leaving Prince Rupert, you take the Yellowhead Highway (Hwy. 16) east for 240 KM (149 miles), and turn north to continue via the Stewart/Cassiar Highway (Provincial Route 37) for 733 KM (456 miles). The highways between Prince Rupert and Upper Liard are covered in the final highway log for this access route.

# HIGHWAY LOG
## *Victoria to Parksville, B.C.*
### 147 KM (91.3 miles)—1 hour, 50 minutes

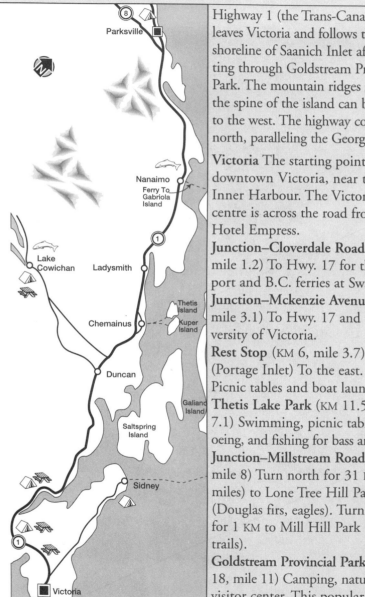

Highway 1 (the Trans-Canada) leaves Victoria and follows the shoreline of Saanich Inlet after cutting through Goldstream Provincial Park. The mountain ridges forming the spine of the island can be seen to the west. The highway continues north, paralleling the Georgia Strait.

**Victoria** The starting point is downtown Victoria, near the Inner Harbour. The Victoria Infocentre is across the road from the Hotel Empress.

**Junction–Cloverdale Road** (KM 2, mile 1.2) To Hwy. 17 for the airport and B.C. ferries at Swartz Bay.

**Junction–Mckenzie Avenue** (KM 5, mile 3.1) To Hwy. 17 and the University of Victoria.

**Rest Stop** (KM 6, mile 3.7) (Portage Inlet) To the east. Picnic tables and boat launch.

**Thetis Lake Park** (KM 11.5, mile 7.1) Swimming, picnic tables, canoeing, and fishing for bass and trout.

**Junction–Millstream Road** (KM 13, mile 8) Turn north for 31 KM (19 miles) to Lone Tree Hill Park (Douglas firs, eagles). Turn south for 1 KM to Mill Hill Park (hiking trails).

**Goldstream Provincial Park** (KM 18, mile 11) Camping, nature trails, visitor center. This popular park has stands of very high Douglas firs amid a mixed forest. There is an annual chum salmon run on the Goldstream River.

**Junction–Shawnigan Lake Cutoff** (KM 28, mile 17.4) To a resort and recreation area that includes Memory Island Provincial Park (beaches) and Shawnigan Lake Provincial Park (swimming, boating, picnicking). The scenic drive over Malahat Mountain begins here.

**Bamberton Provincial Park** (KM 35.5, mile 22) Camping, swimming, picnic tables.

**Mill Bay** (KM 45, mile 28) Visitor Infocentre on Hwy. 1. The ferry travels to Brentwood Bay near Butchart Gardens. Gas, stores.

**Junction–Cobble Hill Road** (KM 48, mile 29.8) West to Cobble Hill and Shawnigan Lake. East to Cowichan Bay.

**Cowichan River** At the south entrance to the city of Duncan. This popular fishing river has a 19 KM trail offering anglers great fishing for rainbow, steelhead, and salmon.

**Duncan** (KM 62, mile 38.5) Gas, stores, motels. Infocentre on Hwy. 1 downtown (604) 746-4421. A city of 20,000, Duncan is home of the Cowichan Indian Tribe, best known for crafts including Cowichan sweaters.

**B.C. Forest Museum** (KM 64, mile 39.8) A popular attraction with indoor and outdoor displays.

**Junction–Highway 18** (KM 65, mile 40.3) To the town of Lake Cowichan (28 KM, 17.3 miles), Bamfield, Carmanah Park, the West Coast Trail, and Port Renfrew.

**Crofton** (KM 74, mile 46) A pulp mill town with ferry to Salt Spring Island. Infocentre at the museum, next to ferry terminal.

**Junction–Highway 1A** (KM 89, mile 55) Gas, stores, Infocentre in a rail caboose on Chemaines Rd. The town is famous for the historical murals on the downtown buildings. A ferry runs to Thetis and Kuper islands.

**Ladysmith** (KM 91, mile 51.5) Infocentre on Hwy. 1. Stores, cafés, gas, arboretum, and museum.

**Junction–Yellow Point Road** (KM 96, mile 59.6) To Roberts Memorial and Hemer day-use parks.

**Nanaimo** (KM 112, mile 70) The "Harbour City." Gas, hotels, motels, restaurants, stores. Travel Infocentre at Hwy. 19 and Bryden St. At Nanaimo, the Island Hwy. to Port Hardy becomes Hwy. 19. Ferry terminal at Departure Bay, at the end of Hwy. 1. Ferries run to the Vancouver area.

**Lantzville Road** (KM 134, mile 83) A small seaside community. Gas, a great pub, stores, camping.

**Parksville** (KM 154, mile 95.6) Gas, stores, motels, restaurants, pub, camping. A resort community with golfing and a popular beach.

# HIGHWAY LOG
## *Parksville to Campbell River*
### 117 KM (73 miles)—1 hour, 45 minutes

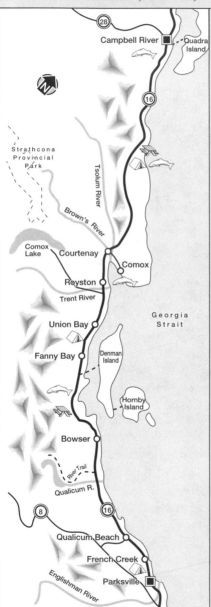

Parksville, a resort and retirement town, has a long, wide beach, golfing, and many recreational adventures within a few kilometers' drive. The Infocentre is on Highway 19 at the south end of town.

**Junction–Highways 16 and 4** From Parksville, Hwy. 16 runs through a continuous series of resort communities with frequent gas stations, stores, cafés, and campgrounds.

**French Creek** (KM 6, mile 3.7) Take Lee Road east for camping, motels, and café.

**Lasqueti Island Ferry** Take Lee Road to the terminal. A foot-passenger ferry runs to this small gulf island daily except Tuesday and Wednesday. General store on the island. Squitty Bay Provincial Park is 25 KM from the ferry dock.

**Qualicum Beach** (KM 11, mile 6.8) A resort town, known for its golf courses and salmon fishing. Infocentre on the hwy. marked by a totem pole (604) 752-9535. The Little Qualicum River, just north of town, is a favorite trout fishing stream.

**Junction–Horne Lake Road** (KM 25, mile 15.5) To Spider Lake and Horne Lake Caves provincial parks. Spider Lake Park is an excellent picnic park with canoeing and trails. The caves are open daily in summer, with a fee charged. This route provides a scenic sidetrip using logging roads.

**Bowser** (KM 29, mile 18) Village named after a B.C. premier, or the local pub owner's dog, depending on whom you ask. Gas, store, accommodations.

**Rosewall Creek Provincial Park** (KM 40, mile 24.8) West off the hwy. Picnic tables, fishing.

**Fanny Bay** (KM 49, mile 30.4) Seaside village on Bayne Sound. The Fanny Bay Inn is an early building. The *Brico,* a cable-laying ship, now operates as a restaurant.

**Ferry to Denman and Hornby Islands** (KM 51, mile 31.7) The ferry from Buckley Bay runs to Denman Island, with wildlife, sandstone beaches, and salmon fishing. There is a small campground in Fillongley Provincial Park. A second ferry runs between Denman and Hornby islands. There are private campsites on Hornby, which is one of the most scenic of the gulf islands.

**Union Bay** (KM 59, mile 36.6) Gas, motels, campgrounds, and a boat launch used for trips to Sandy Island Provincial Park.

**Junction–Cumberland Road** (KM 66, mile 41) To Cumberland, a former coal mining town. Some of the Chinatown buildings from the early 1900s still stand. Take Comox Lake Road from Cumberland to this major fishing lake.

**Royston** (KM 67, mile 41.6) An oceanfront village off the hwy.

**Courtenay** (KM 73, mile 45.4) The recreation center of the mid-island area, Courtenay is close to excellent lake and saltwater fishing, two ski areas, and other outdoor activities. Strathcona Provincial Park, B.C.'s oldest park, is a superb wilderness area. The Infocentre is in Courtenay, at 2040 Cliffe Avenue, off Hwy. 19.

**Miracle Beach Provincial Park** (KM 96, mile 59.6) A busy park with camping, swimming, trails, picnic sites, and coho fishing.

**Saratoga Beach** (KM 97, mile 60.3) A sandy beach with golf course, private campground, and boat launch on the Oyster River.

**Mitlenatch Island Provincial Park** (KM 109, mile 72.1) Access by boat with seabirds in abundance.

**Campbell River** (KM 116, mile 72.1) Canada's "Salmon Fishing Capital," this town has a variety of motels, hotels, fishing resorts, restaurants, pubs, and stores. The Infocentre is in the Museum building in Tyee Plaza on the hwy. The town overlooks Discovery Passage. Quadra Island lies across the passage, with a ferry running to it from downtown Campbell River.

# HIGHWAY LOG
## Campbell River to Port Hardy
### 237 KM (147 miles)—3 hours

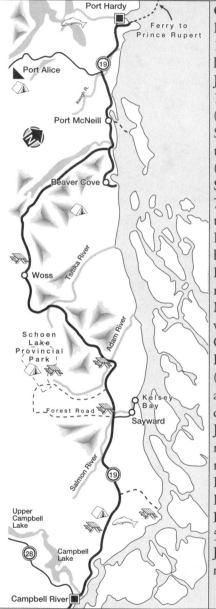

**Campbell River** (KM 0, mile 0) Infocentre in Tyee Plaza, off Hwy. 19. The ferry to Quadra Island leaves from downtown.

**Junction–Highway 28** (KM 2, mile 1.2) This road runs west for 92 KM (57.1 miles) through Elk Falls and Strathcona provincial parks, to the town of Gold River. Infocentre (604) 238-7123.

**Seymour Narrows** (KM 12, mile 7.5) Two trails lead to cliffs above the narrows, near where Ripple Rock, a shipping hazard, was blown to smithereens in 1958.

**Rest Area** (Ripple Rock) (KM 14, mile 8.7) Picnic tables.

**Morton Lake Provincial Park** Turn west onto Adams Resort Road. Camping, fishing, trails, swimming.

**Rest Area** (Roberts Lake) (KM 32.5, mile 20.2) Picnic area. Good fishing for Dolly Varden, cutthroat, and kokanee.

**Junction–Rock Bay Road** (KM 39, mile 24.2) Runs for 21 KM (13 miles) beside McCreight Lake to Rock Bay and Chatham Point Lighthouse.

**Rest Area** (Big Tree Creek) (KM 50, mile 31) Picnic area.

**Junction–Sayward Road** (KM 66, mile 41) Gas, café. The road leads to Kelsey Bay, a village with a boat launch and wharf.

**Rest Area** (Keta Lake) (KM 75, mile 46.6) Picnic tables.

**Rest Area** (Adam River Bridge) (KM 81, mile 50.3) A picnic area is two KM south of the bridge.

**Rest Area** (Eve River) (KM 95, mile 59) Picnic tables.

**Junction–Schoen Lake Logging Road** (KM 128, mile 79.5) This gravel mainline runs to Schoen Lake and several other prime fishing lakes. Schoen Lake Provincial Park has campsites, mountain trails, canoeing, and a striking alpine meadow filled with masses of wildflowers in July and August.

**Rest Area** (Hoomak Lake) (KM 134, mile 83.3) Picnic area.

**Junction–Woss Road** (KM 140, mile 87) To Woss (2 KM). Gas, store, café, camping. This is an old logging town. A logging railway has four-hour tours through the Nimpkish Valley during the summer.

**Rest Area** (Eagle's Nest) (KM 146, mile 90.7) Picnic tables.

**Junction–Zeballos Road** (KM 156, mile 96.9) West to village of Zeballos, at the head of Zeballos Inlet (21 KM, 13 miles). **Little Hustan Cave Regional Park** A short distance along Zeballos Road, with several caves and a river flowing through. **Fair Harbour** Located 35 KM beyond Zeballos is the launching point for canoeists and sea kayakers exploring Kyuquot Sound.

**Junction–Beaver Cove Road** (KM 190, mile 118) Runs southeast to Beaver Cove and Telegraph Cove.

**Port McNeill** (KM 197, mile 122.4) Gas, motels, cafés, store. Infocentre on Beach Drive next to ferry terminal. A government ferry runs to Alert Bay.

**Rest Area** (Misty Lake) (KM 211, mile 131) To Port Alice (motels, cafés, store, boat launch). Camping on Alice and Victoria lakes.

**Beaver Harbour** Take the airport turnoff. This is the site of the Hudson's Bay Company's Fort Rupert, founded in 1849.

**Road to Bear Cove** (KM 216, mile 134.2) The terminal for the ferry to Prince Rupert is 5 KM.

**Junction–Coal Harbor Road** (KM 217, mile 134.8) East is a scenic route to Port Hardy. Coal Harbor is a former whaling station (café and fishing wharf).

**Port Hardy** (KM 220, mile 136.7) The largest community on the North Island, with motels, cafés, private campgrounds, and stores. Infocentre on Market Street.

# HIGHWAY LOG
## Prince Rupert to Stewart Junction
337 KM (234 miles)—4 hours, 15 minutes

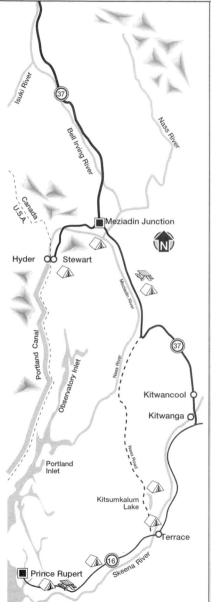

The drive begins in downtown Prince Rupert. The first 245.2 kilometers (152.4 miles) are on the Yellowhead Highway (Hwy. 16), traveling east. We then pick up the Stewart/Cassiar Highway (Highway 37) to head north.

**Rest Area** (KM 12, mile 7.5) Picnic tables.

**Diana Lake Provincial Park** (KM 20.4, mile 12.7) Located 2 KM south of Hwy. 16. Scenic day-use park with picnic tables, swimming.

**Prudomme Lake Provincial Park** (KM 21.9, mile 13.6) Camping, picnic tables.

**Rest Area** (KM 93.2, mile 58) Picnic tables. Enter west of the Exchamsiks River bridge.

**Exchamsiks Provincial Park** (KM 94, mile 58.4) Picnic area and overnight RV parking. No tent camping.

**Junction–Kalum Lake Road** (KM 146.2, mile 90.8) This logging road leads to several fishing lakes and the Tseax lava beds. A circle route is available by returning to Terrace via Cranberry Rd. (221 KM, 137 miles).

**West Access to Terrace** (KM 149.2, mile 92.7) Infocentre on Yellowhead Hwy. Terrace is a large town with restaurants, stores, gas stations, hotels and motels.

**Bridge** (KM 150.3, mile 93.3) Over the Skeena River to Ferry Island Municipal Campground. Picnic tables.

**Rest Area** (KM 183.1, mile 113. 7) Picnic tables and historical marker on Skeena River steamboats.

**Rest Area** (KM 236, mile 146.6) Picnic tables.

**Junction–Stewart/Cassiar Highway** (KM 245.2, mile 152.4) Gas, café. Bridge across Skeena River to village of Kitwanga. New Hazelton is 43 KM (26.7 miles) west on Hwy. 16.

**Turnoff–Village of Kitwanga** (KM 249.5, mile 155) Totem pole collection, tourist kiosk.

**Turnoff–Village of Kitwancool** (KM 266.8, mile 165.8)

**Turnoff to Kitwanga Lake** (KM 281, mile 174.6) Rough road leads to campsites, boat launch, fishing road, and exits to hwy. at KM 290.3.

**Rest Area** (KM 346.2, mile 215) At north end of Kitwanga Lake, with picnic tables.

**Picnic Area** (KM 394.2, mile 245) South end of Nass River bridge.

**Meziadin Lake Provincial Park** (KM 407.2, mile 253) Campsites on lake, picnic tables, fishing.

**Junction–Meziadin** (KM 408.5, mile 253.8) Turn west on Hwy.

37A to Stewart. Café, gas, motel, Infocentre at junction.

**Picnic Area** (KM 430.2, mile 267.3) View of the Bear Glacier and its lake.

**Bear Glacier** Turnouts along the lake at KM 434 (mile 269.7).

**Bear River Canyon** (KM 445.6, mile 277) Narrow road, look for rocks on road.

**Bear River Bridge** (KM 468, mile 290.7) Entrance to town of Stewart. Museum and Infocentre in the old fire hall at 6th and Columbia. Continue through Stewart and down the road to reach Hyder, Alaska. There is no border crossing station between the towns.

**Stewart** At the head of the Portland Canal, a long fjord leading from the Inside Passage, Stewart has overnight accommodations, stores, bars, and cafés.

**Hyder** Located 2.3 miles beyond Stewart, Hyder has a small population of 85 residents. The tidal flats at Hyder reveal the remains of the extensive mining industry that developed here after the discovery of silver in 1917. You will see many pilings along the flats, on which buildings perched during the busy mining era. The only mining operation left in the area is a gold and silver mine owned by Westmin Resources.

# HIGHWAY LOG
## *Meziadin Junction to Upper Liard*
### 575 KM (357 miles)—7 hours

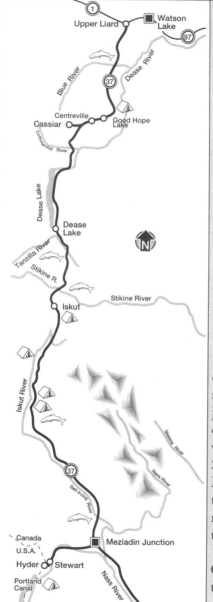

North of Meziadin Junction, the Stewart/Cassiar Highway quickly runs out of pavement and moves into mountainous country, with the Coast range to the west and the Skeena Mountains to the east. Ningunsaw Pass (466 meters, 1,530 feet) is the divide between the Nass and Stikine watersheds. Found 13.4 KM (8.3 miles) beyond the pass is a historical marker noting the Dominion Telegraph Line, which linked Dawson City with Vancouver in 1901.

After another 34 KM (21 miles) you drive into a burn area where a large fire destroyed 78,000 acres of forest in 1958. The berries in this area are huckleberries; it's B.C.'s largest huckleberry patch.

Dease Lake is the nearest large community to the enormous Spatsizi Plateau Wilderness Park, enjoyed by thousands of hikers and canoeists each year. The largest wilderness preserve in Canada, Spatsizi is joined at the highway by Mount Edziza Provincial Park (to the west). The best place for information on this wilderness area is the Infocentre in Iskut.

The road now climbs into the Cassiar Mountains and descends to the Yukon Plateau after passing

Boya Lake Provincial Park. The highway joins the Alaska Highway at Upper Liard, just across the Yukon border. Watson Lake, Y.T., is 31 KM (19 miles) east (right) of the junction.

**Paved highway ends** (KM 1.8, mile 1.1) The road is almost totally graveled until the Alaska Hwy. junction.
**Picnic Area** (KM 32.7, mile 20.3)
**Picnic Area** (KM 91.7, mile 57) Table and boat launch
**Highway Services** (KM 94, mile 58.4) Gas, food, lodging.
**Access to Bob Quinn Lake** (KM 142.7, mile 88.6) At the maintenance camp. Picnic table and toilet.
**Rest Area** (KM 192, mile 119.3) Picnic tables at Eastman Creek. The creek was named for Kodak inventor George Eastman, who hunted and fished in here.
**Kinaskan Lake Provincial Park** (KM 210, mile 130.5) Camping, picnic tables, boat launch, fishing.
**Tatogga Lake Resort** (KM 237.4, mile 147.5) Gas, café, RV park, cabins. Turn northeast on to Ealue Lake Road for a sidetrip to the Spatsizi wilderness area.
**High Watermark Campsite** (KM 249.8, mile 155.2) Private campground.
**Iskut** (KM 253.2, mile 157.3) Small Tahltan village. Gas, store, post office, camping, Infocentre.

**Forty Mile Flats** (KM 265.5, mile 165) Café, gas, store, private campground.
**Turnout** (KM 284.3, mile 176.6) **Roadside Display** Map of Iskut Lakes Recreation Area.
**Gnat Pass Summit** (KM 316.7, mile 196.8)
**Rest Area** (KM 327.3, mile 203.4) Picnic tables.
**Junction–Telegraph Creek Road** (KM 336.7, mile 209.2) Access to the town of Dease Lake. Gas, food, motels, restaurants, post office.
**Ghost Town of Laketon** (KM 380, mile 236) Seen across the lake at the mouth of Dease Creek. Laketon existed during the Cassiar gold rush (1872-80).
**Dease River Wilderness Park** (KM 404, mile 251.3) Private campground, gas, store, showers.
**Mighty Moe's Place** (KM 421.7, mile 262) Private campground.
**Picnic Park** (KM 439.7, mile 273.2) On Simmons Lake, fishing for lake trout.
**Junction–Cassiar Road** (KM 454, mile 282.1) This road runs for 15.7 KM (9.7 miles) to a longtime asbestos mine and village of Cassiar. Gas, bank, stores.
**Site of Centreville** (KM 468.3, mile 291) During the gold rush days of the 1870s, some 3,000 people lived here. The present population is two.

# Access Route 3

## Alberta/Montana Border to Dawson Creek

Montana offers two border crossings connecting the Great Falls/ Glacier Park region with southwestern Alberta. The first in this series of highway logs covers the route from the Piegan/Carway border crossing (just east of Glacier National Park). This route enters Canada at Carway and takes Highway 2, the fast road to Calgary and Edmonton, and then leads northwest through the Peace River watershed to Dawson Creek and "Mile 0" of the Alaska Highway.

From Great Falls, Montana, take Interstate 15 north, and cross the international border at Sweetgrass, entering Alberta at Coutts. Drive north on Alberta Route 4 to Lethbridge, switch to Highway 3 for a few miles, and pick up Highway 2 for the remainder of the drive to Calgary and Edmonton. Between the border and Edmonton, the drive is flat and generally empty of scenery, compared to the scenery to come in the more northern parts of this route and along the Alaska Highway. This entire drive to Dawson Creek, a distance of 1206 KM (750 miles), runs through plains, east of the Rocky Mountains, in Alberta's vast prairie region. The Rocky Mountains and their foothills will be in view to the west, between the Montana border and Calgary.

### Along the Way

**Glacier and Waterton Lakes National Parks**   It would be difficult for travelers headed for Alaska, driving right beside these superb national parks, not to enjoy them for at least a day. The famed Going to the Sun Road, leading through Glacier National Park, is located less than an hour's drive from the international border crossing. Waterton Lakes National Park is the Canadian component of this unusual pair of joined parks. The Canadian Rockies landscape is every bit as scenic as the Glacier landscape to the south.

**Tour of Kananaskis Country**   North of Waterton Lakes, along the eastern foothills of the Rockies, lies a huge tract of wilderness area, now becoming better known for its recreational facilities. Running all the way north to the Canmore/Banff area, west of Calgary, Kananaskis Country is found on both sides of Provincial Route 40, which leads south from the town of Seebe (on Highway 1), joining Route 541 at the south end near High River. Peter Lougheed Provincial Park, nestled against the high walls of the Rockies, is the centerpiece of this fabulous recreation region.

**Highway 2 to Calgary and Edmonton**    The large Alberta cities are modern, clean, and full of attractions for visitors. You may wish to time your trip north in order to be in Calgary for the famous Stampede, Canada's largest rodeo and agricultural fair, held over 10 days around the second week of July each year. Edmonton, the provincial capital, boasts the largest shopping mall in Canada, the West Edmonton Mall, with 800 stores.

**Highway 43—River Country**    While the flat route to Edmonton is accomplished over a fast divided highway (Highway 2), the rest of the journey is over two-lane highway, a slower, more meandering route through northwestern Alberta's river and lake country. Over the 591 KM (367 miles) between Edmonton and Dawson Creek, you'll cross a half-dozen major rivers, including the Smoky, Athabaska, and McLeod, drive past many small lakes, and pass through a baker's dozen of little towns, plus one big one—Grande Prairie. Several of the towns, including Whitecourt, are there because of the nearby forests. Grand Prairie is in the middle of a huge oil and gas field, and has long been an agricultural center.

**Highway 34 and 2–Northern Prairie**    In the final 134 KM (83 miles) between Grand Prairie and Dawson Creek, the highway enters the Peace River Valley, the wide, rolling prairie known for its honey production. This stretch of road offers a steady succession of public campgrounds and outpost towns including Beaverlodge and Pouce Coupe. Both communities offer visitor services, including motels, gas stations, grocery stores, and cafés. The Alberta/British Columbia border, 38 kilometers (24 miles) from Dawson Creek, is crossed between these two small towns.

# HIGHWAY LOG
## *Montana Border to Calgary*
### 321 KM (199 miles)—3 hours, 40 minutes

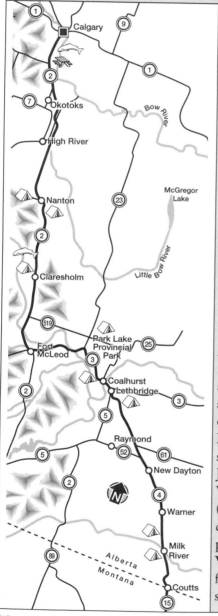

This route begins at the U.S./ Canada border, north of Great Falls, Montana. The fastest passage through northern Montana is via Interstate 15, which crosses the border into Alberta at Sweetgrass. The more scenic route leads northwest along Highway 89 through Browning and then beside Glacier National Park to the border crossing at Piegan. From there, Highway 2 leads north to Calgary. This first of three logs covers the fastest route through Lethbridge, Alberta, to Calgary. With a lack of kilometer-posts along these highways, we have omitted kilometer-post numbers on the following logs.

**U.S.–Canada Border** At Coutts, Alberta. The customs station here is open 24 hours a day. Gas, food, and motel accommodations are available at the border. We're now on Alberta Hwy. 4.

**Milk River** A small town with gas, store, café, motel, and camping.

**Junction–Road 501** Leads east to Writing-in-Stone Provincial Park (42 KM, 26 miles). The park has campsites and contains Indian petroglyphs.

**Warner** Village 40 KM (24.5 miles) from the border, with gas, food, store.

**New Dayton** Another small village, with hotel.

**Junction–Highway 61** Leads east to Cypress Hills Provincial Park, on the Alberta/Saskatchewan border. The park is slightly less than 200 KM (125 miles) from the junction.

**Lethbridge** City of 60,000 people with gas, stores, shopping malls, motels, restaurants. Camping is available at Henderson Lake Park (via Mayor McGrath Drive, to the east of the hwy.).

**Junction–Highway 5** Leads south to Cardston, and on to Waterton Lakes National Park with connections south to the Montana border and Glacier National Park. The Lethbridge tourist information center is north of downtown beside Brewery Gardens.

**Junction–Highway 3** Hwy. 4 comes to an end. Take Hwy. 3 (Crowsnest Hwy.) northeast, for 43 KM (26.7 miles), until reaching the junction with Hwy. 2.

**Junction–Highway 25** Leads north to Park Lake Provincial Park, camping, boat launch (9 miles, 14 KM).

**Coalhurst** Town just north of junction, with gas, cafés, store.

**Fort McLeod** Gas, hotels, motels, stores, and cafés. The Fort Museum is a reproduction of the original Northwest Mounted Police station built in 1874. The fort is open from May to September.

**Junction–Highway 2** Take Hwy. 2 north to Claresholm and Calgary.

**Oldman River Bridge** Public campground to the west. The Head-Smashed-In Buffalo Jump is 16 KM (10 miles) off the hwy. to the west via a sideroad.

**Junction–Road 519** This sideroad leads west to Granum, a small community with camping.

**Claresholm** Gas, accommodations, cafés, stores. There is a campground at Centennial Park.

**Road to Willow Creek Provincial Park** To the west. Large campground, swimming, fishing.

**Junction–Road 533** Leads west to Chain Lakes Provincial Park (camping).

**Nanton** Small town with gas, motels, stores, cafés, and camping.

**Junction–Highway 2A** This hwy. is an alternative route north, to the town of High River.

**High River** Off the hwy. to the west (on Hwy. 2A) with gas, motels, cafés, stores.

**Junction–Highways 2A and 7** Hwy. 2A leads south to High River. Hwy. 7 leads west to the community of Black Diamond and the Turner Valley.

**Sheep Creek Provincial Park** At the Sheep Creek Bridge, with picnicking, fishing, and swimming.

**Calgary** Stay on Hwy. 2 through the city to continue our drive north toward Edmonton and Dawson Creek.

# HIGHWAY LOG
## *Calgary to Edmonton*
### 294 KM (183 miles)—3 hours, 30 minutes

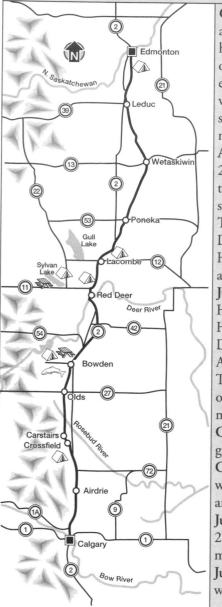

**Calgary** The Stampede City, with a population of 620,000. Calgary has full visitor services. Hwy. 2, our route to Edmonton, is a modern freeway with few visitor services right on the hwy. There are services off the hwy. at several nearby communities.

**Airdrie** Town just west of the hwy., 27 KM (17 miles) north of downtown Calgary. Gas, motels, cafés, stores.

**Tourist Information Centre** At the Dickson-Stephenson Stopping House (Old Calgary Trail). Picnic area.

**Junction–Highways 2A and 72** Hwy. 2A leads west to Crossfield. Hwy. 72 runs east to the town of Drumheller, the center of the Alberta Badlands and site of the Tyrrell Museum of Paleontology, one of the world's best dinosaur museums.

**Crossfield** Small community with gas, café, and hotel to the west.

**Carstairs** Exit west to this town with gas, stores, motel, camping, and cafés.

**Junction–Highway 27** Take Hwy. 27 west to the town of Olds. Gas, motels, cafés, stores.

**Junction–Road to Bowden** (to the west). The road also leads west to

Red Lodge Provincial Park with camping, swimming, and fishing. **Picnic Area** At the junction, with an information center.
**Junction–Highway 54** Leads west to the town of Innisfail which has gas, motels, cafés, and stores. The RCMP Dog Training Centre is open to the public daily, 5 KM (3 miles) south of town.
**Junction–Highway 42** Leads west to Penhold, a small community. **Highway Services** Found 4.5 miles north of the junction.
**Junction–Highway 2A** Leads east to the city of Red Deer with full visitor services including motels and a municipal campground, Riverside Drive, which includes a laundry, picnic area, and dump station.
**Junction–Highway 11** At the north end of Red Deer, leading west 6 KM (10 miles) to Sylvan Lake and 82 KM (51 miles) to the town of Rocky Mountain House. Sylvan Lake Provincial Park features picnicking, swimming.
**Blackfalds** A small community off the hwy. with gas, motel, café, and store. To the east of the hwy.
**Junction–Highway 12** Drive east on Hwy. 12 to the town of Lacombe, which has gas, motels, cafés, and stores. Campsites are available at Mitchener Park.
**Aspen Beach Provincial Park** is 10 KM (6 miles) west of the hwy.

on Hwy. 12 with camping and swimming.
**Junction–Highway 53** Leads east to the town of Ponoka. Gas, motels, cafés, stores. Ponoka Stampede Trailer Park has campsites.
**Exit to Wetaskiwin** The town is just off the hwy. There is a picnic area at the junction, with a summer information booth.
**Junction–Highway 13** Leads east to Wetaskiwin.
**Junction–Edmonton Bypass** Exit to Hwy. 39 for the Devon Bypass, which leads to Hwy. 60 and the junction with the Yellowhead Hwy. (see next hwy. map and log). **Leduc** Town accessed via Hwy. 39. Gas, motels, cafés, stores.
**Junction–Highway 19** Leads west to Devon and the Devon Bypass. From Devon, drive north on Hwy. 60 (bypass).
**Whitemud Drive** This is the continuation of Hwy. 2, which becomes 170 Street after crossing the Saskatchewan River Bridge.
**Edmonton** Alberta's capital city, with a population of 605,000. The city operates several tourist information centers: on Hwy. 2 south, two on hwy. 16 (east and west), and downtown at 9797 Jasper Avenue. Edmonton has full visitor services including hotels, motels, and the Rainbow Valley Campground (public) on Whitemud Drive.

# HIGHWAY LOG
## Edmonton to Dawson Creek
### 589 KM (366 miles)—7 hours

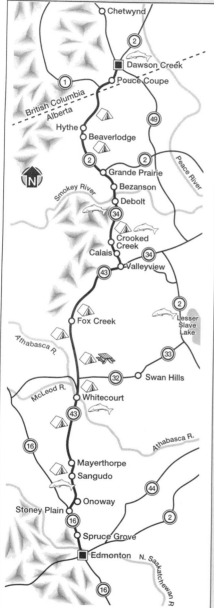

This drive begins in downtown Edmonton, taking Jasper Avenue westbound, which becomes the Yellowhead Highway (Hwy. 16) at the city limits. The route is a divided highway for 27 KM (17 miles) until we turn onto Highway 43.

**Spruce Grove** A large town with gas, motels, cafés, and stores.
**Stoney Plain** To the south of the hwy. with gas, motels, restaurants, shopping mall and other stores. The Multicultural Heritage Centre is a museum and art gallery with a café serving pioneer food. Andrew Wolf Winery is located to the north of the hwy., offering tastings daily except Sundays.
**Junction–Highway 43** Turn north onto this hwy. for Dawson Creek.
**Junction–Highway 633** Leads west to the Alberta Beach Recreation Area (Lac St. Anne).
**Onoway** Small town with gas, cafés, laundry, motel. Elks Campground has a few sites in town. The Alberta Government Campground (west of town) has more sites and a dump station.
**Lessard Lake Campground** County campsites and boat launch, fishing (perch and pike). Golf course nearby.

**Sangudo** Small community to the south with gas, café, motel, and laundry. Public campground.

**Mayerthorpe** Small town, 1.6 KM (1 mile) north of the hwy. with hotel, motel, gas, café, laundry and store. Public campground (free) and golf course are located 1.6 KM (1 mile) south of town.

**Junction–Highway 658** Gas and café at junction, 3.2 KM (2 miles) beyond Mayerthorpe access road.

**Whitecourt** A town with gas, motels, stores, restaurants. Camping, on Hwy. 43 west of the town center with a tourist infocenter and dump station.

**Junction–Highway 32 North** Carson-Pegasus Provincial Park is located 23.5 KM (14.5 miles) northwest of Whitecourt.

**Two Creeks Campground** A small campground with picnic tables, located 12.9 KM (8 miles) beyond Chickadee Campground.

**Iosegun Campground** Picnic tables and fire pits, 19.3 KM (12 miles) beyond Two Creeks Campground.

**Fox Creek** Small town with gas, hotel, motels, stores and nine-hole golf course, summer info center.

**Pines Campground** 16 KM (10 miles) North of Fox Creek.

**Little Smokey** Small village with motel, gas, and store.

**Waskahigan River Campground** At the bridge, with picnic tables and fire pits.

**Valleyview** Town with full services. Information center and picnic area 0.6 KM (1 mile) south of town on Hwy. 43.

**Junction–Highway 34** Turn left onto Hwy. 34 west for the remainder of our drive to Grande Prairie and Dawson Creek. Hwy. 43 north leads to the Mackenzie Hwy. route to Yellowknife.

**Junction–Road to Sturgeon Lake** Williamson Provincial Park offers camping, fishing, boat launch, and dump station.

**Calais** Village with store.

**Sturgeon Heights Road** leads north to Young's Point Provincial Park (10 KM, 6 miles). Camping, boat launch, fishing, and dump station.

**Debolt** Small town north of hwy. with store. Gas and café on hwy.

**Smoky River Campground** At bridge.

**Bezanson** Gas, café, store.

**Grande Prairie** Large town at junction of hwys. 34 and 2. Full services. Infocenter on 3rd Avenue.

**Saskatoon Island Provincial Park** North of hwy. via access road. Camping, boat launch, swimming.

**Beaverlodge** Town with gas, motels, cafés, stores, golf course.

**Hythe** Gas, motel, café, public camping.

**Swan Lake Provincial Park** Camping, picnic area, boating.

**Pouce Coupe** Small town with gas, motels, store and car wash.

# Access Routes
## Destinations

T he following pages contain information on the major cities and towns along the three southern access routes leading to the Alaska Highway. Recommended restaurants are found at the end of the descriptions for the larger urban areas. Many of the smaller towns in British Columbia and Alberta have small cafés and family-operated restaurants and diners that offer basic food for travelers, including families. Fast-food chains are represented in most of the towns with populations over 5,000. We have included a few unexpected gems in several smaller communities. Otherwise, we have not recommended the basic cafés and roadside diners. You may take your choice, they're all essentially the same.

## Ashcroft and Cache Creek (B.C.)

Ashcroft, a small cowtown, is located 4 KM (2.5 miles) east of the Trans-Canada Highway (Highway 1), just south of Cache Creek on the main highway. This is near-desert country with sagebrush on the hills and some of the largest ranches in Canada. Ashcroft Manor, an original roadhouse, sits by the Trans-Canada Highway, and is still in operation as a restaurant. The Infocentre is at 404 Brink Street downtown and is open during summer months, (604) 453-9232. The Ashcroft Museum is in an old federal building and houses displays on the old Cariboo Wagon Road and local history, including the town's main street at the beginning of the 1900s.

Cache Creek is nearby, at the junction of the Trans-Canada (Highway 1) and the Cariboo (Highway 97) highways. Several fine guest ranches are located in this region, including the historic Hat Creek Ranch. Also in the area is the huge Lornex Copper Mine, which offers tours of its open-pit operation.

A backroad drive from Ashcroft leads to Logan Lake in a scenic foothills setting. The main industry is the enormous Highland Valley Copper Mine, the largest open-pit copper mine in North America. Tours of the mine are featured. Farther along the road is Lac le Jeune Provincial Park, with a camping area, good fishing for rainbow trout, an archeological site, and swimming. Nearby is Lac le Jeune Resort, offering downhill and cross-country skiing (100 KM of groomed trails). The Stake-McConnell Recreation Area, north of the park turnoff, has excellent trout fishing, boating, and trails for feet and bikes. Logan Lake and the Lac le Jeune area are also accessible from Highway 5 (the Coquihalla), a few miles south of Kamloops.

# Calgary (Alberta)

Calgary is a city of 700,000, with a modern, high-rise downtown It was not much more than an overgrown cowtown in the 1960s when the Canadian oil and gas industry made the city its headquarters, and Calgary became the prosperous corporate city it is today.

Best known around the world for hosting the 1988 Winter Olympics, Calgary is the gateway to an incredible range of recreation opportunities in the Rocky Mountains, which lie just west of the city. Not only is Banff National Park less than two hours' drive from town, but the newly developed Kananaskis Country on the eastern slopes of the Rockies offers skiing, summer hiking, and other pleasures even closer than Banff.

Calgary sits at the edge of the great Canadian prairie, with the foothills of the Rockies almost touching the city. Because of the climatic effect of the mountains, Calgary often enjoys mild winter temperatures, caused by the Chinook winds that blow over this area of southwestern Alberta.

The city's history goes back to 1875 when the Northwest Mounted Police arrived to establish law and order in an area where buffalo hunters, whiskey traders, and Native Americans had clashed. Typical of the rest of Canada, there was never any great conflict, but the NWMP (the predecessor of the RCMP) brought an added measure of security. Calgary became a center for neighboring ranchers, and a stopping place for travelers on their way to Banff National Park.

The city's tourist information center is downtown, at 237 8th Avenue SE. It's easy to find, at the base of the Calgary Tower. The center stays open year-round. Other info centers are located along the main highways into the city. These outlying kiosks are all seasonal operations. For advance information call the Calgary Convention and Visitors Bureau at 800-661-1678.

### Things to See and Do

Calgary is a social and cultural center which boasts the finest museum in Western Canada—some say in all of Canada: the Glenbow Museum. Located at 130 9th Avenue SE, across the street from the Calgary Tower (another popular attraction), the Glenbow houses displays documenting the history of western Canada, including Native American history and cultures, the great European explorers who mapped the west and the Rockies, the Northwest Mounted Police, and western settlers. The museum also features displays on the building of the Canadian Pacific Railway which tied Canada together shortly after the nation was founded.

The Calgary Science Centre offers interactive displays and traveling exhibits directed at children as well as adults. It's located at the corner of 11th Street and 7th Avenue SW.

Calgary's annual celebration is the Calgary Stampede, a rodeo and exhibition held during 10 days in early July. The site of the rodeo, Stampede Park, hosts other events year-round. The Olympic Saddledome is home to the city's hockey team, the

Flames, while The Grandstand has thoroughbred and harness racing. Find Stampede Park at 17th Avenue and 2nd Street SE.

Travelers interested in natural history should drive south of Calgary to visit the Royal Tyrrell Museum of Paleontology, situated in the Alberta Badlands near the town of Drumheller. The Dinosaur Trail is found 6 KM (3.7 miles) north of Drumheller. Drive 160 KM (100 miles) south of Calgary via Highways 2 and 785 to Head-Smashed-In Buffalo Jump, a world heritage site and the best preserved buffalo jump in North America. An interpretive center contains displays on prairie life and wildlife. The buffalo jump and badlands can be explored in a one-day trip from Calgary.

Bow Valley Ranch also offers exhibits that cover the past 8,000 years of history in the area. Located in Fish Creek Park, south of town on Bow Bottom Trail, the ranch house was built by William Roper Hull in 1902. There are guided tours available from the visitor center.

Heritage Park is another historical exhibit, comprised of more than 100 buildings and exhibits that re-create a village from early Canada, prior to 1915. There's a steam train ride, a paddle wheeler that plies the Glenmore Reservoir, and antique fair rides, making this park a terrific place to bring kids for a half-day or more of looking at the past through having fun. The park is located at 1900 Heritage Drive SW. It's open weekdays until 10 P.M.

Devonian Gardens is a 2.5-acre indoor park in downtown Calgary that displays 200,000 plants, including local and tropical varieties, reflecting pools, waterfalls, and fountains. What is interesting about this garden is that it's on the fourth floor of the Toronto Dominion Square, at 8th Avenue and 3rd Street SW. Also interesting is the admission price: Zero.

Kananaskis Country is the name given to a year-round recreation area located 90 KM (56 miles) west of Calgary (and 60 KM, 37 miles, south of Banff). On the eastern slope of the Rockies, this area combines a ski hill built for the Calgary Olympics, cross-country skiing, camping, staying at resort lodges, and mountain hiking. There is also good fishing in the area, which is less populated by tourists than Banff National Park and has scenery almost as exciting.

The Kananaskis region includes Peter Lougheed Provincial Park (named for a former Alberta premier). The province's largest park, it boasts a setting of high peaks, a beautiful valley, and a number of high lakes, including Upper and Lower Kananaskis lakes. Park campgrounds are available, with hiking trails (ski trails in the winter), picnic areas, a store, and cafeteria. All of this is reached by taking the Trans-Canada Highway (Highway 1) west from Calgary and turning south onto Highway 40. Farther along Highway 40 you'll encounter Highwood Pass, the highest driveable pass in Canada, with an elevation of 2,227 meters (7,306 feet). The road to the pass is open from about June 15th to November 30th and interpretive trails start at the pass. You can continue on Highway 40 as a loop trip via High River to Calgary.

As a large city, Calgary offers accommodations of every type, from hotels (with good dining rooms) to nearby guest ranches and RV parks.

A morning's drive of 264 KM (164 miles) south of Calgary, is Waterton Lakes National Park, which joins Glacier National Park at the U.S. border as an International Peace Park. Waterton shares with Glacier the wondrously rugged beauty of the Rockies. A resort hotel with an 18-hole golf course operates inside the park, plus camping, alpine riding, good fishing, tennis, and mountain trails. To reach Waterton Lakes, take Highway 2 south from Calgary and turn west onto Highway 6 at Cardston. To continue on to Glacier National Park, stay on Highway 2, crossing the border with Montana at Carway. There's a shorter route from Waterton Park via Highway 6 to the border at Chief Mountain.

### Where to Eat

You can get a good meal, even fine cuisine, in almost any mainline hotel in the city. Calgary also boasts many smaller and less auspicious cafés and bistro-style restaurants, many with an international focus. Here are a few of the best, plus an outstanding fast-food drive-in.

**Coyote Grill**, at 1411–17th Avenue, is a great barbecue house, also specializing in such Southwestern dishes as smoked chicken quesadillas and home-smoked chicken salad sandwiches. Before it's smoked, the meat is rubbed with a combination of spices. The piquant, smoky barbecue sauce served with the meat is rich with tomato and has a deep, spicy flavor. Don't expect fancy surroundings; this place used to be a fish-and-chips restaurant, and has retained the counter and stools, with a few tables filling the other spaces.

The **Elephant and Castle**, at 8th Avenue and 4th Street SW, is one of about 20 similar restaurant operations located in Canada and the U.S. This one, like the rest, is a large English pub-style place, divided into smaller rooms. They manage to make it look like a cozy little pub. Food includes traditional English fare such as bangers and mash, but they add to the menu with steak sandwiches and other North American pub dishes. Beer is a strong suit, with a good selections of draft brews, in mugs or jugs.

**Trong Khanh**, located at 1115 Centre Street North, is a fine little Vietnamese noodle restaurant, not much to look at with vinyl-clad dinette furniture, but the food more than makes up for the basic ambiance. This place has no pretensions, and serves food just as good as, but at a cheaper price than, the ritzier East Asian restaurants in Calgary. Look for the lemongrass chicken and wonderful soups.

**Boogies Burgers**, at 908 Edmonton Trail NE, is an original burger stand, revered locally for its tasty grilled burgers, and crisp, fresh french fries, with espresso and cappuccino to add a little sophistication. Be prepared for loquacious restaurant staff, fine old-fashioned milk shakes, and memories of better fast-food days.

# Campbell River (B.C.)

If your trip northward on the Island Highway is to take two days, Campbell River is an excellent place to stay overnight and is midway between Victoria and Port Hardy. You may wish to stay longer if fishing is a serious hobby. Campbell River is known as the "Salmon Capital of the World" and salmon fishing here is the best in Canada. There is good steelhead and trout fishing in nearby lakes and streams.

This town of 25,000 is close to Strathcona Provincial Park and to Quadra Island via a short ferry ride. The Kwakiutl Indian Museum in Quathiaski Cove on Quadra displays traditional masks and carvings, created by local Native Americans over the past centuries. If you're staying on Quadra Island, Rebecca Spit Provincial Park provides beachcombing and swimming. Another ferry runs to Cortes Island.

The regional tourist Infocentre is found at 1235 Island Highway (Highway 19).

# Courtenay and Comox (B.C.)

These sister towns are separated by only a few miles, with Courtenay on Highway 19. Logging, agriculture, and fishing support their economies. Skiers come to Mount Washington and Forbidden Plateau ski resorts. Forbidden Plateau is open during summer months, with a scenic sky-ride. The B.C. Ferry to Powell River on the mainland leaves from Little River, 11 KM (6.8 miles) northeast of Courtenay.

Strathcona Provincial Park is nearby, with a variety of wilderness experiences available, including viewing of black bears, a reserve of Roosevelt elk, and hiking trails. Miracle Beach Provincial Park has family and wilderness camping. The Oyster River provides trout, coho, and steelhead fishing.

A travel Infocentre for the two towns is located at 2040 Cliffe Avenue in Courtenay.

The nearest B.C. Ferry Corp. terminals are at Buckley Bay, 20 KM (12.5 miles) south of Courtenay, and at Little River, 13 KM (8 miles) north of Comox.

## Where to Eat

Sometimes you find unexpected pleasures in the most unlikely places. The **Old House Restaurant**, at 1760 Riverside Lane in Courtenay, is a case in point. The attractive room models the West Coast lodge style, featuring four fireplaces and a summer patio. Game is the specialty here, in addition to the more normal seafood and steak cuisine served in most of the pricier restaurants on Vancouver island. The Old House is open for lunch and dinner, and reservations are recommended, (604) 338-5406. Prices are moderate to expensive.

The **Gaff Rig Restaurant**, at 1984 Buena Vista Avenue in Comox, has a menu based on seafood dishes, and an additional focus on Swiss specialties. This restaurant is open for dinner only, and is closed Mondays.

# Edmonton (Alberta)

The capital city of Alberta lies in the central part of the province, 294 KM (183 miles) north of Calgary and 590 KM (366 miles) southeast of Dawson Creek, B.C.—"Mile 0" of the Alaska Highway. Jasper National Park lies almost due west of Edmonton, and is easily reached by taking the Yellowhead Highway (Highway 16) to the Jasper townsite 362 KM (225 miles) from the capital. Not benefiting from warm winter Chinook winds as Calgary does, Edmonton is a northern city with cold winters but a very pleasant summer climate. The North Saskatchewan River flows through the city, past the downtown city-center, and through the Edmonton suburbs. The drive northwest to the Alaska Highway departs from downtown Edmonton, via Highway 16. The turnoff onto Highway 43, which leads toward Grande Prairie and Dawson Creek, is 27 KM (17 miles) from Edmonton.

Edmonton Tourism, the large visitor information center, is at 104–9797 Jasper Avenue North. There are three other information centers on major highway entrances to the city.

### Things to See and Do

One of Edmonton's claims to fame is that it is the site of the world's most famous shopping mall—and the world's largest until 1992. The West Edmonton Mall contains about 800 stores including 11 major department stores, 110 restaurants and cafés, a large amusement park, a hotel with bizarre theme rooms, and a water park complete with submarine rides, a large wave pool, and hot tubs.

The city has an enviable succession of festivals throughout the summer and fall months. The long-running Klondike Days (July) sets off dancing, costume parties, raft races, gambling, and more, as the city celebrates the 1898 Gold Rush (which took place far from here in Dawson City, and barely affected Edmonton). The city was a starting point for a few adventurous and foolhardy souls, who left for the Klondike by the tough (and deadly) overland route.

Early July brings the Jazz City Festival and in early August Edmonton is the site for the large Folk Music Festival. The first weekend in August are Heritage Days, when the city celebrates its ethnic diversity. A large number of Ukrainian immigrants settled in this area and if there is a place to eat piroshkies, this is it!

One of the more interesting sights in the city is seen only on holidays, when the historic High Level Bridge over the North Saskatchewan River becomes the Great Divide Waterfall, installed in 1980 for Alberta's 75th anniversary. The cascade is best seen from downstream, on the south side of the river. The waterfall operates on Sunday evenings and Saturday afternoons during Klondike Days.

A stay in Edmonton could include sightseeing, and one of the most fascinating ways to spend a few hours is by visiting Fort Edmonton Park. The fort is a full-scale replica of the old fort, which was a major fur trading post constructed by the Hudson's Bay Company in 1846. Not one but three historical villages, the park depicts Edmonton as the original fur trading post, as the new capital city in 1905, and as a "modern" prairie community in 1920. You can ride an old streetcar and a steam train. The fort is reached by driving to Whitemud Drive and Fox Drive, at the south end of the Quesnel Bridge. It's open for summer hours from 10 A.M. to 6 P.M. and from 11 A.M. to 5 P.M. on Sundays and holidays during the winter months.

The Muttart Conservatory, with displays of arid, tropical, and temperate plants, is a series of four glass pyramids at 9626–96 A Street. Three of the pyramids hold permanent displays. The fourth changes every few months. The conservatory is open daily during the summer period from 11 A.M. to 9 P.M. and during the winter Sunday through Wednesday from 11 A.M. to 9 P.M. and Thursday through Saturday from 11 A.M. to 6 P.M. The Valley Zoo (134th Street and Buena Vista Road) is a 20-acre zoo with relatively natural exhibit areas featuring, among other animals, Siberian tigers. This is one of the rare zoos where one can see peregrine falcons, an extremely endangered species. The John Janzen Nature Centre (next to Fort Edmonton) features nature exhibits of flora and fauna, with nature walks on Sunday afternoons.

The Provincial Museum of Alberta has four large galleries that depict Alberta's history through displays of artifacts, ranging from Native American history and culture, the fur-trading era, railroad history, and the settling of the Canadian West. The provincial archives are also located in the building. It's open from Tuesday through Sunday.

Edmonton's excellent theater complex, the Citadel Theatre, offers dramatic productions throughout the year. It's located at 9828–101 A Avenue with information and reservations obtained by calling (403) 426-4811.

There are 30 golf courses in Edmonton, most of them open for public play. Major city courses are Riverside at Rowland Road and 86th Street, Rundle Park (2902-118th Avenue), and Victoria, at River Road and 120th Street. For family thrills, jet boat rides are available on the North Saskatchewan River. For reservations phone (403) 486-0896.

To catch a view of what this part of Canada looked like before European settlers arrived in the mid-1800s, drive a few miles east of Edmonton to Elk Island National Park. The park is home to 1,600 elk, 500 plains bison (buffalo), and 400 wood bison, as well as deer and moose. There are 100 KM (60 miles) of hiking and walking trails throughout the park and a boardwalk over part of a lake. An interpretive center offers displays and films. Golfing is available, as are several picnic areas. Located within the park at the Astotin Recreation Area is a Ukrainian pioneer home with museum displays inside. The Sandy Beach Campground has 80 sites. For information on the park, phone (403) 922-5790. It's reached by driving east along Highway 16 (the Yellowhead) from downtown Edmonton, or by taking Highway 15 from the north end of town.

## Where to Eat

The large Canadian cities, particularly those in the west, are blessed with many great Vietnamese cafés. **Lemon Grass Cafe**, at 10417 51st Avenue on the city's South Side, is one of the best. It opened in 1995 and has been busy ever since. Noodle dishes, seafood entrées, and wonderful hot (both ways) soups make a stop in this small but pleasant restaurant a special treat. Another fine little Vietnamese café is **Saigon Terrace**, at 11607 Jasper Avenue.

**Moroccan Gardens**, 6427 112th Avenue, is perhaps the finest ethnic restaurant in Edmonton. It is linked to another restaurant, La Boheme, but the two operations are very different. Moroccan Gardens has the required North African ambiance, and what you eat is a six-course Moroccan feast. In this leisurely paced restaurant, you can expect to spend an entire evening.

One of the best family eateries in town is **Fargo's**, at 10307 82nd Avenue (at 103rd Street). All seats have a good view of television sets scattered throughout the large room, so it's a good place for those who are missing their sports while traveling. The menu focuses on pizzas, burgers, and a selection of Mexican dishes.

For fine dining, you couldn't do better than to spend at least three hours in **L'Anjou**, at 10643 123rd Street. This is definitely a restaurant for those special (especially romantic) occasions. Like Moroccan Gardens, this restaurant has a prix fixe menu, with a five-course meal that makes a full evening here go by in what seems a few minutes. The price is surprisingly reasonable, for one of the best meals you'll ever eat.

# Grande Prairie (Alberta)

Called the "Commerce Centre of the Peace Country," Grande Prairie is a growing city on the northern Alberta prairie, with an agricultural economy enhanced by natural gas and oil production in the area. Founded as a village in 1914, it became a city in 1958 when the oil and gas revolution took place. This is quite a modern community, although it maintains some of the rough-and-ready qualities it had 30 years ago. You can find gas, several cafés, and shopping in the city.

The Chamber of Commerce office, with information for visitors, is located at 10011 103rd Avenue. A seasonal (July and August) information center operates off the Highway 2 Bypass on 106th Street, at the Bear Creek Reservoir.

Bear Creek flows through the city, widening to create Bear Creek Reservoir. The creek is a focus for recreational facilities. Muskoseepi Park is comprised of five separate units spread along the creek. Access to the reservoir, where you will find most of the park attractions, is via 106th Street, off the Highway 2 Bypass. The park offers canoeing on the reservoir, picnicking, and bicycling. Centennial Park, nearby, has public tennis courts and is the site of the Pioneer Museum, which features displays of fossils, rocks, stuffed wildlife, and pioneer farming implements. The regional community college was designed by the noted Canadian

Native American architect Douglas Cardinal, and is well worth a look.

# Hazelton (B.C.)

There are two Hazeltons: "Old" Hazelton, located 6.5 KM (4 miles) off Highway 16 (Yellowhead), and New Hazelton, which straddles the Yellowhead Highway. K'san Village is a few hundred yards from old Hazelton.

This is Upper Skeena Country and the Skeena River dominates the area. Two other rivers, the Bulkley and Kispiox, have earned fame for their varieties of salmon and steelhead trout. It is also the best area in which to view the Native American heritage of northern B.C. Nowhere else can visitors see so many historic totem poles.

K'san Village provides an authentic glimpse of the Native culture of the Northwest Coast Indians, and is open daily for public viewing. It is a combination museum, Native American carving school, cultural center, and gift shop. The village contains seven authentic longhouses that face Mount Roche DeBoule. Hourly tours are given during summer months. "Old Town" Hazelton is nearby. It was established by the Hudson's Bay Company in 1866 and remains a functioning business center. A pioneer museum and antique machinery displays show the early pioneer settlement.

The tourist Infocentre sits beside Highway 16 in New Hazelton. Pick up a copy of the "Hand of History" self-guided-tour map. This 60-mile route features signposts describing important pioneer and Native American events.

# Hope (B.C.)

This town of 4,000 is nestled in the mountains north of Chilliwack and makes an excellent holiday base. The town's visitor center is in the Chamber of Commerce office, beside Highway 1 at the south end of town. The mountains in the immediate area

(Ogilvie, Thacker, Hope, and Holy Cross) offer hiking and alpine picnics. Several lakes close to Hope offer a variety of activities. Kawkawa Lake, a five-minute drive from downtown, has a park with picnic tables, boat launch, and fishing. Lake of the Woods, just north of Hope on Highway 1, has a roadside picnic park, canoeing and fishing.

The Coquihalla River Valley is accessible from two routes—either from Hope by taking Kawkawa Lake Road and Union Bar Road, or from the new Coquihalla Highway (Highway 5). The Quintette Tunnels, near the old Othello Station of the Kettle Valley Railroad, provide a thrilling heritage walk through the Coquihalla Canyon. The path follows the rail bed of the Kettle Valley line through a deep canyon where the river has worn a chasm 300 feet deep. This is an outstanding experience—not to be missed.

Hope also serves as a starting point for driving to the Skagit Valley Provincial Recreation Area southeast of town. Follow the Silver Skagit Road as it leads 60 KM (37 miles) to Ross Lake and the U.S. border. Ross Lake features campsites, hiking trails, boating, and fishing.

North of Hope in the Fraser Canyon is the First Bridge Trail, a fine hiking trail that leads to an elevation of 900 meters (2,952 feet). The trailhead lies 300 meters north of Alexandra Lodge, which is north of the Alexandra Bridge and Provincial Park. This trail dates back to 1848 and was one of the early pioneer trails of the region. The 13-KM (8-mile) path rises above the canyon and ends at a small lake.

# Nanaimo (B.C.)

Nanaimo was a coal town when it was founded by the Hudson's Bay Company in 1852. With a population of 50,000, Nanaimo is the island's second largest city and a year-round fishing, logging, and transportation center. An important confection was invented here in 1950 when a local housewife won a contest for dessert squares and the "Nanaimo Bar" was born. The B.C. Ferry docks in nearby Departure Bay. Newcastle Island, a provincial park with good hiking and tent camping, is a short ferry ride from the city. Downtown Nanaimo offers a walking tour with several historic buildings.

The Visitor Infocentre is at 266 Bryden Street (on the Trans-Canada Highway downtown). The B.C. Ferry Corp. terminal is located on Departure Bay, off the Trans-Canada Highway, the end of Stewart Avenue.

### Where to Eat

**Harbour Lights Restaurant**, at 1518 Stewart Avenue, is a steak and seafood house, and a popular one at that, with a good salad bar. It is located in Nanaimo's downtown area, and is closed on Sundays.

The **Lighthouse Bistro and Pub**, at 50 Anchor Way, is a fine place to eat, drink, and take in the harbor atmosphere. Cross a walkway to this pier-top restaurant. Seafood is the specialty.

**Chez Michel**, at 10 Front Street on the waterfront, is a small and classy restaurant specializing in French cuisine, and featuring piano music. Be prepared to spend some time here, and to spend more money than you would at almost any other Nanaimo restaurant (604) 754-1218.

# Port Hardy (B.C.)

While whaling has disappeared from the North Island scene, Port Hardy thrives as a prime fishing area, with coho salmon in abundance. The B.C. Ferries terminal is located at Bear Cove, south of town. The Coal Harbour museum captures the whaling era with relics of those days. There is good picnicking at Beaver Harbour near Fort Rupert, just south of Port Hardy. Only a few tall chimneys remain of an old Hudson's Bay Company fort established at this site. Miles of hiking trails in Cape Scott Provincial Park link Queen Charlotte Strait and the Pacific coast. Beware of the rough access road. Wildlife abounds here, including bald eagles, bears, seals, sea lions, and orcas (killer whales). The town's tourist Infocentre is at 7250 Market Street downtown, via Hardy Bay Road. Tour maps are available. The historical museum, also downtown, provides lots of information about the fascinating history of Native American and European settlement in the North Island region.

## Where to Eat

**Snuggles**, at the Pioneer Inn on Old Island Road, south of town, has a pleasant ambiance and reasonable prices. Seafood, steaks, and salads are menu mainstays.

**Sportsman's Steak and Seafood House**, on Market Street near the Infocentre and bus depot, has no surprises, but serves seafood and beef, and fresh greens from a salad bar.

The North Shore Inn has a prominent location on the Port Hardy waterfront, at 7370 Market Street. The dining room here is called the **Sign of the Steer**, but its seafood is what makes the room stand out—this is, after all, a fishing port. Port Hardy being a long way from market sources other than fish makes dining here an expensive proposition. There is a lounge in the same hotel.

After a long drive from the southern part of the island, ordering a delivered pizza is very tempting. That was my situation one night, after arriving in Port Hardy dog-tired and hungry. **Plato's Pizza**, located downtown, makes its own dough, has several tempting combinations, and (best of all) delivers to local hotels. Call (604) 949-8688.

# Prince George (B.C.)

This major trading and forestry center for northern B.C. is located at the junction of the Yellowhead (Highway 16) and the north/south route (Highway 97). The Nechako River joins the Fraser at Prince George. The local travel Infocentre is at 1198 Victoria Street, at 15th Avenue, or call (604) 562-3700. A summer booth operates at the junction of highways 97 and 16.

Originally called Fort George by explorer Simon Fraser, this was an early Northwest Company fur trading post, founded in 1807. It is a fine place to explore the outdoors, and several back-road forest tours are available. Prince George has 116 parks, including the Forests for the World Park on Cranbrook Hill. Here, visitors learn about tree planting and forest management techniques.

A guided tour starts at the Travel Infocentre. Stops on the tour include the Prince George Art Gallery, and the Fort George and Railway museums. Cottonwood Island Park is a natural area with waterfront trails amongst a grove of cottonwood trees. Two industrial tours are available: at the Northwood Pulp and Timber plant (including a tree nursery), and the North Central Plywood factory.

Just 15 KM (9 miles) east of the city is the splendid Tabor Mountain Recreational Preserve. More than 56 KM (35 miles) of walking trails thread through this park. They are used for cross-country skiing in the winter, and the Tabor Mountain Ski resort offers downhill skiing. A five-minute walk takes you to a raised platform just off Highway 16, 9.5 KM (6 miles) east of the ski resort, for viewing the moose that range throughout this area.

Fort George Park, located on an old Carrier Native American burial site, is the largest park in the city and has playgrounds, picnic tables, barbecue facilities, and a museum. The Fort George Regional Museum opens daily in summer months from 10 A.M. to 5 P.M. The Fort George Railway in the park offers rides for visitors on weekends and holidays.

The Prince George Railway Museum is located next to Cottonwood Island Park, with an extensive collection of antique railway stock, a restored dining car, and 1914 Grand Trunk Railway station.

### Where to Eat

Nick's Place, at 363 George Street, is rife with low-cost decor, and low-cost but very good food, Italian and otherwise. Earl's, a noisy, glitzy place at 15th Avenue and Central Street, serves gourmet burgers and other trendy food, with beer and other potables at moderate prices.

Few pizza joints are recommended in this book (although we felt compelled to do it for Port Hardy), but the two **Boston Pizzas**, at 3339 8th Avenue and 751 Brunswick Street, are upscale pizzerias with modern interiors and friendly staff. By far the best of many fast-food chain restaurants in Prince George, they are fine places to take the kids for lunch or dinner.

The Coast Inn of the North, the city's most modern hotel, has three restaurants. **Winston's** serves American cuisine in its high-quality dining room. The **Coffee Garden** is the normal hotel coffee shop. The standout here, however, has to be **Shogun**, a Japanese steak house where the food and the art of preparation bear equal importance. All of these restaurants are recommended, but the show is at Shogun. For reservations at either Winston's or Shogun, call (604) 563-0121. The hotel is located downtown, at 770 Brunswick.

# Prince Rupert (B.C.)

Known as the "Gateway to the North," Prince Rupert is the jumping-off point into Alaska via the Alaska ferry system, as well as for the unique and scenic Queen Charlotte Islands, and as the beginning of the drive up the Stewart/Cassiar Highway, which joins the Alaska Highway near Watson Lake. Prince Rupert is a city situated on Kaien Island just 73 KM (45 miles) south of the tip of the Alaska Panhandle. Because of this fortuitous location, the city has a good trade with southeastern Alaska, as well as serving as a Pacific Ocean port.

The regional travel Infocentre is found at 1st Avenue and McBride Street. It's open daily from 9 A.M. to 5 P.M. To get there, turn left from Highway 16 onto McBride. Everything you need for a full visit to Prince Rupert is available here, and the museum next door includes displays and relics of the Tsimpshian and Haida people.

The locals call Prince Rupert the "City of Rainbows." More correctly, it's a city of mists and frequent rain. Founded as a company town by the Grand Trunk Pacific Railway, by 1914 Prince Rupert was a bustling young seaport. It started as the dream of Charles Hays, a visionary entrepreneur who promoted the idea of a second trans-Canada railroad that would ship goods to the Pacific Ocean for access to Asia. Hays and his plans went to the bottom of the Atlantic on the *Titanic* in 1912, but others realized his dream. Today, more than 250,000 tourists visit the city each year by cruise ship, ferry, car, and RV, enjoying the scenery of the North Coast and reliving some of the pioneer history of the area. Festivals are held during the summer months and the city attracts thousands of anglers who come to the area to fish the Pacific and the Skeena River. Prince Rupert is also the access point for catching the ferry to the Queen Charlotte Islands.

### Things to See and Do

The rains don't seem to bother the residents who fully enjoy life in this mild climate zone. Museums, the public gardens, and Native American artisans provide a focus for visits to Prince Rupert. The Skeena River, named "River of the Mists" by the Tsimpshian, is one of the exceptional scenic highlights with an outstanding fish run. Charter boats and flightseeing tours are available throughout the year.

A totem pole walking tour is provided by the Infocentre and Museum (Market Place and 1st Avenue). The tour covers 15 blocks in the downtown area. The Museum of Northern B.C. has a good collection of northwest coast Native American (Tsimpshian and Haida) artifacts. The Sunken Garden, originally excavated as the foundation of a courthouse, merits a visit, as does the Native American carving shed behind the museum. This museum organizes a tour of important archeological sites in the inner harbor. Sites number more than 150 in the area, many dating back 5,000 years. The tour stops at the historic Metlakatla Village, where snacks and souvenirs are available. Travel is by an enclosed boat that also provides a great tour of the inner harbor.

Ten miles to the west of the city along Highway 16 is Diana Lake Park, with picnic facilities in a beautiful lake setting. A 20-minute drive from downtown Prince Rupert along Skeena Drive takes you to the old North Pacific Cannery, the oldest existing fish cannery on the coast, now a museum and historic site with walkways over the water and restored fish packing exhibits and displays.

The Mount Hays Gondola Lift takes winter skiers to the top of this ski hill, and also travels the 1,850 feet during the summer for tourists who want to see panoramic views of this part of the North Coast, including the Queen Charlotte Islands to the west. There's a restaurant at the top of the lift, and walking across the meadows makes a sunny day a pleasure. To get there, drive east on McBride Street and turn right onto Wantage Road, driving on the gravel road past the golf course to the base. Mount Hays is the site of an annual Canada Day celebration on July 1st.

The North Pacific Cannery is a restored heritage site at Port Edward, near the city. Once a major salmon canning operation, the docks, boardwalks, and cannery buildings have been restored as a North Coast museum. Live performances highlighting the history of the cannery are presented twice each day, and there are many displays on cannery history and the general history of development along B.C.'s north coast.

Seafest is a major celebration held during the second weekend in June. The fun centers around bathtub races, a parade, and water competitions, including a jousting match. Seafest includes Indian Culture Days, a two-day event featuring traditional dances, Native American food, and crafts displays.

## Ferry Services

The B.C. Ferries office is at 1045 Howe Street. The terminal is at the end of 2nd Avenue. The government ferry operation has service to the Queen Charlotte Islands and to Port Hardy (see Access Route 2, page 276). For information on ferry schedules, call (604) 624-9627.

The Alaska Marine Highway operates ferries that sail north to southeast Alaska (the panhandle) and stop in Ketchikan, Wrangell, Petersburg, Juneau, Haines, and Skagway. Ferry service also runs south to Bellingham, WA. For information on local schedules, call (604) 627-1744. For general information on all Alaska Marine Highway routes, call 800-382-9229 or (907) 235-8448.

### Where to Eat

When in a seaport and fishing community, always try out the seafood. That's my personal motto, and I recommend it to you. I tend to visit the smaller cafés rather than the places that offer pretension with their expensive menus. The **Green Apple,** at 301 McBride Street, is an unpretentious little café with halibut and chips the specialty. The halibut is fresh for the north coast seas, and you can have a large plate of fish and chips for a small amount of money. A local favorite, **Smile's Seafood Café,** at 11 George Hills Way, serves seafood fresh from the local waters, and is a bit more sophisticated than at the Green Apple. Prices are in the moderate range. If you're adverse to seafood, **Cu's Steak House,** at 816 3rd Avenue, serves standard burger and steak house cuisine, but also features seafood and has a salad bar.

# Queen Charlotte Islands

One hundred kilometers (62 miles) offshore from Prince Rupert lie the Queen Charlotte Islands, the ancestral homelands of the Haida people. The islands form a unique archipelago, providing a variety of misty mountains, forests, inlets, and an abundance of wildlife. If time is available, plan to spend at least two days in this unusual and fascinating island homeland. The islands are accessible by B.C. Ferry or by air from Prince Rupert. The ferry to Skidegate makes five return trips each week during the summer, taking six hours. The tourist Infocentre in Queen Charlotte City is located on 3rd Avenue, in Joy's Island Jewellers shop. For advance information, write the Chamber of Commerce, P.O. Box 357, Queen Charlotte, B.C. V0T 1S0. To obtain information on Masset events and accommodations, drop into the information center at Highway 16 and Old Beach Road.

## Things to See and Do

The islands are called *Haida Gwai,* the Haida way of saying "islands of the people" and to many, they are the Canadian Galapagos. The Haida consider the islands a special place of great spiritual value, and to others they are such a special place that they have been declared a World Heritage Site by UNESCO. Canada's newest national park is being created on South Moresby island. About 2,000 Haida people live on the islands, most on the northern island.

The islands escaped the last ice age and the temperate rain forests have flourished throughout the ages, giving a home to unusual animals and plants. Some of the largest trees on earth live here, along with special varieties of daisies and mosses that are found elsewhere only in the alpine regions of China or the Himalayas. Bald eagles soar over the landscape and the sea. Half of B.C.'s sea lions live here and the islands are home to enormous black bears.

There are two main islands in the archipelago, Graham and Moresby, and smaller but significant islands include Lyell, Kunghit, Louise, and Skungwai.

The west coast of the Charlottes is wild, rocky, and devoid of human settlement. The more sheltered east coast features long stretches of sandy dunes and long flat beaches. Moresby Island, to the south of Graham, has thousands of little inlets.

In all, the Charlottes have a population of about 6,000 people. They live in the small towns of Haida, Masset, Port Clements, Tlell, Queen Charlotte City, and Skidegate—all on Graham Island. Sandspit is a town on Moresby Island. Thousands of miles of logging roads lead through the thick rain forests; this has been a profitable lumber area for several major companies. Only 150 KM (94) miles of public road connect the communities.

Graham Island, with its highway and logging roads, is the preferred island for car explorations. Queen Charlotte City and Skidegate are only a few miles from the ferry landing. The Queen Charlotte Islands Museum is located near Skidegate Landing on a high point overlooking the water. Cedar totem poles here are more than 100 years old. The collection of Haida canoes in the museum longhouse includes Loo Taas ("wave eater"), designed by the renowned Haida artist, carver, and jewelry maker Bill Reid for display at EXPO '86. After the fair, Reid and a group of Haida men paddled the huge canoe home from Vancouver, a journey of 960 KM (600 miles).

Tlell is a perfect spot for beachcombing before continuing beside Naikoon Provincial Park to Port Clements. Highway 16 winds north to the fishing town of Masset (the largest community on the islands) and the Haida village of Old Masset. A gravel road runs from there to the end of Rose Spit with more wonderful ocean views. Just north of Masset is the Delkatla Wildlife Sanctuary, the home of transient birds traveling the Pacific Flyway. Naikoon Park is blessed with a wonderful beach, rain forest, picnic ground, and campsites.

Moresby Island has many abandoned Haida village sites. An additional 160 smaller islands lie off Moresby. A ferry ride connects Skidegate Landing on Graham Island with Alliford Bay on North Moresby. A circle tour taking a half to a whole day leads from Sandspit to Cooper Bay.

# Quesnel (B.C.)

The town of Quesnel (pronounced *kwa-nell*) is at the north end of the Cariboo—situated where the Quesnel River meets the Fraser River. Originally a gold rush town founded in the late 1800s, Quesnel became a commercial and transportation center with the building of the railway (now B.C. Rail). Much of the history of the town is evident. The old Hudson's Bay trading post is over 100 years old and is being restored. Bohanon House is one of the original homes in the area. The Quesnel Museum reflects the gold rush era and the more recent logging and ranching pioneers of this area. Quesnel provides a staging point for trips to Wells, Barkerville, and the Bowron Lakes area. The city's LeBourdais Park is a pleasant place for picnicking and walking. There are two golf courses here as well as downhill and cross-country skiing.

The big blow-out of the year comes in the third weekend in July with the Billy Barker Days festival, when the town relives the rambunctious gold rush period with a parade, dances, saloons, concerts, and other events. The Quesnel Infocentre, open from May through September, is located at the south end of town opposite the B.C. Rail station (604) 992-8716. During the off-season, phone (604) 747-2244.

Visitors can pan for gold by contacting the Gold Commissioner's office at 350 Barlow Street, Suite 102, (604) 992-4301. A map is available here for those who would like to pan for gold along the Quesnel River near its mouth.

The Quesnel and District Museum is on Highway 97 at Carson Avenue, (604) 992-9580. Heritage Corner, at Carson and Front streets, has some interesting artifacts of times past, including the remains of the old steamboat *Enterprise,* the Old Fraser River Bridge built in 1929, and a waterwheel used in sluicing for gold.

# Smithers (B.C.)

The Bulkley River Valley is a destination for skiers and anglers. Canoeists and kayakers also come to this northern area to run two of the major rivers of northern B.C.: the Bulkley and the Skeena.

The Bulkley is known for its steelhead, and a number of rustic fishing lodges service the ardent anglers who come here to catch a big one. Exploring the Bulkley Valley by canoe is an exciting adventure. Canoe trippers usually put their canoes in the water at Houston and paddle down to Smithers. This 50-mile stretch is the same route that canoeists race during the Bulkley Valley Fall Fair.

The Babine River, which runs northeast of Smithers, is known as the finest steelhead river on the continent. The Babine also provides a white-water rafting and kayaking adventure, and local operators will take you down the river from June to September. Driftwood Canyon Provincial Park, 20 KM (12 miles) north of Smithers, contains a fossil bed that reveals fossils of insects, fish, plants, and prehistoric birds. Visitors are allowed to dig and to keep their fossil finds. Smithers, with its Bavarian architecture, is dominated by Hudson Bay Mountain. This is part of the region of the Gitksan-Wet'suwet'en nation, which stretches along and beyond the Yellowhead Highway. Native American art and crafts are available in Smithers. Hudson Bay Mountain features downhill skiing.

The town's travel Infocentre is the Canadian National railway car, on the east side of Highway 16. It's open from May through September. In the off-season, contact the Smithers Chamber of Commerce in the Central Park Building behind the Infocentre. The year-round address is Smithers Chamber of Commerce, P.O. Box 2379, Smithers, B.C. V0J 2N0.

### Where to Eat

The dining room in the **Hudson's Bay Lodge** is as good a place to eat as any in town, and better than most. Prices are in the moderate range. **Savala's Steak House**, at 1338 Main Street, offers steak and Italian dishes at moderate prices.

# Stewart (B.C.) and Hyder (AK)

A spur off the Stewart/Cassiar Highway, Route 37A is the most scenic short drive in northern B.C. This road, which traverses

Bear Pass, starts at Meziadin Junction on Highway 37. In 67 kilometers, visitors travel through several ecosystems, over the Coast mountain range and into the mild climate of the coast region. These border towns were founded in the gold rush period. Gold, then silver and copper, were mined (on and off) until 1950. First named Portland City, Hyder burned to the ground (or to its pilings) in 1948. Thousands of pilings on which the town was built over the water can be seen today.

Hyder, three kilometers down the road from Stewart, calls itself "The Friendliest Ghost Town" in Alaska. It is set in the midst of the Tongass National Forest. Mount Rainey rises almost perpendicularly from the canal. The major activities for visitors to the two neighboring towns are fishing, hunting, and sightseeing. Looking for bears and eagles is part of the experience. Four types of salmon spawn here. Most of all, it's a scenic paradise, well worth the drive for the scenery alone. Most services are in Stewart. There is an open border between the two towns.

Before you reach the turnoff to Stewart and Hyder, you'll come across the travel Infocentre, at the Meziadin Lake Campground (on Highway 37). There is another Infocentre in Stewart, in the Old Firehall (6th and Columbia Street), the home of the local museum.

### Where to Eat
**Portland City Dining Emporium** is located in the tiny rustic community of Hyder. Seafood is a specialty, with the restaurant offering large servings at reasonable prices. **Border Café**, also in Hyder, serves burgers and good breakfasts. The **Dutch Pastry Shop** in Stewart sells some of the best bread, donuts, pastries, and turnovers available in the north.

# Terrace (B.C.)

On the Skeena River, Terrace was originally a firewood stop for the many paddle wheelers that used to ply the river. This is a handy stop for travelers before catching the Alaska Marine Highway or B.C. Ferries on the north coast, or before beginning the long trip up the Stewart/Cassiar Highway.

The town is known for its fish (salmon) and for the white Kermode bears, a light-colored sub-species of the ordinary black bear. Terrace is a good place to look for Native American handicrafts in retail stores and in special crafts shops run by local bands. Travel Infocentre: 4511 Keith Road. Open 9 A.M. to 5 P.M. during summer season, (604) 635-2063. The center has lists of licensed fishing guides and information on nearby Native American villages.

Things to do include a visit to Heritage Park, a collection of pioneer buildings showing several forms of log architecture, capturing the spirit of pioneer days along the Skeena. Be sure to visit the restored Kalam Lake Hotel and Dance Hall, the centerpiece of the park. Fishing is the big recreational sport here, with jet boats on the river, lake fishing in Lakelse Lake, or fly-in to a remote lake. One of the largest thermal pools in B.C. is located at Mount Layton Hotsprings Resort. An interesting sidetrip along Kalum Lake Road (3 KM west of the Infocentre) leads 80 KM (50 miles) to the Tseax lava beds, formed around 1750 B.C. A logging road will take you north of Terrace to Kitsumkalum Provincial Park, on the west shore of Kitsumkalum Lake, where volcanic action created red sand beaches.

# Vancouver (B.C.)

Vancouver is by common consent one of the most striking city locations in the world. It is Canada's third largest city, surrounded by the waters of the Georgia Strait and flanked by the dramatic Coast Mountains. Blessed with a mild climate, Vancouver is a city of beaches, great views, outdoor restaurants, a vigorous artistic scene, and a lifestyle that often makes permanent residents out of visitors.

Just over 100 years old, Vancouver was the home of several Native American settlements before Spanish explorer José

Narvaez anchored off Point Grey in July 1791. Captain George Vancouver charted Burrard Inlet and then made rendezvous with Spanish captains Galiano and Valdes on June 21, 1792. Vancouver was established as a village when "Gassy Jack" Deighton received a saloon permit in 1869, and the community at Burrard Inlet was in business where the restored Gastown area is now situated.

Vancouver is now a young, modern city, based on its large port facility and its role as the financial center for western Canada. Tourism is a very large industry in Vancouver. The 1986 world's fair, EXPO '86, brought major improvements to the region and a steady increase in tourists and tourist facilities. However, what still attracts visitors to Vancouver is its basic charm, the spectacular scenery, and the attractions that this environment promotes: sightseeing, boating, Canada's largest Chinatown, several excellent museums, gardens, wonderful parks, and excellent shopping.

### Practical Information

The central visitor Infocentre is at the corner of Burrard and Hastings streets in downtown Vancouver, close to the waterfront and several major hotels as well as to the main shopping district a few blocks north. Information is available for the Vancouver area and other parts of B.C. Other smaller Infocentres are located on the major highways leading into Vancouver.

B.C. Ferries terminals are located at Tsawwassen (the town of Delta) for service to Vancouver Island (Victoria and Nanaimo) and the Gulf Islands, and also in Horseshoe Bay (city of West Vancouver) for service to Bowen Island, Vancouver Island (Nanaimo), and Langdale (Sunshine Coast).

One of the best ways to get to know Vancouver is by taking a guided bus tour to get your bearings. Gray Line Tours is located in the Vancouver Hotel, 900 West Georgia Street, downtown. This long-established tour operator has basic daily tours that last two hours, with longer tours available.

### Getting Around Vancouver

Vancouver is surrounded by water, so bridges are a basic fact of life in the area, although traffic jams rarely occur outside of rush hours. Two bridges link Vancouver and the north shore of Burrard Inlet: the Lions Gate suspension bridge from Vancouver's West End, and the Second Narrows Bridge to the east. The Burrard, Granville, and Cambie Street bridges cross False Creek in downtown Vancouver, while a series of bridges cross the arms of the Fraser River, leading to the suburbs of Richmond, Delta, and Surrey. City maps are available at the downtown Vancouver Infocentre or can be purchased at gas stations.

B.C. Transit operates an effective transit system throughout Vancouver and the Lower Mainland area.

Two special forms of transit offer tourists special rides. SkyTrain, the region's rapid transit system, is an elevated, automated light rail service running from downtown Vancouver through the cities of Burnaby and New Westminster to the far suburb of Surrey. This half-hour ride provides some exciting views of the city and mountains and is well worth taking. Catamaran ferries, called Seabuses, take passengers across Burrard Inlet from the downtown Waterfront Station to Lonsdale Quay in North Vancouver.

### Major Vancouver Areas

The Lower Mainland of B.C. is divided into several cities by natural barriers including the Fraser River and Burrard Inlet. On the Vancouver side, Burnaby lies to the east and Richmond to the south. Vancouver International Airport is located on Sea Island in Richmond. Farther south are Delta and Surrey, on the U.S. border.

To the north, across Burrard Inlet, are the North Shore communities of North and West Vancouver. Here, scenic residential areas are situated on the Coast Mountains. Interesting smaller communities on the North Shore include Deep Cove, where Indian Arm joins Burrard Inlet, and Horseshoe Bay. Bowen Island is the closest of the Gulf Islands and is a 20-minute ferry ride from Horseshoe Bay.

The City of Vancouver is divided into distinct communities, each with its own ambiance. Kitsilano, Kerrisdale, and Point Grey form the West Side of Vancouver, with great beaches and, at the tip of Point Grey, the University of B.C. Kitsilano is an almost nonstop parade of good restaurants. The West End is Vancouver's downtown, with an amazing mixture of high- and low-rise apartment buildings, tall office towers, hotels, restaurants and bistros, chic shopping streets, and beaches on English Bay and Stanley Park. The East Side features several immigrant communities including Chinatown and Commercial Drive, with its cappuccino bars and continental atmosphere.

## Things to See and Do

Vancouver is a city of parks and gardens, aided by the mild climate and lack of frost during most winters. Outstanding gardens include the Asian and Nitobe (Japanese) gardens at the University of B.C., as well as the U.B.C. Botanical Garden. The Dr. Sun Yat Sen Classical Garden is the only traditional Chinese garden built outside China. Located in Chinatown, this garden was designed in the Ming Dynasty style. Other garden areas include Queen Elizabeth Park and VanDusen Botanical Gardens in central Vancouver.

Beaches are found on English Bay in the downtown area (English Bay and Sunset beaches), in Stanley Park, and from Kitsilano Beach to Spanish Banks beach on the West Side. Wreck Beach at Point Grey is the renowned nude beach. Stanley Park in the downtown West End is the world-famous natural park, mainly forest with nature trails, but including a fine rose garden and the Vancouver Aquarium, Vancouver's top visitor attraction. Several good restaurants are located within the park, as well as lots of picnic areas and places for relaxing. Pacific Spirit Park is a purely natural forest park near the University of B.C.

The Capilano Suspension Bridge in North Vancouver spans a deep chasm, with gardens and waterfalls. For a complete picture of the area, take the Grouse Mountain Skyride from the top of

Capilano Road, with views overlooking Vancouver and the Fraser River delta.

Several museums are well worth visiting. The best is the Museum of Anthropology at U.B.C., containing a re-created Haida village and displaying historical artifacts and the Native American heritage of the province, with totem poles, carvings, dugout canoes, jewelry, and ceremonial gold objects. Shopping is centered in the downtown West End area. Robson Street is filled with fashion boutiques and interesting restaurants, continental and otherwise. The nearby Canada Place—a convention center located on the cruise ship pier in the harbor—offers great views of the mountains and bustling harbor life. Granville Island, on False Creek, has a public market, fishing boats, restaurants, art galleries, and shops; it's a great people place. Gastown is the restored early-Vancouver district, with restaurants, clubs, pubs, and shopping.

### Where to Eat

Over the past 10 years, Vancouver has become a very good place to eat. Its multicultural community has burst out with a range of international cuisine that matches the finest cities in the world. We can only give you a sampling of the exceptionally wide selection of good dining available in the area and have listed the city's top eating places, along with a couple of moderately priced restaurants suitable for family dining or for sampling on a short stay in the city.

**Bishop's Restaurant**, 2183 West 4th Avenue, is a fine small restaurant in the Kitsilano area. John Bishop and his staff are famed for personal service and fresh, seasonal dishes. Reservations required, call (604) 738-2025. This restaurant cannot be recommended too highly. Bishop has made this restaurant a personal triumph, and a delight for diners. Prices are in the expensive range.

The **Cannery Seafood House** seems to have been in Vancouver forever, although it's just a little more than 20 years since this deceptively rustic, shanty-style place opened on the Burrard Inlet waterfront. The restaurant offers fine seafood dishes, simply prepared with superb seasoning. In recent years, the chefs have added a mesquite grill and a slight Southwestern touch to the menu mixture. Costs range from moderate to expensive. It's located at 2205 Commissioner Street. For reservations and directions, call (604) 254-9606.

There are two **Keg Boathouses**; the Vancouver-city version is at 566 Cardero Street just east of Stanley Park. The second incarnation is in Horseshoe Bay, the terminus for the B.C. Ferries ships (6695 Nelson Avenue). Both boathouses serve seafood in picturesque waterfront settings, providing good eating and seaside fun for families and couples.

**Settebello**, at 1133 Robson Street, upstairs in the Robson Fashion Court building, is one of several fine restaurants established in this city by Umberto Menghi. This relaxed, informal place specializes in Italian cuisine with a light touch. There's an outdoor patio for summer dining. Prices are moderate.

**The Teahouse**, at Ferguson Point in Stanley Park, is a special experience, offering dining in the spectacular park. The restaurant has a scenic location, fine views of English Bay, and reasonably good food. You'll find that the view and location make the prices high.

The **Timber Club**, in the Hotel Vancouver on Georgia Street, is a long-time institution. This dining room, just off the main lobby, has been a local standby for many years, and has recently been re-done. It still retains its famed service. At the top of the same hotel is **The Roof** restaurant, which has dining and dancing on weekends, more often during summer months. Both restaurants are in the expensive range.

A few years ago Hidekazu Tojo opened his eponymous restaurant in midtown Vancouver, at 202-777 West Broadway. **Tojo's** was filled from the second day of operation, thanks to great reviews and word of mouth about the superb sushi served in this elegant restaurant. Tojo is a true master of the sushi art, and if you're a dedicated sushi fan, you'll let the maestro choose your menu for you.

Gastown is the restored pioneer settlement, located just to the east of the downtown waterfront area. Gastown is now a series of cobblestone streets, boutiques, restaurants, and nightclubs. One of the best places to eat in this historic sector is the **Water Street Café**. This is a fine place for seafood, particularly the crab cakes. There is also a slight Southwest slant to the eclectic menu. Phone for reservations and ask for an outside window; the street scene adds to the dining experience, (604) 689-2832.

The **William Tell Restaurant**, in the Coast Georgian Court Hotel at 765 Beatty Street (604-682-5555), is tops in continental cuisine, with a focus on Swiss entrees. This fine restaurant is close to the B.C. Place stadium and to G.M. Centre, the home of the Vancouver Canucks and Grizzlies. For reservations call (604) 682-5555.

# Vancouver Island (B.C.)

Stretching north and south for 480 kilometers (300 miles), Vancouver Island is the largest island off the west coast of North America. Its spine is the mountain range that separates the island into two zones: the sheltered and mild east coast, with its beaches and resort communities, and the wild, rugged west coast, which is largely uninhabited.

Near the southern tip of the island is Victoria, a decidedly non-Canadian city with its quaint Victorian-English charm: the many tea rooms, woolen shops, double-decker busses and other accouterments of English life that set Victoria apart from other B.C. cities. While there are such pseudo-English tourist establishments as a replica of Anne Hathaway's Cottage and the Royal London Wax Museum, this part of Vancouver Island is filled with unique things to see, like Fort Rodd Hill, a British fort built to keep Americans south of the border during the short and silly

"Pig War" with the U.S., and the renowned Butchart Gardens in Sidney, north of Victoria. With its light rainfall (27 inches average) and temperate climate, Victoria is a prime tourist destination for Americans and Canadians. The Trans-Canada and Island highways (highways 1 and 19) provide the route to the North Coast, steering you to varied tourist centers, including:

- Sooke, along the road to the southwest corner of the island;
- Cowichan, with its Native American crafts and Cowichan sweaters;
- Chemainus, with murals depicting local history and culture painted on many of the town's buildings;
- Nanaimo, the "harbor city" and home of the renowned Nanaimo Bar (not a pub—it's a famous dessert square);
- Parksville and Qualicum Beach, offering sheltered beaches and lazy living.

As you reach the northern half of the island you'll find:

- Comox, Courtenay, and Campbell River, at the top of the Georgia Strait, where the salmon fishing is unparalleled;
- The north coast and small fishing towns: Port McNeill and Port Hardy.

The West Coast is reached by taking Highway 4 past Port Alberni to two small fishing villages, Ucluelet and Tofino. In between the communities lies Long Beach, part of Pacific Rim National Park, providing campers with truly super-natural vacation experiences. Tofino is a salmon fishing center and the take-off point for short cruises and expeditions along the coast.

A cruise will take you to natural hot springs pools, located on a coastal island. Other boat rides take visitors to scenic Meares Island. Most visitors just want to fish, while surfers work out in the waves at Long Beach.

# Victoria

Established by the Hudson's Bay Company when the Oregon Treaty was signed, Victoria has lost its rough-and-ready atmosphere and is an oasis of English gentility, where the Union Jack waves in the summer breezes and high tea has become a standing tradition. The best way to observe the mores and manners of the high tea tradition is to have a "cuppa" in the lobby of the Empress Hotel.

Because Victoria has developed this more-English-than-England theme, it has become an extremely popular tourist city. The people are friendly, the pace is leisurely, and a variety of attractions and recreation opportunities bring people back to Victoria again and again. It is also a popular retirement place. For visitors on their way to more northern travels, Victoria is a handy overnight stopping place.

The city's Visitor Infocentre is at 812 Wharf Street, located downtown on the Inner Harbour. The harbor provides a focal point for visitors, with the local Infocentre located under an art deco tower. Here are the terminals for ferries to Seattle and Port Angeles, Washington, and seaplane flights to Vancouver. Across the harbor are the B.C. Parliament buildings, which sparkle at night with hundreds of lights. The Empress Hotel, also on the harbor, is another major landmark, one of many picturesque buildings in the city. The downtown shopping district is two blocks from the harbor and many other hotels are located nearby.

An excellent introduction to the province is a visit to the Royal British Columbia Museum, located next to the Parliament buildings. This major museum concentrates on the province's natural history and Native American heritage. More history can be soaked up at Fort Rodd Hill, a former British bastion from 1896 now operated as a national historic site. Bastion Square in the downtown area is the site of old Fort Victoria from 1843. Craigdarroch Castle, a Victorian mansion built by coal magnate Robert Dunsmuir, is open for tours.

The Victoria area is a wonderland of gardens and parks. The most famous of these is Butchart Gardens, located in Sidney near the Swartz Bay ferry docks. At any time of the year Butchart Gardens provides a spectacular panorama of flowers, trees, and shrubs. The gardens of Government House, the residence of B.C.'s lieutenant governor, are open to the public daily.

The city has a wide range of hotels, motels, and bed-and-breakfast places, some of them surprisingly inexpensive, particularly during the non-summer months. Traveling by car to the outskirts of Victoria is recommended: to Saanich Inlet, Sidney, and Cowichan Bay, where boat rentals, guides, and tackle are available. Sooke, due west of Victoria, is a scenic natural area, perfect for picnics or for more sophisticated dining. The University of Victoria, on a hill overlooking Cadboro Bay, is worth a visit. Several golf courses within the city include Uplands, Cedar Hill, and Gorge Vale. Glen Meadows Golf Club is outside of the urban area, at West Saanich Road and McTavish Road.

### B.C. Ferries

The government's B.C. Ferry Corporation operates car ferries from Swartz Bay, 37 KM (23 miles) north of Victoria, to Tsawwassen (near Vancouver) and to the Gulf Islands. Recorded information: (604) 656-0757. General information: (604) 386-3431. A fast new harbor-to-harbor passenger service started linking Victoria with Vancouver in 1992. Black Ball Transport has service from Victoria to Port Angeles, WA, throughout the year; 430 Belleville Street, (604) 386-2202. Washington State Ferries operates from Sidney to Anacortes, WA, stopping in the San Juan Islands along the way, (604) 381-1551.

### Where to Eat

There are restaurants everywhere in the Victoria area. The following is a small selection of places with atmosphere and scenery.

Several **Fogg and Suds** restaurants operate in the Vancouver and Victoria areas, and this one is much like the others: an informal place with super-relaxed staff, with a modern pub-style menu on the lighter side including gourmet burgers, and with a wide selection of beers, both bottled (domestic and lots of imports) and microbrews on draft. You'll find it at 1630 Store Street.

The **Captain's Palace** is a series of large old homes turned into a B & B operation, next to the Inner Harbour and close to the provincial Parliament Building, at 309 Belleville Street. The dining room here, decorated in Victorian period style, specializes in seafood, largely focusing on what's in season. For reservations call (604) 388-9191.

The **Dining Room and Greenhouse Restaurant**, in Butchart Gardens, north of Victoria in Sidney, is open for lunch, afternoon tea, and dinner. The gardens' Benvenuto Buffet opens each evening, from 5 P.M. The gardens are renowned as the finest show gardens in Canada, if not in all of North America. The two dining rooms provide a colorful setting, with good food and service. Visitors to the gardens make reservations at the reception desk when they arrive. Prices are in the moderate range.

**Rattenbury's** is at Douglas and Belleville streets downtown. If you like to eat in the middle of everything, this is the place! Named for the architect who designed the Parliament buildings, Rattenbury's serves fish and chips, crêpes, quiche, and salads for lunch, beef and seafood for dinner. It's located in the Crystal Garden, next to the Royal B.C. Museum, and near the Inner Harbour.

**Sooke Harbour House,** at 1528 Whiffin Spit Road in Sooke, is (without doubt in my opinion) the finest place to eat—certainly on Vancouver Island, and probably in all of B.C. While this hotel dining room is a one-hour drive from downtown, it's worth the trip and the required reservations. The food is seasonally fresh and service is superb. The dining room is part of a deluxe bed-and-breakfast inn, with package rates that include dinner and breakfast. Prices match the level of the food and service. For reservations call (604) 642-3421.

# Williams Lake (B.C.)

A town of 10,000 people, Williams Lake sits in the center of the Cariboo country: a ranching, lumbering, and mining community. The local Infocentre is at 1148 South Broadway (Highway 7 at the south end of town). Several sawmills produce lumber and specialty woods, and the Gibraltar Mines produce copper and molybdenum. Cattle ranching is the prime form of agriculture here, and the ranching background of the community is reflected in the famous Williams Lake Stampede—the rodeo held the first weekend in July. One of the largest rodeos in Canada, it attracts performers and onlookers from across the country and the U.S. The community dresses up for the Stampede, putting false fronts on some of the downtown buildings and the citizens wear western garb. The new Williams Lake Museum is at 113 North 4th Avenue, near City Hall. Displays include artifacts of Coast Salish Native American life, grist mill equipment, and other reminders of the period between 1850 and 1920. The Scout Island Nature Centre is located at the south end of town off Highway 20, with trails and activities for children.

# Access Routes
## Places to Stay

### ASHCROFT AND CACHE CREEK (B.C.)

**Ashcroft River Inn**
P.O. Box 1359
Ashcroft, B.C. V0K 1A0
(604) 453-9124

This modest motel operation offers standard air-conditioned units with satellite TV. There is a licensed restaurant, and a pub. Pets are permitted. The motel is located beside the Thompson River, at the edge of town. ($)

**Bonaparte Motel**
P.O. Box 487
Cache Creek, B.C.
V0K 1H0
(604) 457-9693

The Bonaparte is found along Highway 97, north of the built-up area of Cache Creek, offering air-conditioned standard and housekeeping units, rooms with queen beds, morning coffee, whirlpool, and a heated pool. ($)

**Brookside Campsite**
P.O. Box 737
Cache Creek, B.C.
V0K 1H0
(604) 457-6633

This medium-size operation on Highway 1 is open May to October, with RV and tentsites, full and partial hookups, showers, sanitation station, laundry, store, and playground.

**Cache Creek Campgrounds**
P.O. Box 127
Cache Creek, B.C.
V0K 1H0
(604) 457-6414

This large campground and RV facility is located 4 KM (2.4 miles) north of Cache Creek on Highway 97. Facilities include RV and tentsites, full hookups, sani-station, showers, laundry, heated pool, whirlpool, mini-golf, store, and car wash.

**Desert Motel**
P.O. Box 339
Cache Creek, B.C.
V0K 1H0
(604) 457-6226

One of the larger motels in this sagebrush town, the Desert has air-conditioned units (some no-smoking) and a heated pool. As with the other motels clustered around the highway junction, restaurants and stores are nearby. ($)

**Sandman Inn**
P.O. Box 278
Cache Creek, B.C.
V0K 1H0
(604) 457-6284 or
800-726-3626

One of a chain of motels stretching from Vancouver to Prince George, this place is a basic roadside motel operation, with air-conditioned units, some with kitchenettes, a licensed restaurant, and seniors' discounts. ($)

**Sundance Guest Ranch**
P.O. Box 489
Ashcroft, B.C. V0K 1A0
(604) 453-2422

Located eight miles south of Ashcroft, off Highland Valley Road, this popular guest ranch offers air-conditioned rooms with private baths, horse riding, cookouts, and a heated pool, plus tennis and children's activities. ($$$)

*Cache Creek has a wider range of accommodation, and is conveniently located at the junction of the two major highways in the region, the Trans-Canada (Highway 1), and the Cariboo (Highway 97).*

## CALGARY (ALBERTA)

**Delta Bow Valley Inn**
209 4th Avenue SE
Calgary, AB T2G 0C6
(403) 266-1980 or
800-268-1133

This deluxe hotel has large rooms and recreational facilities, including a children's creative activity center. There is a fine dining room, coffee shop, lobby lounge, indoor pool, sauna, and whirlpool. ($$$)

**International Hotel
of Calgary**
220 4th Avenue SW
Calgary, AB T2P 0H5
(403) 265-9600 or
800-661-8627

This all suite-hotel has one- and two-bedroom units, an indoor pool, health spa, dining room, lounge, and special weekend rates. ($$ to $$$)

**KOA Calgary West Kampground**
P.O. Box 10, Site 12, SS #1
Calgary, AB T2M 4N3
(403) 288-0411

This very large KOA offers all the trimmings, including full hookups and tentsites, laundry, barbecues, store, and dump station. It's off Highway 1 (Trans-Canada), 4 KM (2.5 miles) west of downtown Calgary. The campground is open from April 15th to October 15th.

**Lord Nelson Inn**
1020 8th Avenue SW
Calgary, Alberta T2P 1J2
(403) 269-8262 (collect)

The Lord Nelson is an inexpensive downtown hotel with standard rooms and suites, queen beds and water beds, free underground parking for guests, a licensed dining room, and pub-style lounge. Children stay for free. ($$)

**Mountain View Farm Campground**
P.O. Box 6, Site 8,
Rural Route 6
Calgary, AB G2M 4L5
(403) 293-6640

This large rural operation offers full hookups and tentsites, a store, dump station, fishing, laundry, and hay rides. Open year-round, the campground is located 4 KM (3 miles) east of downtown Calgary, on Highway 1, the Trans-Canada.

## CAMPBELL RIVER (B.C.)

**Anchor Inn**
261 Island Highway
Campbell River, B.C.
V9W 2B3
(604) 286-1131 or
800-663-7227

This motor hotel offers sea views, and some rooms are equipped with kitchens. The operation includes a dining room, an outdoor patio/lounge, indoor lounge, pool, sauna, and whirlpool. ($$)

**Austrian Chalet Village**
462 South Island Highway
Campbell River, B.C.
V9W 1A5
(604) 923-4231

This sizable motel operation with an Austrian or Tyrolean flair overlooks Discovery Passage. Facilities include standard rooms and housekeeping units, some with lofts, in-room coffee, a restaurant and pub, pool, whirlpool, and sauna. ($ to $$)

**Coast Discovery Inn**
975 Shoppers Row
Campbell River, B.C.
V9W 2C5
(604) 287-7155 or
800-663-1144

Located in the downtown area next to the shopping mall (Tyee Plaza), this is a high-rise hotel offering full services, including whirlpool suites, a restaurant, coffee shop, pub, health club, and a cold beer and wine store. ($$ to $$$)

**Holiday Shores RV Park**
3001 Spit Road
P.O. Box 274
Campbell River, B.C.
V9W 5B1
(604) 286-6142

Located 3 KM (2 miles) from downtown Campbell River, this medium-size campground offers full and partial hookups, showers, a laundry, boat launch, and floats.

**Painter's Lodge and Resort**
P.O. Box 460
Campbell River, B.C.
V9W 5C1
(604) 286-1102 or
800-663-7090

Painter's Lodge is one of B.C.'s most noteworthy fishing resorts, located at the north edge of Campbell River. The resort features lodge rooms and comfortable cottages, plus a dining room, lounge, pub, and pool. When you arrive you'll notice the long lineup of fishing boats at the resort's dock; fishing is on the minds of most visitors to Painter's. Fishing packages are available. ($$$)

**Ripple Rock RV Park**
15011 Ripple Rock Road
c/o 277 Ripple Rock Road
Campbell River, B.C.
V9W 1N5
(604) 287-7108

This adult-oriented campground is located in a scenic setting 20 KM (12 miles) north of Campbell River. The park offers full hookups, cement pads, showers, laundry, hot tub, clubhouse, a barbecue area, shuffleboard, a smokehouse, moorage, and fishing pier. Pets are permitted.

**CLINTON (B.C.)**

*Located at the southern end of the Cariboo-Chilcotin area, Clinton is a small, atmospheric town that services the large cattle ranches of the area. The Coast Mountains provide a backdrop for this town, a far more interesting place to spend some time than around the highway junction at Cache Creek.*

**Cariboo Lodge**
P.O. Box 459
Clinton, B.C. V0K 1K0
(604) 459-7992

This long-time fixture is a large old log structure with dining room, coffee shop, and pub. The units have queen and king beds, and the restaurant has real old-west atmosphere—the closest such thing to some of the older saloons in southeastern Arizona. ($$)

**Gold Trail RV Park**
1602 Highway 97 North
Clinton, B.C. V0K 1K0
(604) 459-2519

Located right in Clinton, this medium-sized campground has RV sites with full and partial hookups, grassy tenting sites, restrooms, showers, and dump station. Restaurants and stores are nearby.

**Lakeview Campsite and Trailer Park**
P.O. Box 98
Clinton, B.C. V0K 1K0
(604) 459-2638

A medium-size operation, this campground in Clinton offers partial hookups, grassy and shaded sites, restrooms, showers, laundry, and dump station. Kids can enjoy the playground and lake activities. The campground has a small store and gift shop.

## COURTENAY AND COMOX (B.C.)

**Arbutus Pacific Hotel**
275 8th Street
Courtenay, B.C. V9N 1N4
(604) 334-3121

Centrally located in Courtenay, this motor hotel has a dining room, coffee shop, pub, heated pool, whirlpool, and sauna. Some rooms are handicapped-equipped. A cold beer and wine store is located on the premises. ($)

**Kingfisher Oceanside Inn and RV Park**
4330 South Island Highway
Rural Route 6, Site 676,
Compartment 1
Courtenay, B.C. V9N 8H9
(604) 338-1323 or
800-663-7929

Located south of Courtenay with a seaside location, the Kingfisher offers a sea view from every room. Other features include free continental breakfast, whirlpool, heated outdoor pool, and a waterside seafood restaurant with lounge. ($$) The small RV park offers full hookups for RVs and trailers.

**Maple Pool Campsite**
Rural Route #4, Site 403,
Compartment 14
Courtenay, B.C. V9N 6Z8
(604) 338-9386 or
fax: (604) 338-9370

Located at 4701 Headquarters Road, the campground is a half-kilometer off Highway 19. Features include grassy sites, some with electrical hookups. Some are pull-through sites, and there are level spots for tent campers.

**Port Augusta Resort Hotel**
2082 Comox Avenue
Comox, B.C. V9M 1P8
(604) 339-2277

Overlooking the bay and adjacent to the hospital, this motel has been recently renovated, and offers standard rooms and housekeeping units, non-smoking rooms, a restaurant, lounge, laundry, and heated outdoor pool. ($$)

**Seaview Tent and
Trailer Park**
685 Lazo Road
Comox, B.C. V9M 3X2
(604) 339-3946

A medium-size campground operation, the Seaview is located 5 KM (3 miles) east of Comox, offering full hookups, showers, laundry, and a store. It is located near a beach and boat ramp. Pets are permitted on-leash.

## EDMONTON (ALBERTA)

**Chateau Louis Hotel**
11727 Kingsway Avenue
Edmonton, AB
T5G 3A1
(403) 452-7770 or
800-661-9843

This downtown hotel is less expensive than its neighbors, with more than a hundred rooms and suites, full room service, a dining room and lounge, in-room coffee, and free parking. ($ to $$)

**Crowne Plaza Edmonton**
10111 Bellamy Hill
Edmonton, AB
T5J 1N7
(403) 428-6611 or
800-661-8801

Formerly the Chateau Lacombe, the Crowne Plaza is located in downtown Edmonton, with standard hotel rooms and suites, including non-smoking units. Other facilities include a dining room and lounge, and indoor heated parking for those long Edmonton winters. Children stay without charge. ($$$)

**Fantasyland Hotel and Resort**
17700 87th Avenue
Edmonton, AB
T5T 4V4
(403) 444-3000 or
800-661-6454.

This hotel is part of the huge West Edmonton Mall, with more than 350 rooms, including theme rooms with fanciful beds, suites with whirlpool, more stores than you will ever want to visit, plus an amusement park and a water park, all under the same roof. ($$$)

**Half Moon Lake Resort**
21524 Township
Road 520
Sherwood Park, AB
T8E 1E5
(403) 922-3045

This campground and RV park provides hookups, tentsites, a sandy beach, wading pool, ball diamonds, store, laundry, riding stables, and paddle boat rentals. Located 3.2 KM (2 miles) east of Sherwood Park, 6.4 KM (4 miles) south on Highway 21, and 10.4 KM (6.5 miles) east on Township Road 520.

**Journey's End Motel**
**(Comfort Inn)**
17610 100 Avenue West
Edmonton, AB
T5S 1S9
(403) 484-4415 or
800-228-5150

Comfort Inns have taken over this northwest Edmonton motel. Facilities include large rooms and low prices, plus complimentary morning coffee. Children stay free. ($$)

**Klondike Valley Tent**
**and Trailer Park**
1660 Calgary Trail
Edmonton, AB
T6W 1A1
(403) 988-5067

South of Edmonton, this campground has 155 sites, full hookups, laundry, and store with hiking trails nearby. Near Highway 2 south. Take Ellerslie Road west to Service Road south 1 KM (0.6 mile), parallel to Highway 2 south.

**Shaker's Acres**
21530 103rd Avenue
Edmonton, AB
T5G 2C4
(403) 447-3564

This large campground is at the western city limits, off Highway 16 (Yellowhead Highway) at the Winterburn Road exit. Facilities include RV and tentsites, snack bar, dump station, store, and playground. Open year-round.

## GRANDE PRAIRIE (ALBERTA)

**Grande Prairie Inn**
11633 100 Street
Grande Prairie, AB
T8V 3Y4
(403) 532-5221 or
800-661-6529

This large hotel has standard rooms and suites, cable television, licensed dining room and lounge, pub, swimming pool, and whirlpool. ($$ to $$$)

**Igloo Inn**
11724 100 Street
Grande Prairie, AB
T8V 4H5
(403) 539-5314 or
800-665-0769

Another large motel, this one features standard rooms, executive suites, and units with kitchenettes, plus an indoor heated pool with waterslide and hot tub, exercise room, movie bar, and complimentary coffee and toast in the morning. Another useful feature is a private patio and barbecue area. The Prairie Mall with shopping and restaurants is nearby. ($$ to $$$)

## HAZELTON (B.C.)

**K'san Campground**
P.O. Box 440
Hazelton, B.C. V0J 1Y0
(604) 842-5940

Located in Hazelton, off the highway, you get to this interesting location by turning north at New Hazelton. The campground is situated at the confluence of the Bulkley and Skeena rivers, with full hookups, showers, flush toilets, and dump station. The campground is close to the museum and K'san Village, a fascinating Native American cultural site.

**Robber's Roost Lodge**
P.O. Box 555
New Hazelton, B.C.
V0J 2J0
(604) 842-6916

On Highway 16, the Robber's Roost is a fairly new hotel on the edge of town. Units have queen beds and some rooms have kitchen facilities. A restaurant is located next door. ($ to $$)

**28 Inn and 28 Inn Annex**
4545 Highway 16
P.O. Box 358
New Hazelton, B.C.
V0J 2J0
(604) 842-6006

This downtown motel features rooms with twin, double, or queen beds, and combination baths. Some units have kitchenettes, and complimentary coffee is available. The inn has a restaurant, pub, and a cold beer and wine store. ($ to $$)

## HOPE (B.C.)

**Coquihalla Campground**
P.O. Box 308
Hope, B.C. V0X 1L0
(604) 869-7119

This family campground and RV park is located on the Coquihalla River, with a treed, park-like setting, riverfront sites, electrical and water hookups, flush toilets, showers, laundry, a small store, video games room, playfield, and dump station.

**Hope KOA Kampground**
62280 Flood Hope Road
Rural Route 2
Hope, B.C. V0X 1L0
(604) 869-9857

South of the town of Hope, off Highway 1, this large KOA operation features full hookups, tenting sites, showers, a store, sani-station, swimming pool, and laundry.

**Maple Leaf Motor Inn**
377 Old Hope-Princeton
Highway
P.O. Box 438
Hope, B.C. V0X 1L0
(604) 869-7107

This motel has standard rooms and housekeeping units, a dining room, coffee shop, indoor pool, sauna, and whirlpool. Complimentary coffee is offered in the morning. ($ to $$)

**Slumber Lodge**
250 Fort Street
Hope, B.C. V0X 1L0
(604) 869-5666

Located in downtown Hope, this motel is one of a regional chain, with indoor pool, sauna, and restaurant. The facility is handy to stores and restaurants. ($)

# NANAIMO (B.C.)

**Best Western Northgate**
6450 Metral Drive
Nanaimo, B.C. V9T 2L8
(604) 390-2222

Located just off Highway 19, near two shopping malls, this modern and recently built motel features standard motel rooms and units with kitchenettes, a family restaurant, pub, sauna, exercise room, and whirlpool. ($$).

**Brannen Lake Campsites**
4228 Briggs Road
Nanaimo, B.C. V9R 5K3
(604) 756-0404

This small campground is located 6 KM (4 miles) north of the Nanaimo ferry terminal. Facilities include shady and sunny sites on 153 acres of working farm, with lake access, pull-through sites, partial hookups, flush toilets, showers, laundry, dump station, store, and hayrides.

**Coast Bastion Inn**
11 Bastion Street
Nanaimo, B.C. V9R 2Z9
(604) 753-6601 or central
reservations: 800-663-1144

The Coast Bastion is a full-service hotel belonging to the respected regional chain of West Coast hotels, featuring rooms with water views, a café-style restaurant, lounge, pub, sauna, whirlpool, and exercise facilities. ($$ to $$$)

**Day's Inn Harbourview**
809 Island Highway
South
Nanaimo, B.C. V9R 5K1
(604) 754-8171 or
800-329-7466

This handy motel features standard rooms, suites, and units with kitchens. Rooms have a harbor view, queen beds, and complimentary coffee. The inn has a restaurant, laundry, indoor pool, and whirlpool. ($$)

**Inn of the Sea Resort**
3600 Yellow Point Road
Rural Route #3
Ladysmith, B.C. V0R 2E0
(604) 245-2211

Located on Yellow Point Road, south of Nanaimo and 13 KM (8.7 miles) north of Ladysmith off Highway 1, this seaside resort has rooms and suites (some with kitchens) with views of Georgia Strait, a swimming pool, whirlpool, tennis, and a waterfront dining room and lounge. This is a fine spot for beachcombing. ($$ to $$$)

## PORT HARDY (B.C.)

**Kay's Bed and Breakfast**
7605 Carnarvon Road,
P.O. Box 257
Port Hardy, B.C. V0N 2P0
(604) 949-6776

This home with an ocean view has four units including self-contained suites, with private and shared baths. ($)

**North Shore Inn**
7370 Market Street,
P.O. Box 1888
Port Hardy, B.C. V0N 2P0
(604) 949-8500

This hotel in downtown Port Hardy offers rooms with great views of the ocean, balconies, and double beds. Five-day fishing packages are available. There's a superior dining room with lounge. ($$)

**Pioneer Inn**
4965 Byng Road,
P.O. Box 699
Port Hardy, B.C. V0N 2P0
(604) 949-7271

This motel and RV park are located in a wooded setting in the country across from the Quatse River. The inn is a large rustic building with big two-room units with kitchens, in-room coffee, a restaurant and coffee shop, laundry, and playground ($ to $$). The campground has sites with full hookups.

**Quatse River Campground**
5050 Hardy Bay Road,
P.O. Box 1409
Port Hardy, B.C. V0N 2P0
(604) 949-2395

The campground is five miles from the ferry dock with power and waterside sites, tenting sites, flush toilets, showers, laundry, dump station, fire pits, and ferry pickup.

## PRINCE GEORGE (B.C.)

**Coast Inn of the North**
770 Brunswick Street
Prince George, B.C.
V2L 2C2
(604) 563-0121 or
800-663-1948

Another of the Coast chain of modern hotels, the Inn of the North is in downtown Prince George, with air-conditioned rooms and suites, an indoor pool, sauna, whirlpool, gym, gift shop, coffee shop, dining room, and a Japanese Steak House. Another Coast hotel is located in Prince Rupert. ($$ to $$$)

**Connaught Motor Inn**
1550 Victoria Street
Prince George, B.C.
V2L 2L3
(604) 562-4441 or
800-663-6620

The large downtown motor hotel has standard rooms and housekeeping units, an indoor pool, whirlpool, sauna, and a licensed restaurant. The inn is conveniently located close to downtown shopping, other restaurants, and city parks. ($)

**Esther's Inn**
1151 Commercial Drive
Prince George, B.C.
V2M 6W6
(604) 562-4131 or
800-663-6844

Entering this motel causes culture shock when you find yourself in a South Seas environment. This otherwise ordinary motor hotel is set around an indoor tropical garden with palm trees, flowering tropical plants, and a pool with waterslides. The inn also offers a restaurant, lounge, coffee shop, and sauna. ($$)

**KOA Spruceland**
P.O. Box 2434
Prince George, B.C.
V2N 2S6
(604) 964-7272

Open from April 1st to October 31st, this large KOA campground is located 5 KM (3 miles) west of the Highway 97 junction, on Highway 16 (the Yellowhead). Features include full hookups, pull-through sites, shaded tenting sites, showers, laundry, heated outdoor pool, store, playground, mini golf, and games room, plus a dump station. A shopping center is nearby.

## PRINCE RUPERT (B.C.)

**Aleeda Motel**
900 3rd Avenue West
Prince Rupert, B.C.
V8J 1M8
(604) 627-1367

This basic and inexpensive motel is located on the edge of the downtown shopping district, with standard rooms and housekeeping units (with queen beds available), complimentary morning coffee, and car storage for those wanting to take the ferry tour of southeast Alaska without their vehicles. The motel offers a discount to seniors. ($ to $$)

**Coast Prince Rupert Hotel**
118 6th Street
Prince Rupert, B.C.
V8J 3L7
(604) 624-6711 or central
reservations: 800-663-1144

Like its Coast counterparts in other B.C. cities, the Prince Rupert version is a full-service hotel, this one overlooking the harbor, with a licensed dining room, lounge, coffee shop, and movie rentals, with pets permitted. ($$ to $$$)

**Moby Dick Inn**
935 2nd Avenue West
Prince Rupert, B.C.
V8J 1H8
(604) 624-6961 or
800-663-0822

A hotel on Highway 16, the Moby Dick offers standard rooms overlooking the Prince Rupert Harbour, with a licensed dining room, bar (with live entertainment), whirlpool, sauna, and guest laundry. ($$)

**Park Avenue Campground**
1750 Park Avenue
P.O. Box 612
Prince Rupert, B.C.
V8J 3R5
(604) 624-5861

Located 1 KM (0.6 mile) east of the ferry terminal, via Highway 16, this is the only RV park and campground within the city boundaries. The large campground offers hookups and unserviced sites for trailers and RVs, a tenting area, flush toilets, showers, a playground, and laundry.

## QUESNEL (B.C.)

**Good Knight Inn**
176 Davie Street
Quesnel, B.C. V2J 2S7
(604) 992-2187 or
800-663-1585

This downtown motel offers standard rooms and housekeeping units, extra-long queen and king beds, a licensed family restaurant, complimentary in-room coffee, heated indoor pool, whirlpool, and discounts for seniors. ($)

**Robert's Roost Campground**
3121 Gook Road
Quesnel, B.C. V2J 4K7
(604) 747-2015 or
fax: (604) 747-0015

Located 10 KM (6 miles) south of town, this medium-size campground is on the west side of Dragon Lake, off Highway 97, with full hookups, pull-through sites, showers, laundry, beach, boat rentals, boat launch, moorage, and dump station. One- and two-bedroom trailers are also available for overnight visitors.

**Talisman Inn**
753 Front Street
Quesnel, B.C. V2J 2L2
(604) 992-7247 or
800-663-8090

You get a lot for your money in this motel set next to a park. Features include standard and housekeeping units, plus executive suites containing whirlpool baths, refrigerators, microwave ovens, toasters, and extra long queen and king beds. Other features include an indoor pool, whirlpool, and sauna. Restaurants are nearby. ($ to $$)

## SMITHERS (B.C.)

**Hudson's Bay Lodge**
P.O. Box 3636
Smithers, B.C. V0J 2N0
(640) 847-4581 or
800-663-5040

This large Tudor-style motel, at 3251 East Highway 16, has standard rooms, plus one of the best dining rooms in this part of British Columbia, a coffee shop, lounge, whirlpool, and saunas. ($$)

**Riverside Recreation Centre**
P.O. Box 4314
Smithers, B.C. V0J 2N0
(604) 847-3229

This private campground found on Highway 16 East (Yellowhead Highway), offers shaded pull-through sites on the river, water and electrical hookups, showers, and dump station. The campground is beside a par-3 golf course with driving range and restaurant.

**Sandman Inn**
P.O. Box 935
Smithers, B.C. V0J 2N0
(604) 847-2637 or
800-726-3626

This standard motel is part of a regional chain, with regular rooms and units with kitchens. It's located at 3932 Highway 16 (the Yellowhead). ($ to $$)

## STEWART (B.C.)

**King Edward Hotel and Motel**
P.O. Box 86
Stewart, B.C. V0T 1W0
(604) 636-2244 or
800-663-3126

The motel is located on Columbia Avenue, while the hotel is on 5th Avenue. Both have rooms with private bath and queen beds. The hotel contains a dining room and coffee shop. ($ to $$)

**Stewart Lions Campground**
8th Avenue
P.O. Box 431
Stewart, B.C. V0T 1W0
(604) 636-2537

Open from May 1st through September 30th, this campground offers shaded graveled sites, some with full hookups, fire pits, flush toilets, tenting area, picnic tables, dump station, showers, nature trails, and a museum. The park is located next to a trout stream. Reservations are accepted and recommended.

## TERRACE (B.C.)

**Alpine House Motel**
4326 Lakelse Avenue
Terrace, B.C. V8G 1N8
(604) 635-7216 or
800-663-3123 (in B.C.)

Off the highway, offering a quiet place to stay, the Alpine House has regular motel rooms and units with kitchenettes, rooms with queen beds, and complimentary coffee. A restaurant is located next door. Turn at the junction of highways 16 and 37 onto the old bridge. ($)

**Coast Inn of the West**
4620 Lakelse Avenue
Terrace, B.C. V8G 1R1
(604) 638-8141 or central
reservations: 800-663-1144 or
800-549-3939 (in B.C.)

This downtown hotel has air-conditioned units, including non-smoking rooms, queen and king beds, licensed dining room, and a cold beer and wine store. ($$ to $$$)

**Slumber Lodge**
4702 Lakelse Avenue
Terrace, B.C. V8G 1R6
(604) 635-6302 or
fax: (604) 635-6381

Another motel in the regional chain, the Slumber Lodge has standard units, including non-smoking rooms, an indoor pool, and licensed restaurant, and serves a complimentary breakfast. The motel is in downtown Terrace, across from shopping. ($ to $$)

**Timberland Trailer Park**
4619 Queensway Drive
Terrace, B.C. V8G 3X5
(604) 635-7411

A small campground, 5 KM (3 miles) from Terrace, Timberland offers pull-through sites, full hookups, cable TV, showers, laundry, a clubhouse, and fish-cleaning facilities. To get there, turn north from the junction of Highway 16 and Highway 37 south, and drive 100 yards to Queensway Drive. Follow Queensway west to the campground.

## VANCOUVER (B.C.)

*Downtown Vancouver is the business, shopping, and hotel center for the Lower Mainland region, and the large and higher-priced hotels are close to the business and waterfront district in Vancouver's West End. Several of the newer deluxe hotels have positions with wonderful views on or near the waterfront. Other fine hotels and several campgrounds are located in the suburban cities.*

**Dogwood Campground**
15151 112th Avenue
Surrey, B.C. V3R 6G8
(604) 583-5585

This large RV park offers full hookups, tenting sites, a swimming pool, and laundry. The operation also arranges seasonal bus tours of the Vancouver area. To get there from the Trans-Canada Highway (Highway 1), take Exit 50 north on 160th Street to 112th Avenue, and then drive west on 112th Avenue to 152nd Street. From 152nd Street, take the Highway 1 overpass, make a right turn, and follow signs to the RV park.

**Four Seasons Hotel**
791 West Georgia Street
Vancouver, B.C. V6C 2T4
(604) 689-9333 or
800-268-6282 (in Canada) or
800-332-3443 (U.S. only)

The Four Seasons gets more stars and diamonds than any other Vancouver hotel, and it has been doing so for more than a dozen years. This fine hotel is close to everything in the shopping and business district, and is connected to the Pacific Centre shopping mall. The restaurants are excellent, and the hotel has pools, sauna, whirlpool, cocktail lounges, and an exercise room ($$$ to $$$+)

**Hotel Vancouver**
900 West Georgia Street
Vancouver, B.C. V6C 2W6
(604) 684-3131 or
800-441-1414

This Canadian Pacific operation is Vancouver's venerable landmark hotel, located in the center of downtown near the Vancouver Art Gallery, Pacific Centre Shopping Plaza, the chic fashion boutiques of Robson Street, and only a 10-minute walk to the waterfront. Hotel features include rooms and suites, swimming pool, sauna, an arcade of shops, plus restaurants including roof-top dining, and the memorable Timber Club, located off the lobby. ($$ to $$$)

**Inn at Westminster Quay**
900 Quayside Drive
New Westminster, B.C.
V3M 6G1
(604) 520-1776 or
800-663-2001

This modern hotel is set beside the Fraser River, in the historic town of New Westminster (B.C.'s first capital city), beside a public market with shops and restaurants, and a riverfront walkway. A station for the SkyTrain light rail service is nearby, making it easy to travel to downtown Vancouver without your car. ($$$)

**KOA Vancouver**
14601 40th Avenue,
Rural Route #1
Surrey, B.C. V4P 2J9
(604) 594-6156

This large KOA operation is in the eastern suburb of Surrey, where the regional bus system can take you into Vancouver. The campground offers full hookups, pull-through sites, a tenting area, showers, laundry, dump station, games room, access to a nearby beach, heated outdoor pool, and mini-golf. The campground is at the junction of Highway 99 and Highway 99A (King George Highway).

**Pan Pacific Hotel**
300-999 Canada Place
Vancouver, B.C. V6C 3B5
(604) 662-8111
800-663-1515 (in Canada)
or 800-937-1515 (in U.S.)

Located on a harbor pier overlooking Burrard Inlet, beside the Vancouver Trade and Convention Centre with its huge roof looking like sails, this deluxe hotel is part of a Japanese chain of resort hotels. Restaurants serve French, North American, and Japanese cuisine. The hotel offers a pool, sauna, health club, lounge, and great views from the Canada Place promenade. ($$$ to $$$+)

**Park Canada RV Inn**
4799 Highway 17,
P.O. Box 190
Delta, B.C. V4K 3N6
(604) 943-5811

Located south of Vancouver, close to the Tsawwassen ferry terminal (where you catch the cruises to Victoria, Nanaimo, and the Gulf Islands), this huge RV park and campground features full and partial hookups, tenting sites, full rest rooms, showers, laundry, dump station, heated outdoor pool, store, and recreation lounge. The campground is located next to a popular waterslide park.

**Stay 'n' Save Motor Inn**
10551 Saint Edwards
Drive
Richmond, B.C. V6X 3L8
(604) 273-3311 or
800-663-0298

This motel beside Highway 99, the main route to Vancouver from Interstate 5 and Seattle, provides basic but modern accommodations at reasonable prices (there's another Stay 'n' Save in Victoria). A family restaurant is located on the property, and the large motel has laundry facilities, and some rooms have kitchen units. ($$)

**Sylvia Hotel**
1154 Gilford Street
Vancouver, B.C. V6G 2P6
(604) 681-9321

This ivy-covered hotel is an older, cozy place facing the beach and English Bay, at the corner of Beach and Gilford. It also has a new, modern wing attached to the older hotel. The Sylvia, a long-time stopping place for notables, including the literary crowd, has rooms (some with kitchens) and suites, plus a restaurant and lounge overlooking the bay, where sunsets are usually spectacular. ($ to $$$)

**Waterfront Centre Hotel**
900 Canada Place Way
Vancouver, B.C. V6C 3L5
(604) 691-1991 or
fax: (604) 681-1838

Another Canadian Pacific Hotel (this national company also operates the Hotel Vancouver and the Chateau Whistler), the Waterfront Centre is located across the street from the Pan Pacific (see above), on the shore of Burrard Inlet. It's close to the shopping and the business

**Waterfront Centre Hotel**
*(continued)*

district. This large modern hotel has standard rooms and suites with harbor and mountain views, queen and king beds, a heated pool, health club, and a restaurant specializing in West Coast cuisine. ($$$ to $$$+)

**Wedgewood Hotel**
**845 Hornby Street**
**Vancouver, B.C. V6Z 1V1**
**(604) 689-7777 or**
**800-663-0666**

For a change of pace from the larger, busier hotels, try this small, cozy hotel in the central part of downtown, across from Robson Square. The hotel is in the European romantic tradition, with maid service twice a day, a breakfast room, piano lounge, and a dining room serving Italian cuisine. ($$$ to $$$+)

## VICTORIA (B.C.)

**Captain's Palace Inn**
**309 Belleville Street**
**Victoria, B.C. V8X 1X2**
**(604) 388-9191**

This B & B operation has three historic mansions, on the Inner Harbour across the street from the Port Angeles (Black Ball) ferry terminal. Rooms have private baths. There is morning coffee service, and full breakfast in the dining room is included. ($$ to $$$)

**The Empress**
**721 Government Street**
**Victoria, B.C. V8W 1W5**
**(604) 384-8111 or**
**800-441-1414**

This fine hotel on the Inner Harbour was built by the Canadian Pacific Railway and is one of the grand old railway hotels of Canada, and a tourist attraction on its own. It has been recently renovated from top to bottom. There are rooms and suites, with indoor pool, whirlpool, several dining rooms, lounges, health club, and a magnificent lobby where afternoon tea is served. The hotel is across the street from the Royal B.C. Museum and the

Parliament buildings, and close to downtown shops and restaurants. Small pets are allowed. (**$$$ to $$$+**)

**Fort Victoria RV Park**
340 Island Highway 1A
Victoria, B.C. V9B 1H1
(604) 479-8112

This large private RV park is located 6.4 KM (4 miles) north of downtown Victoria, with full hookups, cable TV, laundry, dump station, showers, flush toilets, playground, and shopping nearby.

**Grand Pacific Hotel**
450 Quebec Street
Victoria, B.C. V8V 1W5
(604) 386-0450 or
800-424-6423 or
800-663-7550

This modern high-rise hotel is a Clarion operation, with rooms and suites, dining room, lounge, pool, sauna, whirlpool, fitness center, and underground parking. It's adjacent to the Inner Harbour and across the street from the Parliament buildings. (**$$$**)

**James Bay Inn**
270 Government Street
Victoria, B.C. V8V 2L2
(604) 384-7151 or
800-836-2649

This historic old hotel is a mainstay of the downtown Victoria area, and is located near the Parliament Building and Beacon Hill Park. As an older hotel, some rooms have shared bath but rates are the most reasonable in the Inner Harbour area. A popular pub and a restaurant are also in the building. (**$ to $$**)

**Oak Bay Beach Hotel**
1175 Beach Drive
Victoria, B.C. V8S 2N2
(604) 598-4556

Why go to Victoria and stay in a standard motel? There are plenty of motels but this fine old Tudor hotel is a standout. Located on a quiet bay, with fine views, the rooms have antique furnishings. The dining room is renowned for its scenic setting and fine food. There's a tiny English pub, and gardens to walk in. The hotel is located on Victoria's Marine Scenic Drive. (**$$$ to $$$+**)

**Stay 'n' Save Motor Inn**
3233 Maple Street
Victoria, B.C. V8X 4Y9
(604) 475-7500 or
800-663-0298

This is a standard motor hotel for those who prefer quick getaways and standard facilities. This motel does have some extras, including suites and queen and king beds. Some rooms have kitchen units. There's a family restaurant and laundry on-site. A large shopping mall is nearby. ($$ to $$$)

## WILLIAMS LAKE (B.C.)

**Fraser Inn**
285 Donald Road
Williams Lake, B.C.
V2G 4K4
(604) 398-7055 or
800-452-6789

Located within easy view of the highway, this full-service hotel has a good restaurant specializing in steaks and seafood, as well as a salad bar. The hotel also offers a whirlpool, sauna, and weight room. There is a pub on the premises. ($$)

**Overlander Motor Hotel**
1118 Lakeview Crescent
Williams Lake, B.C.
V2G 1A3
(604) 392-3321 or
800-663-6898

Offering air-conditioned rooms and suites, this motel provides complimentary morning coffee, and has on the premises a pub, coffee shop, licensed dining room, whirlpool, and sauna, plus a cold beer and wine store. ($$)

**Sandman Inn**
664 Oliver Street
Williams Lake, B.C.
V2G 1M6
(604) 392-6557 or
800-726-3626

One of the regional chain of motor hotels, the Williams Lake Sandman has standard units, all air-conditioned, an indoor pool, sauna, and a 24-hour family restaurant. The chain offers discounts to seniors. ($ to $$)

**Wildwood Campsite**
P.O. Box 50
Williams Lake, B.C.
V2G 4M8
(604) 989-4711

This RV park and campground is located 13 KM (8 miles) north of Williams Lake on Highway 97, offering pull-through sites, trailer and RV hookups, shady tenting sites, cable TV, rest rooms, showers, laundry, dump station, ice, freezer, and store. A gas station is located across the street.

# Index

The listings in this index cover the scenic drives, in addition to the cities, towns, and significant attractions that are found in the Destinations pages for the British Columbia section of the Alaska Highway, Alaska, the Yukon and Northwest territories, and the access routes to the Alaska Highway. When information on attractions is included in the Drives section for each region, these attractions are also included in the index with page numbers shown in bold type. Public parks (camping and day-use) and fishing places along the scenic routes are listed in the highway logs which accompany maps in the Drives pages.